GUERRILLAS
AND GENERALS

GUERRILLAS AND GENERALS

The "Dirty War" in Argentina

Paul H. Lewis

Westport, Connecticut
London

Library of Congress Cataloging-in-Publication Data

Lewis, Paul H.
  Guerrillas and generals : the "Dirty War" in Argentina / Paul H. Lewis.
    p. cm.
  Includes bibliographical references.
  ISBN 0–275–97359–X (alk. paper)—ISBN 0–275–97360–3 (pbk. : alk. paper)
    1. Argentina—Politics and government—1955–1983. 2. Civil-military
relations—Argentina—History—20th century. 3. Argentina—Armed Forces—Political
activity—History—20th century. 4. Guerrillas—Argentina—History—20th century. 5.
Political violence—Argentina—History—20th century. 6. Human
rights—Argentina—History—20th century. I. Title.
  F2849.2 .L475   2002
  982.06—dc21   2001021650

British Library Cataloguing in Publication Data is available.

Library of Congress Catalog Card Number: 2001021650
ISBN: 0–275–97359–X
       0–275–97360–3 (pbk.)

First published in 2002

Praeger Publishers, 88 Post Road West, Westport, CT 06881
An imprint of Greenwood Publishing Group, Inc.
www.praeger.com

Printed in the United States of America

The paper used in this book complies with the
Permanent Paper Standard issued by the National
Information Standards Organization (Z39.48–1984).

10 9 8 7 6 5 4 3 2 1

For Anne

Contents

Abbreviations

AAA	Argentine Anticommunist Alliance
ALN	Nationalist Liberating Alliance
ALUAR	Aluminum Company of Argentina
APDH	Permanent Assembly for Human Rights
BIR	Banco de Intercambio Regional
CATS	Committees in Support of the Tupamaros
CELS	Center for Legal and Social Studies
CGE	General Economic Confederation
CGT	General Confederation of Workers
CN	National Leadership Committee
COFAPPEG	Commission for Families of Political, Student, and Labor Prisoners
CONADE	National Council for Development
CONADEP	National Commission on Disappeared Persons
CONASE	National Security Council
CONICET	National Council for Scientific and Technical Research
EGASA	Empresas Graiver Asociadas
EGP	Guerrilla Army of the People
ELN	Army of National Liberation
ENR	National Revolutionary Army
ERP	People's Revolutionary Army
ESG	Superior War School
ESMA	Naval Mechanics School

EUDEBA	Editorial Universitaria de Buenos Aires
FAL	Fuerzas Armadas de Liberación
FAP	Fuerzas Armadas Peronistas
FAR	Fuerzas Armadas Revolucionarias
FORES	Forum for Studies on the Administration of Justice
FOTIA	Tucumán Sugar Workers' Union
FRAP	Chilean Popular Action Front
FREPASO	Frente para un País Solidario
FRIP	Frente Indoamericano Popular
FUA	Argentine University Federation
GAN	Grand National Alliance
GOU	Group of United Officers
GRN	Guardia Restauradora Nacionalista
IAPI	Argentine Institute for Production and Trade
JAEN	Argentine Youth for Emancipation
MEDH	Ecumenical Movement for Human Rights
MIR	Movement of the Revolutionary Left
MNRT	Tacuara Revolutionary Nationalist Movement
MTP	Movimiento Todos por la Patria
OAS	Organization of American States
OLAS	Organization of Latin American Solidarity
P-2	Propaganda-2
PCA	Argentine Communist Party
PO	Palabra Obrera
PPA	Authentic Peronist Party
PRT	Revolutionary Party of the Workers
SEGBA	Greater Buenos Aires Electrical Services
SERPAJ	Servicío Paz y Justicia
SIDE	State Intelligence Bureau
SMATA	Auto Mechanics' Union
UBA	University of Buenos Aires
UCR	Unión Cívica Radical
UCRI	Unión Cívica Radical Intransigente
UCRP	Unión Cívica Radical del Pueblo
UDELPA	Union of the Argentine People
UOM	Metallurgical Workers' Union

ONE

The "Oligarchy" and the "People"

At a few minutes before 6:00 P.M., on 9 December 1985, Jorge Rafael Videla, 60 years of age, former president of Argentina, retired lieutenant general, and former commander in chief of the Argentine army, stood with eight other generals and admirals in the Federal Court of Criminal Appeals in Buenos Aires, awaiting his sentence. Nine years earlier, he had been popular with the great majority of Argentines, having led a coup to oust a corrupt government floundering in economic chaos and guerrilla terrorism. Now he and his eight colleagues who had served on three of the military juntas that ruled Argentina from March 1976 to December 1983 were charged with kidnapping, robbery, torture, and murder. The trial had started in the third week of April 1985, and for the next four months newspapers and television had given full coverage to the courtroom drama. Testimony ended in mid-August; prosecution and defense summations carried over into September. Now at last León Arslanián, president of the six-man tribunal, read the verdict to a packed courtroom: for General Videla, life imprisonment and the same for Admiral Emilio Massera, former head of the navy and Videla's frequent rival for power on the junta. General Roberto Viola, who supported Videla and succeeded him as president of the junta after his five-year term, was condemned to 17 years in prison. Admiral Armando Lambruschini, who succeeded Massera, got eight and Brigadier Orlando Agosti, who represented the air force on the first junta, got four. The other four officers were absolved.

The court further decreed that Videla and his four other guilty colleagues were to lose their rights as citizens to vote or hold office and were to face "destitution": the loss of their military status and the right to wear their uniforms or to draw a military pension—however, their wives could claim a widow's pension. In brief, they were "civically dead."

The sentences, like the trial, were controversial. The junta officers had argued that they took over the government in 1976 to prevent the triumph of communist subversion. They had fought a war, and in a war the essential thing is to win, whatever the cost. Moreover, this was a new kind of war in which the enemy remained hidden, fought from ambush, and used terrorist tactics to subvert institutions. To fight such an enemy unfortunately required equally unconventional, or "dirty," tactics, as distinct from those used in ordinary warfare. The court rejected these claims. While recognizing that a problem of terrorism had existed, it insisted that the fight against it could have been carried out within the boundaries of legality. The Constitution provided for emergency powers in the event of a severe threat to internal order; clandestine torture centers and mass executions were unnecessary. The court even doubted whether a state of war had existed; but if it had, the armed forces should have adhered to the principles of the Geneva Convention, to which Argentina was a signatory.[1]

The Argentine Left, while agreeing with the court's logic, wanted harsher sentences. Chief Prosecutor Julio Strassera expressed his dismay that evening over the lightness of the sentences. Rumors of the decision had leaked out earlier in the day, and some two hundred human rights activists had already gathered outside to protest the court's leniency. That night Hebe de Bonafini, president of the Madres de la Plaza de Mayo, the most vocal human rights group, led some three thousand demonstrators in a sit-in before the Congress.

The Argentine Right had even less respect for the court and its procedures. Emilio Hardoy, head of the conservative Partido Democrático, expressed his doubts about the judges' impartiality. The military had saved Argentina from terrorism and subversion, and now it was being subjected to revenge by the Left. His criticism was echoed by former President Arturo Frondizi, who called the trials "a political show" and warned that their real intention was to demoralize the armed forces so as to "favor the forces of the Left." General Reinaldo Bignone, president of the last military junta and himself under indictment for human rights violations, described the proceedings as resembling the "popular justice" meted out in Castro's Cuba. The entryways of the court building had been filled with crowds holding placards, threatening the accused and harassing them with catcalls. Years later, recalling the trial, Haydeé Jofre Barroso, a journalist, demanded to know, "How could we have accepted the shameful prosecution of the former highest authorities of our country, which led to a scandalous public trial before 2,500 journalists from around the world: ex-magistrates spat on and insulted by the spectators, broken in their military rank, humiliated as human beings, and degraded in their capacity as former members of a government?"[2]

INSTITUTIONAL DECAY

The trial reflected a nation divided and haunted by its past. When the military took power in March 1976, the country was approaching a complete institutional breakdown: the culmination of a long process of decay. Nearly 46 years had passed since General José Félix Uriburu overthrew the constitutional government of Hipólito Yrigoyen in 1930. That coup interrupted Argentina's evolution toward democracy and set a precedent for future military interventions. From Uriburu to Videla, 19 different presidents had occupied the Casa Rosada. One of them, General Juan Domingo Perón, served for all or part of three constitutional periods, which added up to 21 different administrations. Although the Constitution called for a six-year term, the average life of a presidential administration was only slightly more than two years. Eight of those 21 administrations began with an election, but two of the elections were patently fraudulent. Four vice presidents succeeded to power when the incumbent president died in office, resigned, or was overthrown. Out of this total of 12 constitutional administrations, only two completed the full term. Of the nine administrations that originated with coups, not a single one remained in power for the whole six years. Five were overthrown by their military colleagues; the others bowed to popular pressure and allowed elections to be held. All in all, civilians held office for only about 15 of those 46 years, oftentimes as figureheads.

For 27 of those 46 years, Congress was either dissolved or so reduced in its powers that it did not function as a real deliberative body. Similarly, the courts were often purged or had their jurisdiction severely limited so as to exclude the government's acts from review. Even under elected governments, the ruling party or coalition often manipulated the polls or intimidated the opposition, so Congress and the courts were packed with political yes-men. The president, as "boss," could abuse the emergency powers of the Constitution—such as the state of siege power, the power of federal intervention in the provinces, or the right of the president to issue executive orders—to avoid checks on his power.

People who had something to gain or lose by government action came to disregard laws, institutions, or even political parties as being lesser factors in the power game. All attention was focused on using organized power to influence the executive. Pressure groups—the military, labor, landowners, the Catholic Church, business—became the crucial actors in the political system. Without Congress or the courts as effective mediating and legitimating institutions, the clash of raw interests could turn violent. All of them had their contacts in the barracks, so the threat of violence or simple noncompliance always lurked in the background, threatening the life of one brittle government after another. On paper, Argentina was a model liberal democracy, with a Constitution dating back to 1853 and a federal system of national government divided into the classical three branches, checking and balancing one another. In reality, political institutions were little more than a façade for a naked power struggle, with the military acting as arbiter.

FEAR OF THE MASSES

Endemic political instability, characterized by frequent military intervention, was the sign of a deeper social malaise. It was not caused by economic or cultural backwardness. At the time that General Uriburu marched his troops on the Casa Rosada, Argentina was a rich and confident nation, seemingly on its way to becoming the leader of the South American continent and a significant actor on the world scene. Predominantly agricultural, it was among the world's leading exporters of meat, wheat, corn, and linseed. It also was a major importer of machinery and fuels, to service its modern and efficient agricultural producers as well as a steadily growing manufacturing sector. Buenos Aires, the country's capital and principal port, was a beehive of offices, banks, insurance firms, warehouses, meatpacking plants, and dockyards. It also was a beautiful, cosmopolitan city of broad boulevards, leafy parks, imposing government buildings, smart boutiques, hotels, and commercial shops of every conceivable kind. Nightlife was a glittering world of movies, opera, theatre, dance halls, restaurants, cafes, art galleries, and vaudeville houses.

What lay at the bottom of Argentina's subsequent decline was the refusal of its entrenched elites, the so-called oligarchy, to accept the age of mass politics. The oligarchy was used to running Argentina and was liberal, up to a point. Its close commercial ties with Europe, especially England, made it appreciate capitalism, but its liberalism did not usually extend to politics. The typical Argentine oligarch could accept civil marriage, the separation of church and state, and secular education. He could even accept parliamentary institutions as being "modern," as long as the ballot was restricted to the educated elite. Otherwise, he viewed the classes below him with fear, contempt, and loathing. They were not "the people," as reformist Radical Party politicians liked to call them, but *el populacho, la chusma, los guarangos*—the rude, dirty riffraff. Nonetheless, as Argentina's economy surged forward and the urban population expanded, the oligarchy reluctantly conceded universal male suffrage in 1912. Four years later the Radical Party swept into power behind its leader, Hipólito Yrigoyen.

Instead of forming a mass-based conservative party to rival the Radicals, the Argentine oligarchy retreated from politics, grumbling about the Radicals' corruption and demagoguery. When the Great Depression hit, however, the oligarchs saw their chance to regain power. Yrigoyen, at 77, was too feeble to offer leadership. As his popularity plummeted, many military officers with oligarchic ties began to plot. On 6 September 1930, General Uriburu, a patrician member of the exclusive Jockey Club and Círculo de Armas, reinstated elite rule.

The oligarchy's hold on power was never secure, however. Elections had to be held, although they were carefully manipulated. Radical Party conspiracies and trade union strikes were met with force. One way of maintaining order was through a paramilitary organization called the Argentine Civic Legion, whose members wore fascist-style uniforms, gave the Roman salute, and marched in military formation. Another was through the Special Section of the Federal Police, which achieved a truly ominous reputation for its torture sessions. The methods of torture were brutal and primitive, but they presaged the "Dirty War's" tactics: pincers to squeeze the testicles, a press that crushed fingers, and a leather belt that tightened across the body—all this in addition to the usual beatings. There were mock executions, powerful jets of water directed at the prisoner's sensitive body parts (*el pinchazo*), and soaked sacks of grain (*la toalla mojada*) placed over the ankles to cut off circulation to the feet. But the Special Section's most famous and lasting contribution was the *picana eléctrica*, the electric cattle prod, which could be applied to a prisoner's genitals, nipples, teeth, or any other sensitive place. If the victim were first soaked, or placed on a wet metal surface or in a tub full of water, the effects were all the more excruciating. Thousands of people were put through torture over the next quarter of a century, until the Special Section was shut down in September 1955. Every president from Uriburu through Perón used it.[3]

MAN OF THE PEOPLE

Although the oligarchy was restored to power, it depended on the military. As the Great Depression exposed the flaws in Argentina's traditional agrarian economy, the army became restive. The example of the European fascist powers made it clear that industrialization was the sine qua non for military power, and there was a spreading feeling among the officers that the oligarchy was too tied to Great Britain, both commercially and culturally, to lead the necessary crusade for national greatness. In June 1943 the officers launched the second major coup of the century and brought oligarchic rule to an end.

The real brains and spirit behind the new government was Colonel Juan Domingo Perón, the leader of a secret military lodge called the Group of United Officers (GOU). Tall, athletic, and extroverted, he had charisma, and he was also a man with ideas. His plan for Argentina was a full-scale mobilization of society in every respect: economic, political, and cultural. The state would control every institution so as to enhance national power. Those who would undermine national unity, whether in the name of class war or individual rights, had to be suppressed. In brief, the nation would be organized and disciplined, like an army; and like an army it would follow the orders of a supreme commander.[4]

Perón assured his colleagues that, as a military attaché in Mussolini's Italy, he had actually seen his ideas at work. If only the Argentine armed forces could avoid Mussolini's mistakes, fascism would provide the way to national economic independence and military supremacy on the continent. Perón moved up quickly in the new military government. As war minister, he moved his friends into crucial army posts. He also took over the National Labor Department, a previously unimportant office, and used it to control labor conditions, wages, public health, pensions, low-cost housing, rents, migrant labor, and the Postal

Savings Bank. Unlike the usual antilabor military officer, Perón enforced labor laws that previously had been ignored: laws prohibiting child labor, indexing the minimum wage to the cost of living, guaranteeing an eight-hour day, establishing annual paid vacations, requiring decent and healthy working conditions, providing for severance pay and accident insurance. Social security was extended to virtually all workers. A new system of labor courts was created to handle claims about worker's compensation for injuries on the job, unpaid salaries, and unfair dismissals. Perón also used his power during strikes to achieve favorable terms for the workers. New unions were set up in those areas of the economy in which labor was previously unprotected, and they were extended in the areas in which labor organization was still weak. Even rural labor was brought under the government's protection. Eventually, all workers had to belong to unions, and all unions had to obtain government recognition. Moreover, the government undertook to collect all dues, supervise the disbursal of all monies in the unions' accounts, and dictate the terms of labor contracts. Some of the older unions that predated the regime protested this loss of their independence, but for the great majority of workers, Perón was a great beneficent *patrón*.[5]

By the time that Perón's military colleagues realized that he had grown too powerful and had his eye on the presidency, it was too late. An attempt to remove him from the government backfired on 17 October 1945, when his *descamisados* ("the shirtless ones") converged on the Plaza de Mayo from all the industrial suburbs, filling the entire space and the streets leading into it, demanding his return. The army, caught off guard, caved in, leaving him master of the situation. In February 1946 he was elected president; his supporters claimed almost two-thirds of the seats in the Chamber of Deputies, all but two Senate seats, all the provincial governorships, and majorities in all the provincial legislatures except one. He could now pursue his program for Argentina.

In order to understand the societal breakdown that led to the "Dirty War," it is necessary to appreciate why Perón's years in power were so controversial and why he retained a polarizing yet pivotal influence over Argentine politics after he fell. So far as labor was concerned, Perón's rule represented a golden age. The General Confederation of Workers (CGT) grew from a little more than half a million in 1945 to some three million by 1951, mainly by forming new unions to protect unskilled workers. Real wages rose by about one-third; fringe benefits added another 30 to 50 percent. Job security was practically absolute. Even when a worker was fired for "just cause," the employer had to pay a severance allowance for each year of service. Employers had to collect the union's dues from the workers' paychecks, give time off with pay for union officers, provide space on the premises for union meetings, and even contribute to special union fundraisers. Any attempt at resistance would result in a factory shutdown, and labor courts almost always favored the workers.[6]

Naturally, employers were angry over losing control of their enterprises, in which discipline was breaking down, absenteeism was on the rise, and productivity suffered. Although Perón tried to win them over through protectionism and easy loans, they resented having to join the official General Economic Confederation (CGE). Agriculturalists hated having to sell all their produce to a state monopoly, The Argentine Institute for Production and Trade (IAPI), at government-set prices. IAPI would buy from Argentine farmers and ranchers at the lowest possible price and resell the goods on the world market for big profits, which supposedly financed industrialization.

Not content with controlling capital and labor, Perón created official organizations for students, artists, writers, teachers, women, lawyers, and doctors. Every profession, intellectual endeavor, and social group was to be harnessed to the pursuit of national power.[7] In each of these organizations, internal elections were carefully controlled by the government. Anyone who resisted was "antinational" and therefore an "enemy of the people." Perón's wife, Evita, loved to whip up the lower classes' hatred of the rich and educated, who clung to "outworn" liberal ideas about individualism. She also won their undying affection with her charitable projects, all managed through the Eva Perón Foundation. Proud of their latent power and amused by the oligarchy's fear of them, Peronist demonstrators liked to strip off their shirts, display their darker skins, and beat the Indian *bombo* drums at their parades—aware of how ominous the deep "boom, boom, boom" of the *bombos* sounded to their enemies.

Perón's opponents accused him of totalitarianism, and, indeed, he was no democrat. Although he was freely elected, once in office he moved quickly to ensure that his hold on power would be permanent. He shut down the opposition press, purged the Supreme Court and lower courts, and cowed Congress with a law penalizing speeches that expressed disrespect (*desacato*) toward the government or its policies. The official Peronist Party was completely obedient. Other parties led a precarious existence, without newspapers or access to the media, their meetings often disrupted, their leaders harassed into exile or jailed. Alongside the Peronist Party, but not formally linked to it until 1953, was a heavily armed paramilitary organization known as the Nationalist Liberating Alliance (ALN), which carried out most of the violent acts against dissenters. There was also, of course, the dreaded Special Section of the Federal Police.

Perón's opponents had an uphill fight, but the regime became vulnerable as the economy began to crumble under excessive regulation. Workers wouldn't work, employers wouldn't invest, and ranchers and farmers wouldn't produce at IAPI's prices. Also, the railroads and utilities, which had been bought from their previous foreign owners by Perón in a burst of economic nationalism, were running at a loss. Unfavorable trade balances, falling production, deteriorating services, and inflation began to undermine the system—as did corruption, which spread everywhere as the government extended its controls. As grumbling rose in volume, Perón tried to crack down even harder.

The Catholic Church and the military were two major institutions that managed to retain their autonomy. By 1953, however, there were signs that Perón intended to force them into his lockstep. The Church had resented Evita Perón's attempts to monopolize charity, and when she died of cancer in 1952 the clergy refused to consider canonizing her as a saint, despite popular demonstrations on her behalf. Then the Church really provoked a confrontation when, to combat the regime's totalitarian tendencies, it began to organize trade unions in competition with Perón. Perón went on the attack, forbidding religious processions and expelling priests. Street clashes finally led, on the night of 16 June 1955, to ALN thugs setting fire to many downtown churches. Meanwhile, opposition to Perón had been growing within the military. The officers resented mandatory courses in Peronist political indoctrination at the academy and the regime's new program of encouraging the sergeants and enlisted men to join the Peronist Party. They feared, rightly, that their own men would be encouraged to spy on them.[8]

The Church's struggle with Perón provided a rallying point for all of his opponents: the employers, middle-class professionals, Radicals, Conservatives, Socialists, devout Catholics, and restive military officers. On 16 September 1955, Eduardo Lonardi, a retired general, raised the banner of revolt in Córdoba. On the following day other garrisons in the interior joined him, as did the navy. Although the bulk of the army was still with Perón, when the naval fleet blockaded Buenos Aires's harbor and threatened to shell the city, his chief officers induced him to quit rather than fight. On 20 September he took refuge aboard a Paraguayan gunboat and claimed diplomatic asylum.

POLARIZATION AND DECAY

After ousting Perón, the armed forces were divided over what to do next. General Lonardi, the provisional president, wanted to preserve the Peronist system while eliminating its corrupt elements, but others had endured the last 10 years seething with inward rage against the regime and its *descamisados* and were in no mood to forgive and forget. They found their leaders in Admiral Isaac Rojas, the vice president, and General Pedro Aramburu, who originally conceived the plot to overthrow Perón but failed to act as quickly as Lonardi. When Lonardi balked at undoing Perón's social and economic legislation, the heads of the three armed services forced him from office on 13 November 1955 and replaced him with Aramburu while retaining Rojas as vice president.

Aramburu took a middle position between "soft-liners" like Lonardi and "hard-liners" like Rojas, who favored an extended period of military rule to purge Argentina of Perón's influence. He wanted to return the soldiers to the barracks as soon as possible, before they got caught up in politics. However, civilian rule must not lead to a Peronist restoration, so Aramburu went along with proscribing the Peronist Party and its component organizations. He also encouraged non-Peronist trade unions, in the hope that they would capture the workers' loyalties. The Unión Cívica Radical (UCR), the only other mass-based party, was to provide a firm, popular foundation for constitutional government. Elections were scheduled for February 1958.

Every one of Aramburu's plans went awry. In June 1956 he faced a Peronist revolt by some army officers and union leaders. The rebels planned to seize control of army units and distribute weapons to the workers while terrorists would assassinate government leaders and their more prominent supporters, whose houses were painted with red crosses beforehand. The revolt was crushed in a few hours, but Aramburu was so outraged that he ordered the captured ringleaders shot without trial. Nine civilians and two officers were immediately put to death; another nine officers and seven NCOs were summarily executed over the next two days.[9] Such a bloody reprisal was unprecedented in 20th-century Argentina. It fixed an unbridgeable gulf between the Peronists and anti-Peronists and doomed any attempts to purge Peronism from the labor movement. With open resistance outlawed, clandestine shop committees formed, led by a new generation of militants. Industrial sabotage was on the rise. Go-slow movements soon escalated into full-blown wildcat strikes that were increasingly co-ordinated through an underground Inter-Syndical Committee.

The UCR upset Aramburu's electoral plans by splitting into two antagonistic parties. Arturo Frondizi, a left-wing Radical, aimed at winning over the old Peronist coalition by promising to restore labor's "social conquests," nationalize large industries and all energy resources, begin land reform, and—to regain Church support—encourage parochial schools and private universities. Blocked by the more conservative Radicals, Frondizi and his followers formed their own Unión Cívica Radical Intransigente (UCRI) to promote his presidential candidacy. His opponents formed the Unión Cívica Radical del Pueblo (UCRP) and chose Ricardo Balbín, who had run against Perón in 1952, as their leader.[10]

Aramburu supported the UCRP as the party most likely to carry on his policies. The first test of its strength came on 28 July 1957, when elections were held to a constitutional convention whose purpose was to restore the pre-Peronist 1853 Constitution. This would be a preview of how the UCRI and UCRP would fare in 1958. The Peronist Party was excluded, but voting was obligatory, so working-class voters faced a dilemma. Perón, who was rebuilding his movement from exile, solved their problem by instructing his followers to go to the polls and cast blank ballots. They obeyed, with the result that blank ballots were 24.3 percent of the total vote, outpacing both the UCRP, which got 24.2 percent, and the UCRI, which ran third with 21.2 percent.[11]

Soon afterwards Frondizi sent emissaries to Perón, who was then in Caracas, with offers of a deal: in return for Peronist votes in February, he would legalize Peronism and permit Perón to return from exile. Perón agreed, and, not surprisingly, Frondizi was elected president by a landslide. Nevertheless, his mandate was never solid: everyone knew that Peronist ballots had made his victory possible. Henceforth the military would view him as a stalking horse for Perón and plot incessantly against him, although once in office Frondizi forgot almost all of his promises to the Peronists. For the next four years he used all of his considerable ingenuity to try to carve out a third position between these two powerful camps. Finally, with the March 1962 midterm elections upon him, he took a desperate gamble and allowed the Peronists to run, surmising that the upper and middle classes, thrown into a panic at the prospect of Perón's return, would stampede to the government's party as the only viable alternative. Unfortunately for him, the Peronists won. That was too much for the military, which deposed Frondizi on 21 March and placed him under arrest.

After the coup, 12 high military officers met in the Casa Rosada to decide what kind of government Argentina would have. Some argued that the Frondizi experience proved that Argentina was not ready for civilian rule; others favored giving democracy another chance. While they debated, the Supreme Court hurriedly swore in as president José María Guido, head of the Senate, who was constitutionally next in line to succeed Frondizi. The generals were then informed of this fait accompli. Having no agreed-upon plan of their own, they reluctantly acquiesced.[12] For the next 16 months, Guido bobbed like a cork atop a stormy sea as the military legalists and hard-liners struggled for supremacy. Eventually they would clash in the streets as two rival armies. Adopting the terminology of war games, the legalists became the "Blue" army, while the extreme anti-Peronists became the "Reds." After three such clashes, the "Blues," led by General Juan Carlos Ongania, the commander of the Campo de Mayo cavalry, won out, thus allowing a return to civilian rule.

The elections, held on 7 July 1963, excluded the Peronists and all other "totalitarian" parties. Electoral coalitions that included the Peronists were banned as well. That left three major contenders: the UCRP, which had chosen Arturo Illia, an elderly country doctor who had been governor of Córdoba; the UCRI, now headed by the leftist former governor of Buenos Aires, Oscar Alende; and a new party, the Union of the Argentine People (UDELPA), whose standard-bearer was ex-President Aramburu. The results produced a weak, minority government, for Illia was elected with only 25.8 percent of the vote, and his party controlled only 72 out of 192 seats in the Chamber of Deputies. Illia should have offered to form a coalition government, because otherwise he had little prospect of getting his bills through Congress, but he proved curiously stubborn. It was an inauspicious start for Argentina's second try at liberal democracy, for without a majority behind him, Illia had no firm mandate and would be in a poor position to deal with either the military or the Peronists.

THE PERONIST RESISTANCE

The measure of Perón's genius was his ability, even in exile, to retain his hold over the movement. Though he was thousands of miles from the scene, he kept a close watch on events back home and exercised his leadership through a voluminous correspondence, constant visits by Peronists, and the dispatch of personal delegates to Argentina bearing his commands. By soliciting information from a variety of sources, Perón was able to adjust to shifts in the political climate and change his tactics accordingly. Scattered incidents of working-class resistance broke out within days after Perón fell, but they were too spontaneous and uncoordinated and so were stamped out one by one. Aramburu arrested hundreds of union leaders and Peronist party officials; he also forbade the display of Peronist symbols or posters, the singing of Peronist songs, the use of Peronist slogans, or the possession of Peronist books and pamphlets. Such persecution actually strengthened the resistance by convincing Peronists that only a workers' state could give them justice. The elimination of the older leadership also brought a new generation to the fore, one that proved to be even more combative and fully aware of the enormous political power that a united labor movement could wield. Their initial tactics were sabotage, terrorism, and underground propaganda. Factory sabotage took the form of destroying machinery, raw materials, or finished products—such as putting ground glass into cans of processed food. Bombs exploded at railroad tracks, power lines, gasoline pipelines, public buildings, military installations, and political party offices. Resistance committees sprung up spontaneously in the industrial suburbs, turning out crude mimeographed or handwritten sheets, always with the same message: "Perón will return." This slogan was painted all over the walls of Argentina's cities. The tension and hysteria of those times produced the widespread belief that Perón would soon return, in a black airplane (*el avión negro*), to lead an uprising of the people.[13]

Perón himself recovered his old political drive and began guiding the Resistance. The shock of exile seemed to revitalize him, and his plans were greatly helped when some prominent Peronists escaped from a Patagonian prison in March 1957. One of them was Jorge Antonio, who had made a fortune by profiteering during the Peronist years, had money stashed away in overseas accounts, and would become the movement's financial backer. Another was John William Cooke, who, with his courage and fanatical dedication to social revolution, would become Perón's personal representative to the Argentine underground.

Perón outlined to Cooke in a letter the strategy he was to follow: "Our way is simple: organize carefully underground. Instruct and prepare our followers, . . . grouping ourselves in disciplined organizations, well-formed by capable, brave, and decisive leaders." Furthermore, "we must plan our actions minutely and prepare for their execution by permanent practice and exercises": acts of sabotage, strikes, anything to provoke repression by the rulers so as to radicalize the masses. "If it's necessary to use the Devil, then we'll use the Devil as we must. The Devil is always ready for such work." Only through the creation of chaos could there arise a revolutionary situation that would allow the people to take matters into their own hands. "But," Perón emphasized, "it is necessary that the struggle be based on guerrillas. The forces of reaction should never find a place to land a blow, and every day they should feel the force of resistance."[14]

Soon Cooke was sending Perón a stream of information from underground sources: statistics on meat production, government finances, the balance of political forces within various labor unions, factions within the military, internal struggles in the various political parties, organizational problems inside the Peronist movement, political trends inside countries bordering on Argentina where Peronist exiles were living. "The country is sprinkled with cells," he wrote Perón, "which work with enthusiasm, although anarchistically." There were many acts of sabotage and "such an excess of volunteers that we have to fight off people demanding bombs." The early bombs were poorly made, "with the result that a few have failed to explode while others did so prematurely, badly wounding a couple of our boys." However, he assured Perón, "now we have a very good chemical, so we hope that won't happen again. Right now we're making 30 time-bombs which we'll use within approximately fifteen days." Moreover, he bragged, he now had 270 heavy machine guns and plenty of ammunition hidden away in Buenos Aires; regular arms shipments were coming in through Bolivia and Paraguay. The Aramburu regime had a good intelligence apparatus, with modern training and plenty of money, but Peronism "has eyes and ears inside the government." Many of the Federal Police personnel were sympathetic to the movement. The same was true inside the military. Many officers were opposed to Aramburu and Rojas but feared that Perón's return would lead to a bloodbath of revenge. The chief problems for the underground, according to Cooke, were the shortage of good leaders and the tendency for some Peronists to collaborate with the government.[15] Little by little the Resistance was becoming coordinated.

The Cuban Revolution and its cult of the guerrilla hero had a deep impact on the Argentine Resistance because Ernesto "Ché" Guevara—second only to Fidel Castro in fame—was a native son. Cooke and many others in the Peronist underground suddenly saw another route to power. The first Cuban-inspired guerrillas, the so-called Uturuncos ("Tiger-Men") made their appearance on Christmas Day, 1959, when they attacked a police outpost in Santiago del Estero Province. That was the beginning of a series of guerrilla attacks and bombings that was concentrated in the provinces of Buenos Aires and Córdoba. Military intelligence was convinced that the Uturuncos were receiving aid from Cuba and that UCRI Governors Oscar Alende of Buenos Aires and Fernando Zanichelli of Córdoba were secretly protecting them. After Frondizi put those provinces under martial law, the army rounded up a large number of suspects and found sizable caches of arms and explosives. Their interrogations revealed close dealings among terrorists, common criminals, policemen, and provincial government officials. Zanichelli was replaced by federal intervenors, while Alende went abroad for an "extended rest." Using its power to try civilians in military courts, the army soon made short work of the Uturuncos and similar underground Resistance organizations.[16]

Meanwhile, the movement's traditional organizations, such as the CGT, the CGE, and the Feminist Party had reappeared, and in several provinces the Peronist Party had emerged with considerable support. Perón had moved to Madrid, where he received a constant stream of visitors at his home, the Quinta 17 de Octubre, and sent a constant stream of emissaries to Argentina with instructions for his followers. He made it clear that he would continue to head the Peronist movement. His main concern now was the labor unions, the *columna vertebral* ("backbone") of his movement, for the workers provided Peronism with its mass power. Important changes had taken place in the *columna vertebral* since 1955 that rendered it a less dependable weapon. One of those changes was the new breed of labor union boss that had grown up in the post-Perón period and was less inclined to be blindly obedient to the leader, especially when his orders seemed at variance with what was perceived to be reality. Some of those men had become immensely powerful in their unions through their courageous leadership during the Resistance, and their unchallenged position tempted them to use the CGT for their own ends, not Perón's. They were handling large annual sums that—in the case of bigger unions—ran into several billions of pesos. So much financial power, and the political influence that went with it, naturally constituted a temptation. It is hardly surprising that corruption, violence, and gangsterism spread throughout the labor movement in the 1960s. Union bosses were almost always surrounded by *matones*—bodyguards, or, literally, "killers." Many of these were *pistoleros* recruited from the Resistance.[17]

Augusto Vandor, the head of the powerful Metallurgical Workers' Union (UOM), was a good example of the new kind of union leader. Though neither eloquent nor ideological, he was a workingman's man: virile, courageous, a proven fighter during the Resistance, resourceful at the head of strikes, loyal to his friends, tough at the bargaining table, and proud of his proletarian roots. Vandor had little respect for the Illia government, which he considered socially conservative and weak. He dismissed the 7 July 1963 elections as fraudulent because the Peronist Party had not been allowed to run and was determined to bring Illia down. At his urging, the CGT's central committee approved a Plan de Lucha ("Battle Plan") in the face of an ever deepening economic crisis. Between 21 May and 24 June 1964, some four million workers were involved in the occupation of around 11,000 factories and business establishments throughout Argentina.

Meanwhile, the expectation of Perón's return had never been abandoned by the workers, and he kept that hope alive by repeatedly promising that he would be back before the end of 1964. Having prepared the country emotionally for his return, on the night of 2 December Perón and his entourage boarded a plane in Madrid, bound for Buenos Aires. Despite all attempts at secrecy, they were forced to get off when the plane landed at Rio de Janeiro to refuel and were put on the next plane headed back to Spain. That failure convinced Vandor that Perón was a spent force. At the same time, the Plan de Lucha was going badly. The Illia government, armed with the old Peronist labor laws, had struck back, seizing union bank accounts, withdrawing legal recognition, forcibly dislodging the strikers, and dispersing demonstrators. Accordingly, Vandor switched tactics and accepted Illia's offer to legalize the Peronists and allow them to register for the March 1965 midterm elections. Both men hoped to encourage a participationist neo-Peronism that would marginalize Perón. Perón countered by sending his new wife, Isabel, to Argentina as his representative to meet with Peronist politicians and labor leaders. The movement split down the middle, resulting in rival organizations. Vandor temporarily got the upper hand in January 1966, when off-year elections in Jujuy Province gave his neo-Peronist candidate an 11 to 1 majority over the slate Perón backed, but in March Perón's candidate outpolled Vandor's in Mendoza's gubernatorial elections, proving that the Grand Old Man was still able to rally the masses.[18]

Perón had predicted that Illia's government wouldn't last, and he proved to be right. Illia's economic policies were disastrous, and to make matters worse he quarreled with General Onganía. On 23 November 1965, Onganía tendered his resignation as commander in chief of the army, after Illia appointed someone junior in rank to him as war minister. Finally, Illia's legalization of the Peronists turned out to be, as with Frondizi, the last straw. During the night of 27 June the tanks finally rolled through the streets, surrounded the Casa Rosada when Illia was still inside, and forced him to leave. The following day a military junta declared Congress, the provincial governments, and all political parties to be dissolved. Then it summoned General Onganía to assume the presidency.

THE ARGENTINE REVOLUTION

This time the military prepared itself for a long stay in power. The civilians had twice failed, the crisis had deepened, and now the armed forces would save the nation, cost what it might. In the meantime, there were to be no more politics. Political parties were abolished and the press was controlled. On the evening after the inauguration, police invaded the University of Buenos Aires, where communists had taken control of the student government. During the notorious "Night of the Long Clubs" (*Noche de los Bastones Largos*), the dean, assistant dean, several of the faculty, and more than two hundred students at the Faculty of Exact Sciences were battered unmercifully and forced to run a gauntlet between two rows of policemen who clubbed them with rifle butts as they passed.[19]

Worse scenes occurred in Córdoba. On 8 September a particularly violent clash in the city's center left one student fatally wounded with a bullet in his head. On 14 September the students and workers organized a "silent march" in his memory but were intercepted by the police as they approached the downtown area. The police dispersed them with tear gas, but that only set off another riot as the demonstrators regrouped. Cars were pushed into the streets and set afire to form flaming barricades, and police units were showered with stones and bricks. One of the downtown stores was set ablaze. In hindsight, it can be seen that these clashes were a kind of rehearsal for the truly dramatic upheaval that was to become known as the *cordobazo*.[20]

Meanwhile, Onganía's government tightened its political grip. On 10 October 1966 it promulgated the Law of National Defense, which set up two new agencies: the National Council for Development (CONADE) and the National Security Council (CONASE), both of which reported directly to the president.

Their simultaneous creation reflected the regime's belief that economic growth and national security were intertwined. A second national security measure was the Anti-Communist Law of 25 August 1967. Those who went to prison under this law could expect to be tortured with shocks from the *picana eléctrica*.[21]

Argentina's stagnant economy underwent free market reforms that brought inflation down from 40 percent to only 5 percent while productivity rose and exchange reserves reached their highest level in years. Strikes were broken and unions had to accept a wage freeze. Ongania's overconfident advisors began to plan a new Constitution that would institutionalize his kind of government. Then, in mid-1969, the political calm suddenly exploded. Nearly three years of government antilabor actions had radicalized the workers. In Córdoba, some of the largest unions were led by Trotskyites, Maoists, or left-wing Peronists. Parallel to the rise of these "combative" unions, students across the country were once more challenging the regime. During the previous year there had been riots at campuses in Córdoba, Tucumán, La Plata, Resistencia, and Rosario. In Córdoba they had become mingled with a violent workers' demonstration, which ended with the demonstrators taking refuge on the university campus. In Rosario, students took refuge at the local CGT headquarters. Thus, there was an increasingly close cooperation between the students and the radicalized unions of Córdoba and Santa Fe Provinces. On 5 May a student at the Corrientes campus was killed in a clash with the police during a protest march over a rise in cafeteria prices. A general uprising followed, with townspeople and the local CGT joining in to paralyze the city. Two weeks later students and workers were battling with police for the control of Rosario's streets, with the townspeople joining in to help erect barricades and fight the authorities. General Alejandro Lanusse, the army commander, sent in troops and put the city under martial law.

Córdoba was next. Student leaders had been in contact with the radical union leaders. Plans were made for a march on the city's center by the workers and students on 29 May to protest the recent "repression" in Corrientes and Rosario. On the day of the march some five thousand workers joined about eight thousand students as they headed for downtown. Along the route, people came out to their balconies to cheer them on. Spirits were aroused, and extremist elements, having infiltrated the crowd, whipped them up all the more. As the march neared the city center, its organizers lost control. Windows were smashed, cars were tipped over and lighted, and soon there was an orgy of violence. Attempts by the police to control it were met with molotov cocktails and all manner of refuse. Barricades were erected. Mounted troops were sent in next, but were driven back by a barrage of stones. Once the police used up their store of tear gas they were forced to retreat, leaving the streets in the hands of the rioters. Townspeople poured out of their homes to join the revolt, pleading for weapons. Meanwhile, in the district called Clínicas, an area of about 10 square blocks consisting mainly of student housing bordering the university and the Hospital de Clínicas, student militants were manning the barricades and patrolling the streets. Interspersed among them were priests from the Third World movement.[22]

Soldiers finally entered that city late that evening, but another day was to pass before order was fully restored to Córdoba, by which time about a dozen people had been killed and more than one hundred wounded. The *cordobazo* filled Perón with renewed hope. He now knew that all the reports he had been receiving about Ongania's firm grip on the country were erroneous. By contrast, Ongania's confidence in himself and his government was badly shaken. To placate public opinion, he dismissed his entire cabinet, but the effect was simply to make him look like a crumbling dictator, which indeed he was. For the radical Left, the *cordobazo* was an inspiration. During the next year and a half, a number of armed revolutionary organizations would emerge, and their combined impact would be far greater than that of any guerrilla attempts in the past and would heighten the political tension to a level previously unimaginable.[23]

NOTES

1. Amnesty International, *Argentina: The Military Juntas and Civil Rights* (London: Amnesty International Publications, 1987), 61, 71–72; J. Camarasa, R. Felice, and D. González, *El juicio: proceso al horror* (Buenos Aires: Sudamericana/Planeta Editores, 1985), 11–13.

2. Camarasa et al., *El juicio*, 176–77; Reynaldo Bignone, *El último de facto* (Buenos Aires: Editorial Planeta, 1992), 195; Haydeé M. Jofre Barroso, *La política de los argentinos* (Buenos Aires: Editorial Galerna, 1990), 109.

3. Ricardo Rodríguez Molas, *Historia de la tortura y el orden represiva en la Argentina* (Buenos Aires: EUDEBA), vol. 1, 95–98; vol. 2, 193; Raúl Lamas, *Los torturadores: crimenes y tormentos en las cárceles argentinas* (Buenos Aires: Editorial Lamas, 1956), 146–55.

4. Juan Domingo Perón, *Apuntes de historia militar: parte teórica* (Buenos Aires: Círculo Militar, 1934), 105–6, 123–25, 138–39, 158, 160–61, 233–36, 242–46. See also Peter Ranis, "Early Peronism and the Post-Liberal Argentine State," *Journal of Inter-American Studies and World Affairs*, vol. 21, no. 3 (August 1979), 318–19; and *Nuevo Confirmado* (10–16, July 1973), 11, for excerpts from some of Perón's early lectures at the Superior War School.

5. Samuel Baily, *Labor, Nationalism, and Politics in Argentina* (New Brunswick: Rutgers University Press, 1967), 72–73, 75; Gino Germani, "El surgimiento del peronismo: el rol de los obreros y de los migrantes internos," *Desarrollo Económico*, vol. 13, no. 51 (October–December 1973), 473; Walter Little, "La organización obrera y el estado peronista, 1943–1955," *Desarrollo Económico*, vol. 19, no. 74 (October–December 1979), 332–35; Bertram Silverman, "Labor and Left-Fascism: A Case Study of Peronist Labor Policy" (Ph.D. diss., Columbia University, 1967), 140–41, 151–57, 173–76, 219–20, 228; Robert J. Alexander, *Labor Relations in Argentina, Brazil, and Chile* (New York: McGraw-Hill, 1962), 177–79.

6. Alexander, *Labor Relations*, 204; Baily, *Labor, Nationalism, and Politics*, 98–99, 111–12; Tomás Roberto Fillol, *Social Factors in Economic Development: The Argentine Case* (Cambridge: MIT Press, 1961), 64–65.

7. Martin S. Stabb, "Argentine Letters and the Peronato: An Overview," *Journal of Inter-American Studies*, vol. 13 (July–October 1971), 434–55; Alberto Ciria, *Política y cultura popular: la Argentina peronista* (Buenos Aires: Ediciones de la Flor, 1983), 214–16, 230, 234, 248, 251–52.

8. Noreen Frances Stack, "Avoiding the Greater Evil: The Response of the Argentine Catholic Church to Juan Peron, 1943–1955" (Ph.D diss., Rutgers University, 1976), 284–85, 315–24; Virginia Leonard, "Church-State Relations in Education in Argentina since 1943" (Ph.D. diss., University of Florida, 1975), 170, 175–79; Robert A. Potash, *The Army in Politics in Argentina, 1945–1962: Perón to Frondizi* (Stanford: Stanford University, 1980), 98–99, 107, 112, 115–18, 127, 140, 153–54, 158, 171–72, 177–78; Alain Rouquie, *Poder militar y sociedad política Argentina, 1943–1973* (Buenos Aires: Editorial Emecé, 1982), 86–87, 94, 96, 108.

9. Potash, *Army in Politics*, 230–35.

10. Peter Snow, *Argentine Radicalism* (Iowa City: University of Iowa Press, 1965), 71–77.

11. Eduardo Zalduendo, *Geografía electoral de la Argentina* (Buenos Aires: Ediciones Áncora, 1958), 31–32.

12. James W. Rowe, *The Argentine Elections of 1963* (Washington: Institute for the Comparative Study of Political Systems, n.d.), 13.

13. Peter Ranis, *Parties, Politics, and Peronism: A Study of Post-Peron Argentine Development* (Ph.D. diss., New York University, 1976), 42–43; Daniel James, *Resistance and Integration: Peronism and the Argentine Working Class, 1946–1976* (Cambridge: Cambridge University Press, 1988), 50, 54, 76–80; Ricardo C. Guardó, *Horas difíciles* (Buenos Aires: Author, 1963), 55, 59–61.

14. Perón to Cooke, 12 June 1956, in Juan Domingo Perón, *Perón-Cooke correspondencia* (Buenos Aires: Gránica Editor, 1972), vol. 1, 8–9, 11–15.

15. Cooke to Perón, 11 April 1957; 11 May 1957; 28 August 1957; and 14 November 1957, in *Perón-Cooke*, vol. 1, 58–61, 111, 250; vol. 2, 16.

16. James, *Resistance and Integration*, 143–44; *Nuevo Confirmado* (18 December 1975), 22; Rosendo Fraga, *El ejército y Frondizi, 1958–1962* (Buenos Aires: Editorial Emecé, 1992), 138–41.

17. James, *Resistance and Integration*, 126, 162–63, 167–68, 170–71; Jorge Correa, *Los jerarcas sindicales* (Buenos Aires: Editorial Obrador, 1974), 51–64.

18. Viviana Gorbato, *Vandor o Perón* (Buenos Aires: Tiempo de Ideas, 1992), 102–7; Osvaldo Calello and Daniel Parcero, *De Vandor a Ubaldini* (Buenos Aires: Centro Editor de América Latina, 1984), vol. 1, 76.

19. Gerardo Bra, "La noche de los bastones largos: el garrote y la inteligencia," *Todo es Historia*, vol. 18, no. 223 (November 1985), 8–26.

20. Gregorio Selser, *El onganiato* (Buenos Aires: Hyspamerica, 1973), vol. 1, 182, 248–250, 255–57; vol. 2, 29–44.

21. Alicia S. García, *La doctrina de la seguridad nacional (1958–1983)* (Buenos Aires: Centro Editor de América Latina, 1991), vol. 1, 85–97; Rodríguez Molas, *Historia de la tortura*, vol. 1, 130–32, 146–49; vol. 2, 202–9.

22. *Análisis* (Buenos Aires), 10–16 June 1969, 14–17.

23. Samuel Blixen, *Conversaciones con Gorriarán Merlo: treinta años de lucha popular* (Buenos Aires: Editorial Contrapunto, 1988), 89, 103, 105.

TWO

The Seedbed of Terrorism

The *cordobazo* opened up possibilities for Augusto Vandor, who had backed out of joining it at the last moment. With the radical union leaders in jail, the way was clear to unite labor under his leadership, if he could get Perón's blessing. So on 23 June Vandor slipped out of Argentina and flew to Spain. The two men eventually agreed that Vandor would head a unified CGT. Meanwhile, ex-President Aramburu was meeting with political party leaders to discuss replacing Ongania with a provisional government that would schedule elections. It was well known that he had the backing of General Alejandro Lanusse, the army's commander in chief.[1]

On Monday morning, 30 June, five well-dressed young men walked into the UOM headquarters and showed their Federal Police credentials. Once inside, they pulled out pistols and revolvers, reduced the guards, and disconnected the telephones. Three of them ascended the stairs to the second floor, where Vandor's office was located. When shouts from the corridor prompted him to open the door, a young man shoved a .45 against his chest and fired. The others then burst in, pumped two more bullets into the fallen Vandor, and placed a bomb between his legs. Then they fled to where a car was waiting with its motor running. Friends managed to haul Vandor away from the bomb, which exploded five minutes later, destroying a large part of the building. He died in a police van on the way to the hospital.[2]

Not until February 1971 did a hitherto unknown guerrilla organization calling itself the National Revolutionary Army (ENR) claim the "credit" for what it called "Operation Judas." The ENR had a brief existence as the "hit squad" of yet another organization known as the Descamisado Command, formed by left-wing Peronists Horacio Mendizábal and Norberto Habegger in 1968. Shortly before Operation Judas, the Descamisado Command was taken over by Dardo Cabo, an experienced *pistolero* from the Resistance and a former bodyguard of Vandor. Cabo's role in Operation Judas was to provide the assassins with details about the interior of UOM headquarters, where he had worked for more than eight years. The chief planner of the operation was said to be Rodolfo Walsh, a prominent journalist and author who had written a best-selling exposé of Vandor's complicity in the murder of two UOM rivals. Walsh had some earlier experience in guerrilla movements, having belonged to the Peronist Armed Forces, which in 1968 had tried to set up a rural guerrilla *foco* in Tucumán Province but was uprooted before it really got started. The Descamisados hated labor union "bureaucrats" like Vandor, whom they saw as selling out the revolution and the working class. All of them would merge with the Montoneros early in 1973.[3]

Vandor's death was a serious setback for a government that was trying to regain its balance, but worse was soon to come. On 29 May Aramburu was kidnapped by a small band of urban terrorists calling itself "the Montoneros," after the guerrilla irregulars who fought for Argentina's independence from Spain. When they seized Aramburu, they numbered no more than a dozen, but their cold-blooded audacity succeeded. Around 9:00 A.M. on 29 May two young men, dressed as an army captain and first lieutenant, appeared at Aramburu's apartment in the Barrio Norte to offer themselves as his bodyguards, because only a few days before, the Ongania government had withdrawn his police protection. The general received them amiably, served them coffee, and chatted for a few minutes until the "captain" pulled a machine gun from under his raincoat and ordered him to come with them. Aramburu was taken to a farmhouse and put on "trial" by the Montoneros for the executions of those Peronist officers and civilians who rose up against his government in June 1956. According to the Montoneros's own account, Aramburu was neither nervous nor contrite. On Sunday, 31 May, the Montoneros informed the public that Aramburu had been condemned to death. Early in the morning of 1 June he was taken to the basement, put against a wall, and killed with a 9 mm bullet in the chest, with two more in the head as a coup de grace. The Montoneros dug a grave in the dirt floor of the basement and dumped his body inside. Then they informed the press of his "execution."[4]

General Lanusse and other officers were convinced that Ongania had ordered Aramburu's murder. For some time, the Interior Ministry had been in contact with former members of a violent right-wing group called Tacuara, and the fact that it had withdrawn police protection from Aramburu looked suspicious. On 6 June troops surrounded the Casa Rosada and forced Ongania to resign. Meanwhile, as some 22,000 security agents scoured the country for Aramburu's body, another guerrilla group, called the Revolutionary Armed Forces, struck, firebombing 15 Minimax supermarkets owned by the Rockefeller family to protest a fact-finding visit by Nelson Rockefeller. Then the Montoneros attempted another spectacular feat. On 1 July, during a cold winter's morning in the mountains of Córdoba, Emilio Maza, the "captain" who kidnapped Aramburu, led a band into the resort town of La Calera just before daybreak. Wearing blue-and-white armbands inscribed with the word *Montoneros* and shouting "Viva Perón," they surprised a sergeant and his assistant at the local police station. They also took over the telephone system cutting off the town from the outside world. Two other policemen in a jeep were captured. Then the guerrillas burst into the local bank, forced the manager and employees into a back room, and began emptying the cash drawers. Just then another police car, which had been called out to investigate a minor complaint, happened to cruise by the bank and was fired on by one of the guerrillas. The driver was only slightly wounded and sped away to a nearby outpost of the Third Army Corps. After stuffing some 10 million pesos into their bags, the guerrillas fled but one group ran into an army roadblock. Some of the guerrillas escaped, but two were captured. Two others were arrested later in the day when a witness from La Calera recognized their car in the nearby village of Villa Rivera Indarte. Taken into custody, they gave information that led to hideouts in the city of Córdoba and the roundup of more Montoneros. During one gun battle, Maza was wounded and died.[5]

By this time, the police had considerable information about who composed this underground organization. Many of them, like Maza, were from well-to-do Córdoba families. One of those arrested was a priest, Father Fulgencio Rojas. The information trail also led back to Buenos Aires, to the apartment of Carlos Maguid, a photographer for Channel 11 TV, and to a parish house where Father Alberto Carbone, the general secretary of the Movement of Third World Priests, resided. At Carbone's place the police discovered the typewriter that had been used to write the Montonero communiqués during Aramburu's kidnapping. Carbone was arrested but denied any part in the Aramburu kidnapping. The typewriter had been loaned, he said, to a former student of his at the National High School, Mario Firmenich. Meanwhile, Maguid and his wife were picked up. Both denied being Montoneros but admitted that Maguid's sister-in-law, Norma Arrostito, belonged to the group and had been living at the apartment with her boyfriend, Fernando Abal Medina, another Montonero. They also identified Firmenich and Carlos Gustavo Ramus as being part of the Montonero circle. That piece of information led the police to the Ramus family farm, where Aramburu's body was found.

The Montoneros went underground, taking refuge in different hideouts provided by the Peronist Armed Forces. Other guerrilla groups went into action. On 30 July, the Revolutionary Armed Forces carried out an operation similar to that of La Calera in the small Buenos Aires town of Garín. Guerrillas descended upon the town and took over the police station, the post office, the telegraph office at the railway station, the home of a radio ham operator, and the local bank. During the bank robbery they killed a policeman and a bystander. A month later, on 27 August, the Descamisados' ENR assassinated José Alonso, the CGT's new general secretary. The assassins pulled alongside his car while he was on his way to work and asked for help with a flat tire. When Alonso and his driver stopped to help, Alonso was shot in the face. As he lay sprawled across the car seat, the guerrillas pumped another 14 bullets into him.[6]

Meanwhile, the Montoneros lost their best fighters as the police continued their relentless search. One of the participants in the La Calera attack committed suicide in Córdoba on 8 July as the police approached his home; another was captured in Rosario a month later. The worst blow came on 7 September, when the police, acting on a tip, ambushed a group of seven Montoneros who were meeting at a pizzeria in the *porteño* suburb of William Morris. In the ensuing gunbattle, Fernando Abal Medina and Carlos Gustavo Ramus were killed, and a third Montonero, Luis Rodeiro, was captured. The other four managed to escape.

The military was astonished by the outpouring of public sympathy for the Montoneros. In July, some three thousand people had attended Emilo Maza's funeral in Córdoba, and collections were held in the factories, schools, and shantytowns to pay the legal expenses of the captured La Calera guerrillas. The funeral for Abal Medina and Ramus surpassed that. It was attended by contingents from nationalist and Peronist groups of every sort. Arturo Juaretche, a famous Peronist writer on the Left, was there and so were prominent left-wing Peronist trade unionists. Perón himself sent a large wreath of flowers. The funeral Mass was said by Father Carlos Múgica, a popular Third World priest who referred to Abal Medina and Ramus as "my brothers . . . who chose the hardest and steepest path for the cause of human dignity." They were, he said, "an example for all youth, because we have to fight to reach a just society and overthrow this system that wants to turn us all into robots." Not to be outdone, Evita Perón's former confessor, Father Hernán Benítez, asked God's mercy for the two young men, "murdered by a Nation that could not understand them." "Give them a chance," he pleaded, "and quench their thirst for justice. . . . Thank you, Lord, for these two young men. They didn't choose an easy road." As the flag-draped coffins were lowered into their graves, the young nationalists present shouted, *"Viva el nacionalismo argentino!"* On 14 September a thousand youths paraded in the shantytown of Barrio Casas in a show of support for the Montoneros, and 7 September became an annual day of remembrance for the Peronist Left.

A CULTURE IN CRISIS

The guerrilla violence that followed the *cordobazo* partly reflected the deepening political crisis that began with the overthrow of Perón, but it was also a local version of the worldwide New Left movement of the 1960s. Like the New Left everywhere, it was a youth rebellion against traditional social institutions and an idealization of socialism as being ethically superior to capitalism. Young radicals viewed the capitalist system as a vast network of exploitative relationships extending around the world, with the United States as its headquarters.

The United States was perceived to be scheming to capture Argentina's economy through its multinational corporations and, even worse, to dominate it culturally. Intellectuals on the Left (and even some on the Right) expressed their revulsion for American "consumer society," "godless materialism," and hedonism.

Such attitudes were reactions to signs of change in Argentina's traditional social life, especially in the cities. Modernization was eroding the position of the family, once the basic social institution, with new values that placed individual freedom and self-fulfillment ahead of personal responsibility. The old idea that marriage was a lifetime commitment, and that its primary purpose was the raising of children able to fit into society, was under attack. Whereas people in smaller communities once had relatives, friends, neighbors, and the Church to buttress the family and maintain it, now, in the anonymous secular environment of the cities, unhappy marriage partners turned increasingly to separation or divorce. Often they were advised to do so by a rapidly growing number of psychiatrists and psychoanalysts who encouraged them to free themselves from society's artificial constraints. As the schools were filled with more and more children of broken marriages, they too were undergoing radical change. The traditional mission of outfitting children with useful skills to make a living and become productive citizens was being replaced by the idea that schools ought to function as promoters of social change.[7]

High schools, especially the more prestigious ones, were highly politicized. The new alienation in Argentina was greatest in the upper middle class. Many future Montoneros started their political careers in elitist high schools like the Colegio Nacional in Buenos Aires by becoming active in Catholic nationalist youth organizations like Tacuara, a right-wing anti-Semitic gang that used clubs, brass knuckles, and sometimes even guns to battle with the communist and Maoist clubs. Teachers and administrators were just as politicized as the students, with the Left and Right constantly battling for control of the classroom and the curriculum. Each side tried to enlist the support of students and parents, but the communists usually dominated the PTA, which they used to harrass "elitist" teachers who gave hard tests and graded strictly.[8]

Even where liberalism continued to thrive, as in the pages of a new weekly magazine called *Primera Plana*, which was designed to be a *Time* or *Newsweek* look-alike, it did so in a modern form that was pernicious for Argentina's traditional values. Launched in 1962 with support from the army, and edited by the talented Jacobo Timerman, *Primera Plana*'s business and financial pages held up U.S. enterprise as a model and encouraged businessmen to study the new field of marketing and become "go-getters." In its social and cultural sections, however, "modern liberalism" was more subversive. It favored birth control and spread information about contraceptives so that more women could enter the workforce. Naturally, it held the traditional family to be outdated and advocated more "open" lifestyles. *Primera Plana* was especially fascinated with psychoanalysis, which provided answers to the problems of adjusting to the process of "modernization." As for culture, *Primera Plana* liked modern art and modern literature. In those areas it played no political favorites. Marxist writers like Julio Cortázar or Gabriel García Márquez were received as enthusiastically as conservatives like Jorge Luis Borges or Mario Vargas Llosa. In national politics, however, it relentlessly attacked the Illia administration as weak and bureaucratic, much preferring a strong government able to clear away all obstacles to "modernization." General Ongania was its candidate for the job.[9]

One of the most surprising changes in Argentina's intellectual life during the 1960s was the growing acceptance of Peronism by the university educated. A generation before, almost all university students, faculty, and graduates were bitterly anti-Peronist, but times had changed. Now Peronists were able to combine with Marxists to control the national universities' self-governing institutions and agitate for increasing the size of the student body to incorporate more lower middle-class and working-class students. As a result, the total enrollment at Argentina's national universities rose from 82,500 in 1950 to 180,000 by 1960 and 274,000 by 1970. Along with this went a "modernization" of the curriculum. While there was practically no increase in law school enrollments, and an actual decline in the numbers going into medicine, the natural sciences and the social sciences expanded rapidly. The most popular programs were psychology and sociology.[10]

The move toward mass education produced a downward pressure on standards. "Strict" professors came under attack as "elitists," and if they also happened to be political conservatives or simply apolitical, they were doubly damned. Within the faculty, the inevitable struggle between Left and Right was intensified by a parallel split between "teachers" and "researchers." Researchers had the better-paid senior positions, had often studied in the United States, and insisted on "scientific" and "objective" standards, which led them to be condemned as defenders of cultural imperialism and the oligarchic status quo. Teachers, on the other hand, were usually lower-paid, less secure in their employment, and politically on the Left. The classroom gave them an opportunity to proselytize, and after class they liked to sit in cafes with their students and talk about politics. Although the universities were growing, modernizing, and turning out more graduates, the career prospects for their students were not very bright. The first graduates who came out of the psychology and sociology departments found jobs easily, but as the decade wore on, the economy stagnated and the market for such skills became saturated. There was a growing number of university graduates who had to settle for part-time work, dead-end clerical jobs, or unemployment. Many of them had to live with their parents; others hung around the university, postponing their graduation. Their anxiety and frustration were translated into radical criticism of society and the capitalist system. Their alienation took various forms: retreating into mysticism, sex, consumerism, or, in some cases, politics.[11]

A 1965 best-seller, *Buenos Aires: vida cotidiana y alienación* (Buenos Aires: Daily Life and Alienation), portrayed the anxieties of this middle-class youth. Its author, Juan José Sebrelli, a former president of the Argentine University

Federation (FUA), noted that their parents, in most cases, had risen out of the proletariat and therefore displayed the mixture of fear (of falling back into the lower class) and hope (of rising further in the social scale) that characterizes the socially insecure. Their children, though overtly rejecting their parents' conservatism, in reality were driven by the same fear of being sucked down into the lower class. Where they differed was in their determination to wrest power from the rich and bring society under their own control. However, they were badly disoriented and torn between extreme solutions.[12]

Some reform-minded young people did become active in the democratic political parties, but in most cases they were soon disillusioned. The Marxist and Catholic nationalist parties at either end of the spectrum were poor alternatives: the Argentine Communist Party was an aging, conservative bureaucracy, like its masters in Moscow, and the right-wing parties were only small cliques of intellectual snobs who had no real contact with the nation—the mass of ordinary people—that they wrote about in their small-circulation magazines. The trade unions were closer to the common people, but there was little hope for university-educated youth to find a future in them. What outlet remained, then, for the energy and idealism of a frustrated, angry generation that felt unable to find a place for itself in society?

For some, only a small number at first, the answer was revolution. One could read Trotsky on the Bolshevik Revolution in Russia, or Mao on guerrilla warfare in China, but it was the Cuban Revolution that proved to be the catalytic agent in this seething brew of frustration. It offered a myth to inspire the disillusioned young reformer who was tired of the futile chatter of politicians, priests, labor leaders, journalists, and armchair radicals: a handful of dedicated guerrillas, struggling in the mountains with the help of the humble peasants, had overcome the corrupt army of capitalism's puppet regime and opened up an exciting new path to socialism, much different from the oppressive Stalinist regime in Russia. Fidel Castro and Ché Guevara—the latter actually an Argentine—were romantic heroes in the Latin American tradition of revolution and machismo. These khaki-clad warriors, with their theory of the rural guerrilla *foco*, provided a formula for a revolution led by middle-class intellectuals in the name of the oppressed but inert masses.

This approach involved what traditional Marxists, like those in the Communist Party, condemned as "voluntarism." Voluntarism held that the Cuban Revolution was proof that it was not necessary to wait until the dialectical processes of history produced the objective conditions for revolution. On the contrary, violence, properly carried out, could create the conditions that were originally absent. The New Left gave the leading revolutionary role to a self-selected elite who would seize and exercise power in the name of the masses. The true revolutionary was said to feel the "essence" of the masses and, with his superior grasp of "objective reality," to understand their true interests even better than they. There would be heavy costs, of course. "All struggles, all revolutions, inevitably demand the sacrifice of a generation, or of a community," Sebrelli warned. Revolutions are not made with highfalutin phrases but "with dirt, with blood, with sweat, with human lives."[13]

THE IDEOLOGUES

The path to revolution began in the field of ideas. By a series of small logical steps the alienated Argentine intellectual came to identify his plight with that of the working classes, and from there to all the peoples of the world who were struggling against global capitalism. One more small step brought him to Lenin's theory of imperialism, and the next step led to Trotsky's idea of permanent world revolution. Mingled in with those were heavy borrowings from the Peronist tradition that made Argentina's version of the New Left quite distinct. Instead of a class struggle between proletariat and bourgeoisie, Argentine radicals thought in more nebulous categories of the people versus the oligarchy, with the former comprising both the working and lower middle classes and the latter embracing landowners as well as urban executives. Like Peronism, too, there was a large measure of anti-intellectualism in the New Left, of the sort reminiscent of fascism with its emphasis on action over theory. Politics was war, and only force could settle the outcome.[14]

Contemporary Marxism's latest metamorphosis in the form of Gramsciism provided a strategy. The Argentine Left began to read Antonio Gramsci in the 1950s, when Héctor P. Agosti, a communist intellectual, translated *The Prison Notebooks* into Spanish. Gramsci appealed to intellectuals because he made the cultural world the main battleground in the struggle between capitalism and socialism; therefore, he assigned the leading role in the revolution to those same intellectuals rather than to the proletariat. Even so, liberation required working within the national culture, which meant going to the Peronist masses. When the Argentine Communist Party (PCA) condemned this as "deviationist," the Gramscians retorted that Marxism-Leninism was too foreign an ideology for the Argentine proletariat to embrace. Many Gramscians eventually would join the Montoneros, precisely because the latter had positioned themselves inside the Peronist movement. The Cuban Revolution intensified this generational dispute. The PCA leadership dismissed Castro contemptuously as an "adventurer," whereas the Gramscians joined left-wing Peronists, Liberation Theology Catholics, and Trotskyites to declare their support for him.

Besides Gramsci, perhaps the greatest intellectual impact on this New Left version of Peronism was Juan José Hernández Arregui, who stirred the academic and literary worlds in 1960 with *Formación de la consciencia nacional*, a hefty, five-hundred-page survey and critique of nationalist thought over the last three decades. Hernández Arregui, though claiming to be on the Left, was surprisingly gentle in his criticism of the Catholic nationalist Right. It was correct in its attacks on liberalism as an antinational doctrine, he maintained, although it failed to grasp the possibilities inherent in a synthesis between nationalism and socialism or to perceive the regenerative potential of the working class—the only sector of society still uncorrupted by compromise with foreign capital. By contrast, Hernández Arregui's lash came down hard on the socialist and communist parties. Marxism was a foreign import, essentially the work of Jews, he said. Jews were the ultimate cosmopolites, and their influence was especially pernicious because they came to dominate urban intellectual life—in the universities, the press, and the theatre, as well as in the art and literary worlds. Worst of all, Jews headed the socialist and communist parties, which explained their failure to support a true nationalistic movement of the masses like Peronism.[15]

If Hernández Arregui's writings built a bridge over which the Right and Left could meet, a second span was created by an ideological shift in the Roman Catholic Church that began in 1961 with Pope John XXIII's encyclical *Mater et Magistra*. This warned of a new kind of global imperialism by which rich capitalist nations were forcing the rest of the world into dependency. In 1963 another encyclical, *Pacem in Terris*, called upon Catholics to involve themselves in the struggle for social justice and to collaborate with other social reformers, even Marxists. From there the Church proceeded leftward to *Populorum Progressio* (1967), which expressed sympathy with the violent upheavals in the Third World and called for audacious, fundamental changes in the world economy. The ideology that expressed this shift was called Liberation Theology, and the organization that arose to put it into practice was the Movement of Third World Priests. On 15 August 1967, five months after *Populorum Progressio*, 18 bishops from Latin America, Asia, and Africa, under the leadership of Bishop Helder Câmara of Brazil, initiated the Movement of Third World Priests to put the pope's words into action. In Argentina, some four hundred priests and bishops joined. Because the total number of Catholic clergy in Argentina was around five thousand, these radicals were a decided minority; nevertheless, they attracted much attention and exercised a disproportionate amount of influence.[16]

While accepting an essentially Marxist view of society, *tercermundistas* preferred to work inside the Peronist movement rather than the Marxist parties because Peronism was heterogeneous, essentially undisciplined, and thus easier to penetrate. The question of violence was more divisive. The new theology already had its first martyr: Father Camilo Torres, the Colombian priest-turned-guerrilla, who was killed in 1967. Most *tercermundistas* did not formally approve of violence, but they usually supported popular revolts against the status quo. Others more openly advocated guerrilla warfare. One of those was Father Carlos Múgica, a Jesuit priest who had been to Cuba and had said the funeral Mass for Fernando Abal Medina and Carlos Gustavo Ramus. "A Christian cannot remain passive to the institutionalized violence surrounding him," Father Múgica asserted. "A Christian may decide to kill, for reasons of conscience, of information, or ideology." His heroes were Mao Zedong, Camilo Torres, and Ché Guevara. Rather than engaging in violence himself, he encouraged others to do it. As confessor to the Catholic Youth Organization students at the Colegio Nacional, he knew many who were in Tacuara, like Carlos Gustavo Ramus and Fernando Abal Medina. Múgica would take his young charges with him on his visits to Buenos Aires's shantytowns and preach to them that Christianity required fighting for the rights of the poor. Later, he was replaced at the Colegio Nacional by Father Alberto Carbone, who had a similar influence on Mario Eduardo Firmenich and would one day be implicated through him in the murder of Aramburu. Inspired by such Third World priests, these students left the Catholic Youth Organization and formed their own proto-guerrilla group, the Camilo Torres Command, which would later evolve into the Montoneros. Nor were they the only future Montoneros who adopted the guerrilla mentality by way of involvement with the radical Catholic clergy. Emilio Angel Maza, who was fatally wounded at La Calera, had been a medical student at the Catholic University in Córdoba and a leader in the local Catholic Integralist Youth.[17]

Juan García Elorrio, a former seminarian who, like Father Múgica, was from an upper-class *porteño* family, became another spiritual model for the Montoneros. Formerly a Catholic nationalist, he had travelled to Cuba, met John William Cooke, and became a left-wing Peronist. In September 1966 he started an influential magazine called *Cristianismo y Revolución* to preach the gospel of Catholic revolutionary violence. Its articles praised Cuba, the Black Power movement in the United States, the Viet Cong, the memory of Eva Perón, and the "martyred" Camilo Torres and Ché Guevara. Meanwhile, the Camilo Torres Command made a small stir in the press when García Elorrio and Abal Medina led a group of protesters to disrupt a May Day Mass being held in 1967 at the National Cathedral. President Ongania and his chief cabinet ministers and advisors were in attendance, which made the incident potentially serious, but although the protesters were arrested, they were let off leniently. García Elorrio explained that they were attempting to protest the Church's complicity with Ongania's repressive government. Soon afterwards, Abal Medina and Norma Arrostito went to Cuba to attend an international conference for the purpose of starting guerrilla movements all over Latin America. They stayed until the following year to receive guerrilla training. Upon their return, preparations for guerrilla war moved ahead, the first step being the "expropriation" of weapons from a Federal Police shooting gallery in Córdoba. Beyond that, however, the Montoneros avoided acts that would attract attention, until they suddenly made history by kidnapping Aramburu.

Argentina's guerrillas were nurtured by still another ideological source: Trotskyism, which originally made its appearance in the 1930s as a splinter from the Communist Party. The Trotskyites were never a large group, but they attracted a circle of capable intellectuals such as Hugo Bressano (better known under his alias, "Nahuel Moreno"), Jorge Abelardo Ramos, and Silvio Frondizi, brother of Argentina's future president. Unlike the Stalinist PCA, the Trotskyites were never much bothered by the police, perhaps because they quarreled so much, split frequently into tiny factions, and spent most of their time in sterile pamphleteering. Perón posed a special dilemma for them. Some, like Ramos, decided to join him; others remained pure and independent. Ramos explained his adherence to Peronism in an essay that laid down the strategy of *entrismo* (infiltration), which so many Marxists would follow over the next three decades. Given the absence of any other viable working-class party, he argued, it was necessary for revolutionary Marxists to become Peronists if they wanted contact with the masses. Eventually they would take over the movement and lead the the workers to communism.[18]

Some Trotskyites followed this strategy successfully after 1955, when the Peronist movement temporarily found itself without a leader and in disarray. They managed to exert influence over some of the new generation of union leaders, especially those in Córdoba; but *entrismo* got a setback in 1962 when President Frondizi was overthrown and Peronist electoral victories were cancelled by the military. The failure of the Peronist masses to rise up in protest spread disillusion in Palabra Obrera, the Trotskyites' party, forcing them to conclude that the proletariat had lost its will to fight. Many, inspired by the Cuban Revolution, advocated an elitist insurrectionist strategy. The Cuban and Chinese Revolutions were not accomplished by the proletariat, they pointed out, but by a handful of determined young revolutionaries willing to risk their lives.[19]

Palabra Obrera (PO) would soon divide over whether to actually engage in guerrilla warfare. In 1963 the younger members, led by Cuban-trained Angel Bengochea, revolted against Nahuel Moreno, PO's leader who still favored *entrismo*. Bengochea's schism was short-lived, however, because he soon blew himself up in his fashionable Barrio Norte apartment while trying to construct a bomb. In 1965 Moreno, still prodded by his younger followers, agreed to merge PO with a Tucumán-based group called the Frente Indoamericano Popular (FRIP), led by Mario Roberto Santucho. The resulting Revolutionary Party of the Workers (PRT) quickly split on the issue of guerrilla warfare. After Moreno was forced out, in 1968, Santucho got the PRT to launch a guerrilla force, the People's Revolutionary Army (ERP).[20]

THE CHATTERING CLASSES

As educated people living in an age of worldwide communications, young Argentines were aware of what youth in other countries were doing and what fashions were "in" with respect to dress, music, movies, and ideas. By the beginning of the 1970s, it seemed that everyone in Argentina was involved in protest and revolution. Imitating campuses from California to Paris, students and professors at the University of Buenos Aires demanded an "open university" where informal classes, held in nearby parks or bars, could be taken for credit. The radical historian Juan Carlos Portantiero packed as many as three thousand students into his lectures. In La Plata, the refusal by university authorities to grant a week's vacation in 1971 in homage to the memory of Ché Guevara touched off a major riot, replete with barricades and molotov cocktails. University elections everywhere became more violent as clashes between leftists and rightists threw the various faculties into convulsions. Most students stayed away; turnout for the elections rarely exceeded 20 percent. However, that only made it easier for the activists to take over. During 1971 Montonero and ERP militants were openly recruiting on the campuses.[21]

Among the young and chic of the urban upper middle class, it was highly fashionable to identify with the guerrillas and other figures of the radical Left. Artists, writers, journalists, designers, psychiatrists, architects, and even engineers joined the growing body of alienated intelligentsia calling for revolution. Many lawyers lent their services pro bono to captured terrorists, who were now labeled "political prisoners." A generation ago such people would have been horrified to be thought of as Peronists; now they expressed their radicalism by making a hero of Perón. Perón himself got into the act by eulogizing Ché Guevara after his death, comparing him to the patriot soldiers who fought for independence against Spain or to the more modern resisters of U.S. imperialism like Pancho Villa and Sandino.

Roberto Aizcorbe wrote sarcastically:

The model Chunchuna Villafañe is a Peronist revolutionary. The first-class actor Alfredo Alcón is a Peronist revolutionary, the actress Alicia Bruzzo is a Peronist revolutionary, the first-class actor Sergio Renan is a Peronist revolutionary, the singer and filmstar Leonardo Favio is a Peronist revolutionary, the ballad singer Piero is a Peronist revolutionary, the well-to-do fashion designer Mary Tapin, creatress of the "Gaucho Look," is a Peronist revolutionary. Are they fashionable because they are revolutionary Peronists, or are they revolutionary Peronists in order to be "with it"? It is difficult to find out. Nevertheless, they create a "new attitude" which becomes a new type of intellectual conformity.

"You must!" This is at the same time a suggestion and a command. *You must* read *La Bastarda* because its authoress, Violette Leduc, is "ugly, a kleptomaniac, and a lesbian." (*Primera Plana*) *You must* see the film *Diary of a Chambermaid* by Buñuel because "the wickedness occurs in this film so naturally that it comes almost as a relief." (*Primera Plana*) *You must* go and see the play *La Granada* by Rodolfo Walsh because the soldier, a martyr for the proletarian cause, pulls the pin of his grenade. He dies but succeeds in killing his captain.

It is not that members of Buenos Aires cafe society were anarchist assassins themselves, Aizcorbe quickly assures us. "Nothing of the kind! In fact, none of them would kill a fly. But they are fascinated by violence against established things and people. Above all, they love the language of violence."[22]

So they helped to promote it, whereas the artists and writers who did not go along with it were not "fashionable" and were ignored by television and the slick magazines. Only the outrageous became celebrities. They may have been only playing at revolution, but they were influencing others who took their posturing more seriously.

NOTES

1. *Primera Plana* (6 February 1968), 18; (12 March 1968), 12–13; (23 April 1968), 12; (30 April 1968), 13–14; (7 May 1968), 14, 20–22; (27 August 1968), 13–15; (8 July 1969), 13–16; Calello and Parcero, *De Vandor a Ubaldini* vol. 1, 118.

2. Roberto García, *Patria sindical versus patria socialista* (Buenos Aires: Editorial Depalma, 1980), 73–76; Gorbato, *Vandor o Perón*, 141–42.

3. Richard Gillespie, *Soldiers of Perón: Argentina's Montoneros* (Oxford: Clarendon Press, 1982), 65, 108–9, 170–71; Juan Gasparini, *Montoneros: final de las cuentas* (Buenos Aires: Puntosur Editores, 1988), 56; Eugenio Méndez, *Aramburu: el crimen imperfecto* (Buenos Aires: Sudamericana/Planeta Editores, 1987), 141–43, 145–54, 159–63; Gorbato, *Vandor o Perón*, 142–64, expresses doubt about the ENR's responsibility for the assassination, after interviews with Delia Parodi, Miguel Gazzera, and Héctor Villalón. Villalón put the blame on "certain sectors of the military." There is no evidence to support such a theory, however.

4. Méndez, *Aramburu*, 64–66. Two Montoneros, Mario Firmenich and Norma Arrostito, published an account of the kidnapping and assassination of Aramburu in a journal called *La Causa Peronista*, on 3 September 1974. My copy is from another publication, *La Argentina y sus derechos humanos*, published by the Asociación Patriótica Argentina (no date or place of publication given; presumably Buenos Aires, c. 1979–80).

5. Armando Alonso Pineiro, *Crónica de la subversión en la Argentina* (Buenos Aires: Editorial Depalma, 1980), 73–77; Eduardo Crawley, *A House Divided: Argentina, 1880–1980* (London: C. Hurst & Co., 1984), 325–26.

6. Pineiro, *Crónica*, 77–79; García, *Patria sindical*, 85–89.

7. María Matilde Ollier, *Orden, poder, y violencia (1968–1973)* (Buenos Aires: Centro Editor de América Latina, 1989), vol. 2, 257–58.

8. Gustavo Landivar, *La universidad de la violencia* (Buenos Aires: Editorial Depalma, 1983), 55–57.

9. Oscar Terán, *Nuestros años sesentas* (Buenos Aires: Puntosur Editores, 1991), 81–86, 163.

10. Silvia Sigal, *Intelectuales y poder en la década del sesenta* (Buenos Aires: Puntosur Editores, 1991), 86–87.

11. Sigal, *Intelectuales y poder*, 89, 97.

12. Juan José Sebrelli, *Buenos Aires: Vida cotidiana y alienación* (Buenos Aires: Editores Siglo Veinte, 1965), 70–71, 75–76, 86–88, 98–103, 108–9.

13. Claudia Hilb, "La nueva izquierda, política, democracía," in Claudia Hilb and Daniel Lutzky, eds., *La nueva izquierda Argentina: 1960–1980* (Buenos Aires: Centro Editor de América Latina, 1984), 29–30: Daniel Lutzky, "Una visión de la sociedad," in Hilb and Lutzky, *La nueva izquierda Argentina*, 50–52; Terán, *Nuestros años*, 137.

14. Claudia Hilb, "La legitimación irrealizable del sistema político y la aparición de la izquierda de los años 60," in Hilb and Lutzky, *La nueva izquierda Argentina*, 14–17; Lutzky, "Una visión," 42–48, 57, 60–61. On Peronist Manichaeanism, see especially Victoria Itzcovitz, *Estilo de gobierno y crisis política (1973–1976)* (Buenos Aires: Centro Editor de América Latina, 1985), 13–19.

15. Juan José Hernández Arregui, *La formación de la conciencia nacional (1930–1960)*, 3rd. ed. (Buenos Aires: Editorial Plus Ultra, 1973), 78–98, 198, 279–80, 382–91.

16. Gustavo Pontoriero, *Sacerdotes para el Tercer Mundo: "El fermento en la masa" (1967–1976)* (Buenos Aires: Centro Editor de América Latina, 1991), 10–13, 33–36; Jimmie M. Dodson, "Religious Innovation and the Politics of Argentina: A Study of the Movement of Priests for the Third World" (Ph.D. diss., Indiana University, 1974), 45, 57–58, 61.

17. Gillespie, *Soldiers of Perón*, 54–59; Méndez, *Aramburu*, 23–25; Gasparini, *Mon-*

toneros, 31, 73; Pontoriero, *Sacerdotes*, 31–32, 80–81, 83–88, 94, 97, 102–3. Carbone was arrested again, in 1972, as an alleged machine-gun wielding participant in a guerrilla attack on the Zarate naval base, but was released. A few years later he was assassinated by the Right.

18. Norberto Galasso, *La izquierda nacional y el FIP* (Buenos Aires: Centro Editor de América Latina, 1983), 43, 63–64; Osvaldo Coggiola, *El trotskismo en la Argentina (1960–1985)* (Buenos Aires: Centro Editor de América Latina, 1986), vol. 1, 15, 28.

19. Coggiola, *El trotskismo*, 41–42.

20. María Seaone, *Todo o nada* (Buenos Aires: Editorial Planeta, 1991), 47–48; Galasso, *La izquierda nacional*, 142, 146, 149–51, 157–61.

21. Landivar, *La universidad*, 6, 9–13, 17–18, 31, 36, 61, 71.

22. Roberto Aizcorbe, *Argentina, the Peronist Myth: An Essay on the Cultural Decay of Argentina after the Second World War* (Hicksville: Exposition Press, 1975), 124–26.

THREE

The Guerrilla Emerges

The Argentine guerrilla, emerging in the late 1960s, viewed his country in the same way that a French Resistance fighter might have viewed the Vichy regime. To liberate the nation was a glorious cause worth any cost, even an occasional atrocity. Being a revolutionary presupposed a total commitment: a complete sacrifice of one's private life to the cause. Friends, family, job—all had to be expendable. In addition, there had to be a willingness to commit violent acts, including robbery, arson, and cold-blooded murder. That was a fork in the path that necessarily excluded the nonviolent proponent of change, however radical. For the guerrilla-terrorist, nonviolent action was insufficiently revolutionary because it assumed a fundamental link in values between the oppressor and the victim. Only violent action could strip away the mask of illusion, revealing the unbridgeable gulf, exposing the vulnerability of the ruling class, and stimulating the masses to revolt. The violent deed turned out to be equally liberating for the formerly frustrated intellectual who felt cut off from the real world of doers. He now ceased to be an impotent, irresolute critic or spectator and became an actor at the center stage of history.[1]

THE FIRST STEPS

The Peronist Resistance was an important source for some of the earliest figures of the guerrilla movement. Besides giving rise to the Uturuncos, the Resistance trained a large number of young men in the use of firearms and explosives and gave them a taste for violence. Three of the most prominent—Gustavo Rearte, Dardo Cabo, and Envar El Kadri—came out of the labor movement. Rearte briefly worked in the shipyards before becoming general secretary of the Soap and Perfume Workers' Union in 1956, when he was only 25. Cabo was the son of a high UOM official. El Kadri worked for the UOM as one of Vandor's bodyguards, but before that he belonged to the construction workers' union. All were strongly influenced by John William Cooke's revolutionary brand of Peronism, moved to the Left along with him, and tirelessly worked to rebuild the bases of the movement. In 1957 Rearte and El Kadri joined with another *pistolero* named Carlos Caride to revive the Peronist Youth, which later would become the Montoneros's main recruiting ground. When the military smashed the Resistance in 1960, all three men were arrested but would soon reemerge to help foster the rise of guerrilla warfare and terrorism.

The Movimiento Nacional Tacuara, which came out of the Catholic nationalist Right, was another source. Many *tacuaristas* in the 1950s were the children of former members of the Civic Legion or ALN and had inherited from them a passionate anticommunism as well as anti-Semitism. Their leader was Alberto Ezcurra Uriburu, a 20-year-old descendant of ex-President Uriburu, and their spiritual mentor was Father Julio Meinvielle, a Jew-baiting priest who had supported the Axis during the war. Tacuara adopted the Nazi salute, accepted the view that capitalism and communism were but two pincers of an international Jewish conspiracy to destroy Christianity, and embraced a creole type of fascist romanticism that celebrated gaucho violence and dressing up in uniforms for secret nighttime initiation rites in dark corners of cemeteries. It took the Maltese cross instead of the swastika as its emblem. This was not simply adolescent play-acting; the *tacuaristas* were violent, sinister, and lethal. When the Israeli secret service kidnapped Adolf Eichmann from Argentina in May 1960, Tacuara went on an anti-Semitic rampage, attacking Jewish theatres, synagogues, and students. After Eichmann was executed two years later, there was another round of attacks, climaxing in the kidnapping of a Jewish girl, Graciela Sirotta, who was beaten and had a swastika carved on her back.[2]

Tacuara suffered splits, as there was a growing recognition by some *tacuaristas* that Catholic nationalism was too elitist to ever have a chance at power, whereas Peronism, with its base in the lower middle and working classes, was more truly representative of the nation. Many *tacuaristas* admired men like Envar El Kadri, Gustavo Rearte, and Dardo Cabo, who had risked their lives in the Resistance, and so they began enlisting as Vandor's shock troops in his battles to block leftist infiltration of the CGT.[3] Tacuara "purists" looked with disfavor on this alliance with the traditional Peronist enemy, however. Blaming the new policy mainly on José ("Joe") Baxter, a 20-year-old law student and Ezcurra's personal secretary, whom they labelled a "Trotskyite, *fidelista*, and atheist," they left to form the Guardia Restauradora Nacionalista (GRN). The GRN organized itself in a strictly military fashion and continued to carry out attacks on Jews, communists, and Peronists. Besides Meinvielle, it drew for advice and inspiration upon Jordán B. Genta, a professor of philosophy and history who once had been the rector of the National University at Rosario. A former Marxist and Freemason, Genta had converted to the extreme Right and became convinced that the Jews were using both groups as instruments in their drive for world domination. He was a popular lecturer at the School of Military Aviation, where he preached the superiority of agrarian and military virtues and developed close ties to senior air force officers. Through them, he was able to secure protection and military training for the GRN.

Tacuara split again when a faction led by Dardo Cabo accepted the sponsorship of Vandor's metallurgical union. Though short-lived, *Nueva Argentina* provided bully-boys for fights with leftist unions. In September 1966, 18 of its members, led by Cabo, hijacked a plane and flew to the Falkland Islands to plant the Argentine flag. This occurred while Prince Philip was visiting Argentina and coincided with an attack on the British embassy that destroyed its front windows. The Ongania government, deeply embarrassed, gave Cabo a three-year jail term.[4]

The next big split in Tacuara happened near the end of 1963, when Joe Baxter, now a self-confessed Marxist-Leninist, formed his own group, called the Tacuara Revolutionary Nationalist Movement (MNRT) and immediately sought cooperation with the Peronist Youth. Meanwhile, Baxter and a close friend named José Luis Nell were being hunted by police after a daring robbery of the Bank Employees' Union Clinic. Both eventually managed to get out of Argentina and flee abroad. Many of those who joined the short-lived MNRT, including Nell, would later go on to become Montoneros—although Baxter himself became a Trotskyite.

While many young nationalists were moving leftwards from the Catholic Right, Trotskyism found a heroic leader in Mario Roberto ("Robi") Santucho. Santucho came from a well-to-do and very political family in the province of Santiago del Estero. His father had been a UCR militant, and his brothers ran the whole ideological gamut, from extreme Left to extreme Right. Through them, Santucho became acquainted with the national-socialist ideas of men like Jorge Abelardo Ramos, Arturo Juaretche, and Juan José Hernández Arregui. FRIP, founded in 1961 by his brothers, Francisco René and Oscar Asdrubal, was intended to spread the ideas of the Cuban Revolution, which at that time was perceived as a new and independent road to socialism. Santucho meanwhile, was at the University of Tucumán and active in student politics. As president, in 1959, of the student body of the Faculty of Economic Sciences, he was elected a delegate to the national congress of the FUA, at which he proposed a formal declaration of support for Castro's Cuba.[5]

Santucho visited Cuba in April 1961 and was so impressed by what he saw there that he enlisted for guerrilla training and remained until September. In turn, he impressed his Cuban trainers because he already had done military service in Argentina as a paratrooper and was reportedly a deadly shot. That same military service had left him with a dislike of Argentine army officers, whose treatment of the conscripts he considered cruel. On his return he landed a job as an accountant with the Tucumán Sugar Workers' Union (FOTIA), through which he began to establish a base for FRIP in Argentina's most densely populated province. Tucumán was fertile soil for radical messages in the 1960s, for its monocultural economy was constantly agitated by the federal government's threats to cut off its costly sugar subsidies—which finally happened when Ongania came to power. FOTIA was active in all the protests, and Santucho was one of its most tireless workers. His proselytizing for FRIP brought him into contact with PO. An informal alliance between FRIP and PO in Tucumán eventually led to the merger into the PRT in 1965. The PRT was not an easy marriage, however, and it did not last very long. Nahuel Moreno, the PO leader, opposed violent action, action whereas Santucho pushed the PRT further in the direction of terrorism. As the sugar mills closed, protests mounted, and the PRT was busy behind the scenes supplying strikers with guns and explosives. Santucho himself was arrested in February 1967 on charges of leading a "terrorist cell" and was sent to jail for 24 days. When he got out, his prestige had greatly increased. Many of his friends, like Luis Pujals and Enrique Gorriarán Merlo, were urging him to start a guerrilla *foco* right away. Finally, in January 1968, Moreno was ousted from the party, and Santucho promptly committed it to armed insurrection.[6]

During the early part of 1968, Santucho was busy reorganizing the PRT's directorate and bringing out its newspaper, *El Combatiente*. He went to Cuba again for more guerrilla training, and from Cuba he went to France for talks with the leaders of the Trotskyite Fourth International, which proclaimed the PRT as its only legitimate representative in Argentina. To prepare for guerrilla war, the PRT needed money to buy arms, explosives, and supplies. That was to be had through "expropriations" (bank robberies), which began in January 1969. The first job was bungled and several of the participants were caught, but Santucho managed to escape. The *cordobazo*, later that year, raised the issue within the PRT as to whether more attention should be paid to the industrial proletariat, but Santucho held firm to his original strategy: the revolution would not get diverted into the labyrinth of trade union politics. Meanwhile, the Federal Police were on the PRT's track, and at the end of October they captured a student member who furnished them with a great many details. Lightning raids throughout Tucumán resulted in the arrest of several members, including Santucho. A first attempt to free him failed, but he then made a sensational escape from prison with a pistol that his wife smuggled in to him in a hollowed-out book.

From jail, Santucho went straight to a secret hideout in the Paraná River delta, accompanied by Joe Baxter, who had returned from Vietnam by way of Uruguay, where he had been involved with the Tupamaro guerrillas. At the hideout, some 50 PRT activists decided to form the People's Revolutionary Army (*Ejército Revolucionario del Pueblo*—ERP). It would be a handpicked regiment led by Santucho, who would continue to head the PRT as well. Like any army, its members would be subject to strict discipline and severe penalties for breaking it. It would be an underground terrorist force, using code names and secret hideouts. Overall strategy would still be decided by the PRT's directorate and

central committee, which would coordinate the ERP's military tactics with actions undertaken by the "mass front organizations" that operated in the universities, high schools, factories, and working-class barrios.

THE CUBAN CONNECTION

In January 1966 Fidel Castro played host in Havana to the First Conference
of Solidarity of the Peoples of Asia, Africa, and Latin America. The two-week
convention was attended by 512 delegates representing 82 countries and colonial
territories, including Communist China, the Soviet Union, North Vietnam, North
Korea, Tanzania, Egypt, and Algeria. Political parties and movements still seeking power, like the Palestine Liberation Organization, the Viet Cong, and the
Chilean Popular Action Front (FRAP) also sent representatives. Other "observers" were Regis Debray, the French propagandist for the Cuban Revolution, and
Robin Blackburn, an English spokesman for Bertrand Russell's World Peace
Council. John William Cooke, who was living in exile in Havana and still calling
himself a Peronist, headed the Argentine contingent, composed of a *surtido* of
Stalinists, Trotskyites, Maoists, *fidelistas*, and hard-to-classify radicals. The delegates and journalists were lodged at the old Havana Hilton, now the "Hotel
Havana Libre," and were serviced by hundreds of clerks, typists, translators,
waiters, cooks, and chambermaids. For two dazzling weeks they were treated
lavishly to their choice of food and drink. To the scores of reporters attending
the event, as well as to the participants themselves, the very size and diversity
of the attendants "gave the impression it could change the course of history."[7]

One of Castro's chief aims was to start other guerrilla movements all over
Latin America, so on the day after the Tricontinental conference adjourned, he
brought the Latin American delegations together for a special session to set up
a network to be known as the Organization of Latin American Solidarity
(OLAS). In the following year they met again in Havana to discuss how armed
struggle could be promoted throughout the hemisphere. With Chile's Salvador
Allende presiding, the audience included such notables as the Colombian guerrilla priest, Father Camilo Torres, and Brazilian communist Carlos Marighela,
who would become the main theoretician of urban guerrilla warfare. The Argentine delegation, again led by John William Cooke, included Gustavo Rearte,
Father Juan García Elorrio, Joe Baxter, Emilio Maza, Fernando Abal Medina,
Norma Arrostito, and Roberto Quieto. One of the most dramatic moments of
the conference came when the delegates were read a letter from Ché Guevara,
whose whereabouts had been a mystery for more than a year. He had been
absent from the Tricontinental conference, which caused much surprise and
comment. Now, however, the OLAS delegates were informed that Ché was with
a guerrilla band in the mountains of Bolivia. His letter called upon them, in
ringing words, to return to their respective countries and create "many Viet-
nams" throughout the hemisphere, which would oblige U.S. imperialism "to

disperse its forces, pounded by the waves of the increasing hatred of the peoples of the world."[8]

Even before the Tricontinental and OLAS conferences there were attempts in Argentina to emulate the Cuban rural guerrilla *foco*. In 1962, Ricardo Masetti, a journalist who had gone to Cuba with Rodolfo Walsh and helped to set up Castro's news agency, Prensa Latina, organized a guerrilla band in Bolivia with support from fellow Argentines Ché Guevara and John William Cooke. In September 1963, the dozen or so men, calling themselves the Ejército Guerrillero del Pueblo (Guerrilla Army of the People—EGP), crossed the border into Argentina's Salta Province and set up operations near the town of Orán. Apparently, they were infiltrated by military intelligence, because they were quickly wiped out by troops from the National Gendarmerie, Argentina's border guards, in April 1964. About the same time, the police in Córdoba Province discovered a rural guerrilla camp of *fidelstas*. Seven young men were arrested, and all the equipment in the camp was seized.[9]

The OLAS conference led directly to another attempt. Two of the conference participants, Roberto Quieto and Marcos Osatinsky, gathered a group of dissidents from the Communist Party and the Argentine Socialist Party of the Vanguard to form the Ejército de Liberación Nacional (Army of National Liberation—ELN) in the mountains of the northwest, with the expressed purpose of aiding Ché Guevara's campaign in neighboring Bolivia. The ELN was in touch with the executive committee set up by OLAS in Cuba, the Ejército de Liberación Continental, as well as with the Junta Coordinadora Revolucionaria, a regional coordinating committee composed of the Uruguayan Tupamaros, the Bolivian ELN, and the Chilean Movimiento de Izquierda Revolucionaria (Movement of the Revolutionary Left—MIR). The whole project was thrown into confusion, however, when Ché Guevara was ambushed and killed in Bolivia on 8 October 1967. The Argentine ELN never recovered from this blow and soon broke up. Quieto and Osatinsky quickly started another organization, the Fuerzas Armadas Revolucionarias, which drew closer to the Peronist movement. The other guerrilla organizations of the Junta Coordinadora Revolucionaria continued to operate with financial support and training from Cuba, and eventually Mario Roberto Santucho's ERP would be included.[10]

In 1968 another rural guerrilla *foco* appeared, called the Fuerzas Armadas Peronistas (FAP). Some of its 14 members had attended the OLAS conference: Jorge Lewinger, Eva Gruska de Lewinger, and Arturo Lewinger, a former staff writer for *Primera Plana*. The main organizers, however, came out of the Peronist movement: Envar El Kadri and Carlos Caride, who had earlier set up the Peronist Youth, as well as Rodolfo Walsh and José Luis Nell, the former Tacuara militant. There were also two ex-seminarians imbued with the spirit of Liberation Theology. FAP's rural operation was located in Tucumán, near the town of Taco Ralo, but it was hardly launched when the local police swept down on it. Most of the members were arrested and jailed and the police seized a sizable quantity of automatic weapons, antitank guns, and explosives. They also found a diary on one of the guerrillas killed in the attack that included the description of an execution of two comrades for "indiscipline." Caride and Walsh escaped. Caride was taken into custody a year later after a shootout with the police, but Walsh and a few others went underground. FAP would reemerge in early 1970 as an urban terrorist organization, robbing banks to get money for weapons and working through left-wing Peronist unions to set up revolutionary cells in factories. On the Day of the Three Kings, in 1970, FAP gained some brief popularity by taking over a slum neighborhood in Buenos Aires and distributing toys to the children. However, without El Kadri and Caride, it lacked leadership and began falling apart. Most of its members joined the Montoneros in 1972.[11]

THE URBAN GUERRILLA

Ché Guevara's capture and execution by the Bolivian Special Forces was a setback for the rural guerrilla strategy. Some revolutionaries would continue adhering to it—Santucho's ERP was a notable Argentine example—but many others would lose their faith in its efficacy. Rural guerrilla tactics had failed in Argentina, Ecuador, the Dominican Republic, Guatemala, Paraguay, Brazil, and Venezuela mainly because the United States had redefined its military assistance program in Latin America. Instead of conventional military equipment designed to prevent an attack from a foreign army, it now emphasized items more suitable to counterinsurgency: helicopters, highly mobile landing craft, spotter planes, sophisticated communications equipment. Latin American military and police officers were brought to the United States for counterintelligence training, or to the School of the Americas in the Canal Zone, where they learned jungle warfare. There was also greater emphasis on civic action to win popular support in rural communities through the army's involving itself in improving local transportation, education, and health services. Despite left-wing propaganda decrying such programs, they succeeded, in most cases, in depriving the guerrillas of a receptive population.[12]

Guevara's debacle in Bolivia rubbed in another painful truth: most guerrillas were urban middle-class intellectuals who were easily conspicuous in a rural setting and, moreover, were viewed with suspicion by the peasants. The myths surrounding the Cuban Revolution made the would-be liberators expect a warm welcome from the "oppressed" peasantry; instead they were shunned. Indeed, as in Guevara's case, the peasants often informed the army or police of the intruders' whereabouts. So it began to dawn on the more reflective revolutionaries that the "objective conditions" for an insurrection were not present in most rural situations and that they were not so easily created as Guevara had promised. By contrast, the revolutionaries could easily blend into urban settings like Buenos Aires, Montevideo, Rio de Janeiro, or São Paulo. The urban guerrilla looked just like everyone else, and in those sprawling cities he was anonymous.

If he were caught, there would be "progressive" lawyers and journalists to defend him.[13]

One of the earliest revolutionaries to recognize the advantages of urban guerrilla warfare was Carlos Marighela, a Brazilian communist who broke with the party upon his return from the OLAS conference. Marighela and many of the younger Brazilian Communist Party members were impatient to launch a guerrilla movement, the Nationalist Liberating Alliance (ALN). Rural guerrilla tactics had already been tried in Brazil between 1964 and 1966 and had failed in every instance. Marighela decided, therefore, to switch the focus to the cities. His *Minimanual*, written in June 1969 as a guide for other Latin American revolutionaries, became the classic textbook for urban guerrilla warfare. For Marighela, rural guerrilla warfare could succeed in the more industrialized countries only after a period of urban terrorism had sapped the existing regime's morale. By creating chaos, frightening off foreign investors, disrupting the economy and the administrative machinery, and pinning down the security forces to the cities, the urban guerrilla would bring about the conditions that would make it possible for rural guerrillas to spread and eventually link up with the urban underground. Then it would be possible for the guerrillas to create a regular army to deliver the ultimate crushing blow.[14]

Urban guerrilla warfare would be carried out, according to Marighela, by small armed groups who would do the actual fighting, but they would be supported by mass action groups of students and workers who would contribute to the struggle with strikes, street demonstrations, sabotage, and propaganda. Beyond them would be a network of sympathizers, drawn from every walk of life, who would provide information, supplies, and money. These three levels of participation, from the core outward, were called the "guerrilla front," the "mass front," and the "support network." Urban guerrillas would be constantly active, because "action creates a vanguard" by weeding out the incompetent, creating a sense of solidarity, and gaining prestige for the group. They always had to be on the attack, never on the defensive, and had to use the advantages of surprise, careful preparation, and a thorough knowledge of the terrain to carry out successful operations. They had to be mobile, never sticking to a fixed base. Each guerrilla was required to undergo a thorough ideological indoctrination so as to give him the morale to risk his life. That was supposed to give him an advantage over the ordinary policeman or military conscript, who was thought to lack any idea of the objective for which he was fighting. The guerrilla was also to be trained in the use of a variety of weapons, vehicles, machinery, and explosives. He had to accept discipline and be in top physical condition, because he would be expected to participate in a wide range of tactical operations that would test his skills and endurance, from bank robberies to arms seizures, from kidnappings to ambushes.[15]

Even before the *Minimanual* appeared, however, some guerrilla groups already had dedicated themselves to urban terrorism. One of the earliest of these was the Uruguayan Tupamaros. Formed originally in 1962 by Raúl Sendic, a law student, they gradually built up a supply of arms and an intelligence network until, by 1969, they were ready to go into action. From the very beginning, Uruguay's topographic and demographic character indicated the appropriateness of an urban strategy. The land is flat and open, like the Argentine pampa, and there is only one sizable city, Montevideo, the capital, where 40 percent of the population lives.

The Tupamaros became a model for Argentina's urban guerrillas. Men like Joe Baxter, who returned to Argentina to join ERP, and José Luis Nell, who became a Montonero by way of FAP, served first in the Uruguayan underground and brought with them their experience of Tupamaro tactics. The Tupamaros divided their organization into three layers. The inner core was made up of "combatants": experienced, reliable, dedicated full-time militants engaged in commando-type operations. The next layer consisted of cells of activists engaged in providing various support services: supplying arms, ammunition, food, clothing, medical attention, and hideouts. They could also provide vehicles, make explosives, print propaganda, repair cars and weapons, and gather intelligence. The outer layer was a network of sympathizers, or "peripherals," who worked for it only part-time. Many business firms and government agencies had secret cells called CATs (Committees in Support of the Tupamaros). They helped to obtain arms, supplies, documents, and information; in addition, they distributed propaganda and identified potential recruits. Coordinating all three layers was an executive committee headed by Sendic, which handled all the finances, decided upon strategy and tactics, and applied discipline.

As the Tupamaros gained experience and confidence, their operations became more ambitious. They attacked police and military outposts; bombed the homes, offices, and clubs of conservative opponents; and carried out reprisals against members of the security forces considered guilty of directing the repression against them or of using torture. Sometimes those reprisals were taken against their family, friends, or bodyguards. There were spectacular attacks on jails to free captured guerrillas and there were dramatic kidnappings of prominent government officials, businessmen, and foreign diplomats. According to Arturo Porzecanski, by May 1972 the Tupamaros were running a shadow government in Montevideo, and they felt so invincible that they even published lists of their intended victims in advance.[16]

THE ARGENTINE GUERRILLAS

Even before Joe Baxter and José Luis Nell put their experience with the Tupamaros at the service of ERP and the Montoneros, other Argentine guerrilla organizations had been forming: the Fuerzas Armadas de Liberación (FAL), the Descamisado Command, and the Fuerzas Armadas Revolucionarias (FAR). FAL was started in 1966 but did not engage in any armed actions until 4 April 1969, when it attacked the First Infantry Regiment in the Buenos Aires neighborhood of Palermo and got away with some weapons. In March 1970, FAL also kidnapped the Paraguayan consul, Waldemar Sánchez, but later released him. The group, composed of dissident Communist Party youth and some left-wing Peronists, merged with ERP in 1972.[17]

The Descamisado Command was originally founded by radical dissidents from the youth wing of the Christian Democratic Party. Guided by two older men, Dardo Cabo and Rodolfo Walsh, the Descamisados carried out the assassinations of Augusto Vandor and José Alonso. Despite these "achievements," the organization decided in 1973 to merge with the much larger Montonero movement. FAR's origins go back to the ELN, founded in 1967 to support Ché Guevara's band in Bolivia. The ELN broke up after Guevara was killed, but many of its principal figures decided to switch to urban guerrilla tactics and form a new organization. After bombing the Minimax stores in Buenos Aires in 1970, FAR made news by seizing an army truck in 1971 that was carrying weapons, killing the driver in the attack. FAR's Cuban-trained founders, Roberto Quieto and Marcos Osatinsky, were joined later by Carlos Enrique Olmedo, who rose from a humble background to obtain a university degree in philosophy and Juan Pablo Maestre, who led the column that briefly took over the small town of Garín in July 1970. The following year proved disastrous for FAR, however. Maestre, Osatinsky, and Quieto were arrested in July 1971, and Olmedo was killed in a shootout with the police. Maestre "disappeared," but human rights lawyers rallied to Quieto and Osatinsky's case, so they were brought to trial and sent to the military prison at Rawson, Chubut. From there they made a sensational escape, together with other guerrilla leaders, and returned to Argentina under an amnesty in May 1973 to help the remnants of FAR merge with the Montoneros. By the end of 1973 a series of mergers had reduced the number of significant guerrilla groups to only two: the Montoneros and ERP. They seldom collaborated, however, because the Montoneros had positioned themselves inside the Peronist movement and had been accepted by Perón as his "special formations," whereas ERP rejected him as a "bonapartist" and false revolutionary.[18]

The Montoneros's organization hardly differed from the *Minimanual*'s ideal. The core consisted of combat units called *comandos*, which were underground cells capable of combining to form larger units. Later, when the movement grew and had to be more carefully structured, these were called "platoons." Surrounding these nucleii of combatants was a complex layer of mass front organizations known collectively as the "Revolutionary Tendency." These were all controlled and coordinated by the Montoneros's legal organization, the Peronist Youth, which in turn was divided into eight "regionals." Each "regional" was responsible for the following groups in its area: the Peronist University Youth, the Peronist Worker Youth, the Union of Secondary Students, the "Evita Group" of the Feminist Party, the Peronist Shantytown Dwellers' Movement, and the Peronist Tenants' Movement. Above all this was a National Leadership Committee (*Conducción Nacional*—CN), headed by Mario Eduardo Firmenich and supported by a National Secretariat that linked the national leaders to the regional and local committees. The CN, the national secretaries, and the secretaries of the "regionals" constituted the National Council, which planned the movement's political and military strategy. The entire organization operated on the lines of a military hierarchy, with no pretense of democracy. The mass front organizations were subordinate to the combatants, and the local combat units took orders from above. At every level officers were chosen by the national leadership, and the same was true of the recruitment of new members: front organizations could propose names, but the national leadership made the actual selection. Only in on-the-spot tactical matters did local combat units have some decisional leeway. Each platoon and regiment had an executive committee, or "war department," headed by a senior officer, that assigned tasks in a military operation.[19]

For really big military operations, the Peronist Youth regional would mobilize its front organizations as "militia" to provide support services for the platoons, in which case the total fighting unit was called a "column." Whereas platoons specialized in heavy combat, using sophisticated weapons, the militia were armed with only handguns, molotov cocktails, and walkie-talkies. Their job was to keep open escape routes, provide warnings about reinforcements, and create diversions. When not supporting combat operations, the front organizations were urged to supply needed services, for which they were divided along functional lines. Certain members were responsible for acquiring and maintaining vehicles, others specialized in fabricating documents, and still others wrote manifestos and communiqués as dictated by the national leadership. Eventually the Montoneros were able to operate several clandestine factories capable of producing a wide variety of equipment, from rifles, revolvers, and grenades to machinery and replacement parts. Unlike the full-time guerrillas who composed the combat units and lived underground, people belonging to the front organizations were expected to lead normal lives in public, attending classes or holding steady jobs. They were to dress neatly and conventionally and to engage in no behavior that would call attention to themselves.[20]

Beyond the mass front organizations lay a broad support network of sympathizers: the "eyes and ears of the People," as the Montoneros's tabloid *Evita Montonera* put it. The Montoneros sought out older people who had lived for a long time in their neighborhoods or who had worked at a particular establishment for many years. "Such people have a large amount of information that is useful," *Evita Montonera* remarked. "They know a lot about people who live around them and about their co-workers." Such people could identify informers, police infiltrators, or even secret sympathizers with the Montonero movement. They could furnish information about where police and military officers live, their daily routine, the number of people in their families, what their neighbors say about them, what their wives say to the local shopkeepers; whether they have bodyguards and if so, how many, what they look like, and what sort of weapons they carry. "There may be many people out there who would never say anything if they knew it would help the Montoneros, but they might reveal interesting things in a friendly conversation over a glass of wine to a secret

Montonero sympathizer who would pass it on." Such information might be useful, for example, in drawing floor plans and organizational charts of places they intended to attack—or for kidnapping someone or assassinating him, or intimidating a shop steward who wasn't forceful enough in representing his fellow factory workers.[21]

The Montoneros also referred to their support network as the "rear guard" of their military operations, the "geopolitical space" into which they could retreat after a confrontation with the government's forces. They also drew upon their sympathizers as occasional sources of logistical aid and specialized services. Sympathizers sometimes helped to write, print, store, or distribute propaganda. Gunsmiths, mechanics, lathe operators, and other skilled workers were especially valuable. "We lack shops to manufacture all kinds of materials, from the little barriers (*miguelitos*) that we use during a getaway or to cut off a street, to machine gun barrels. Everything helps, from a small wirecutter to a soldering iron or a screw. We need auto repair shops." There was always a need for doctors and nurses to help *compañeros* wounded in combat or stressed by life in the underground. To facilitate military operations, "*compañeros* who understand the workings of radio transmitters or walkie-talkies are as useful as *compañeros* who lend us their telephones to keep in touch with operatives, or who receive and transmit messages." Again *Evita Montonera* underscored the need to receive information about the Montoneros's opponents and the government's counterrevolutionary plans, as well as the layout of telephone exchanges, utilities plants, and underground sewer systems.[22]

The PRT-ERP was organized in a similar fashion to the Montoneros. The PRT was the movement's political arm and supreme decision-making body. At its top was a seven-man politburo, headed by its general secretary, Mario Roberto Santucho. Below that was an executive committee, composed of the politburo plus four other members; and below that (though theoretically the PRT's ultimate authority) was the central committee, made up of the executive committee plus all of the 12 regional secretaries. The central committee's work was divided up among specialized committees consisting of propaganda, labor affairs, international affairs, legal affairs, and solidarity work.

The propaganda committee's main task was to produce the PRT-ERP's news organs. The PRT had acquired a daily newspaper, *El Mundo* ("The World"), in addition to which it published two weeklies: *El Combatiente* ("The Combatant") for the PRT and *Estrella Roja* ("Red Star") for ERP. There was also a nominally independent magazine, *Revista Nuevo Hombre* ("New Man Review"), edited by Silvio Frondizi and Manuel Gaggero, who also edited *El Mundo. El Combatiente* and *Estrella Roja* were turned out in (literally) underground printing houses, located in subterranean chambers. One of those, described by Luis Mattini (whose real name was Arnold Kremer), a former *erpista*, was in an enormous cavern about 25 feet below the street level, consisting of two arched corridors about 10 feet high, 10 wide, and 45 feet long that formed a cross. Besides the printing presses, the corridors contained a conference room, sleeping quarters for 12 bathrooms, a kitchen, a library, storerooms, a guard station, and an exit leading to Buenos Aires's sewer system.[23]

The labor affairs committee focused on the unions, where PRT-ERP had much more success than the Montoneros did. Its leaders were more experienced in labor matters to begin with, because FRIP and PO had been involved in strikes and agitation for years. The PRT made it a policy to recruit more proletarians to its ranks and promote them to leadership positions. Julio Santucho calculated that as of 1974, about 30 percent of PRT's membership and 50 percent of its central committee were from working-class backgrounds. The PRT also urged its members to get factory jobs, concentrating especially in areas like cleaning services, quality control, or freight, which would give them a reason to move about the plant and get in touch with people in every section. They were to form cells that would put pressure on the old, moderate shop stewards at contract time and agitate for more internal democracy in the local unions. Consequently, by mid-1974 PRT had made significant inroads into the labor organizations of Córdoba, Rosario, Tucumán, and the industrial complex around Villa Constitución in southern Santa Fe Province.[24]

The international affairs committee was the PRT's link to the Tupamaros, the Chilean MIR, and the Bolivian ELN. It also maintained ties with Cuba, the Soviet bloc countries, Third World liberation movements, and Western European communist parties. It had offices in Paris and, briefly, in Lisbon, as well as contacts to terrorists operating out of Stockholm. The legal affairs committee supervised the mass front organizations like the Anti-Imperialist Front for Socialism, headed by Silvio Frondizi. The Movimiento Sindical de Base was the PRT's labor front, while shantytown dwellers were represented through the Cómites de Base. Among the youth, the PRT's university organization was relatively weak; but its high school front, the Juventud Guevarista, was very active and was an important source for recruiting future guerrillas. Finally, the solidarity work committee involved PRT with various human rights organizations, such as the National Movement Against Repression and Torture and the Commission for Families of Political, Student, and Labor Prisoners (COFAP-PEG). These carried on agitation against the use of torture and "disappearances," which were becoming more common under the Lanusse government. They also arranged for the services of human rights lawyers to defend captured guerrillas and tried to pressure the courts to release those prisoners.[25]

Below the PRT's national level structures were 12 regional committees: four for the Greater Buenos Aires area, three for Santa Fe Province, and one each for Tucumán, Salta, Mendoza, Neuquén, and Córdoba Provinces. Those regions were then subdivided into zones, which were in turn subdivided into neighborhood and workplace cells. A cell usually consisted of three members, with no more than six, and perhaps three candidate members. As with the Montoneros, orders flowed from the top down, in military fashion. ERP was the movement's military wing and Mario Roberto Santucho was its "commandant," the highest ranking officer, thus combining in his own person the supreme political and military powers. Below him, ERP's structure resembled that of any army. Its basic units were squads of 5 to 10 guerrillas, led by a sergeant. Those could be combined into platoons of 15 to 20 guerrillas, under a lieutenant; platoons could form companies of 30 to 90 guerrillas, under a captain.[26]

ERP's operations were divided into a rural front and an urban front. The rural front, headquartered in Tucumán, had two companies, each with two platoons and four squads. The urban front consisted of five companies: one for Córdoba, one for Rosario, and three for the Greater Buenos Aires area. One did not have to belong to PRT to be in ERP, but one did have to accept the PRT's leadership and undergo intensive political indoctrination. The PRT's military committee, an offshoot of the central committee, had cells in all ERP units. Every unit also had both a military and a political captain. That occasionally caused some problems, but in general the political captains did not interfere in military decisions. Santucho insisted on instilling a military attitude in his "soldiers." They all wore uniforms, "presented arms when officers arrived," used the formal manner of address toward superiors, and observed a strict code of discipline.

Despite their structural similarities, there were important differences between the Montoneros and the PRT-ERP. In addition to their ideological differences, the Montoneros were much more middle class in their social composition. Not many proletarians were to be found either in their rank-and-file membership or among their leaders, although there were a few important Montonero figures from the working class. By contrast, the PRT-ERP made a greater effort to incorporate workers. They were fairly successful in getting blue-collar laborers into their mass front organizations, but much less so in enlisting them in ERP. According to Luis Mattini, most workers considered guerrilla tactics as too "leftist" and "infantile."[27]

Of the two organizations, the Montoneros were universally conceded to be the larger, by far. Unfortunately, their actual number is a matter of guesswork, because no exact membership figures were ever made public. Army estimates of guerrilla strength tended to be high. General Ramón Genaro Díaz Bessone put total guerrilla fighting capacity, at the beginning of 1975, at about 30,000 combatants, with another 150,000 people active in the mass front organizations and support networks. His colleague, General Osiris Villegas, was more conservative in his estimates: 15,000 combatants, backed by another 25,000 collaborators. This latter figure came close to an estimate offered by the weekly British publication *Latin America*, in January 1976, of around 20,000 "incorporated into the military structures of the guerrilla organizations, at one level or another." The magazine went on to note: "Certainly they are not all adequately armed or trained, but this puts them potentially on a footing with the Argentine regular army which consists of some 6,000 officers and 19,000 non-commissioned officers. Except in a few specialized units, the ordinary soldiers are all conscripts, of whom there are around 65,000. The army is particularly concerned at the possibility of many new recruits already belonging to guerrilla organizations." Even a careful political scientist like Kenneth Johnson accepted the higher figures. He estimated Montonero strength in the spring of 1975 at 250,000 members, of which only 25,000 actually bore arms. ERP was estimated to have 60,000 members and sympathizers, but only 5,000 actual combatants. The latter were thought to be more heavily armed than the Montonero platoons, however.[28]

At the other extreme, human rights activists preferred to minimize the guerrillas' strength. D. Frontini and M. C. Ciai, in a report entitled *El mito de la guerra sucia* ("The Myth of the Dirty War"), written for the Center for Legal and Social Studies, calculated the combined guerrilla forces at the beginning of 1976 to number only somewhere between two and three thousand. That presumably referred only to combatants. That was not much below the estimates of some other military men—Generals Jorge Rafael Videla and Roberto Viola—who led the 1976 military coup. Videla thought there were perhaps four thousand guerrilla fighters, while Viola put their number at closer to three thousand. María Seoane, who wrote the most careful study of Santucho and ERP, estimated ERP's peak strength at six hundred to one thousand combatants, backed up by another two thousand to five thousand activists in front organizations and perhaps as many as 20,000 sympathizers in the support network. Martin Andersen guessed there were three hundred armed ERP combatants for the Greater Buenos Aires area, which is about 50 fewer than Seoane estimated.[29]

As for the Montoneros, Moyano put their fighting strength in 1974 at "at least 3,000 active combatants," out of a total guerrilla combatant population of 5,000. Richard Gillespie, combining both commandos and militia, estimated that the Montoneros could mobilize "at least five thousand people." He admitted, however, that other knowledgeable observers might put the figure higher. Robert Cox, the former editor of the English-language *Buenos Aires Herald*, thought that the Montoneros might have as many as 10,000 guerrilla fighters. Cox's estimate may have been more accurate, if Juan Gasparini's calculations are right. Gasparini, a former Montonero militant, asserted that the Montoneros lost as many as 5,000 combatants in the first few months after the 1976 coup, suggesting that their numbers were much greater at the peak of their strength. As for the mass front organizations and support network, guessing at their numbers is even more difficult. Peronist Youth rallies often attracted more than 100,000 people, and Martin Andersen estimated that at the 1974 May Day Rally, "fully half of the more than 150,000 who filled the Plaza de Mayo" were Montoneros, Peronist Youth, and activists in the various front organizations constituting the "Revolutionary Tendency."[30]

Whether one accepts the higher or lower estimates, Argentina's guerrilla organizations, backed by multimillion dollar war chests, were formidable—and lethal. Sustained, at least until Perón returned in 1973, by a favorable public opinion, they grew in numbers, organizational sophistication, and fire power. Their collaborators reached into every level and every sector of society, and no one was safe from their vengeance. As they moved, within a few short years, from small scattered bands engaging in isolated terrorist acts to large-scale military operations, they became a credible threat to the established order, including the military's traditional monopoly of violence.

NOTES

1. Richard E. Rubenstein, *Alchemists of Revolution: Terrorism in the Modern World* (New York: Basic Books, 1987), 8–9, 93–97, 99–100, 145, 148.

2. *Tacuara* means "lance" in the Araucanian Indian language. Marysa Navarro Gerassi, *Los nacionalistas* (Buenos Aires: Editorial Jorge Álvarez, 1968), 148–53, 203, 225–27; Christian Buchrucher, *Nacionalismo y Peronismo* (Buenos Aires: Editorial Sudamericana, 1987), 49, 203; Leonardo Senkman, "The Right and Civilian Regimes, 1955–1976," in Sandra McGee Deutsch and Ronald H. Dolkart, eds., *The Argentine Right: Its History and Intellectual Origins, 1910 to the Present* (Wilmington: Scholarly Resources, 1993), 126; Gorbato, *Vandor o Perón*, 55, 72. Tacuara had imitators, such as the Concentración Nacional Universitaria, a right-wing student organization that formed in La Plata under the leadership of Carlos Disandro and Alejandro Giovenco.

3. Gorbato, *Vandor o Perón*, 54–55, 73, 75, 84; Ramón Prieto, *El pacto* (Buenos Aires: Editorial En Marcha, 1963), 170–71, states that Perón approved of Vandor's use of Tacuara against leftist infiltrators of the movement.

4. Gorbato, *Vandor o Perón*, 122–26.

5. Seoane, *Todo o nada*, 28–41, 49.

6. Coggiola, *El trotskismo*, 57–59; Seoane, *Todo o nada*, 35, 39, 50–51, 64–65, 72–73, 98, 104–5; Antonio Petric, *Así sangraba la Argentina: Sallustro, Quijada, Larrabure* (Buenos Aires: Editorial Depalma, 1983), 27.

7. Maurice Halperin, *The Taming of Fidel Castro* (Berkeley: University of California, 1981), 186, 188–89; Luis A. Leoni Houssay, *La conexión internacional del terrorismo* (Buenos Aires: Editorial Depalma, 1980), 174–82; Hugh Thomas, *The Cuban Revolution* (New York: Harper & Row, 1977), 702–3.

8. Ramón Genaro Díaz Bessone, *Guerra revolucionaria en la Argentina* (Buenos Aires: Editorial Fraterna, 1986), 74, 75; Leoni Houssay, *La conexión*, 184–85; Seoane, *Todo o nada*, 103; Halperin, *Taming*, 192, n. 10; Thomas, *Cuban Revolution*, 704.

9. Seoane, *Todo o nada*, 350–51; *Nuevo Confirmado*, (18 December 1975), 22.

10. Familiares y Amigos de los Muertos por la Subversión (FAMUS), *Operación Independencia* (Buenos Aires: FAMUS, 1988), 29–31, 34–35.

11. Gasparini, *Montoneros*, 24–25, 29; Richard Gillespie, *Soldiers of Perón*, 67, 106–7.

12. Brian Loveman and Thomas M. Davies, Jr., "Introduction: Guerrilla Warfare, Revolutionary Theory, and Revolutionary Movements in Latin America," in Ernesto "Ché" Guevara, *Guerrilla Warfare* (Lincoln: University of Nebraska, 1985), 19–28.

13. James Kohl and John Litt, eds., *Urban Guerrilla Warfare in Latin America* (Cambridge: MIT Press, 1974), 6–10; Díaz Bessone, *Guerra revolucionaria*, 42–43.

14. Carlos Marighela, "Problems and Principles of Strategy," in Kohl and Litt, *Urban Guerrilla Warfare*, 81–86; and Carlos Marighela, *For the Liberation of Brazil* (Baltimore: Penguin Books, 1971), 37–38, 47. The letter is the English language translation of the *Minimanual*.

15. Marighela, *For the Liberation of Brazil*, 31–32, 34–35, 55–56, 64–66, 73–78.

16. On the Tupamaros's organization, strategy, and operations, see Arturo C. Porze-

canski, *Uruguay's Tupamaros: The Urban Guerrilla* (New York: Praeger, 1973); and Carlos Wilson, *The Tupamaros: The Unmentionables* (Boston: Branden Press, 1974).

17. Donald C. Hodges, *Argentina, 1943–1987: The National Revolution and Resistance* (Albuquerque: University of New Mexico Press, 1988), 67; María José Moyano, *Argentina's Lost Patrol: Armed Struggle, 1969–1979* (New Haven: Yale University Press, 1995), 26; Seoane, *Todo o nada*, 352; Raúl Tomás Escobar, *Estrategia contrarevolucionaria* (Buenos Aires: Editorial Fraterna Internacional, 1984), 71–72.

18. Roberto Baschetti, ed., "La guerrilla en la Argentina: Quién fué quién, 1959–1973," *Documentos (1970–1973): De la guerrilla peronista al gobierno popular* (Buenos Aires: Editorial de la Campana, 1995), 34–39; Roberto Cirilo Perdía, *La otra historia: testimonio de un jefe montonero* (Buenos Aires: Grupo Ágora, 1997), 179–80. Indeed, Perón assured the Montoneros that he approved of Aramburu's "execution" and urged them forward in their guerrilla strategy. See Baschetti, "Montoneros a Perón, 9 de febrero, 1971," and "Perón a Montoneros, 20 de febrero, 1971," *Documentos*, 123–28.

19. Perdía, *La otra historia*, 117–21.

20. Gillespie, *Soldiers of Perón*, 84, 134, 177–78, 182–83; Moyano, *Argentina's Lost Patrol*, 149–51; Gasparini, *Montoneros*, 74–75.

21. "Los ojos y oídos del pueblo," *Evita Montonera*, vol. 2, no. 12 (February–March 1976), 26–27.

22. "La participación del pueblo en la guerra," *Evita Montonera*, vol. 1, no. 7 (September 1975), 9–11.

23. Luis Mattini, *Hombres y mujeres del PRT-ERP* (Buenos Aires: Editorial Contrapunto, 1990), 321, 372; Seoane, *Todo o nada*, 371. These underground publications constantly took a "triumphalist" tone, much to Mattini's annoyance. In his view as a pragmatic, proletarian, metallurgical worker, their bragging about their strategy and strength often furnished the military and police with useful information.

24. Luis Santucho, *Los últimos guevaristas: surgimiento y eclipse del Ejército Revolucionario del Pueblo* (Buenos Aires: Editorial Puntosur, 1988), 207; Mattini, *Hombres y mujeres*, 254–55; García, *Patria sindical*, 15, 50, 52.

25. Seoane, *Todo o nada*, 367–71; Mattini, *Hombres y mujeres*, 250–58; Moyano, *Argentina's Lost Patrol*, 148.

26. For a description of PRT-ERP's structure, see Mattini, *Hombres y mujeres*, 245–46, 293–95; Seoane, *Todo o nada*, 360–61.

27. Mattini, *Hombres y mujeres*, 256.

28. On estimates of guerrilla strength, see Díaz Bessone, *Guerra revolucionaria*, 25, n. 17, 34–35, 38–39; Osiris Villegas, *Testimonio de un alegato* (Buenos Aires: Author, 1990), 186; *Latin America*, vol 10, no. 5 (30 January 1976), 35; Kenneth Johnson, "Guerrilla Politics in Argentina," *Conflict Studies*, vol. 63 (October 1976), 15.

29. Seoane, *Todo o nada*, 262; Martin Andersen, *Dossier Secreto: Argentina's Desaparecidos and the Myth of the "Dirty War"* (Boulder: Westview Press, 1993), 233.

30. Moyano, *Argentina's Lost Patrol*, 2, 41; Gillespie, *Soldiers of Perón*, 120, 178; Gasparini, *Montoneros*, 206; Andersen, *Dossier Secreto*, 109.

FOUR

The Guerrillas' World

Bombings, shootings, kidnappings, bank robberies, and armed ambushes grew more frequent as the guerrilla organizations grew and spread. There are no precise statistics on such acts of violence; those that exist are only estimates, and they vary considerably. Nonetheless, they all point to a similar pattern: a sudden, sharp upsurge in guerrilla violence beginning in 1969 that would hit a peak in 1971. Then it would decline in 1972, as the military government began to apply tough, counterguerrilla tactics, including the use of special tribunals, torture, and "disappearances." In 1973, however, an exhausted, unpopular military held elections and turned the government over to Héctor Cámpora, Perón's designated stand-in. On inauguration day, Cámpora declared an amnesty and released all the captured guerrillas. Although the Montoneros pledged their support to the new Peronist government, ERP simply renewed its campaign. As a result, guerrilla violence rose once more in 1973; after the Montoneros broke with Perón in mid-1974, it shot up to unprecedented levels and remained high throughout 1975. Only after the military returned to power, in March 1976, were the guerrilla organizations finally uprooted and smashed.

VARIETIES OF TERRORISM

María Ollier's study of guerrilla violence, which ends with the Peronist restoration in 1973, noted 1,243 cases of terrorist attacks of all kinds, for an average of slightly fewer than one a day, or about two every three days. It is important to keep this frequency in mind in order to understand the extreme tension behind the upward spiral of terror and counterterror. Of those 1,243 cases, 659 (53 percent) were attributable to a particular guerrilla band, or bands acting together, either because some of the attackers were caught or because the perpetrators claimed credit afterwards. Of all those groups identified with these attacks, ERP was the most active, accounting for 262 (40 percent) of the total. The Montoneros (67 attacks) and FAL (61) were the next most active forces, followed by FAR (39), FAP (26), and the Descamisado Command (10). The rest were committed by small, ephemeral Marxist or Peronist groups. According to Ollier's calculations, these guerrilla attacks reached a peak of 603 in 1971, as compared to 282 in 1970 and 368 in 1972.[1]

María Moyano's statistics, though recording more incidents, revealed a pattern similar to Ollier's. From 114 "armed operations" in 1969, there was a sharp increase to 434 in 1970, rising even higher to 654 in 1971, then dropping to 352 in 1972. On the other hand, Guillermo O'Donnell recorded a steady increase in "acts of political violence" from 349 in 1969 to 443 in 1970, 619 in 1971, and 745 in 1972. When bombings were subtracted from these figures, however, leaving only acts of armed political violence, the pattern was the same as in the other studies: 49 acts of armed political violence in 1969, 156 in 1970, 275 in 1971, and 206 in 1972. The decline in 1972 found by all three authors was only temporary. Moyano, the only one of the three to offer figures after 1972, recorded a sharp upswing in armed operations in 1973: 413, as opposed to 352 the year before. That almost doubled, to 807, in 1974 and it remained high, at 723, in 1975.[2]

O'Donnell didn't separate his figures on armed violence into categories like bank robberies, kidnappings, or assaults on military and police installations, but he did isolate statistics on political assassinations. Those averaged only 5 a year from 1960 to 1968 but then rose sharply to 39 in 1969, 41 in 1970, 64 in 1971, and 68 in 1972. Moyano classified her armed operations more carefully into arms thefts, attacks on property, takeovers (of towns, buildings, broadcasting stations, or police and military posts), bombings, kidnappings, hijackings, and deaths (i.e., assassinations). She found that bombings (855 incidents), arms thefts (278), and takeovers (200) were the most frequent kinds of guerrilla action between 1969 and 1973. There were also many incidents of arson. In general, this earlier period saw more attacks on property than on persons, although there was a greater number of political assassinations (129) and kidnappings (85) than Argentina had ever experienced. By contrast, from 1973 to 1976, political assassinations by guerrillas almost quadrupled, to 481, and kidnappings almost doubled, to 140. In the latter case, the guerrillas were able to demand, and get, huge ransoms for their victims, which enabled them to purchase large quantities of weapons. That resulted in a drop in the number of arms thefts to only 107. Takeovers also changed in nature. In the earlier period, guerrillas commonly took over school buildings, movie theatres, or radio and television stations in order to get their message before the public by haranguing the audience. From 1973 on, the emphasis shifted to military bases, so that while the number of takeovers dropped to only 143, the scale of operations was more significant.[3]

About half of all guerrilla attacks happened in the city of Buenos Aires and the surrounding province. Córdoba and Santa Fe Provinces added another 30 percent, and Tucumán and Mendoza another 10. Of the 687 people killed in guerrilla attacks between the start of 1969 and the end of 1975, 523 were policemen and soldiers. Of those, 105 were from the army, 19 from the navy, 10 from the air force, 9 from the National Gendarmerie (border guards), 119 from the heavily armed Federal Police, 141 from the Buenos Aires provincial police, and the remaining 112 from all other local police forces. The next largest category of victims consisted of businessmen, whether merchants, industrialists, or *estancieros*: 54 in all. Then came labor union officials (24), politicians and public functionaries (21), guerrilla deserters (11), and innocent bystanders who happened to get hit in a shootout. These included 3 wives and 3 children of security officers who were killed with their husbands or fathers. Guerrillas also took heavy casualties during these operations. According to the *Review of the River Plate*, security forces killed 136 of them in 1970, 270 in 1971, and 242 in 1972. However, those figures might be inflated by the inclusion of common criminals killed during robberies.[4]

The assassinations of Vandor, Aramburu, and Alonso opened up this bloody period. No such prominent victims were killed in 1971, but 51 policemen and 6 prison guards were gunned down, and Lieutenant Marcos César Azua lost his life trying to prevent the hijacking of his army truck carrying a load of weapons. Another 38 policemen were killed during 1972, and on 17 March, ERP guerrillas in Quilmes broke into the home of Abel Pedro Agarotti, head of the National Gendarmerie, and killed him. It was ERP's first "execution," justified on the grounds that Agarotti was a notorious torturer during his stint as the head of Tucumán's provincial police back in 1970. The next day the Montoneros invaded the Olivos home of Roberto Uzal, a prominent member of the probusiness "Fuerza Nueva" party, to kidnap him. Instead of surrendering, Uzal grabbed a pistol, killed one Montonero, and wounded two others before being gunned down himself.[5] Three days later, on 21 March, ERP struck again, kidnapping Oberdán Sallustro, Fiat's chief executive officer, as he was being driven to work in Córdoba.

Sallustro was intercepted in the usual way, with his car blocked by two guerrilla vehicles. His chauffeur, José Fuentes, was wounded while attempting to struggle as Sallustro was pushed into one of the waiting cars. After the guerrillas drove off, Fuentes made his way back to the Sallustro residence and reported what had happened. No word came from the guerrillas for days, although the Sallustro family made a public appeal for his kidnappers to immediately obtain certain drugs for the victim's weak heart. Finally, ERP released a photograph of the executive sitting in a "people's prison," with ERP's red-star flag in the background. The group also announced that Sallustro would be put on trial for slave-driving his workers and dismissing their rightful labor representatives. A few days later came another announcement: he had been found guilty and would be executed within 48 hours unless Fiat rehired all the workers it had fired, including the strike leaders, and unless 50 ERP guerrillas being held in jail were released. In addition, Fiat would have to pay ERP an "indemnity" for Sallustro's release and distribute a billion pesos worth of clothing and school supplies to poor children in the neighborhoods around the plant.[6]

Although the company and the family were ready to meet their share of the guerrillas' demands, President Lanusse dug in his heels, arguing that giving in to the abductors would only encourage more such incidents. Not only would the Argentine government refuse to free its imprisoned guerrillas, but it ordered Fiat and the Sallustro family not to give in, either. In the meantime, the government launched a massive dragnet that rounded up more than 40 members of ERP, FAR, and Montoneros, but it found no strong leads as to Sallustro's whereabouts. Then Lanusse appointed Alberto Villar, a tough police inspector who had formed a special Anti-Subversive Brigade, to head the investigation. Villar was known as a man who was equally handy with a gun, his fists, or an electric prod. One of his first acts was to arrest Silvio Frondizi, who at the time was a chaired professor of "human rights" at the University of La Plata's journalism school. Frondizi was at the police station only a few hours, but that was sufficient for Villar to get 14 names out of him, people who were later proven to be directly involved in Sallustro's kidnapping. One of them had shot Fuentes, the chauffeur, and several of the group also had taken part in other kidnappings. The group's leader, Osvaldo Debeneditti, was arrested a few days later, but the chief planner, Joe Baxter, escaped. Nor was Sallustro found.

While human rights lawyers were gathering to defend the captured guerrillas, the police continued their search, patiently going over the records of recent apartment leases in the Greater Buenos Aires area and checking out the locations. On 11 April, as four policemen approached the door of one of the buildings on their list, they were met by a volley of pistol fire that left one of them mortally wounded on the sidewalk. Before reinforcements arrived to seal off the area, three of the four guerrillas inside escaped through an underground passage. The fourth, an elegant young Brazilian woman of Scandinavian descent, surrendered with a revolver in her hand. Smiling complacently, she directed the police to a bedroom at the back of the house, where they found Sallustro's still-warm body with two bullets in his chest and one in his head.[7]

On the same day that Sallustro was found, ERP also gunned down General Juan Carlos Sánchez, commander of the Second Army Corps, in Rosario. As he was on his way to work, a pickup truck ahead of him suddenly stopped and another car pulled alongside his car. Suddenly the other car's roof hatch popped up and a guerrilla appeared with a machine gun. He sprayed Sánchez's car with bullets that ricocheted in every direction, killing the general, his chauffeur, and a news vendor standing on the corner. In this case, ERP's motive was revenge. Santucho held the general responsible for the suppression of a second *cordobazo* that had erupted in March 1971.

Military operations were considered different from operations directed at killing or kidnapping a particular individual. Earlier in the evolution of guerrilla organizations, the chief purpose of such attacks was to obtain weapons or money. Guerrilla organizations robbed gun stores, banks, armored trucks, suburban police outposts, and clinics (to obtain medical supplies). During 1970 they tried more ambitious projects, such as the takeovers of La Calera and Garín. On 28 March 1971, ERP took over Channel 10 in Córdoba to broadcast a 20-minute speech outlining its political program. On 1 July the Montoneros seized the town of San Jerónimo in northern Santa Fe Province, robbing the local bank and the police station's arsenal. Becoming even bolder, ERP seized the women's prison in Córdoba, on 1 July, to free some guerrilla *compañeras* and on 26 July the Montoneros did the same in Buenos Aires. The takeover of Villa Urquiza prison in Tucumán by ERP, on 6 September, was a bloodier event. Five guards were killed in order to free 16 ERP and 2 FAP guerrillas.[8]

Every month throughout 1971, 1972, and 1973 was filled with similar kinds of killings, kidnappings, bombings, and assaults. Here a bank was robbed, there a police station was taken, a radio or a television station was invaded and made to broadcast a message, letter bombs were mailed out to businessmen or public officials, a policeman was killed, an executive was kidnapped for ransom, an office was bombed, a private club was bombed, a factory was bombed, someone's home was bombed. Fiat continued to be a favorite target: the Fiat-Concord plant was hit with bombs, and the home of its personnel director was destroyed. Other companies suffered, too. In 1972 and 1973 the Minimax grocery stores were hit again with firebombs. So was a *confitería* (cafe) in Córdoba, a movie theatre in Buenos Aires, a federal courthouse in Rosario, the Journalists' Union headquarters, a Coca-Cola plant, a Cessna airplane belonging to the air force, and the headquarters of the San Juan Province military district. Many homes were destroyed, too, including those of a radio news commentator, a conservative politician, the mayor of Resistencia, an United Press correspondent, a naval captain, a railway union leader, the dean of the Faculty of Exact Sciences at the University of La Plata, the Peronist Party's adjunct secretary, the rector of the National University of Bahía Blanca, and the director of the University of Santiago del Estero's Computer Institute—and these were only the most publicized incidents. There were, literally, hundreds of others every year. O'Donnell recorded 1,470 from the beginning of 1969 to the end of 1972, making an average of one per day.[9]

Some bombings were in the nature of reprisals. Companies involved in bitter strikes with their workers were prime targets, and such strikes and work stoppages almost doubled between 1970 and 1971. Guerrillas might then bomb a factory, an office, or the home of some executive to demonstrate solidarity with the workers. Guerrillas also took reprisals against moderate labor officials who resisted leftist takeovers of their unions or who compromised with management. Dirk Henry Kloosterman, the national secretary of the Automotive Mechanics' Union, (SMATA), had been getting death threats because he was determined to break the Trotskyites' control of SMATA's Córdoba branch. He ignored them, not even bothering to protect himself with bodyguards or an armed chauffeur.

Then, one day as he was backing out of his driveway on the way to work, his wife and three children saw three men approach his car. They had been pretending to be working on a malfunctioning car across the street, but now they had drawn their revolvers. Kloosterman saw them coming from his rearview mirror and tried to pull his car around to escape, but in doing so he struck a tree, and before he could back away the three men ran up and emptied their revolvers into him. The children had meanwhile run into the street toward their father, but by the time they reached him there was glass and blood all over the pavement. The killers fled to the corner, where a green Chevrolet was waiting for them. After the funeral, SMATA declared a day off from work for its members, to mourn Kloosterman, but the Córdoba branch refused to obey the work stoppage.[10]

The bombing of foreign embassies and consulates, or the kidnapping of their staff, were intended to create chaos, discredit the government in foreign eyes, and drive away foreign investment. The Paraguayan consul in Ituzaingo and the Uruguayan consul in Córdoba were released unhurt, but John Patrick Egan, a retired businessman who served as honorary U.S. consul in Córdoba, was "executed," and Alfred Laun, the director of the U.S. cultural center in Buenos Aires, was shot in the stomach while resisting his abduction. On the other hand, the kidnapping of the National Gendarmerie's commander, Jacobo Nasif, was meant to show that the guerrillas were capable of meting out punishment to anyone in the regime, no matter how highly placed. Colonel Héctor Iribaren, the Third Army Corps' chief of intelligence, was "executed" while resisting a Montonero kidnapping in Córdoba. Other prominent Argentines were kidnapped in order to make them issue damaging "confessions" that would discredit the Lanusse government. Héctor García, the publisher of the *porteño* daily newspaper *Crónica*, was seized in March 1973 and made to sign a statement condemning the regime. Admiral Francisco Alemann, the former head of naval intelligence, was held in a "people's prison" for 60 days until he "confessed" that the Ongania government had been a dictatorship. And Hugo D'Aquila, the director of psychiatry at the Villa Devoto prison, had to sign a confession that he had routinely induced mental disorders in political prisoners.

Most kidnappings were about money. The first recorded kidnapping from this period was in August 1970, when a local businessman, Carlos Baltazar, and his family were abducted. It was not reported how much was paid to secure their release, but the sum must have been sufficiently impressive, because this was followed by a great many other kidnappings. In May 1971 Stanley Sylvester, the manager of the Swift Meatpacking Company and honorary British consul in Rosario, was seized by ERP guerrillas in the lunchroom of his factory. They held him in a "people's prison" for several weeks, until Swift ransomed him for $250,000. In the meantime, they made him pose for a photograph in front of a poster of Ché Guevara. Swift's ransom was topped in September 1972, when the Montoneros kidnapped Jan van der Palme, the manager of Phillips-Argentina, and got half a million dollars for his release. The guerrillas hit the million-dollar mark in December when the Vesty meatpacking company paid ERP that much for Ronald Grove, and ITT paid the Montoneros the same for Vicente Russo. In 1973 there was a rash of kidnappings that cost the Bank of Boston $750,000; Coca-Cola, $1 million; Amoco, $1 million; Kodak, $1.5 million; the British-American Tobacco Company, $1.7 million; Firestone, $3 million; and Esso (Exxon), $14.2 million. On 19 September 1974 the Montoneros hit the biggest jackpot of all when they captured two brothers, Juan and Jorge Born, heirs to the Bunge and Born food processing conglomerate, an Argentine multinational corporation. Juan Born was soon released because of his poor health, but Jorge was held in a "people's prison" until June of the following year, when he was finally turned over at a clandestine press conference. By then the Montoneros had received $61.5 million in ransom money—a record never to be broken in that era, although other multimillion dollar ransoms followed. In July 1975 Charles Lockwood, the chief executive officer of the Roberts Group, an Argentine conglomerate, was ransomed for $10 million. It was his second abduction, for he had been kidnapped in 1973 for $2.3 million. The year 1975 ended with the kidnapping of Enrique Metz, the manager of Mercedes-Benz, who was to cost his employers $5 million for his life. Failing to pay the ransom was equivalent to consigning the victim to death. Such was the fate of Alfredo Miotti, a Córdoba *estanciero* (rancher) who was killed in September 1974 after being held for several months in a "people's prison." Nor were the guerrillas hesitant about killing their captives in the event of a rescue attempt. In addition to Sallustro, there was the example of David Kraiselburd, the editor of *El Día*, a La Plata daily. Kidnapped by the Montoneros in June 1974, he was murdered a month later when the police discovered the guerrillas' hideout and surrounded them.

Guerrillas had little compunction about killing a kidnap victim who tried to resist, nor were they hesitant about shooting anyone in the vicinity of their target, whether it was an assassination or a kidnap attempt. On the morning that the Born brothers were seized, they were accompanied in their car by Alberto Bosch, one of their managers, and a chauffeur, Juan Carlos Pérez. Suddenly they were directed into a side street by a guerrilla posing as a policeman, while other guerrillas dressed as workmen closed off the street with barricades and surrounded the car. When the victims realized their danger and tried to escape, the Montoneros opened fire, killing Pérez and Bosch with shotgun blasts at close range.[11]

Sometimes the guerrillas killed someone as an example to make it easier to "shake down" other businessmen. On 25 May 1973, ERP guerrillas attempted to kill two Ford Motor Company executives but only wounded them. Two days later, however, they succeeded in murdering Ford's Luis Giovanelli. ERP then demanded $1 million from the company in "protection money" and received it, but the greedy guerrillas made even more demands for payoffs, and Ford balked. So on November 22 John Swint, the manager of Transax, a Ford subsidiary in Córdoba, was killed. In the usual fashion, two carloads of guerrillas

blocked his vehicle and machine-gunned the occupants, killing Swint, his chauffeur, and two bodyguards. It was all done very coolly and professionally: to
make sure that Swint was dead, a blond youth got out of one of the cars and
let him have another machine-gun blast. Afterwards, Ford got a call saying that
unless ERP received $4 million, more of Ford's executives would be killed.
Instead, Ford moved 22 of its managers and their families out of the country.
The Otis Elevator Company was similarly threatened; so was the Editorial Abril
publishing house; so were Coca-Cola, Kodak, General Motors, IBM, and dozens
of others. In most cases they moved their top executives and their families out
of Argentina, and some even closed down their Argentine operations altogether.
The technique was so common that it acquired a name, *apriete*, which means
"the squeeze."[12]

Sometimes, when it was too difficult to kidnap a CEO or some other prominent figure, the guerrillas would seize a member of his family instead. Santiago
Soldati, the son of a bank president, was abducted in April 1973 and held for
$1.5 million in ransom. León Grinchpun, the son of another Argentine busi-
nessman, was kidnapped that same month and later ransomed for an undisclosed
sum. On 26 June this happened to Alberto Mazzarella, the son of a local merchant; and on that same day two wives, Mirta Graciela Rubin and Liliana Aerin,
were kidnapped. Nestor Parmasso, an *estanciero*'s son, was picked up by guerrillas in August. During 1974 family victims included Eugenia de Denovos,
whose husband owned a Córdoba printing firm; and Elcira de Laplana, the wife
of a candy manufacturer.[13] These incidents were only the most dramatic among
those that were known. Others were never reported by their intimidated victims.

People in the upper class drastically changed the way they lived. The children
went to school with bodyguards, the women were afraid to leave their houses,
and the men went to work each day with bodyguards, always making sure to
change their route. Some families even moved across the La Plata River to
Uruguay, where a military government had come to power in 1973 and crushed
the Tupamaros. The executives would commute between Buenos Aires and
Montevideo by plane. Nevertheless, whatever precautions the wealthy took, they
still lived in fear and when a kidnapping did occur, "the families of those who
were kidnapped tried desperately to conceal the abduction from the police and
even from their friends, convinced that their best hope was to pay the ransom
in silence."[14]

For the guerrillas, this was a truly lucrative business. The conservative magazine *Somos* estimated in 1985 that extortive kidnappings and "squeezes" on
wealthy families brought in a total of around $100 million to the Montoneros
alone, most of which was laundered out of the country. Those sums permitted
the Montoneros to equip an army with weapons, "medical supplies, hideouts,
arms depots, clandestine presses, logistical support, and a vast network of international contacts." ERP was almost as well-financed.[15]

THE PEOPLE'S PRISONS

The British ambassador to Uruguay, Geoffrey Jackson, was kidnapped in Montevideo by Tupamaro guerrillas in January 1971 and spent the next nine months in two different "people's prisons," of which he has published a vivid account. The first prison was "a small two-sided cage, some two metres broad by half a metre deep, built in the corner of a room which itself seemed little more than four metres square. . . ." Sheets of yellow foam plastic covered the floor, and Jackson, dressed only in his underwear, slept on a filthy mattress of black nylon mesh so old and ruined that the stuffing came out. He also had a woolen blanket but no sheet. The cell had been dug out of the foundations of a building and was extremely hot, damp, and close because there were no windows; only a little ventilation came through an air compressor. The ceiling was so low that Jackson could do little more than lie or squat. Sanitary arrangements consisted of a bucket passed inside to defecate in, or left just outside the wire if only urination was required. The rules allowed urinating only once a day. Anytime that the police or soldiers were in the neighborhood, the lights and the air compressor would go off, and a guard would handcuff him, ready to kill him if necessary.[16]

The second "people's prison" was even smaller, consisting of a plank cot hinged to the back wall with barely a foot of space between its edge and the front wall. To exercise, or even move at all, Jackson had to lift up the bed and raise a small table that was hinged from the framework of the grill. The bed had a hard mattress of raw wool covered in clear plastic. This time, however, he had a blue twill sheet in addition to his wool blanket. The ceiling was low, and when he lay down at night, Jackson had the claustrophobic sensation of being stashed away in a coffin, like being buried alive. At a right angle to his cell was another cell, which was L-shaped and contained another prisoner. Jackson was never allowed to speak with him or learn who he was, but when the man was finally released, Jackson was transferred to this slightly larger cell. In it, he exercised as best he could: "two steps to the corner, a right, face-about, and back again." The room outside was lit by a powerful light bulb set in a reflector made from the bottom of a large tin can. There was always an armed guard, and the cells were electronically monitored with microphones and tape recorders.

Jackson's captors impressed and disturbed him by their "essential ferocity." It "represented . . . one of the most exhausting pressures against which the subconscious mind had to stand fast." It was "something animal-plus. The animal's is an innocent ferocity, while that of man contains hate, or madness." Jackson eventually concluded that "the violence, the ferocity, of clandestinity have no intellectual let alone ethical component, but instead are just another symptom of deranged body-chemistry," the products of extreme alienation from society.

"People's prisons" run by Argentine guerrillas were just as cramped and suffocating, and the ferocity was there, too. A prisoner of one of Argentina's guerrilla bands might be, for all practical purposes, buried alive. General Ramón Camps, the head of the Buenos Aires provincial police after the 1976 coup, described a "people's prison" his men discovered during a house search:

In one of the many investigations carried out by the police we went to the house of an apparently ordinary family, on the suspicion, however, that the people had some sort of connection with the subversives. On going through it we noticed that in the master bedroom (a room measuring approximately 3 by 3 meters), there was a difference in the parquet floor under the bed. We tried to lift this piece but it was impossible. On removing the shade of the living room light we found inside a tube with a valve in it. By using a pump we started forcing air into it, and then the floor began to rise. That piece of parquet was attached to lifts which, when inflated, pushed up the floor. On removing that section of parquet, we saw a hole about 1.5 meters deep, with damp earthen walls, and about the length of an army cot—that is to say, between 1.85 and 1.9 meters. There, lying on the cot in total darkness and unable to move or even stand up because of the low height, was a man who had been kidnapped by a Montonero group several days before.[17]

Being buried alive like that was not unusual. Victor Samuelson, the Esso executive who later was ransomed for $14.2 million, was kept in a prison that resembled a gas-station grease pit. The first time that Charles Lockwood was kidnapped, he was taken, blindfolded and wrapped in a rug, to a country house out in Buenos Aires Province, where he was kept in a tent in one of the rooms. Then he was transferred to a house on the outskirts of the city and put in a nine-by-six-foot windowless cellar whose only light came from a fluorescent bulb. However, he was given the luxury of an electric heater on which he could make tea and boil potatoes. The Born brothers were lodged in a cellar beneath a paint store in a Buenos Aires suburb. It was divided into two small cells, each with a toilet and a vent and a guardpost that contained a kitchen, bath, and laundry. Juan Born's health broke down quickly, which led to his early release. Jorge was freed eight months after the kidnapping, at a clandestine press conference called by the Montoneros' leader, Firmenich. Andrew Graham-Yool, from the *Buenos Aires Herald*, stayed with Born afterwards while he waited to be picked up by a company car. The physical and psychological tolls of a "people's prison" were evident: "His legs seemed to shiver, as do those of a convalescent after a long illness. He asked permission to walk, to turn back, to stop. Nine months of being bullied and commanded had created that habit. . . . He had done exercises to keep fit, but he was not fit; the words came between long pauses for thought and formulation of sentences."[18]

Military captives were treated even worse. Colonel Juan Alberto Pita was seized in the late afternoon, when Montoneros forced his van off the road as he was returning home with his family to Buenos Aires after a day's visit with relatives in La Plata. Later that night a guerrilla tribunal sentenced him to death, after which he was taken down to a basement. They put a pistol to his head and fired—with a blank cartridge. They repeated this mock execution, then forced him to crawl through a small, low door into a three-by-six-foot cell with damp, dirt walls. They took away his clothes and gave him pajamas to wear. He had nothing to cover his feet. He could not bathe, shave, or cut his hair, and for the next six months he lived on rice and yerba mate. Trickles of water came through the walls when it rained.[19]

As he lay on his cot, Colonel Pita gradually observed how the rivulets of water were weakening the walls. One day, after the rain had let in more water than usual, he pushed against the dirt and kicked with his feet, finally making a breach in it. Struggling through the opening, he found himself in another narrow chamber, in which a stairway led up to the main floor. Above him was a trap door. At first it refused to budge, but his patient work finally got it open. He found himself on the main floor of a carpentry shop, lying beneath a table. There were voices coming from the back, where the Montoneros were having breakfast. Sliding from under the table, he was able to stand up and look about. There were weapons all around. He took an automatic rifle and slipped quietly out of the shop. About 20 yards away was the gate to a chain-link fence. He passed through it and ran another 60 yards to a road, where he was able to flag down a Provincial Road Department truck, which took him to the nearest police station. Meanwhile, the guerrillas discovered that he was missing and cleared out. By the time the police arrived, the hideout was empty, but reporters got to inspect a real "people's prison."

Major Julio Argentino Larrabure's story, unfortunately, did not have such a happy ending. A 42-year-old military chemical engineer from a *tucumaño* working-class background, he was captured in August 1974 when ERP guerrillas attacked the army's Villa María base in Córdoba, where he worked in an explosives factory. Three sympathetic conscripts let the attackers enter. Most of the soldiers were away, having been given weekend passes. Once inside, the guerrillas attacked the base commander's quarters and the officers' club, where the officers and their families were gathered. The base commander, Lieutenant Colonel Osvaldo Guardone, had detected some strange movements outside and had time to grab a rifle before the guerrillas broke through his door. He shot the first intruder, and two other guerrillas fled. In the meantime, the 60 soldiers on the base, awakened from their sleep, reacted confusedly to the sound of shooting and, because the ERP guerrillas were dressed in army uniforms, were slow to understand the situation. At the officers' club, Major Larrabure and Captain Roberto García held off the attackers until the officers ran out of ammunition and were overwhelmed. Taking the officers as prisoners and shields, the rebels forced them into a truck into which they had already stashed a large number of machine guns, automatic rifles, small arms, explosives, and uniforms from the camp arsenal. Other trucks, waiting outside, spirited away the attackers with their two captives. García, however, had been shot in the abdomen and was too badly hurt to hold prisoner, so he was shoved into one of the damaged trucks that the guerrillas decided to abandon—after having his arms and legs broken, cigarettes burned on his face, and another seven bullets pumped into him.[20]

Larrabure was carried off to a "people's prison" located beneath a corner dry goods store in Rosario, run for the past two years by a young couple with two small children and an "aunt." These apparently ordinary people, who lived in the back of the store, had patiently excavated a hole under their kitchen floor into which they installed two cells that could be reached by a stairway. A sheet of plywood, carefully disguised and fitted into the floor under the table, camouflaged the entrance. The two cells were approximately five feet deep, six feet wide, and six feet high, with plywood floors and cement walls on three sides. On the fourth side was a grill, set in bricks, through which one could see the corner of the adjacent cell and a small passageway leading to the stairs, where a guard sat. Each cell had a cot, a chair, a small table, and a portable toilet. No sunlight penetrated this hole; the only light was from a fluorescent bulb. Two black plastic tubes attached to a small pump brought in some air from the outside, but the atmosphere was always damp and close.

Major Larrabure's jailors, always hooded, lectured him occasionally about politics and gave him revolutionary tracts to read. They also let him have a ballpoint pen and some paper. During the next year he was allowed to send three letters to his wife and children. The rest of the time he wrote poetry, worked crossword puzzles from old newspapers, figured out complicated mathematical and chemical formulas, and devised a deck of cards with which to play solitaire. He also kept a diary; its jottings reveal his constant fear, as he suffered from asthma, that the air tube in his cell would quit functioning. "Oh God," he wrote in one passage, "please don't let me die suffocated, asphyxiated, desperate!" His diary also recorded his fear of losing his mind. Unable to sleep, often confused, hearing the voices of his wife and children, he confessed that he was sometimes out of touch with reality: "I silently pray to God that He won't abandon me to a humiliating insanity." His mental breakdown progressed and took the form of loud singing, especially the national anthem, which he sung repeatedly.

In the cell next to Larrabure's was a businessman being held for ransom. Neither man knew who the other was, because they were not allowed to see or talk to each other. One day, while Larrabure was singing, his neighbor noticed that he suddenly became quiet. In fact, Major Larrabure was being strangled. His body was then taken away, later to be dumped into a vacant lot. During the next few days the businessman, perceiving an unaccustomed silence from the neighboring cell and the absence of any guard, pushed a little on his cell door. To his surprise, it gave way. Seeing no one in the passageway or on the stairs, he ascended and emerged into the kitchen. The house was empty. Though barefoot and dressed only in light pajamas, he slipped quietly out of the house into a damp winter's night and, once out on the street, began running desperately, the shakiness of his legs making him stumble and fall several times. At last he came across a police patrol, which took him to central headquarters. With some difficulty, he helped the police find the store, which had been abandoned.

Days later, Larrabure's body was found after the police received an anonymous phone call. Dressed in pajama pants and a pullover sweater, it was wrapped in a polyethylene bag tied with a cord and tagged with his name. The corpse was emaciated because Larrabure had lost more than 80 pounds, and an autopsy report concluded that he had been garroted (strangled from behind) with a cord. A final coup de grace had been administered with a heavy instrument to the back of his skull. The body also showed signs of previous mistreatment. The genitals were inflamed in a manner suggesting the application of electric shocks, the right eye was damaged, and the face showed signs of frequent beatings. The whole body displayed the visible effects of undernourishment and dehydration. Curiously, it had been frozen for about 36 hours before being abandoned.

THE ANTINOMIANS

Imagine that you are standing on a sidewalk, a short distance from a stranger. You notice suddenly that a roof tile is about to fall on his head. You shout a warning. Suppose the tile strikes him with a sickening crack. You flinch, as if you yourself had received the blow. These are natural responses, because as human beings we are capable of putting ourselves in another person's place, of imagining that danger and pain happening to ourselves. How is it possible, then, that some people can suspend their natural inclinations and even participate in the infliction of pain and death on their fellow human beings? Violence committed in self-defense or even in anger is understandable because it is human, but to kill a stranger or put someone alive into a dark hole under the ground is a cold-blooded act. What sort of mind enables a person to do those things?

Roberto García (no relation to the murdered captain), an Argentine journalist, agreed with Ambassador Jackson that for many terrorists violence was an end in itself, devoid of any real ethical content. Terrorists were psychotics for whom violence was a way of "getting even" with a society they didn't fit into, and they justified their acts by any ideology they found useful. Their frequent need to publish detailed accounts of their bloody deeds were both acts of confession and assertions of importance in the face of a public that once had ignored their existence. The account that Mario Firmenich and Norma Arrostito published in *La Causa Peronista* of how they kidnapped and murdered Aramburu certainly belongs in the category of confessional literature. Its grisly details are told with pride and are even embellished by the authors. Moreover, Graham-Yool's description of Firmenich at the clandestine press conference where Jorge Born was released conveys the same mixture of egotism and anxiousness to claim importance. The Montonero chief "spoke with controlled excitement," Graham-Yool recalled. "The 'imprisonment' of the Born brothers was proof that 'we are now a force to be reckoned with, a political organization that cannot be ignored'.

His preoccupation seemed to be with not being ignored. He was the chief. . . . His smugness seemed to form a cloud around him."[21]

Mario Roberto Santucho, the ERP leader, was outwardly more modest, soft-spoken, and simple than Firmenich. Below the surface, however, they were much alike. Although Santucho lacked Firmenich's background as a militant in Catholic organizations, those who knew him well described him as having many of the qualities of a priest or a monk. Although he briefly had a mistress, he was a moralist about sex, and his guilty conscience drove him back to his wife, Ana María Villareal. Marxism-Leninism was his religion, and he put great emphasis on his followers reading and absorbing its doctrines. Meetings often turned into lectures by him in which the other members of the politburu were treated somewhat as students. On strategy and tactics he was utterly dogmatic, always underestimating difficulties and exaggerating the possibilities that effort and determination could bring about. Like Firmenich, Abal Medina, Arrostito, Maza, and other leading Montoneros, Santucho had a Sorelian fascination with violence for its own sake, as a "cleansing" force. Andrés Pascal Allende later recalled that the leaders of the Chilean MIR guerrillas tried to warn Santucho in 1974 not to directly attack the Argentine army and provoke a coup, as they had done in Chile. Santucho, however, would not listen to reason or facts, so certain was he of the rightness of his strategy. Similarly, Santucho's emphasis on violence ruined his opportunities to work in concert with the labor leaders in Córdoba. As practical men, they refused to adopt his strategy of guerrilla war, so he turned his back on them. Santucho found it impossible to work with anyone who did not share his views. Eventually, he even broke with the Fourth International when the Trotskyites criticized his growing emphasis on "militarism."[22]

Both ERP and the Montoneros tried to turn their guerrilla organizations into full-fledged armies to engage in all-out combat with the Argentine armed forces, and the more they did so, the more they resembled fascist movements. The Montoneros's hostility to foreigners, their exhaltation of the leader, their militant nationalism, their middle-class origins, their worship of violence, their heroic conception of history as the work of elites, their belief in voluntarism or will, and their fascination with death—all of this bore the imprint of fascism. They embraced the military way of life as a kind of liturgy, loving its terminology, uniforms, hierarchy, and discipline, its salutes and its click of the heels. Military camaraderie and its attending dangers gave the Montonero a sense of self-identity and importance; it made him the member of an elite vanguard, someone superior to the mass culture of bourgeois society yet still defending the people. All soldiers are aware that they may be called upon to sacrifice their lives, but for Montoneros the contemplation of death took on the aspects of a cult. The journal *Cristianismo y Revolución* assured them that fallen revolutionaries would be immortal: there would be "a kind of metaphysical existence among 'the people' long after physical death."[23]

ERP's underground society lacked the Catholic religious imagery of the Montoneros, but it had the same sort of asceticism and rough equality of a military band. Its revolutionary morality rejected social distinctions. Middle-class members were expected to become proletarianized, whereas proletarians were supposed to improve themselves intellectually. Every member had to be a tireless worker and a good *compañero* to the others, living modestly and avoiding luxury. *Erpistas* dressed simply; their food was plentiful but ordinary; wine was drunk with meals, but never to excess; and cigarettes were of the cheapest kind. Honesty and prudence were demanded of all who handled ERP's money. Although ransoms brought in millions of dollars, no one was ever found to have appropriated any of it for his personal use. The PRT and ERP leaders received a small salary and had a modest expense account; those with dependents to support also got a family supplement. These leaders were professional revolutionaries. They never rested, never took vacations or holidays. Like soldiers, they rose before dawn and went to bed early. Although there was no sex discrimination in theory, few women rose to leadership positions in either ERP or the Montoneros. Norma Arrostito, a Montonera, stood out as an exception. The women who joined—they constituted about 30 percent—proved to be good fighters. "Revolutionary sexuality" meant that a female militant was expected to satisfy the sexual needs of her male companions, but falling in love with any one of them was frowned upon as being potentially divisive. Children born from such liaisons were cared for by the group.[24]

In both the Montoneros and ERP, discipline was strict, it had to be, if those organizations were to become armies. Each had its strict hierarchy, and subordinates were expected to obey orders without question. This was justified as a necessary but temporary evil in ERP's case, because the ultimate goal was a classless society; but for Firmenich, elitism was official doctrine. The Montoneros did not seek to be a mass movement, he explained, because incorporating the masses would dilute the purity of the doctrine. Both organizations placed a great deal of emphasis on studying Marxism-Leninism—mixed, in the Montonero sessions, with writings by Perón. ERP's sessions, called *rondas*, also included the usual communist practices of group criticism and self-criticism, in which individuals were expected to listen to their own shortcomings and confess to them. Some of the more serious faults might be individualism, uncooperativeness, authoritarianism, moral laxity, lack of discipline, incorrect ideological interpretation, or luxurious habits. Like all closed societies, the guerrillas developed a special vocabulary that helped to cloak the disagreeable tasks they had to perform, so that "expropriate" became a synonym for robbery, "condemn" or "execute" for assassination, "harassing the enemy" for planting bombs, and "arrest" or "sequester" for kidnapping.

There was not perfect unity inside the Montoneros and ERP, however. Each organization suffered its splits, although the departing factions made little difference. However, even among those who remained loyal to the group purpose, there were feelings of dissatisfaction. Pedro Cazes Camarero, who was in the ERP inner circle, complained after the fact that the organization's excessive rigidity and hierarchy led to Santucho being isolated from the membership by a clique of yes-men. Moreover, the practice of democratic centralism meant that even at the grass roots, cell leaders were chosen from above, from members who conformed blindly to the party line. After a while the lower levels of the organization only passed along information that they thought the leaders wanted to hear, with the result that false impressions were "confirmed" and decisions were increasingly based on irrational optimism. Luis Mattini agreed: taking the Marxist-Leninist theories as gospel led to tactical mistakes. Cazes Camarero also disagreed with the practice of "proletarizing" the PRT and ERP, because it brought politically unprepared people into leadership positions. However, if they followed Santucho's orders, he was satisfied.[25]

Ironically, this "proletarization" policy brought the class struggle right into the bosom of the party. A longtime militant who dared to criticize the ERP leadership might find his bourgeois class origins thrown in his face to silence him. The offender would be criticized as a "petit bourgeois deviationist" and forced to undergo a self-criticism session. Those were, Cazes Camarero related, episodes of "true ideological terrorism very much like those practiced under Stalinism." The victim was made to recant and forced to undergo humiliating rituals of public confession. In an oblique allusion to Santucho, Cazes Camarero concluded that the most dangerous party bureaucrat is not the corrupt and cowardly one, but the one who is brave and *simpatico*.

He tries to maintain a humble attitude, takes an interest in his colleagues, often makes his criticisms and observations in a fraternal manner. And his bravery—sometimes an insane bravery—which he boasts of as proof of his militancy, is accompanied in many cases by incessant and self-sacrificing activity. That makes it extremely difficult to criticize him in any way. Where he becomes ferocious and implacable is in the defense of his leadership position, when he feels it threatened."[26]

However, these observations and criticisms were made after ERP had failed. In the early 1970s there was still a feeling of solidarity among the members. Those who formed ERP and the Montoneros had come together gradually, out of mutual affinity. They influenced one another and, as María Moyano emphasizes, their decision to go beyond the bounds of legality was a collective one. Drawn from the "counterculture," they gave one another the sense of "belonging" that they had failed to find in the established society. They formed their own communities, made their own rules and moral codes, and established the trappings of countergovernments and counterarmies to war against the social order that had rejected them. The fact that they often had to go underground cut them off even further from the old society: their parents, brothers and sisters, friends, and spouses.[27]

Gradually, the "organization" became all of life. The deepening involvement proceeded in stages. Beginning with the outermost layer of its system, the "sympathizers," the PRT kept track of all those who received *El Combatiente* and especially those who agreed to take an additional copy to sell to someone else. Those who bought the extra copy of *El Combatiente* were called "readers" (*lectores*). They would be urged to discuss the articles and editorials with the sympathizer to whom they sold their paper, and also to discuss them with other people. Each activist in a PRT cell was to pay special attention to all the sympathizers and readers under his jurisdiction. Ideally, for every three-man cell there would be 12 sympathizers and 12 readers. Eventually, if those sympathizers proved to be good material, they might be formed into another cell. This was also a good system for distributing *El Combatiente*, which had an average weekly distribution of around 10,000 copies. For a brief time in 1973, when it was legal, it sold as many as 50,000.[28]

As the Montoneros and ERP were openly recruiting in the high schools and universities beginning in 1971, they lured sympathizers into more activist roles by first having them pass out leaflets or write graffiti, then getting them to take part in student strikes and protests, confrontations with professors, street marches, and finally the seizure of classrooms and administrative offices. The Montoneros's youth groups were especially active in recruitment, drawing in the curious and sympathetic through consciousness-raising "discussion groups" called *ateneos* ("atheneums"). Each class had its *ateneo*, which was linked to others in the school by a coordinating council. Each school, in turn, sent delegates to the local Peronist University Youth or Union of Secondary Students group. In that way, it was possible to mobilize students for mass protests at the school, community, or national level, depending on the issue.[29]

The guerrillas guided their protégés through progressively more violent stages until, satisfied with the militancy of those who were willing to continue going along, they admitted them into their mass front organizations. At first the protests focused on problems in the schools (student participation in governance, difficult examinations, teaching, admissions, curriculum), some of which were causes of legitimate grievances. Public education had been allowed to deteriorate, with the consequence that decaying buildings, poor teaching, and overcrowded classrooms were common. Those issues were quickly superseded by more political ones, however, such as whether to declare a holiday to mourn the death of Ché Guevara or Evita Perón. As student protests took to the streets, clashes with the police radicalized students into viewing school problems as part of a whole rotten social order. From these kinds of protests, activists were encouraged to join a mass front cell. At that stage they assumed more serious roles as protest leaders and organizers, sometimes even providing logistical support for the combatants' military operations. A militant might be called on to steal guns or cars, guard a guerrilla "safe house," or do volunteer work for a slum dwellers' organization as a teacher or consultant. Finally, for those select few in the mass fronts who appeared to have the makings of a real combatant, there would be training in the handling of guns and explosives before they were allowed into the very inner circle.[30]

A true revolutionary had no loyalties or sentimental attachments outside that circle. When ERP kidnapped Rear Admiral Francisco Alemann on 1 April 1973, the guerrillas were let in by the admiral's favorite nephew, Oscar Ciarlotti, who had come by the apartment ostensibly to introduce his new girlfriend. While they were chatting amiably, the doorbell rang and Ciarlotti let in 19 of his "friends," who surrounded Alemann and his wife and led the elderly couple off at gunpoint. Before leaving, they spray-painted ERP slogans all over the apartment walls.[31]

Just how far guerrillas could suspend normal human feelings is even better illustrated, perhaps, by the June 1976 murder of Federal Police Chief General Cesareo Cardozo and his wife. Ana María González, an 18-year-old friend of their daughter María Graciela, had been arrested previously by the police on suspicion that she was involved with the Montoneros, but at the urging of his daughter, the general obtained her release. The police were right however: González was a Montonera and had deliberately made friends with María Graciela in order to gain access to her home. The Cardozos felt sorry for González because her parents had just separated, so she had been having dinner at their apartment with them since the beginning of May. On 17 June she carried a time bomb of seven hundred grams of trotyl concealed as a box of perfume in her purse. During dinner she excused herself to go to the bathroom, set the bomb, and then tiptoed into the parents' bedroom and slipped it under their bed, making certain that it would go off right under the general's head—which it did, at 1:30 A.M. By then González had gone underground. Later, in a clandestine interview with a European magazine, she expressed no pity for the orphaned María Graciela but complained of having to "make one of the militant's worst sacrifices": being in daily contact with the hated enemy. "During a month and a half I had to frequent Cardozo's home as his daughter's classmate, while he supervised the kidnapping, torture, and assassination of tens of comrades." But then she saw the funny side. "And to think that when the police held me, and then had to let me go thanks to General Cardozo, they gave me chocolates."[32]

NOTES

1. María Matilde Ollier, *El fenómino insurreccional y la cultura política (1969–1973)* (Buenos Aires: Centro Editor de América Latina, 1986), 117–19.

2. Moyano, *Argentina's Lost Patrol*, 27, 36, 53; Guillermo O'Donnell, *Bureaucratic Authoritarianism: Argentina, 1966–1973, in Comparative Perspective* (Berkeley: University of California Press, 1988), 296–300.

3. O'Donnell, *Bureaucratic Authoritarianism*, 296–97; Moyano, *Argentina's Lost Patrol*, 54–61.

4. Ambrosio Romero Carranza, *El terrorismo en la historia y en la Argentina* (Buenos Aires: Ediciones Depalma, 1983), 213–14; *Review of the River Plate*, (21 January 1972), 71; (31 January 1973), 118–19.

5. Gillespie, *Soldiers of Perón*, 113; Seoane, *Todo o nada*, 169–70.

6. Petric, *Así sangraba*, 24, 47–59, 75–81; Pineiro, *Crónica*, 21–23.

7. Seoane, *Todo o nada*, 155, 171–75.

8. Díaz Bessone, *Guerra revolucionaria*, 126, 139–46; Seoane, *Todo o nada*, 147, 151.

9. O'Donnell, *Bureaucratic Authoritarianism*, 296; Pineiro, *Crónica*, 133–40; Moyano, *Argentina's Lost Patrol*, 55–62; and Romero Carranza, *El terrorismo*, 213–28.

10. García, *Patria sindical*, 91–92.

11. Andrew Graham-Yool, *A State of Fear: Memories of Argentina's Nightmare* (New York: Hippocrene Books, 1986), 37; Pineiro, *Crónica*, 63–65; Gillespie, *Soldiers of Perón*, 180, 189.

12. Kohl and Litt, *Urban Guerrilla Warfare*, 362; Pablo Guissani, *Montoneros: la soberbía armada*, 8th ed. (Buenos Aires: Editorial Sudamericana/Planeta, 1987), 74–75, n. 21.

13. Pineiro, *Crónica*, 133–56; Kohl and Litt, *Urban Guerrilla Warfare*, 360.

14. O'Donnell, *Bureaucratic Authoritarianism*, 303.

15. *Somos*, (2 August 1985), 8; Moyano, *Argentina's Lost Patrol*, 59–60.

16. Geoffrey Jackson, *People's Prison* (London: Faber, 1973). This was published in the United States under the title of *Surviving the Long Night* (New York: Vanguard Press, 1974).

17. Ramón J. A. Camps, *Caso Timerman: punto final* (Buenos Aires: Tribuna Abierta, 1982), 34–35.

18. Graham-Yool, *State of Fear*, 48.

19. Pineiro, *Crónica*, 67–71.

20. Petric, *Así sangraba*, 137–63; Díaz Bessone, *Guerra revolucionaria*, 320–24.

21. García, *Patria sindical*, 6–7; Graham-Yool, *State of Fear*, 43–44.

22. Seoane, *Todo o nada*, 84, 86–87, 143–44, 149, 178–80, 191–92, 244.

23. O'Donnell, *Bureaucratic Authoritarianism*, 307; Giussani, *Montoneros*, 67, 93, 100; Gillespie, *Soldiers of Perón*, 58–59, 118; Lutzky, "Una visión," 64–65.

24. Mattini, *Hombres y mujeres*, 232, 239–40.

25. Pedro Cazes Camarero, *El Ché y la generación del 70* (Buenos Aires: Ediciones Dialéctica, 1989), 93, 95, 98; Mattini, *Hombres y mujeres*, 232.

26. Cazes Camarero, *El Ché*, 97.

27. Moyano, *Argentina's Lost Patrol*, 119.

28. Mattini, *Hombre y mujeres*, 392–94; Seoane, *Todo o nada*, 371.

29. *Evita Montonera*, vol. 1, no. 7 (September 1975), 5–7. For a description of how students were recruited into the Montoneros' inner core of combatants, see Eugenio Méndez, *Confesiones de un Montonero* (Buenos Aires: Editorial Sudamericana/Planeta, 1985), chapters 1 and 2.

30. Landivar, *La universidad*, 16, 31, 48–49, 71; Moyano, *Argentina's Lost Patrol*, 121–22.

31. Pablo Hernández, *La Tablada: el regreso de los que no se fueron* (Buenos Aires: Editorial Fortaleza, 1989), 56–57.

32. Revista Somos, *Historias y personajes de una época trágica* (Buenos Aires: Editorial Atlantida, 1977), 179–81; Moyano, *Argentina's Lost Patrol*, 62.

FIVE

The Military Surrenders

The sudden outbreak and spread of terrorism shocked the military. Air Force Brigadier Eduardo McLoughlin, the minister of interior, expressed his "main concern," which was, he said, to rescue those young people who were being seduced by the excitement of violence. "There is a minority, a small minority, that has [already] embarked on this course of [violent] action. I do not think we can convince that small minority. But around that minority there is a much wider circle of people, a very important sector of the youth, who may be sympathetic and share intellectual concerns with the nucleus that has chosen violence. We cannot afford to lose that youth." General Alejandro Lanusse, the army's commander, was less understanding. He had been a close friend of General Aramburu, and now he promised "widespread retribution" against the perpetrators and their accomplices, as well as those intellectuals "who, with their insidious preaching, sheltered by a freedom they violate day after day, encourage the use of violence."[1]

Upon taking over the presidency in March 1971, Lanusse used both legal and counterterrorist methods for dealing with the guerrillas. *Cristianismo y Revolución* and *Primera Plana*, now under Peronist ownership and considered pro-guerrilla, were closed down. Next, Lanusse established a special federal tribunal to handle the prosecution of terrorists. The Federal Criminal Court of the Nation, which began functioning in July, cut through the tedious and cumbersome criminal procedures of Argentina's federal system, which had become bogged down in jurisdictional disputes and appeals. The new Federal Criminal Court of the Nation had overriding jurisdiction throughout Argentina for crimes linked to subversion. In such cases, one of the 12 special judges or three special prosecutors would go to the place where a guerrilla was being held, file the proper papers, and get the accused transferred to Buenos Aires, where the investigation would immediately get under way. The court's trials were public, but there was no appeal of its decisions.[2]

Human rights advocates on the Left attacked the new court's procedures, and even its very existence, as unconstitutional. The Right, especially the military, viewed it as getting in the way of more "efficient methods" of the sort that would become common in the "Dirty War." Moderate opinion, however, accepted it pragmatically as a form of "legal repression" of terrorism. The court did indeed act expeditiously in putting quite a number of arrested Montonero and ERP guerrillas, including Santucho, behind bars. By the time Lanusse left office, the court had dealt with more than two thousand cases, of which some six hundred were found guilty, eight hundred were released, and the remainder were being processed. Naturally, the court's personnel became targets of the guerrillas. The chief judge, Jorge Quiroga, was assassinated in April 1974; Judge Carlos Malbran was shot and wounded in the legs in 1972; Judge Eduardo Munilla miraculously escaped after his car was fired upon in August 1974; and a court secretary named Bicenso was kidnapped in August 1973.

Lanusse also proclaimed a state of siege, which allowed the armed forces to act to "combat internal subversion, terrorism, and related acts" whenever the president became convinced that neither the Federal Police nor the provincial police could preserve order. The military could go into action in any part of the country, and anyone they arrested under the state of siege power was supposed to be turned over to the Federal Criminal Court of the Nation. Less savory methods of combatting subversion also began to make their appearance late in 1970. "Disappearances" and torture became increasingly common. The victims were left-wing activists, intellectuals, or people somehow connected to the guerrilla underground.

Besides the use of these sinister methods, police work in general had become much more efficient over the past couple of years. Instead of roughing up bearded young men with long hair as suspected terrorists, the police now concentrated on compiling data about kidnappings and guerrilla attacks in order to establish patterns. They scoured the records on real estate transactions and bank transfers to locate safe houses, "people's prisons," and staging grounds for attacks. Civilian security agencies like SIDE (the State Intelligence Bureau) and the Federal Police coordinated their actions more closely with those of the three armed forces' intelligence services and that of the National Gendarmerie. These new tactics paid off. Santucho and Gorriarán Merlo were captured, and most of ERP's remaining leaders were either dead or in jail by mid-1972. The Montoneros also suffered some serious casualties. José Sabino Navarro died after a shootout with the Córdoba police; Juan García Elorrio, the founder of *Cristianismo y Revolución*, died in a suspicious car accident; and Carlos Capuano Martínez was killed in a gun battle with the Buenos Aires police. As for FAR leaders, Carlos Olmedo was gunned down in Córdoba, while Roberto Quieto and Marcos Osatinsky were in jail.

The principal ERP, FAR, and Montonero prisoners were kept at the Rawson Military Prison, which lies on a bleak Patagonian plateau. It was said to be impregnable because its thick walls were heavily guarded by soldiers, marines, gendarmes, and federal policemen. Nevertheless, on 15 August 1972, a group of 25 guerrilla prisoners suddenly seized control. Someone had smuggled in a machine-gun pistol, a revolver with a silencer, and an army uniform. (Suspicion later fell on Mario Amaya, a human rights lawyer, who was said to have hidden the items in a container of candied pumpkin that he passed to his client, Marcos Osatinsky.) One guard was shot and several others were taken as hostages. Once outside, the escapees expected to be met by trucks driven by ERP militants that would take them to the nearby Trelew airport. All but one of the trucks had left, however, so only the six leading guerrilla chiefs were able to board; the other 19 were left behind to commandeer taxis or private cars as best they could. Santucho, Gorriarán Merlo, and Domingo Menna of ERP; Osatinsky and Quieto of FAR; and Fernando Vaca Narvaja of Montoneros made it to the airport. There an airplane was awaiting them, having been hijacked by four ERP guerrillas. The six leaders boarded and told the pilot to wait a few minutes for the others but when they didn't appear, the plane was ordered to take off. It was already in the air, en route to Chile, when the other guerrillas finally arrived.

The 19 remaining escapees then took over the control tower, awaiting a second plane. Other guerrillas, led by Jorge Omar Lewinger of the Montoneros, took over the landing field, but the expected plane had already been warned off by the authorities and had returned to its base in Comodoro Rivadavia. Moreover, within half an hour a battalion of marines surrounded the Trelew airport. There was a brief battle, after which Lewinger's guerrillas surrendered, as did the occupants of the control tower. The prisoners were rounded up and taken to the nearby Comandante Zar naval air base. What happened after that is a matter of controversy. According to the few guerrillas who survived, the prisoners were tortured for the next six days. Then, on August 22, 16 of the 19 escapees were gunned down in cold blood. The three badly wounded survivors were rescued by officers arriving unexpectedly on the scene who were "alien to the massacre plan." The official version, on the other hand, was that during an early morning inspection, one of the terrorists made a grab for the weapon of the captain of the guard. A melee ensued, during which the guards opened fire. Thirteen guerrillas died on the spot, three others died later from their wounds, and three survived. Meanwhile, Mario Amaya and a team of human rights lawyers were in Chile, urging President Salvador Allende not to extradite the guerrillas who had escaped. Three days later Allende rejected the Argentine government's extradition request and sent the six escapees to Cuba.[3]

The guerrillas took their revenge for Trelew. Retired Rear Admiral Emilio Berisso, who had been a member of the Junta of Admirals at the time of Trelew, was killed by FAR on 27 December 1972. Retired Rear Admiral Hermes Quijada was targeted for murder because, as chairman of the Joint Chiefs of Staff, he issued the report on Trelew that exonerated the navy. After surviving two assassination attempts, he was killed in Buenos Aires on 30 April 1973. When his car stopped at a traffic light, two young men on a motorcycle pulled alongside and fired six bullets into him.

The Trelew shootings turned public opinion even further against an already unpopular military government, which after five years in office had brought neither political stability nor economic growth. Most civilians, even longtime anti-Peronists, were now desperate for Perón's return as the only way out of a hopeless situation. Lanusse favored elections, too, but he did not want to see Perón return to power. His minister of interior, Arturo Mor Roig, offered a way out of the dilemma by trying to construct an alliance that he called the Gran Acuerdo Nacional (Grand National Alliance—GAN), which would restore democracy gradually. Peronists would be invited to participate but would first have to show their sincere dedication to democracy by repudiating the guerrillas. Nothing specific was said about whether Perón could return to Argentina, run as a presidential candidate, and be allowed to take office if he won. Considering Lanusse's personal antipathy toward Perón, such vagueness was surely deliberate. Yet there could be no peace unless the Peronists participated in the GAN, and without Perón's approval there would be no participation.

THE MAN OF THE HOUR

Perón was 77 years old and not in good health. He had undergone an operation in 1964 to remove a tumor from his prostate, and in March 1970 another tumor was removed from his urethra. Chain-smoking had damaged his heart, and he complained sporadically of chest pains. A physical examination in 1973 revealed that he had suffered a minor, undetected heart attack sometime late in 1972. In mid-1972, polyps were forming again on his prostate and would have to be removed in a few months. He was aging rapidly, and although he maintained an interest in the game of political strategy, he was increasingly dependent on those in his immediate circle.

First, there was his wife, Isabel, who, at 41, was much younger than Perón. She had followed him faithfully through good and bad times during his exile, seemingly taking little interest in politics, but beneath her quiet exterior she harbored personal grudges against those in Perón's entourage by whom she felt slighted. Perón, who liked to play off his sycophants against one another, encouraged her intrigues. Américo Barrios, a journalist who acted as his secretary and confidential aide, was replaced by José Cresto, formerly Perón's gardener, who was said to be Isabel's stepfather. Cresto was a short, unpretentious man who believed in spiritualism, as did Isabel. His wife, who remained in Buenos Aires, was a leading spiritualist in a secret lodge of mystics known as ANAEL.

Spiritualism thus constituted part of the atmosphere of the Quinta 17 de Octubre; but it did not dominate it until the arrival of José López Rega, another member of ANAEL. Soon after joining ANAEL in 1965, López Rega came into contact with Isabel, whom Perón had sent to Argentina to represent him. She was met, as planned, by a reception committee, one of whose members was Raúl Lastiri, who had a fiancée named Norma López Rega. Thus Norma's father, who once had been a corporal in the Federal Police, was included in the body-guard. For the next nine months, José López Rega was constantly at Isabel's side and, unlike the other bodyguards, he displayed social graces. When Isabel was preparing to return to Madrid, López Rega humbly asked to be allowed to go back with her, as a bodyguard and servant of the general. He produced old newspaper photographs showing him close to Perón, as proof that he had once performed those functions. Isabel agreed to take him along, and so López Rega was installed in the Quinta 17 de Octubre.

At first, Perón assigned him only menial tasks. Even so, López Rega slowly gained influence over Isabel. She was isolated in that shadowy world of hard-ened, furtive men who surrounded the general. They treated her with respect as Perón's wife, but they always compared her unfavorably to Evita. The general was usually busy, plotting with his men, but López Rega was always available to accompany her on her shopping trips, carry her packages, listen to her over coffee at the Cafe California, or just chat. He became a kind of spiritual con-fessor and piqued her interest with his knowledge of the occult. She like he, lacked even a high school education; her ideas were a melange of half-digested facts, notions, and superstitions. As López Rega won her over, she in turn de-fended him against the coarse men among Perón's friends who laughed at his astrological charts, called him "the Sorcerer," and made him the butt of their jokes. There is no evidence at all that they ever became lovers, yet they were strongly bound by ties of mutual dependence.[4]

"Isabel is going according to plan," López Rega wrote to his friends in Ar-gentina, and "Don José" [Cresto] was a help, with his "humble and modest spiritualism." However, he noted, there was going to be a struggle to overthrow the influence of Jorge Antonio, whose fortune was the movement's main source of funding. Antonio currently had "a well-organized hold on the General," López Rega wrote, "but, for the Lord, nothing is difficult." Antonio's boastful egotism and bossiness earned him Isabel's hatred, too, although he was scarcely aware of it. Perón himself would have liked to shake loose from Antonio, but he remained dependent on the Syrian financier. Nothing could erode Antonio's position within the movement unless some alternative source of money could be found. That possibility arose late in 1966, shortly after López Rega arrived on the scene, when Perón came into contact with a powerful, secret lodge of Italian Freemasons called "Propaganda-2."

"Propaganda-2" (P-2) originated in the *Risorgimento*, when it was connected to the Piedmontese nobility and banking community. Under Mussolini, who outlawed Freemasonry, P-2 went underground. There it networked with other groups trying to evade Fascist controls, such as the Mafia and the Vatican, both of which helped P-2 members hide illegal fortunes made during the war. At the same time, this did not prevent P-2 from recruiting some well-placed Fascists into its ranks. After the war P-2 reduced its membership to a select few, 40 in all, who included leading Italian and foreign industrialists, bankers, diplomats, military men, and politicians. Among this inner circle was Licio Gelli, who had fought in the Spanish Civil War as a member of a Falangist militia, joined the Fascist Party, and served in Italian-controlled Yugoslavia as an officer in charge of the port of Cattaro. One of his duties was to ship a large quantity of gold, dollars, and jewelry back to Italy. Some of it was never accounted for. After the war, Gelli fled to Buenos Aires, where he stayed until the heat was off. Then he returned to Italy and joined the right wing of the Christian Democratic Party, led by Giulio Andreotti, whose links with the Mafia were a common subject of gossip. In 1964 Gelli became a Freemason, and two years later, with Andreotti as a sponsor, he was inducted into the super-secret P-2. The basis of his importance to the lodge was the network of contacts he had developed in Buenos Aires with former Fascist officers who had been in military intelligence. Many of them still had friends in the Italian armed services, and through them he began to receive information about people in high places, financial transactions, and diplomatic secrets. When P-2's Grand Master died in 1971, Gelli succeeded him and increased the lodge's membership to more than two thousand.[5]

The initial contact between Perón and P-2 came through Giancarlo Valori, a Fiat executive. Gelli, Valori, and Perón had many friends in common in Buenos Aires's Italian emigré community. Perón's motives for this connection were not hard to fathom: he wanted money for his movement and to free himself from Jorge Antonio. P-2's motives were more complicated. According to testimony given later, when P-2 was under investigation, Giulio Andreotti and his Christian Democratic faction were trying to use the organization to set up a power center in the Vatican that would rival Opus Dei, a Catholic lay organization of powerful, worldwide business interests. Already P-2 and Opus Dei were struggling for control of certain Italian banks. Perón, too, was opposed to Opus Dei because it was supporting the Ongania government. For P-2, Argentina was a potential field for investment because of its close cultural ties to Italy, but to clear the way Ongania would have to fall. The Peronist movement was a lever by which he could be toppled. As time went on, however, and Ongania's military successors appeared unable to hold on to power, Perón's stock in P-2 rose even higher, for it was increasingly clear that he would be the most likely beneficiary of a return to civilian rule.

P-2's backing was not sufficient, at first, to make Perón completely independent of Antonio. Still, he needed a trusted contact man to keep exploring the P-2 option, and for this task he picked López Rega. Thus, about a year and a half after arriving in Madrid, "the Sorcerer" was promoted from a household menial to Perón's private secretary. In addition his rival, Antonio, lost a good part of his fortune in 1968 and 1969 on some bad real estate investments. Nevertheless, Perón, ever careful to balance off his subordinates, appointed

Jorge Daniel Paladino to be his personal delegate in Argentina as well as the movement's general secretary. Paladino, who was 38 years old, represented the moderate trade unions, which were now the principal sources of funding. Perón also transferred the supreme command to Buenos Aires, appointed Paladino to head it, and filled it with important labor leaders.

RETREAT TO THE BARRACKS

In 1971, Perón's position suddenly became much stronger. After assuming the presidency in March, Lanusse secretly dispatched a personal representative, Colonel Francisco Cornicelli, to Madrid to test Perón's openess to a rapprochement. No one else in Argentina knew about the mission, not even the top military commanders. At 6 P.M. on 22 April, Cornicelli was whisked into the secluded grounds of the Quinta 17 de Octubre and conducted to Perón's magnificent paneled office. It was the first step in an intricate chess game in which Perón had the advantage. To get his cooperation, the Lanusse government would have to grant Perón an amnesty and let him return to Argentina. Elections would have to be held soon, with no prohibitions on parties or candidates, and all sentences and judgments against Perón would have to be lifted. Finally, the general wanted the return of Evita's corpse, which the military had sequestered after the 1955 coup, and the Argentine government had to unblock the Swiss bank accounts being held under her name.[6]

Lanusse met one of Perón's demands when a federal court overturned all criminal charges against him, and another when the government restored his right to vote. In September, Evita's coffin was exhumed from a Milan cemetery (where it had been buried under a false name) and was delivered to the Quinta 17 de Octubre. With Perón, Isabel, the Argentine ambassador, and two monks looking on, López Rega and Paladino opened the coffin. There was dirt inside, and the shroud was damp and stained, but aside from a flattening of the nose from the coffin lid, which was easily reparable, the corpse was perfectly preserved. Dr. Pedro Ara, the Spanish physician who had embalmed Evita's corpse at great expense nearly 20 years before, examined it the next day. He fixed the nose, covered a scar on the forehead, and resealed a crack in the plastic coating around the throat that had occurred when the head had been jammed against the coffin.[7]

The corpse was washed, combed, dressed in a new shroud, and placed in an upstairs guest room. Mysterious things began to happen. One night Isabel was awakened by a knocking sound, according to friends who knew her in Madrid. She got up and went into the hall. The sound was coming from the room where Evita's corpse lay, but when Isabel opened the door the noise stopped. The casket lay in its place. As soon as Isabel returned to her room, the steady knocking sound started up again. "Evita's body was kicking the coffin," Isabel claimed. She roused López Rega, who explained to her that Evita was bored and lonely. He quieted the cadaver by placing a little doll (of which he had many) inside the coffin. Even so, Isabel slept with her door locked after that. During the daytime, however, Isabel was required to lie on top of Evita's casket while López Rega "burned candles and uttered incantations for the purpose of raising Evita's spiritual essence from the corpse to the psyche of her would-be successor."[8]

In mid-September Lanusse met another of Perón's demands by scheduling general elections for March 1972, with the new president and Congress to take office in May. It was not clear whether Perón could be a candidate, however, so he ordered the CGT to call a one-day general strike for Wednesday, 29 September, as a way of tightening the screws on Lanusse. Calling the strike also was intended to embarrass Paladino and the moderates within the movement, who, in Perón's view, were showing too much enthusiasm for the GAN. Paladino's reports to Madrid were becoming less frequent and suspiciously less informative. Finally, at the beginning of November, Perón suddenly replaced Paladino with Héctor J. Cámpora, an old party warhorse.

A big, genial dentist from Buenos Aires, Cámpora was dull-witted but as obedient as a trained puppy. His two sons, Carlos and Pedro, were active in the Peronist Youth and were in close touch with the Montoneros. Two other friends, Esteban Righi and Jorge Vásquez, were also sympathetic to the Peronist Left. For Perón, Cámpora was the right tool for the moment. As a leftist, he would balance off the moderate trade unionists, who were becoming difficult to discipline and he would be intransigent toward Lanusse. To strengthen the movement's Left even more, Perón appointed Rodolfo Galimberti as head of the Peronist Youth. Galimberti had not yet joined the Montoneros, but the organization he headed, Argentine Youth for National Emancipation (JAEN), worked closely with them.

Taped messages coming from the Quinta 17 de Octubre urged the Montoneros to more violence and eulogized their fallen.[9] Perón had neither abandoned the idea of elections nor committed himself to it until he knew whether he would be allowed to return to Argentina and run for the presidency. As neither Lanusse nor Mor Roig wanted to let him do either, he used the guerrillas as his battering ram. Meanwhile, the Justicialist Party steadfastly refused to nominate anyone other than him to head its ticket.

Lanusse's counterstrategy was to concede as little as possible, crack down more efficiently on the guerrilla Left, and try to detach the more moderate unions from Perón through wage increases. On 7 July, at the annual armed forces banquet, he announced that Perón could be a candidate for the presidency, but only if he returned to Argentina by 25 August 1972. Perón ignored the deadline, saying that he would not be dictated to by the government. Lanusse then stepped up his personal attacks, hinting that Perón was a coward not to return. To Lanusse's great surprise and consternation, Perón suddenly arrived at Ezeiza International Airport at around noon on November 14. Tipped off in advance, soldiers surrounded the area and sealed it off. Perón was conducted to a room at the airport hotel and given strict orders not to leave it. He could receive visitors, however, so for the next 24 hours he met with a stream of labor leaders and politicians. On the next day he was allowed to go to a house he recently had bought in the upscale suburb of Vicente López. A crowd estimated at between twenty and forty thousand jammed into the area—workers, students, men, women, and children—all straining to see and greet "their general." Throughout his stay, the crowds continued to surround the house and were kept from pushing inside or peeping through the windows only by the constant vigilance of the young toughs of the GRN. Perón remained inside most of the time but emerged occasionally, with Isabel and López Rega, to raise his arms in a signal of triumph. This never failed to raise a cheer and start the people chanting Peronist slogans. Inevitably, too, there would come the deep boom, boom of the *bombo*.

Perón's unexpected appearance was an embarrassing defeat for Lanusse and the military. After challenging him to come back, they could hardly send him away, yet the enthusiastic greeting he got from the masses dispelled any doubts about whether his old charisma still held. For many military officers this was a nightmare come true. Lanusse appealed to his fellow soldiers to be firm in their resolve to disengage from power. Like it or not, he told them, Peronism is a reality.

Meanwhile, Perón was firming up his base and building alliances. Then, with no previous announcement, he suddenly left Argentina on 14 December and headed for Asunción, where he was to meet with Paraguay's dictator, General Alfredo Stroessner. From there he flew to Madrid. Years later it was learned that his health had suddenly begun to deteriorate. He was passing blood, and only his athletic constitution and strong will kept him going. He left behind, however, a sealed envelope naming his choices for president and vice president. Many Peronists were dismayed to discover that he was taking himself out of the race. It would be too provocative for the military to swallow, he explained. Instead, Héctor Cámpora would be his stand-in, and Vicente Solano Lima, an old fellow traveler of Peronism from the Popular Conservative Party, would be the vice presidential candidate. Perón's wishes were dutifully ratified by a convention of the Justicialist Party. To mollify the Peronist Youth, Perón appointed Juan Abal Medina, brother of the dead Montonero leader, to be the new general secretary of the Justicialist Party.[10]

Cámpora's links to the guerrilla Left made his candidacy only slightly less repugnant to the military than Perón's would have been. Lanusse told his fellow officers, however, that "we have the distinct feeling that Perón picked this fellow especially so that we'll veto him. If we veto him, he'll be replaced by another and even more irritating candidate. . . . That leaves the armed forces with a choice of either suspending the elections or simply proscribing Peronism. Then we'd be back where we were before." Completely outmanuevered, the military grudgingly let the electoral campaign continue, assuaging themselves with warnings that any future civilian government had better stay within certain bounds. It would have to respect the military's autonomy and keep it informed about its proposed actions. In particular, the officrs warned against any "indiscriminate amnesties" of guerrilla prisoners.

THE CAMPAIGN

The Peronist movement, campaigning on the slogan *Cámpora al gobierno; Perón al poder*, was deeply divided. The unions were angry at having to share places on the ticket with the Peronist Youth, whom they saw as communist infiltrators. The Buenos Aires unions rejected a slate of candidates drawn up by Cámpora and Abal Medina because its gubernatorial nominee, Oscar Bidegain, was a Montonero sympathizer. In Córdoba, the unions balked at supporting Ricardo Obregón Cano, a human rights lawyer with many guerrilla friends, for governor, and Atilio López, a "revolutionary Peronist" union leader, for lieutenant governor. The Peronist Left struck back, accusing the union leaders of being unrepresentative of the workers and corrupt lackeys of colonialism. Both FAR and the Montoneros warned their members that Peronism's certain victory at the polls was not an end in itself but merely a stage in the revolutionary march toward the *patria socialista*. "The popular struggle has no interest in democratic forms," Gustavo Rearte asserted, "but only an interest in real democracy," which he defined as existing only when the "exploited classes, the oppressed classes," are in power. After the election, the true revolutionaries would have to settle scores with the moderate reformists and the traitorous union bureaucracy.[11]

Only Perón's personal authority, his considerable skill at being all things to all factions, and the knowledge that all these factions needed one another to win kept the movement from disintegrating. Recalcitrant union leaders were forced into line, and compromises were hammered out concerning the makeup of electoral tickets. Still, the unions were disgruntled. As the campaign got underway the Peronist Left set the tone with enthusiastic references to the Montonero "heroes," whose songs, slogans, and banners dominated the rallies. López Rega also earned labor's hostility because Paulino Niembro, head of the Buenos Aires metalworkers' union (UOM), was bumped out of fourth place on the congressional ticket in favor of Raúl Lastiri, "the Sorcerer's" son-in-law.

On 11 March 1973, more than 12 million voters went to the polls, an 86 percent turnout. Cámpora got 49.5 percent of the total rate, compared to 21.3 percent for the Radicals' Ricardo Balbín and 14.9 percent for Francisco Manrique, of the conservative Alianza Federalista. The remaining 14 percent was scattered among the other six candidates. Although Cámpora had not quite gotten an absolute majority, he was so close that his opponents agreed to forego a runoff. Some "hard-line" military officers suggested cancelling the results and retaining power, but they were unable to win over a majority of their colleagues, who were heartily sick of politics and anxious to get back to the barracks.

Inauguration Day, 25 May, saw an ocean of young people filling the entire Plaza de Mayo and all the surrounding streets, waving Montonero, FAP, FAR, and Peronist Youth banners. They insulted, spat at, and physically assaulted the soldiers, sailors, and policemen who were lined up for the traditional inaugural parade. They leaped up on tanks and armored personnel carriers, jeering at the drivers and spray-painting the vehicles with Montonero slogans and offensive graffiti. Scuffles broke out between soldiers and demonstrators, as the latter chanted, *"¡Se van, se van, y nunca volverán!"* ("They're going, they're going, and they're never coming back!"). The parade finally was cancelled and the soldiers—roughed up, sore, and dejected—were taken back to camp. It was a shocking confrontation with mass hatred that left a deep impression on many of them. They had been aware that the armed forces had lost popularity, but they never had guessed how wide the gulf was between themselves and the populace. Some of the soldiers, like General Jorge Carcagno, drew the lesson that the army must open itself up to Peronism as the only way to get back in touch with the people. Others, like General Jorge Videla, felt their anti-Peronism rise to new heights.

NOTES

1. Crawley, *A House Divided*, 338–39.

2. Ricardo Burzaco, *Infierno en el monte tucumaño: Argentina, 1973–1976* (Buenos Aires: R. E. Editores, 1994), 33–35; Foro de Estudios sobre la Administración de Justicia (FORES), *Definitivamente Nunca Más (La otra cara del informe de la CONADEP)* (Buenos Aires: FORES, 1985), 43–46.

3. Seoane, *Todo o nada*, 181–83; Gillespie, *Soldiers of Perón*, 116–17; Díaz Bessone, *Guerra revolucionaria*, 156–58; Alejandro Lanusse, *Mi testimonio* (Buenos Aires: Lasserre Editores, 1977), 296–98.

4. Revista Somos, *Historias y personajes*, 162.

5. Martin Berger, *Historia de la lógia masónica P-2* (Buenos Aires: El Cid Editor, 1983), 15, 21–30; Gerardo Bra, "La P-2, en la Argentina," *Todo es Historia*, no. 214 (February 1985), 8–10.

6. Joseph Page, *Perón: A Biography* (New York: Random House, 1983), 421; *La Prensa* (4 July 1972), 1–6, for the transcript of this meeting.

7. Pedro Ara, *El caso Eva Perón: apuntes para la historia* (Madrid: CVS Ediciones, 1974), 263–69; Page, *Perón*, 424.

8. Revista Somos, *Historias y personajes*, 30; Page, *Perón*, 425. In September 1976, when the Quinta 17 de Octubre was repossessed by the bank for nonpayment on the mortgage, a large number of voodoo dolls were found on the premises.

9. Gillespie, *Soldiers of Perón*, 38–41; Daniel James, "The Peronist Left, 1955–1975," *Journal of Latin American Studies*, vol. 8, no. 2 (November 1976), 275; *Análisis* (12–18 November 1971), 14–16; 19–25 November 1971, 18–19.

10. Ramón Prieto, *Correspondencia Perón-Frigerio, 1958–1973* (Buenos Aires: Editorial Machaca Güemes, 1975), 193–95.

11. Baschetti, *Documentos*, 513–15, 517, 519–20, 524, 526, 533.

SIX

The Peronist Restoration

"TÍO" AND HIS "MARVELOUS YOUTH"

In his inaugural speech Héctor Cámpora promised to initiate government economic planning and take over the banking system in order to control investment. Argentina's sovereignty would be protected against foreign companies. He also promised to curtail private education, which he called a privilege of the oligarchy. Just in case the government's opponents were thinking of appealing these measures to the courts, he warned the judiciary that it would not be allowed to remain "outside of the process of national liberation." Above all, Cámpora praised "our marvelous youth" whose "courage and sacrifice" had made it possible for Peronism to return to power.

The "marvelous youth" owned the streets and had prepared for this day. Led by Juan Abal Medina and Rodolfo Galimberti, they went directly from the inaugural ceremonies to the Villa Devoto prison and demanded the release of some eight hundred guerrillas. Although Cámpora had promised to move quickly on an amnesty, the "marvelous youth" were unwilling to wait and became increasingly unruly and threatening. Faced with the possibility of a mass invasion of the building, Cámpora quickly issued a pardon for all those being held for "political crimes," including terrorist acts. Meanwhile, the guerrilla prisoners already had seized control of their cell blocks while the crowd clashed with the police. When the presidential pardon was read, confusion broke out. The crowd surged forward and poured into the jail. Two people were killed in the rush, and nine others were seriously hurt. The chaos inside was so great that many common criminals made their escape with the guerrillas. Among those released that night were Oberdán Sallustro's and Aramburu's kidnappers, as well as General Juan Carlos Sánchez's assassins.[1]

The next day Congress went even further, approving an amnesty for all guerrillas and terrorists, repealing all of the military government's antiterrorist laws, and abolishing the Federal Criminal Court of the Nation. This was a direct challenge to the armed forces, which had warned against "indiscriminate amnesties." Now it became clear to many officers that, if the antiguerrilla war were ever resumed in the future, it would be better to kill captured terrorists outright than to see them released by sympathetic civilians to fight again. Back in Madrid, Perón was stunned by the news. He knew history, and he knew very well what should be done with guerrillas who were no longer useful. He also knew the effect that this would have on the military. Meanwhile, two of the released guerrillas, Envar El Kadri and Juan Carlos Mena, were meeting with Oscar Bidegain, the pro-Montonero governor of Buenos Aires Province. "We've returned to fight," they told him. "There'll be no truce."[2]

Charmed by at last having a government sympathetic to them, the Montoneros adopted Cámpora as "Tío" ("Uncle"). He was surrounded and greatly influenced by his two Montonero sons: Pedro, his chief of staff, and Carlos, his private secretary. They controlled who saw him, they wrote his speeches, and they reviewed all of his decrees. Carlos Cámpora's law partner, Esteban Righi, was the interior minister and in charge of the Federal Police. The education minister, Jorge Taiana, was not himself a Marxist but, like Cámpora, was under the strong influence of his Montonero son, Jorge Junior. The foreign minister, Juan Carlos Puig, was imposed on Cámpora by Perón as a sop to the Catholic Left. He had served on an international commission under Ongania, however, so he was unacceptable to the Montoneros. Their nominee, Jorge Vásquez, had to settle for being undersecretary. The Montoneros had their revenge, however. On the day that Puig was sworn in, armed demonstrators broke into the room, chanting insults. Aiming their guns at the assembled Argentine and foreign diplomats, they forced them to stand at attention while Vásquez laughed and applauded.[3]

Perón also forced Cámpora to include representatives from other branches of the movement and its allies. The unions controlled the Labor Ministry through Ricardo Otero, a UOM leader. The powerful Social Welfare Ministry went to Perón's private secretary, José López Rega. The Justicialist Party organization was represented by Antonio J. Benítez, the new justice minister and a longtime antagonist of Cámpora's. The Ministry of Treasury and Finance (later, the Economics Ministry) was headed by José Ber Gelbard, perennial head of the CGE, who had held the same position back in 1955. Angel Robledo, the defense minister, was a conservative populist with good connections to the armed forces.

Those appointments angered the Montoneros, who were determined to control the government even if they couldn't control the makeup of the cabinet. During the following weeks they seized government offices, state-owned factories, schools, university buildings, hospitals, railway stations, packinghouses, stores, radio and television stations, airports, public housing projects, newspaper offices, prisons, and banks. An employee at the National Council for Scientific and Technical Research (CONICET) recalled a terrifying invasion by guerrillas: "We were at work when a group of young kids with arm bands and machine guns entered. They kicked open the door. Then they smashed everything. There was more than twenty years of work in there. We learned later that they did the same thing to lots of other places." At the Thoracic Surgery Institute, the guerrillas tied up the director, wrapped him in the Montonero flag, and hanged him, head-down, from the third floor of the elevator shaft. Interior minister Esteban Righi took a benign view of such pranks. "Our order is a revolutionary order," he said. "It rests upon the People. It expresses their struggles and their organizations. It doesn't try to repress them." However, the unions struck back, sending their tough guys into action to throw the left-wing invaders out of factories, shops, and offices where they believed their interests to be at stake. Then the clashes really got violent. *La Prensa* noted that in the 20 days after Cámpora's inauguration, 18 deaths had resulted from such confrontations.[4]

The universities were prime targets for "liberation." The halls became scenes of permanent meetings and rallies. Armed guerrillas at building entrances kept out anyone they perceived as an opponent. Ordinary students stopped going to classes, which were usually suspended, anyway. They had no stomach for confronting terrorists and could not count on their professors for support. The professors themselves were either collaborators of the guerrillas or were intimidated. The junior lecturers now settled scores with their seniors, forming flying squads that invaded classrooms to shout down the conservative professors, or breaking into their offices to scatter their books and papers and drive them fleeing down the hall. The new university administrators encouraged such actions. A Marxist sociologist, Rodolfo Puiggrós, was the new rector of the University of Buenos Aires. At his installation, Puiggrós, flanked on the platform by Juan Abal Medina, Rodolfo Galimberti, and Mario Firmenich, urged the students to destroy the old university and build a more popular one on its ruins. His audience responded with the clenched fist salute and then stamped around the hall singing the march of the *Muchachos Peronistas* to the beat of the *bombo*. Puiggrós was heavily influenced by his daughter, Adriana, who was consorting with guerrillas like Roberto Quieto. On her recommendation he made Ernesto Villanueva, a young Montonero, his provost. Villanueva, in turn, began appointing fellow Montoneros and other Marxists to deanships so they could weed out the traditional faculty and replace them with people like themselves.[5]

Mario Kestelboim, a flamboyant human rights lawyer, became the new dean of the University of Buenos Aires Law School. Cámpora disliked him personally and made it a condition of his appointment that Kestelboim get a haircut. So, with television cameras rolling, the law school students hoisted their "first Montonero dean" on their shoulders and carried him to a barbershop to get his flowing locks cut. As soon as he was installed, Kestelboim picked Mario Hernández, a human rights lawyer and former guerrilla (FAP, FAR, Montoneros), as his associate dean. Then they informed conservative law professors that they would have to appear before a "popular tribunal" to answer questions about whether they had been supporters of the military. Knowing in advance what their fate would be, many of those professors never returned to the law school. Others who did were attacked and driven from the building.

At the College of Philosophy and Letters, Father Faustino O'Farrell, a Third World priest, let the Montoneros use the basement as a firing range. Human rights lawyers Rodolfo Ortega Peña and Eduardo Duhalde taught there as well as at the law school. Their philosophy courses heavily emphasized the works of Marx, Lenin, and Gramsci, and they introduced the concept of "group exams," for which students gave oral presentations at the end of the year and graded each other. At the College of Economic Sciences, Dean Oscar Sbarra let the Montoneros have the run of the building to hold their meetings and assemblies. The College of Exact and Natural Sciences was headed by Angel Virasoro, one of the professors purged by Ongania after the "Night of the Long Clubs." Upon taking office, Virasoro rehired as many of his former colleagues as he could find. As a core member of CONICET, he put lots of Peronist Youth and PRT activists on full-time grants so that they could have money while they devoted themselves full-time to politics. He also got CONICET to act as a clearinghouse for fellowships for "scholarly exchange" between communist bloc countries and Argentina, thus enabling guerrillas to travel abroad for more training. The Colleges of Pharmacy & Biochemistry, Medicine, and Engineering were all headed by young men in their 20s who were open supporters of the Montoneros. Even the ultra-traditional College of Agronomy, the "finishing school" for *estancieros*, failed to escape the new trends. Its new dean turned over one of its model *estancias* to the Montoneros to use for rural guerrilla training. The only holdout was the College of Dentistry, where a right-wing Peronist, Dean Alberto Banfi, refused to give in to pressure.

Arturo Juaretche, a left-wing Peronist polemicist, became editor in chief of the prestigious Editorial Universitaria de Buenos Aires (EUDEBA). Juaretche then picked leftist muckraker Rogelio García Lupo as his managing editor. Under them, EUDEBA began bringing out such "scholarly" titles as *La revolución chilena* by Salvador Allende, *La revolución peronista* by Héctor Cámpora, *La revolución peruana* by General Juan Velasco Alvarado, *La batalla de Panamá* by General Omar Torrijos, and *El marxismo* by Henri Lefebvre. Meanwhile, the new university administration was hard at work erasing any signs of hierarchy or authority. Kestelboim ordered the distinguished National Law Academy to leave the law school premises because it was "elitist" and was taking up room needed for student meetings. Faculty clubs and lounges were abolished and turned over to students, although the administration urged professors to continue going to them in order to meet the students and mingle with them. Professors and students were expected to address each other as *compañero* and use the familiar form of the second person.

The Montoneros warned that guerrilla warfare would continue until their rise to power was "definitive." ERP also rejected Cámpora's call in April for a truce. Both groups would continue to attack the armed forces and foreign capitalists, sparing the police and government functionaries only if they "do not collaborate with the army in persecuting the guerrillas or in repressing popular demonstrations." The government had little legal redress against such arrogant threats because the courts had practically ceased to function. The Supreme Court resigned as a body after the elections, and upon Cámpora's taking office, the lower court judges were offered a choice of accepting a generous early retirement package or being impeached. As a result, practically all judgeships became instantly vacant and there were massive resignations of judicial staff. Chaos spread through the court system as Peronists wrangled over appointments and the new judges tried to acquaint themselves with the cases in progress. Because the costs of early retirement were paid for, in part, out of the budget for supplies, courts ran out of pads, legal forms, stamps, typewriter ribbons, and everything else. In addition to this confusion, many of the new judges were unwilling to process cases against terrorists. Throughout 1973 and much of 1974, not a single guerrilla or terrorist was condemned to prison. There was not even an arrest warrant for ERP's leaders, who already had announced their intention of carrying on the revolutionary war, despite the new government's constitutional legitimacy.[6]

Watching the chaos spread, Perón was concerned that the armed forces might be provoked into action before he could return to Argentina. The Montoneros had publicly stated that they intended to replace the regular army with their own and Rodolfo Galimberti announced that the Peronist Youth was forming "popular militias." Those were direct challenges that even the most nonpolitical officers could hardly ignore. Perón's contact man with the army, retired Colonel Jorge Osinde, reported that Galimberti's remarks had raised dangerous questions in military circles. Protests were coming from army garrisons around the country. Perón had to quiet down the situation, so he summoned Galimberti to Madrid and dismissed him as head of the Peronist Youth. Cámpora was blundering, too, however. He defended his "marvelous youth" at the annual military banquet and told the assembled officers that because they had served the oligarchy and imperialists, the guerrilla attacks on them had been excusable. Now they must make up for their past by being active collaborators in building the *patria socialista*. Consequently, when Cámpora flew to Madrid to accompany Perón on his triumphal return, he found an icy reception. Nobody showed up at the airport to meet him, and when the taxi finally brought him to the Quinta 17 de Octubre, Perón gave him a severe reprimand: What was he trying to do, destroy 18 years of struggle and sacrifice? The guerrillas had to be suppressed and the Peronist Youth reined in sharply. Instead of obsequious assent, however, Cámpora gave equivocal and evasive answers that provoked Perón even more. Thoroughly put out with his puppet, Perón refused to attend any of the diplomatic receptions sponsored by the Spanish government for Argentina's new president.[7]

HERO'S RETURN

On 20 June, Perón, Isabel, López Rega, Licio Gelli, and Cámpora boarded a plane for Argentina. After so many years of exile, the general was going home for good. Peronist leaders from all over the country were preparing to bring their followers to the airport to greet him. For days they had been whipping up enthusiasm with rallies and marches; the government declared 20 June a holiday, and the railroads offered free transportation to anyone who wanted to make the trip. Now people began pouring into the capital and proceeding on foot to makeshift camps alongside the airport highway, where the Justicialist Party had set up sanitary facilities and first-aid stations.[8]

Perón, fearing that assassins would mingle with the crowd, ordered that the Ezeiza Airport be free of crowds, so the police set up roadblocks at a point where the airport highway is crossed by an overpass serving Route 205. Plans called for Perón to be taken from Ezeiza to this bridge by helicopter, from which he would be ushered into a bulletproof glass cage outfitted with microphones. These were attached to an elaborate speaker system that extended all the way across the overpass on both sides and down to the highway and fields below, where speakers hung from trees and lampposts. On the bridge itself were huge posters of Perón, Evita, and Isabel. Colonel Jorge Osinde, a former counterintelligence officer with a sinister reputation, had the task of securing the immediate area around the overpass. Working out of the seemingly innocuous position of secretary of sports and tourism in the Social Welfare Ministry, he had assembled a formidable army of some three thousand well-armed toughs drawn from various unions and right-wing paramilitary groups. Osinde set up his command post in the Hogar Escuela, a three-story children's hospital located about five hundred yards from the overpass whose occupants and staff were temporarily removed several days before the event. From the top floor there was a panoramic view of the overpass and surrounding area. Osinde's heavily armed men, wearing green armbands, were posted on the bridge and at its approaches. Others were to mingle with the crowd and keep a lookout for suspicious persons. In the event of trouble, Perón would immediately be ferried away by helicopter.

On the appointed day, the area around the overpass was packed with at least a million people in a holiday mood, many of them waving banners embroidered with Peronist slogans. About one hundred of Osinde's men occupied the bridge, keeping a watchful eye on the crowd while their comrades stood guard at the foot of the embankment. Through the microphone system, the guards urged the people not to crowd too close to the bridge, to stay calm and avoid pushing. Around midmorning they began to notice suspicious movements beyond the fields that flanked the airport highway. Men with different-colored armbands were positioning themselves behind the trees while others were climbing up into them. Then, just before noon, a huge column of armed men, led by Governor Oscar Bidegain, appeared at the southern approach to the overpass, flanked by two Leyland buses and some ambulances. A few minutes later someone fired a shot, and the battle was on. It raged for the next three hours. The guards on the bridge, caught in a crossfire, began shooting in every direction. The crowd stampeded in panic, trampling the dead, the wounded, women, and children. Reinforcements came from the Hogar Escuela. One of the Leyland buses was blown up by a grenade. Later, it was found to be full of weapons, with supports in the windows for machine guns. The other bus went into reverse. As the two sides blasted away at each other, the Federal Police and the provincial police stayed on the sidelines, refusing to get involved without orders from the Ministry of Interior.

Around 3:00 P.M. there was a lull in the fighting. Each side secured its positions. Then, about half an hour later, the Montoneros moved in from the trees and, behind an intense barrage of fire, made an assault on the bridge. It was a frenzied and nearly successful attempt to break the Peronist Right once and for all and establish the Left's supremacy, but the defenders held their ground. Thrown back, the Montoneros began to scatter, pursued by Osinde's men. Some of those who were caught were shot or badly beaten. Most were hauled to the International Hotel at the Ezeiza Airport, where Osinde had set up an emergency interrogation center, and were beaten unmercifully until they revealed who had ordered the attack. In the meantime, the Ezeiza control tower radioed the plane carrying Perón and told the pilot not to land at Ezeiza but to proceed to the Morón air force base, some six miles away. Perón landed there at 4:50 P.M. and was immediately taken to his home under heavy guard. He said nothing that night in his radio and television address to the people about the events at Ezeiza, whose death toll has been estimated at as high as two hundred (there was no official count), but over the next few days his home was the scene of numerous visits, from the UCR's Ricardo Balbín, cabinet ministers, labor leaders, and Justicialist Party representatives.

Posters began appearing the next day all over downtown Buenos Aires with the demand "Perón to Power." Victorio Calabró, the lieutenant governor of Buenos Aires Province, summed up the public mood: "Now that Perón is back, no one else can be president of Argentina." Finally, General Jorge Carcagno, the army's commander, went to Vicente López at Perón's invitation. He was understandably tense when he walked into the room, not knowing where to begin, but Perón turned on the charm. "General," he said, "I want to talk to you as one soldier to another." Immediately the ice was broken, and Carcagno poured out his concerns about the chaos that was spreading. He told Perón that military intelligence believed that the Left was preparing more *cordobazo*-type riots. At the end of the meeting, Perón accompanied his visitor to the garden, where he gave him a prolonged *abrazo* that was reported in all the evening papers. The next day, the navy and air force chiefs confirmed all that Carcagno had said. After they left, Perón contacted the CGT's José Rucci, who then went to the Casa Rosada and told Cámpora that he must either resign or face a massive general strike that would shut down the whole country. Cámpora, knowing that resistance was useless, gave in.

RESURGENCE OF THE PERONIST RIGHT

Because Vice President Solano Lima also resigned, the next in line for the presidency was Alejandro Díaz Bialet, the president of the Senate. However, he suddenly had to go to Spain "indefinitely" on "urgent business," so the succession fell to the president of the Chamber of Deputies, who "happened" to be Raúl Lastiri, López Rega's son-in-law. The swiftness with which control of the government passed to the Peronist Right dumbfounded the Montoneros. After the Ezeiza shootout, Perón issued an ominous warning against "infiltrators" in the movement and followed this up by removing the Peronist Youth representatives from the Supreme Council and dismissing Juan Abal Medina as the movement's secretary. Rucci was ordered to fully "Peronize" the labor movement by eliminating the Marxist unions and imposing order at the shop floor level. Rucci immediately sent gunmen into Córdoba but was forced to retreat when the radical unions obtained arms from Governor Obregón Cano. Similar battles were going on in Buenos Aires Province, this time with the guerrillas and Governor Oscar Bidegain helping the "combative unions." At the end of August, Marcelino Mansilla, one of Rucci's chief lieutenants, was riddled by machine-gun fire from a passing truck.

The Montoneros's only hope of clinging to power was to get Cámpora nominated as Perón's vice presidential candidate at the upcoming 2 August party convention. At the convention, however, Perón chose Isabel to be his running mate. The Montoneros interpreted this as further proof that the general was under "the Sorcerer's" influence. Thus, Firmenich and Quieto became increasingly determined to "break inside the circle" that was preventing Perón from understanding them, but despite their lobbying for Cámpora, on 23 September voters went once again to the polls and the Perón-Perón ticket captured 61.9 percent of the vote.

Firmenich and Quieto now saw no hope for recovering their influence in the movement except by eliminating their rivals. On 25 September, two days after the elections, about a dozen gunmen, positioned in windows and doorways, were waiting for José Rucci as he left the home of a relative, where he had spent the night. As he approached his car, a bullet, fired from across the street, broke his neck. His squad of bodyguards fired back, but other guerrillas with submachine guns and high-powered rifles rained bullets on them, as well as on Rucci, whose body was sprawled by the car. No one claimed responsibility afterward, but suspicion fell on ERP because only a day before Perón had outlawed the organization.[9] Not until years later did the Montoneros finally admit that they murdered Rucci.

Nevertheless, there were those in the government who suspected the truth and were ready to use counterterrorist tactics. In the Ministry of Social Welfare, López Rega and Colonel Osinde had their private army, which came to be known as the "Argentine Anticommunist Alliance," or AAA. Besides having one of the largest budgets in the entire government, the ministry was in charge of combating drug trafficking, which gave it access to U.S. loans for the purchase of arms. It also got light arms from General Numa Laplane, the commander of the army's First Corps and a nationalist who sympathized with the Peronist Right. Arrangements for such secret deliveries were said to be handled by a Special Forces officer, Captain Mohammed Ali Seineldín. The police were instructed not to interfere with the AAA's operations; indeed, SIDE, under General Otto Paladino, actually supplied the death squads with logistical support.[10]

Forty-eight hours after Rucci was killed, Enrique Grynberg, head of the Peronist Youth's Buenos Aires meeting center, the "Ateneo Evita," was gunned down. The AAA's next attempt was against Senator Hipólito Solari Yrigoyen, who had influenced Cámpora to release the guerrillas from Villa Devoto Prison. On 29 September the AAA placed a bomb in his car, set to go off when he turned the ignition. The senator was wounded in the explosion but did not die. Over the next two years, however, the AAA "perfected" its techniques and would seldom fail to kill its intended victim. In addition to assassinations, it also carried out attacks, using bombs and machine guns, against Peronist Youth centers.

THE MILITARY MOOD

General Carcagno survived Cámpora's fall because Perón took the advice of Colonel Osinde and moved cautiously in dealing with the military, but Carcagno was impervious to the change in mood. His chief advisor, Colonel Juan Jaime Cesio, was a fellow paratrooper but also a left-wing nationalist. Cesio convinced Carcagno that Perón was in poor health and would probably die before his term was up, opening the way for the Peronist Left to return to power. Thus, Carcagno started a civic action program called "Operation Dorrego." Some five thousand soldiers and eight hundred Peronist Youth were supposed to cooperate in building drainage canals in some recently flooded slum areas. Colonel Cesio had sold his boss on the idea that such contact between the Peronist Youth and the soldiers would breed mutual understanding and friendship.[11] In fact, Operation Dorrego had negative results in every respect. Colonel Cesio's courting of the Peronist Youth and Montoneros raised concerns among the labor and López Rega factions of the Peronist movement. These were communicated to Perón, who cancelled his appearance at the opening ceremonies at the last moment. (Nor would he attend the closing ceremonies.) The appearance of the Peronist Youth, as they marched onto the scene, reminded the army officers of the Montoneros's threat to build popular militias. During the actual work on the project, officers, non commissioned officers, and soldiers kept their distance from the Peronist Youth. The officer in charge, General Jorge Rafael Videla, a popular professor and director at the Military Academy, avoided all contact with either the Peronist Youth or the press. The entire experiment cost Carcagno a great deal of prestige among his fellow officers.

Worse was to come. While Carcagno was in Caracas excoriating the United

States at the Conference of American Armed Forces, ERP guerrillas captured the army Medical Corps headquarters in the Buenos Aires neighborhood of Palermo. They gained entry by pretending that their van was delivering a load of supplies. Once inside, a soldier who was an ERP collaborator held and disarmed the guards, killing an officer and an enlisted man who resisted. As ERP commandos loaded arms and medical supplies into their van, however, two soldiers managed to escape and run to a nearby police station. The police cordoned off the area while units of the First Infantry ("Patricios") Regiment and other reinforcements arrived. The guerrillas refused to surrender, however, so Lieutenant Colonel Raúl Duarte Ardoy and his men scaled the back wall of the compound, under the cover of heavy fire that drove the guerrillas deep into the building. When Duarte Ardoy forced open one of the doors, he was shot in the stomach. His men retreated, carrying their dying officer with them. By then, however, the army had brought up cannon and heavy machine guns and threatened to demolish the building, whereupon the *erpistas* surrendered. Duarte Ardoy was given a martyr's funeral, during which several officers bitterly attacked the current policy of friendship with the Left. Nevertheless, on his return from Caracas, Carcagno dismissed the U.S. and French military missions, forcing Perón to conclude that the general was political deadweight. At his secret instigation, the Senate refused in December to accept certain names on the promotions list that Carcagno submitted. One of those names was Cesio. Carcagno appealed to Perón to intervene but was told that the Senate's word was final. With that, he submitted his request for retirement, which Perón quickly granted.

Perón and López Rega favored General Numa Laplane, commander of the First Army Corps, as Carcagno's successor, but he was too strongly identified as a sympathizer of the Peronist Right. The bulk of the army was still "professionalist" and opposed to any involvement in politics. They then chose General Leandro Anaya, who was nonpolitical, descended from a distinguished military family, and trained in counterguerrilla warfare. Only a few weeks after his appointment, the country was stunned by a full-scale ERP attack on the Azul army base, in Buenos Aires Province, home of the Tenth Armored Cavalry Regiment and the First Artillery Group. Late in the evening of 19 January 1974, Enrique Gorriarán Merlo attacked, with a force of about 80 guerrillas armed with automatic rifles and antitank grenades and supported logistically by leftist militia from a nearby shantytown. They overpowered the guard at the rear gate of the Tenth Armored Cavalry, entered the base, and split into three groups: two in the direction of the barracks and armory, one toward the officers' quarters. They were spotted, however, by a guard posted on the base water tower, who gave the alarm. The guerrillas were met by heavy fire from the base's 50 or so defenders. Two trucks they had driven onto the grounds for loading arms were immediately destroyed; a third truck retreated. The ERP squad heading for the officers' quarters was met by resistance, led by Azul commander Colonel Arturo Gay. Colonel Gay was killed, and his next in command, Lieutenant Colonel Jorge Ibarzábal, surrendered when he learned that the guerrillas had seized Gay's family and were threatening to kill them. Ibarzábal, shoved into a car and driven off by the guerrillas, had his picture taken in a "people's prison" and displayed a week later in *Estrella Roja*. As for Colonel Gay's family, the guerrillas thrust them into the base machine shop and "executed" his wife. Outside the base, the guerrillas and their supporters held off a contingent of 15 marines from the nearby Azopardo arsenal and several squads of Buenos Aires provincial police while most of the guerrillas inside made a tactical retreat. On the whole, the attack was a failure. ERP lost four guerrillas: three dead and one captured. Its support units, the workers and slum organizers, were left to their fate. About a dozen of them simply "disappeared," and no arms were captured. Human rights lawyers like Rodolfo Ortega Peña and Eduardo Duhalde distanced themselves from the attack, while Santucho himself considered the operation to have been poorly planned and executed, especially the retreat. Although he decorated 28 of the participants for bravery, he demoted Gorriarán Merlo in rank. Nevertheless, the operation constituted a quantum leap in the evolution of the guerrillas' military strategy. More than a mere ambush, it resembled a standard military operation.[12]

The next day Perón appeared on television, dressed in his army uniform, and promised a stepped-up campaign against the "subversive delinquents." He especially targeted Buenos Aires governor Oscar Bidegain, who was harboring guerrillas like Norma Arrostito (staff supervisor), Daniel Vaca Narvaja (agricultural affairs), and Julio Troxler (assistant police chief and head of a left-wing "death squad") in his government. After Perón's attack, the CGT and Justicialist Party forced Bidegain to resign in favor of his lieutenant governor, Victorio Calabró.[13] Perón then called upon Congress to restore the harsh penalties it had eliminated from the penal code back in May. If it didn't, he would still take extreme measures. Many of the same congressmen who had voted enthusiastically to expunge those provisions now obediently reversed themselves. The Peronist Youth bloc resigned in protest, and the Montoneros warned that repression would only provoke reprisals.

Bidegain was only the first of many leftist governors to fall from power in the aftermath of the Azul incident. Next, Córdoba governor Ricardo Obregón Cano and his lieutenant governor, Atilio López, were overthrown by a coup led by the head of the provincial police, Lieutenant Colonel Antonio Navarro. Some 80 known guerrillas and their sympathizers in the government were rounded up. The Marxist unions declared a general strike, gun battles broke out between the police and the guerrillas, bodies lay in the streets, and snipers fired away from the rooftops. Perón quickly gave Colonel Navarro his backing and intervened in the province. Then it was Mendoza's turn to be the scene of turmoil. Governor Alberto Martínez Baca, who had filled his cabinet with Montoneros, was ousted in favor of his lieutenant governor, Carlos Mendoza, a union man.

The new campaign also meant tightening the screws on the press. The Montoneros's *El Descamisado* was closed after its editor, Dardo Cabo, made the mistake of running an editorial attacking Perón and demanding to know, "Why didn't you tell us before, when we were fighting Lanusse, that we ought to join another party? . . . No one has the right to throw us out! No one can dismiss us!"[14] The PRT's *El Mundo* was attacked by AAA gunmen on 23 January after it ran an article praising ERP's assault on the Azul base. When one of its reporters, Ana María Guzzetti, asked Perón at a press conference about "fascist attacks" by "parapolice groups" against "popular activists," he lost his temper and told his aides to have the Justice Ministry start proceedings against her for *desacato* (disrespect). Subsequently, Guzzetti received death threats, was indicted, and was finally abducted by the AAA. After the Buenos Aires Press Association called a protest strike, she was found, six days later on a highway outside the city, drugged, badly beaten, but still alive. *El Mundo* finally was closed by the Interior Ministry and then firebombed to make sure it stayed closed. The police also shut down the Montoneros' *El Peronista*. Juan Abal Medina barely survived an assassination attempt by the AAA, while Firmenich was arrested and roughed up. After being released, he immediately went underground. Even conservative anti-Peronist newspapers were harassed by printers' strikes or the withdrawal of advertising. Some, like *Clarín* or *El Burgués*, were attacked in gangland style, with submachine guns and incendiary grenades.[15]

As for the universities, the last redoubts of the Peronist Youth and Montoneros, Cámpora's fall was not followed immediately by a purge because Perón still harbored the idea that he could somehow hold together the left and right wings of his movement. He was willing to give the Montoneros free rein on the nation's campuses, if only they would obey him. As they resisted, he tightened the screws. Puiggrós was fired, and so was his daughter, Adriana, who had become head of the College of Philosophy and Letters. Rodolfo Ortega Peña and Eduardo Duhalde also were dismissed from all of their university appointments (Duhalde himself held 13). Their classroom antics had become notorious—on the rare occasions when they showed up for class. The Left salvaged something when student demonstrations convinced the conservative Alberto Banfi not to succeed Puiggrós, so that Ernesto Villanueva then became acting rector. He was soon replaced by former Vice President Vicente Solano Lima. However, as rector, Solano Lima was never really in control. Neither he nor Perón was willing to undertake the ruthless purge necessary to free the university of the guerrillas' supporters. Solano Lima was wishy-washy, and Perón hoped to split the Peronist Left by holding out university posts to those who would reject the terrorists.

The Left struck back with a series of dramatic attacks. Rogelio Coría, the former construction workers' leader, was riddled with bullets by the Montoneros on a downtown Buenos Aires street. ERP killed Antonio Magaldi, head of the CGT's San Nicolás branch, and also Judge Jorge Quiroga, former president of the Federal Criminal Court of the Nation. A Brazilian industrialist and Fiat's chief of personnel were assassinated. Kidnappings increased: Victor Samuelson, manager of Esso; A. A. Valocha, Swift's personnel director; Eugenia de Denovoa, proprietress of a printing establishment; Juan Peña Riba, the owner of a San Juan vineyard; and David Kraiselburd, the owner of La Plata's *El Día*. Riba and Kraiselburd would later be killed by their captors.

Perón now found himself a victim of the very chaos that he once had encouraged against others. When he tried to give the usual 1 May Labor Day address from the balcony of the Casa Rosada, the Montoneros and Peronist Youth heckled him: "What's going on, General? The People's Government is full of gorillas!" Perón slashed back, calling them "morons" and hinting at their immaturity by referring to them as "beardless types." Orthodox Peronists in the crowd then began shouting their support for the leader. Perón went on with his speech as the Montoneros and Peronist Youth left the Plaza, chanting, *"Si Evita viviera, sería Montonera"* ("If Evita were alive, she'd be a Montonera"). Although Isabel and López Rega urged him to drum the Montoneros out of the movement and launch a thorough purge of the universities, Perón refused. Instead, on the morning of 12 June he suddenly appeared on television and made a dramatic address to the nation. He outlined all the serious problems Argentina was facing, described their causes, and said that his solutions would take time. Unless he had the support of the people, however, he would resign. That afternoon the Plaza de Mayo was filled again, this time with workers that the CGT leaders quickly mobilized for a show of support. Perón's gamble had paid off; it was just the display he needed. He thanked the crowd and announced, as their reward for backing him, that the traditional end-of-the-year *aguinaldo*, the extra month's wage, would be payable immediately and in full.[16]

It was Perón's last public triumph. On the following day, he flew to Paraguay but arrived so exhausted that the diplomatic ceremonies had to be restricted. Before departing, he insisted on reviewing Paraguayan troops in the rain and refused an umbrella. By the time he returned to Buenos Aires he had caught a cold. He bid good-bye to Isabel and López Rega, who were off on a trip to Europe, and shut himself up in the Presidential Residence, accepting no visitors. Five days later, 20 June, López Rega was called back from Geneva by Perón's doctors. After seeing the general, he issued a statement that Perón only had a bad cold, but on 28 June Isabel was suddenly called back from Madrid and named interim president by her husband, on the advice of his doctors. Despite constant upbeat bulletins that Perón was making progress, there was tension in the air—at Justicialist Party headquarters, in the Congress, at cabinet meetings, in the CGT, at the various army barracks. Finally, at midmorning on Monday, 1 July, Isabel was summoned from a cabinet meeting to her husband's bedside. He had had a cardiac arrest, but the doctors, working feverishly, had managed to restore his heartbeat. Then Perón had another heart failure, shortly past noon, and this time the doctors were not able to keep his heart going. López Rega intervened, seizing the agonizing Perón by the ankles, he began to mutter, "I can't, I can't . . . I did it ten years ago. I gave you strength. . . . He is a pharaoh and always with you . . . but I can no longer. . . . I can't." At 1:15 P.M. Perón was pronounced dead.[17]

NOTES

1. Revista Somos, *Historias y personajes*, 50–51; *Primera Plana* (9 August 1973), 9; Rosendo Fraga, *Ejército: del escarnio al poder (1973–1976)* (Buenos Aires: Editorial Planeta, 1988), 39–40.

2. Julio Santucho, *Los últimos guevaristas: surgimiento y eclipse del Ejército Revolucionario del Pueblo* (Buenos Aires: Editorial Puntosur, 1988), 191; Norberto Beladrich, *El parlamento suicida* (Buenos Aires: Ediciones Depalma, 1980), 11–15, 25–26, for the full text of these congressional acts.

3. Revista Somos, *Historias y personajes*, 55.

4. Moyano, *Argentina's Lost Patrol*, 71–72; Ezequiel Raggio, *La formación del estado militar en la Argentina, 1955–1976* (Buenos Aires: Editorial Losada, 1986), 148–49; Revista Somos, *Historias y personajes*, 46, 49, 51–52.

5. Landivar, *La universidad*, 17, 31–37, 88, 91–95, 97, 99–100, 109, 116, 121–22, 127–28, 131–32, 135, 150, 157, 162.

6. FORES, *Definitivamente Nunca Más*, 47–50.

7. Fraga, *Ejército*, 54, 58–59; Gregorio Selser, *Perón; el regreso y la muerte* (Montevideo: Biblioteca de Marcha, 1973), 18; *Análisis Confirmado* (8–14 May 1973), 18; Revista Somos, *Historias y personajes*, 52.

8. Horacio Verbitsky, *Ezeiza* (Buenos Aires: Editorial Contrapunto, 1986); Roberto Aizcorbe, *El mito peronista* (Buenos Aires: Ediciones, 1976), 237–242.

9. Méndez, *Confesiones*, 53–68; Pineiro, *Crónica*, 27–28; Graham-Yool, *State of Fear*, 34; *Primera Plana* (27 September 1973), 26–27.

10. Ignacio González Jansen, *La Triple-A* (Buenos Aires: Editorial Contrapunto, 1986), 13–15, 35, 48–49; Crawley, *A House Divided*, 384; Alipio Paoletti, *Como los nazis, como en Vietnam* (Buenos Aires: Editorial Contrapunto, 1987), 329–30, 332–33, 337–340; Santucho, *Los últimos guevaristas*, 201–2, 205; Raúl Veiga, *Las organizaciones de derechos humanos* (Buenos Aires: Centro Editor de América Latina, 1985), 114; García, *Patria sindical*, 23–28; Carlos Juvenal, *Buenos muchachos: la industria del secuestro en la Argentina* (Buenos Aires: Editorial Planeta, 1994), 77–78, 90, n. 3, 137–38.

11. Fraga, *Ejército*, 62, 70–75, 110–12; García, *La doctrina*, vol. 1, 40; Seoane, *Todo o nada*, 223.

12. Díaz Bessone, *Guerra revolucionaria*, 214–16; Seoane, *Todo o nada*, 232–34; Mattini, *Hombres y mujeres*, 276–77.

13. Revista Somos, *Historias y personajes*, 60, 180.

14. Liliana De Riz, *Retorno y derrumbe: el último gobierno peronista* (Mexico City: Folios Ediciones, 1981), 108, from an editorial in *El Descamisado* (12 February 1974).

15. Andrew Graham-Yool, *The Press in Argentina, 1973–1978* (London: Writers and Scholars Educational Trust, 1979), 25–28, 32–35; Aizcorbe, *El mito peronista*, 286.

16. Rodolfo Terragno, *Los 400 días de Perón* (Buenos Aires: Ediciones de la Flor, 1974), 182.

17. Pablo Kandel and Mario Monteverde, *Entorno y caída* (Buenos Aires: Editorial Planeta Argentina, 1976), 2–5; *Última Clave* (11 July 1974), 1–2.

SEVEN

Toward the "Dirty War"

Upon Perón's death, his wife, María Estela Martínez de Perón, or "Isabel," succeeded him to the presidency, as the Constitution provided. She had no deep roots in the Peronist movement, either in the Feminist Party or the CGT, as Evita once had; nor did she possess any of Evita's charisma, toughness, or instinct for politics. She was essentially unimaginative, ignorant, and stubborn, but she had the advantage of being Perón's legitimate spouse and the bearer of his magic name. Beyond that, she depended upon José López Rega, who now became her private secretary as well as her minister of social welfare. He possessed a drive for power that Isabel lacked and was well connected through two separate networks, P-2 and AAA.

The government was riddled with P-2 members: naval minister Admiral Massera, the defense minister, several ambassadors, and Raúl Lastiri, head of the Chamber of Deputies (and next in line to succeed Isabel). P-2's economic empire in Argentina was said to include the largest paper company, a domestic airline, an oil company, and two publishing houses, Editorial Korn and Editorial Huemul.[1] The AAA network included the chief of the Federal Police, Isabel's personal bodyguard, and the security guard for the Presidential Residence. In the latter half of 1974, AAA death squads killed more than 70 prominent leftists, including Silvio Frondizi; human rights lawyers Rodolfo Ortega Peña and Alfredo Curutchet; leftist "hit-man" Julio Troxler; Atilio López; and Gen. Carlos Prats, former head of the Chilean army under Allende. The AAA usually sent its victims notification in advance that they were on its "hit list" and warned them to leave the country. Some of them quickly opted for exile; others, like Frondizi, stood their ground. The method of attack varied. Prats and his wife were killed by a bomb that went off in the doorway of their apartment building. Frondizi was dragged out of his apartment, shot and bleeding, and his son-in-law was killed on the sidewalk below while trying to pull him away from his captors. Ortega Peña was gunned down while getting out of a taxi in downtown Buenos Aires. Often the victims were kidnapped, their bodies usually appearing later in vacant lots on the outskirts of town, riddled with bullet holes. (The police counted at least 60 in López's body.) Often the corpses were doused with gasoline and burned beyond recognition.

Despite such terror tactics, Isabel and López Rega were not secure. The Montoneros had gone into open opposition, adding their strength to that of ERP. Two weeks after Perón's death, a Montonero walked up to former Interior Minister Arturo Mor Roig while he was eating in a restaurant and blasted him with a sawed-off shotgun. Montonero guerrillas enjoyed an advantage over ERP by having participated in the Cámpora government, through which they had obtained hundreds of official identity cards and uniforms. They also had established networks of sympathizers in the bureaucracy, the universities, the media, the labor unions, and even children of military officers.

In the meantime, Santucho had finally launched his long-awaited rural guerrilla operation in the mountains of Tucumán Province. Early in May 1974, the first ERP camps appeared to the south and west of the provincial capital. There were about 30 guerrillas in all, well supplied so that they would not have to go down to the villages during this initial phase. They spent most of their time practice-firing and patrolling the region to gain familiarity with it. Santucho remained with them for the first few days and then turned over the leadership of the Companía del Monte "Ramón Rosa Jiménez" to Hugo Iruzún (alias "Captain Santiago"). By the end of May the guerrillas were becoming anxious to do something dramatic, so they procured a truck and, dressed in olive-green uniforms with matching berets, they rumbled into the town of Acheral (population 1,800) on May 29. To the astonishment of the locals, the guerrillas fanned out and swiftly took control of the telephone lines, the police outpost, the train station, and all access roads. Meeting no resistance, they proceeded to put up posters, hang ERP banners, and paint revolutionary slogans on the walls. Then, after haranguing the assembled townspeople, they climbed back into their truck and left, having had a perfectly successful day.

Back in camp, the guerrillas talked over their experience and decided to follow it up by sending some of their *tucumaño* colleagues back into Acheval and some of the neighboring villages to recruit collaborators. The ERP emissaries went by night and found a fairly large number of local residents willing to help with provisions and information. Some ham radio operators, including a few in the capital of San Miguel de Tucumán, promised to keep them informed about the whereabouts of the provincial police and also keep them in touch with other ERP groups in Córdoba, Santa Fe, and Buenos Aires.[2]

The 12 June issue of *El Combatiente* spelled out exactly what Santucho had in mind. It was time to go beyond urban guerrilla terrorism, which by itself would never accomplish the overthrow of the old society, and initiate a higher phase of the struggle, the actual conquest of "liberated zones" in which it would be possible to create a true army of the revolution. Eventually, the revolutionary army would confront the counterrevolutionary army in regular battles. Tucumán, with its dense, impoverished population, its thick jungles, and the Andean mountain chain running its length, seemed to Santucho to offer an impregnable base for launching the revolution.

At the same time that ERP was spreading its network in Tucumán, it was stepping up its operations against the army elsewhere in Argentina, backed by the $14.2 million of ransom money that Esso had recently paid to gain the release of one of its executives, Victor Samuelson. In May it attacked an artillery base in San Luis Province, and on the same day that Acheral was invaded, guerrillas tried to shoot their way into the 121st Communications Batallion in Rosario. So much money and so much initial success made ERP cocky. On 11 August they launched simultaneous operations against the Villa María army explosives factory in Córdoba and against the 17th Airborne Infantry Regiment in Catamarca. The Villa María attack resulted in the kidnapping of Major Julio Argentino Larrabure. Although the guerrillas got away with large stores of ammunition and explosives, much of it was recovered in the next few days. Catamarca was an unmitigated disaster. Part of the attacking force was made up of guerrillas from the Companía del Monte "Ramón Rosa Jiménez," who made the journey in a bus they rented from the School of Agronomy at the University of Tucumán, on the pretext that they were going on a picnic. Once over the border they subdued the unwitting driver, donned military uniforms, and made their rendevous with other ERP units. However, they had been spotted by a farmer who saw them changing their clothes, and he informed the police. Two patrol cars carrying eight policemen were sent out, but they were outgunned by the 70 guerrillas. Nevertheless, there was a fight, resulting in two policemen and two guerrillas dead. Four of the policemen finally escaped, leaving behind two wounded, who saved their lives by pretending to be dead. Several of the guerrillas were hurt, too, so the leaders decided to abandon the operation. The Tucumán contingent took the police cars and made their escape while the others started back to their bases on foot. By this time, however, the entire Catamarcan police force and the 17th Airborne Regiment were alerted and began a manhunt. The 27 rebels traveling on foot were located and cornered. At that point, accounts diverge. The official version was that the guerrillas refused a call to surrender. Eleven managed to escape, and the remaining 16 were wiped out. ERP claimed that the guerrillas did surrender and were then executed on the spot.[3]

Despite these defeats, ERP was making progress in its Tucumán operations. The collapse of the sugar economy a decade before had left more than 40,000 *tucumaños* unemployed, of whom about 70 percent were between the ages of 14 and 28, ripe for recruitment in a revolutionary crusade. Isabel and López Rega sent the Federal Police to take over the counterguerrilla operations from the hopelessly inefficient local police, but the *federales* were scarcely better. Led by the brutal Alberto Villar, they were riddled with corruption and lacking proper training or morale. For months they sporadically chased the guerrillas around the mountains, vainly trying to encircle them, while the ERP extended its control to about a third of the province, sending its guerrillas into towns and villages to collect supplies and mete out "justice" to suspected police informers. Cars and trucks using the country roads could expect to be stopped and forced to pay a "revolutionary tax." Despite the desire of army professionalists like General Anaya to let the Federal Police handle the situation, unease was growing among the officers.[4]

Isabel and López Rega were more successful in winning back the universities from the guerrillas. Solano Lima resigned as rector of the University of Buenos Aires (UBA) immediately upon Perón's death, and Jorge Taiana, the education minister, was replaced by Oscar Ivanissevich, a right-wing Peronist who had held the same post back in the early 1950s. Trying to stave off a takeover, the Montonero provost, Ernesto Villanueva, "elected" Raúl Laguzzi, dean of the School of Pharmacy, to succeed Solano Lima, as some five hundred Montoneros gathered at the University's Superior Council to shout their approval. Expecting a confrontation with the government, the Montoneros and their Peronist Youth then occupied all of UBA's buildings and vowed to resist any attempt to place the university under rule by "fascists." They were well-armed with machine guns, pistols, and hand grenades. The confrontation never happened, however, because on the night of 7 September a bomb destroyed Laguzzi's home, killing his four-month-old son. Although hundreds of saluting Montonero militia filed past the coffin, which was displayed in the hall of the Superior Council, draped in Argentine and Montonero flags, Laguzzi, desolated by the experience, lost interest in being rector and soon left the country. Ivanissevich then named Alberto Ottalagano, another right-wing Peronist, to the post. On going to his office the first day, Ottalagano met no opposition—no demonstrators outside the entrance, no Montonero militiamen blocking his way. The same was true throughout the university. The Montoneros had abandoned the buildings and also had abandoned "their" deans to their inevitable fate. As they disappeared underground, they took with them all of the university's cars and trucks.[5]

LABOR'S DISCONTENTS

Isabel and López Rega also had to deal with an increasingly unruly labor movement. The government wanted to control production, distribution, prices, wages, profits, rent, investment, and international trade, but the world oil crisis, which hit Argentina in late 1973, knocked the entire program to splinters. Inflation reached more than 74 percent by May 1974. By June 1975 it would be 100 percent, and by March 1976 it would be more than 900 percent.[6] Ordinary workers, desperate to feed their families, were not impressed by the government's periodic calls for discipline and belt tightening. Wildcat strikes broke out in defiance of both the Economics Ministry and the CGT leadership, providing opportunities for the PRT-ERP to seize power on the shop floor.

Labor leaders blamed José Ber Gelbard, the economics minister, who was widely viewed as an unsavory character. A few years before, while acting as a go-between for Perón, he had made Lanusse employ one of his companies to build the state-owned aluminum plant, Aluar. That had raised a storm of protest at the time, and the scandal would continue to dog both Gelbard and Lanusse over the next several years. More recently, his foreign trade deals often stipulated that products had to be purchased from companies that Gelbard owned. Without Perón to back him, Gelbard was open to attacks from both Isabel and López Rega, on one side, and the CGT on the other. He fell from office in October 1974, and with his departure the Ministry of Economy lost much of its importance. Five different men would head it over the next 16 months, struggling vainly to control runaway inflation by trying to apply more or less orthodox economic policies in a situation where labor union power made success impossible. Still, this did not reverse the erosion of the labor leaders' authority over the rank and file. Insurgents on the shop floor increasingly disavowed the union bureaucracy, won more and more local elections, and even began winning a few national ones. Strikes were becoming more confrontational, with workers taking over the buildings and seizing hostages. Some of this was spontaneous, but much of it was fuelled by the infiltration of PRT-ERP into the local factory committees. A good example of the latter, and the dilemmas it posed for the top union leadership, was the steel strike at Villa Constitución at the beginning of 1975.[7]

Located in a heavy industrial belt south of Rosario, the city of Villa Constitución depended on two large steel complexes: the state-owned Sociedad Mixta Siderúgica Argentina (SOMISA) mill, and the privately owned Aceros Industría Argentina (ACINDAR). PRT-ERP had been active in the region since 1973, but before that PO, its forerunner, had been busy spreading its propaganda in the bleak factories and the shabby, densely populated neighborhoods surrounding them. PRT-ERP located its headquarters in the neighboring city of Zarate and soon began setting up clandestine factory cells, as well as front organizations in neighborhood clubs, schools, and clinics. This operation was managed by Domingo Menna, a likable former medical student in the PRT politburo. Menna quickly found two energetic, intelligent steelworkers willing to fall in with his plans. One of them was Luis Segovia, a man with long political and union experience, and above all knowledgeable about dealing with fellow workers. Another was Alberto Piccinini, a forceful young man who agreed to head a revolt against the factory's traditional UOM leadership at the ACINDAR plant.

The ACINDAR steel mill union had been under police intervention since 1970 because of a strike. That made it easy for the government to insure that only trusted UOM members would get elected to union offices. In March 1974, therefore, Piccinini called for a strike to protest the exclusion of his slate of candidates from elections earlier that month and to demand the removal of the police. After negotiations between management, the UOM, and Piccinini broke down, Labor Minister Ricardo Otero stepped in. Striving to be fair, he ordered new elections scheduled for November, with participation by all factions. Those elections resulted in a nearly 2 to 1 victory margin by Piccinini's "Maroon List" over the official UOM "Blue List."

Once in power, the "classist" union leaders confronted ACINDAR's management over working conditions and its plans to substitute machinery for much of the existing labor force. To squeeze the bosses some more, Piccinini, Segovia, and Menna called another strike on 20 March, backed by the occupation of the town's center by the workers and their families. Argentina's "establishment" reacted with horror and indignation. The UCR's Ricardo Balbín warned of "industrial guerrilla war." Lorenzo Miguel of the UOM disassociated himself from the "hotheads." Otero called the strike illegal and "subversive." ACINDAR's president, José Martínez de Hoz, complained to Isabel about the "climate of insurrection" at his plant. Isabel went on television and radio to announce that the government had discovered a subversive network in the industrial belts of Santa Fe and Buenos Aires Provinces, "whose epicenter is Villa Constitución."

Approximately four thousand National Gendarmerie, Federal Police, and provincial police, supported by well-armed bands of AAA and Juventud Sindical, descended on Villa Constitución on 26 March. Some of the attackers burst into the ACINDAR buildings and forcibly dislodged the strikers; others spread out through the city, rounding up left-wing labor leaders like Piccinini and the other members of his "Maroon List," as well as the head of the local CGT and the local railway workers' union. Domingo Menna and Luis Segovia escaped, but 117 targeted "agitators" were imprisoned. Nevertheless, the steel plant remained shut down, as did Villa Constitución's stores, banks, and schools. It became an occupied city for the next 39 days. Protest marches were quickly dispersed with brutal force. ERP struck back with bombings and armed attacks on other steel mills and automotive factories in the region. Eventually, Lorenzo Miguel insinuated himself into the situation as a moderator, wheedling Isabel and López Rega into replacing the intractable federal intervenor with a UOM man and negotiating the release of all but 40 of the arrested strike leaders. By June, the exhausted strikers began returning to work, but Villa Constitución remained as a warning. The old labor structures were losing their grip on the proletariat, and there were indeed subversive organizations looking to capitalize on the workers' growing discontent. This was not lost upon the military, for whom a guerrilla–working class alliance was the worst of nightmares.

THE MILITARY SHIFTS

Isabel dismissed General Leandro Anaya, the army's commander in chief, after the Villa Constitución strike because he had refused to send army troops. Backed by the chief of the General Staff, General Jorge Rafael Videla, and by his own private secretary, General Roberto Viola, he had been resisting pressure from the government and from a growing number of military interventionists to use the army in the war against the guerrillas. He had temporary success because the army's interventionists were divided into those who wanted to prop up the floundering Peronist government and those who wanted to push it aside. The pro-Peronists were led by General Alberto Numa Laplane, the man who eventually would replace Anaya, and included Colonel Vicente Damasco, Isabel's secretary for military affairs and a friend of Raúl Lastiri. The anti-Peronist interventionists included men who would become prominent after the military returned to power in 1976: General Luciano Benjamín Menéndez, commander of the Fifth Infantry Brigade; General Ramón Genaro Díaz Bessone, chief of operations at General Staff Headquarters; and General Carlos Suárez Masón, head of army intelligence. This group had a special dislike for López Rega and his corrupt cronies, like defense minister Adolfo Savino (who also belonged to P-2), and Federal Police Chief Alberto Villar, whose ties to AAA were notorious. They condemned AAA as an illegal organization undertaking counterguerrilla tasks properly belonging to the army.[8]

The professionalists' nonintervention policy was eroded by the sharp rise in violence in the latter half of 1974, much of it directed at the military, or at civilians with good military connections such as Mor Roig or the Born brothers, whose sensational kidnapping on 19 September made it plain that even the wealthiest and most powerful were not safe. The attacks of 11 August on the 17th Airborne Infantry in Catamarca and on the Villa María explosives factory in Córdoba were a shock. In the latter case, there were parallels with the attack on Azul in January. In both instances, conscripts had collaborated with the guerrillas, and officers were seized as hostages: Colonel Ibarzábal at Azul, Lieutenant Colonel Larrabure at Villa María. Meanwhile, ERP took revenge for the Catamarcan fiasco by murdering four army officers in various parts of the country in September and October. Each funeral became an occasion to vent anger against the "do-nothing" army leadership.

An especially macabre note was struck on 16 October when visitors to the Recoleta Cemetery discovered that General Aramburu's tomb had been violated and his body was missing. The Montoneros soon claimed "credit" for the deed, announcing that they would keep the corpse until Evita's body was brought back from Spain. (Isabel complied. On November 17 Evita's corpse was brought back and, after a quiet ceremony from which the CGT and Justicialist Party leaders were excluded and which the military boycotted, it was stored in the Presidential Residence in Olivos.) The month ended with ERP assassinating Professor Jordán Bruno Genta, the Catholic nationalist intellectual who had long taught for the air force.

Impatience was growing throughout the military, undermining the "professionalist" position. Joint exercises in counterguerrilla warfare were held between army units in the Andean provinces. The Joint Chiefs of Staff were discussing the possibility of military intervention in the war against internal subversion. Up in Corrientes, General Leopoldo Galtieri, commander of the Seventh Infantry

Brigade, criticized the government for its flabby response to the guerrilla threat and likened subversion to a cancer in the human body, which sometimes required the removal of neighboring cells to prevent its spreading. The speech caused so much concern in government circles that Anaya sent his secretary, General Viola, to warn Galtieri to moderate his language. Anaya had already compromised his position by allowing the army to supply logistical support to the Federal Police in Tucumán, but the war there was still going badly. Then Police Chief Villar himself was assassinated. He and his wife were blown to smithereens in the river resort of Tigre, by a remote-controlled bomb set off by the Montoneros as the couple left the dock in their motor launch.

In mid-November the life of ERP's hostage, Lieutenant Colonel Jorge Ibarzábal, came to a deplorable end. As he was being transported across the city of Buenos Aires, drugged and guarded in the back of a canvas-covered military-looking truck, to a different "people's prison," the vehicle was halted by a police patrol. Rather than surrender his prisoner, the guerrilla guarding Ibarzábal "executed" him with a bullet to the head. What shocked the military even more than his death, however, was Ibarzábal's physical condition. During his 10 months in captivity he had lost about 60 pounds and was extremely emaciated.[9]

The act that finally broke the professionalists' resistance, however, was the murder of Captain Humberto Viola and his three-year-old daughter, María Cristina, on 1 December. Captain Viola, his wife, and two daughters (ages five and three) were leaving their house, about five blocks from the center of San Miguel de Tucumán, the province's capital. They were to have Sunday dinner at his parent's home, after which they would watch a soccer game on television. This time two carloads of ERP guerrillas were waiting for Captain Viola to get out of the car and shut the gate to the street. Instead, his wife got out, so one of the ERP cars drove up and a guerrilla fired a shotgun blast through the left windshield of the car. Another guerrilla fired a .45 caliber pistol. Viola had just time to duck, but the .45 bullet struck María Cristina in the back seat, immediately killing her. In the meantime, another guerrilla approached the car as Captain Viola was trying to get out, holding María Fernanda, his five-year-old daughter, who had been hurt. He pumped four shots into Viola's back before his machine gun jammed. Crouching, Viola managed to get free and escape a second shotgun blast fired from hood level. He headed for San Lorenzo Street, holding his little girl. The guerrilla with the jammed machine gun pulled out a pistol, fired once and missed, then ran forward and fired a second shot that stopped him. As Viola staggered, the car carrying the shotgun-wielding guerrilla pulled up beside him, and a blast fired point-blank blew apart his head. The man with the pistol fired one last shot. María Fernanda lay beside her father in a coma, permanently crippled.[10]

General Luciano Benjamín Menéndez, whose troops had been providing logistical support for the Federal Police, gave an impassioned speech at Viola's funeral. Senior officers listened, weeping, while their juniors cursed and insulted them for not taking action. After that there was no holding back the military interventionists, who now closed ranks against the professionalists. On 5 February 1975, Isabel bowed to the pressure and signed an enabling decree allowing the army to conduct any operations it considered necessary to "neutralize or annihilate" subversive elements in Tucumán. The National Gendarmerie, the Federal Police, and the provincial police were all placed at the army's disposal.[11] Four days later, General Acdel Edgardo Vilas, an officer with many friends in the CGT, arrived in Tucumán to take over "Operación Independencia," the code name for the army's first big organized antiguerrilla campaign.

THE JUNGLES OF TUCUMÁN

The western border of Tucumán Province is formed by the Andes Mountains, whose jagged peaks rise there to about 15,000 feet. Rivers rush down through densely forested valleys to the tropical plains, where sugarcane is grown in hundreds of small farms and sent to mills to be ground by thousands of workers. Santucho believed that the combination of rugged mountain terrain and thick jungle would cancel out the regular army's superiority in men and firepower. With popular support from the impoverished mill workers and small sugar growers, the guerrillas would be able to recruit more fighters, supply themselves, and have eyes and ears everywhere to alert them to the army's intended moves. The Compañía del Monte would draw the soldiers into the jungle, where they would flounder in vain attempts to encircle the more mobile guerrillas and gradually lose their morale as they were picked off. "Following the glorious example of the Vietnamese people and their Army of Liberation," *El Combatiente* explained, ERP would create "liberated zones" spreading north and south along the mountains from Tucumán, then gradually spread eastward. As in Vietnam, the insurrection would gain peasant support and systematically undermine local authorities. The army and police might patrol the area by day, but at nightfall the guerrillas would take over. As peasant support grew, the authorities would be confined to the towns, where terrorism would be on the rise. The government would become demoralized, army officers would quarrel, and the economy would be paralyzed as capital fled the country. The last scene of the drama would be a mad scramble of the army, oligarchy, and imperialists to abandon Buenos Aires, as the advancing People's Revolutionary Army drew near.[12]

Santucho prepared for the army's intervention by dividing the Compañía del Monte into four platoons. There were about one hundred guerrillas as of the end of December, 90 men and 10 women. In an emergency, their number could be raised to perhaps two hundred or slightly more. They were supported by a network of around four hundred people, some local and some brought in from outside, whose job was to recruit more combatants, supply the guerrillas, gather intelligence, and spread propaganda. They busied themselves in the factories, sugar mills, and schools, gradually extending ERP's mass support network to perhaps around 2,500 sympathizers and occasional collaborators. ERP also was working more closely with the Montoneros. The police received reports that representatives of the two groups had met on 30 December in Metán, a town just across the border in Salta. Remnants of the Uruguayan Tupamaros, the Bolivian ELN, and the Chilean MIR also joined up for the campaign. Meanwhile, ERP took advantage of human rights lawyers like Mario Abel Amaya, who demanded an investigation into the deaths of the 16 guerrillas killed in Catamarca; or Raúl Alfonsín, leader of the Radicals' left wing, who protested the legality of Isabel's enabling decree; or Oscar Alende, who offered his small Partido Intransigente for mobilizing antigovernment demonstrations.[13]

The Compañía del Monte's tactical instructions for the opening phase of the coming campaign were to evade direct combat, harry the enemy, draw him into the jungle, and avoid encirclement. When the enemy became tired and stopped to rest, the guerrillas were to hit him and run. There was excitement in the guerrilla camps in anticipation of real action. The police received reports of increased activity all throughout December and January. Armed guerrillas were sighted in the Tucumán towns of Santa Lucía, Los Sosa, and Las Mesadas at the end of December; and in the first week of January they were seen several times in the Río Seco area and around the "La Angostura" sugar mill. Police undercover agents saw them near Río Vacas, and on 7 January a small plane was sighted landing near Famaillá. Subsequent reports said that it was carrying radio equipment. Another secret meeting between ERP and Montonero leaders was reported, this time in Tucumán's capital, on 14 January. Simultaneously, there were sightings of guerrillas in many different towns, buying provisions and distributing propaganda. On 17 January guerrillas took over a ranch in Potreros Las Tablas and executed its owner, who had been acting as an army scout. On 19 January another peasant scout reported seeing "approximately 200 guerrillas" camped on the west bank of the La Sosa River, near Highway 307, which joins San Miguel de Tucumán to Tafi. Eight women were with them, washing clothes in the river. The next day a band of between 20 and 30 guerrillas took over the railway station at San Rafael, cut the telephone lines, and destroyed everything inside the office. On 24 January there were reports of ERP reinforcements heading toward Tucumán from Córdoba.[14]

By the time the army moved into Tucumán, the Compañía del Monte controlled about a third of the province, collecting "taxes" from local merchants in the form of supplies, and "tolls" from motorists using Routes 38 and 307, running north and south. With their network of informers and collaborators, ERP guerrillas moved easily from their many bases along jungle paths, appearing in small towns and villages practically at will to collect provisions, exhort the inhabitants, put up signs and flags, and mete out "revolutionary justice" to those suspected of helping the police. An army captain who arrived in late December described the situation as "grave." The southern part of the province was completely under ERP control—a no-man's land. A police officer and some anticommunist labor leaders had been shot only a few days before, and in the town of Santa Lucía a band of guerrillas had recently forced the inhabitants to witness the execution of a policeman and two suspected informers. Even in his own regiment, one of the soldiers was discovered passing out ERP pamphlets. In Santa Lucía the intendant, the councilmen, and the managers and foremen of two local factories had fled. There were no services, not even garbage collection. This was only 20 miles from San Miguel de Tucumán, the capital.[15]

General Vilas's forces numbered from 3,000 to 3,500, of which General Menéndez's Fifth Infantry Brigade constituted the core. It included about one hundred commandos, divided equally into two companies. They had been trained by U.S. Green Berets at the School of the Americas in the Panama Canal Zone, but had never actually fought a jungle war. The Fifth Brigade also contained engineers and communications specialists. It was supported by a helicopter company, a naval air force Beechcraft B-80 equipped with infrared sensors, and units of the National Gendarmerie, Federal Police, and provincial police. Qualitatively, the Fifth Brigade was no better equipped than the guerrillas. For both sides, the principal weapons used would be 762 mm FAL rifles and 726 mm MAG light machine guns. Both had a few heavy machine guns, which were of limited use in this kind of warfare. The guerrillas also had Itaka and Batan shotguns, and their ammunition was newer. Most of it dated from 1974, whereas the army's had been manufactured in 1969. The guerrillas also wore camouflage uniforms, whereas on Vilas's side only the commandos had them. The guerrillas' communications equipment was superior, too, consisting of U.S.-made walkie-talkies with a 3 km range, compared to the Korean War–vintage backpack radios used by the Argentine army. On the other hand, the army's big advantage was its helicopters, for which ERP had no countersolution.[16]

General Vilas immediately established his headquarters in Famaillá, a medium-size town in southern Tucumán, and designated the nearby towns of Santa Lucía, Los Sosa, Monteros, and Las Fronteritas—all places where guerrillas had recently been sighted—as army operations centers. The National Gendarmerie and Federal Police were sent to secondary locations and to the provincial capital. Vilas was a rough sort, but he was well read in guerrilla strategy. Like his enemy, he could quote from Mao, Ché, and General Giap, as well as from French counterguerrilla theorists like Colonel Roger Trinquier and General André Beaufre, both veterans of the Algerian War. He was well aware that ERP expected to lure him into the mountains and jungle, there to wear him down. He already had planned a different strategy: instead of pursuing the enemy into unknown and difficult territory where the guerrillas would have the advantage, he would uproot their support system in the towns and villages. That would involve both civic action programs to win the allegiance of the local population and counterterrorism to eliminate ERP collaborators and frighten any waverers. The army began by calling on local residents to inform it as to whether "in your neighborhood, town, or settlement there are young couples without children or with very young children" who have "no relationships with their neighbors," "no known families in the province," and "no known occupation or place of work."[17]

Meanwhile, based on police reports he already had received, Vilas ordered hundreds of arrests of labor and student activists, left-wing political figures, journalists, teachers, and anyone else identified as having suspicious connections. The arrested were carried off in army trucks to one of the 14 interrogation centers hastily set up in abandoned schoolhouses, churches, or sugar mills around the province. The great majority of these arrested were tortured, questioned, and then they "disappeared" (i.e., were shot). There were some angry disagreements about these methods among Vilas's staff officers, but the hardliners were the majority. General Luciano Benjamín Menéndez summed up their position: "We have to act drastically. Operación Independencia can't just consist of a roundup of political prisoners, because the army can't risk the lives of its men and lay its prestige on the line simply to act as a kind of police force that ends up by turning over X-number of political prisoners to some timorous judge . . . who will apply lenient punishment which in turn will be cancelled out by amnesties granted by ambitious politicians courting popularity. We're at war, and war obeys another law: he who wipes out the other side wins."[18]

Repression was as systematic as intelligence could make it. The army conducted a careful census of the inhabitants of each village, town, and *barrio*, noting where each individual lived and what his occupation was. In the larger towns the army and police made careful maps of all the streets, identifying places that might be used as hideouts, arms depots, or mail drops. The provincial police concentrated on San Miguel de Tucumán, establishing automobile checkpoints, going over identification papers, noting the description of people and vehicles. Anyone coming from outside the province was questioned. In the smaller towns the police knew the young people and could tell if someone was acting suspiciously. They also knew which merchants had been supplying the guerrillas. All of this information was gathered and collated. When a likely ERP hideout or radio transmitter was pinpointed, specially trained soldiers and the Federal Police were sent to raid the building. There were many shootouts during this uprooting process. Attempts by ERP mass front organizations to disrupt the crackdown by holding violent street demonstrations, as they had done successfully in the past, were met by overwhelming, pitiless force. Luis Mattini, ERP's chronicler, called it "the most bloody repression in Argentina's recorded history." General Vilas's tactics were "hair-raising," he said, but he also had to admit that they worked:

If the golden rule of guerrilla war is that one should "move among the people like a fish in water," then Gen. Vilas responded by removing the water from around the fish. The indiscriminate kidnapping and "disappearing" of innocent people, as well as activists, went beyond any known repressive methods, and to a certain extent surprised the PRT-ERP, which began to feel, behind its seemingly inexhaustible self-confidence, impotent to stop the repression.[19]

Vilas did not depend on repression alone, however. From the very first day the army moved in, San Miguel de Tucumán became a beehive of uniformed men carrying rifles, buckets, and tools. Long-neglected schools, streets, public buildings, parks, and playgrounds were repaired, restored, cleaned and painted. Out in the villages and small towns, roads were resurfaced, bridges repaired, school buildings refurbished, army medical dispensaries and clinics set up. However, this effort to win support would not have worked unless the people were convinced that the army was there to stay. Police contingents had been sent in before, but they never stayed for long. Eventually the guerrillas came back and executed those who had welcomed the police. Thus, fear made the locals hold back now. The soldiers were dismayed to find out, when they first entered the region, that the food and clothing they distributed so freely quickly found its way into the guerrillas' hands. At night, when the army returned to its barracks, ERP sent its men into the villages. Through their information network they knew who had received gifts. Indeed, they themselves often dressed as peasants and mingled in the villages to personally observe the troops.[20]

The army concentrated on the villages lying west of Route 38, where sugar-cane fields ran close to forested mountain spurs. At first the soldiers found the villagers to be "skeptical, indifferent, and timorous," especially the merchants. Some of them may have been sympathetic to the guerrillas, but most were simply afraid. Yet the army needed their cooperation in order to cut off the guerrillas' supplies, so they reached a compromise with the merchants: they could still sell their goods to the Compañía del Monte, but they had to inform the police afterwards. As the army dug in and eventually took the offensive, the local people became increasingly helpful, even the merchants. This made an enormous difference in prosecuting the campaign. A veteran lieutenant colonel observed, "In the anti-guerrilla war there were hardly any spectacular battles. Anyone who thinks it was like the wars you see in the movies is completely wrong. It was nothing like that. Usually, an important, fundamental success— capable of deciding the course of future developments—might consist of inter-cepting a message, or disrupting the sending of provisions like a few kilos of bread or pasta."[21]

Thus, instead of the army thrashing through the jungle to look for guerrillas, the increasingly needy guerrillas were forced to come out of the jungle and scour for provisions in the plain. ERP faced an uncomfortable dilemma: either increase terrorism against the local population in order to keep supplies flowing, or seek alternative sources outside the province. Terrorism would drive the people to the army's side and increase the risk of being ambushed, but supplies shipped in from outside would have to come in such large quantities that it would be a simple matter for the army and police to detect them. Santucho and his lieutenants, who viewed General Vilas as no more than a ruffian, failed to appreciate the dangers in their situation until it was too late, mainly because the army did very little actual jungle fighting, beyond a few daytime patrols, in the first weeks. Vilas was unsure of the quality of his troops. None of them had ever been in combat, and few of them were familiar with the local terrain. Moreover, until the villagers could be made confident of the army's commitment to stay, it was hard to find scouts. So the initial stage of the campaign was limited to learning the jungle paths, making careful maps, and consolidating the army's hold on the population. The navy's spotter airplane, with its infrared sensors, was a great help in gaining information about guerrilla camps and movements. The sensors were able to measure subtle changes in ground temperatures at an altitude of 1,500 feet and record them on heliographic paper. That allowed the commandos to plot where the main trails were and where the guerrillas were heading. Without that, the guerrillas could move through the jungle undetected by helicopters because they would be hidden by the thick canopy of trees.[22]

During March and April the army and police made sweeps through the capital and smaller towns, unearthing arms, propaganda, an underground printing press, and a number of ERP collaborators. ERP fought back with sabotage, booby traps, and executions of army collaborators. Commando patrols still kept close to the villages but were learning the terrain. Various ambushes netted them seven guerrillas, killed either while foraging or acting as couriers. Vilas's strategy of concentrating on the support network was beginning to have its effect on the Compañía del Monte. Mauro Gómez, who was in charge of keeping ERP's urban network intact, told Santucho in May that it was suicidal to keep bringing in activists from outside to replace those captured by army dragnets. Santucho's response was to plan an attack on General Vilas's headquarters, capture Vilas, and deal the army's morale a fatal blow.[23]

On 28 May about 70 guerrillas, led by Hugo ("Captain Santiago") Iruzún, set out for Famaillá in two trucks, intending to camp near the town that evening and launch their attack in the early morning. Late in the afternoon, however, they unexpectedly encountered an army truck, with a lone soldier, coming up the dirt road. Instead of taking the soldier prisoner, the nervous guerrillas opened fire, which alerted a small party of 11 soldiers who were rebuilding a school-house in the nearby hamlet of Manchalá. They grabbed their rifles and hurried to the scene, where they discovered the guerrillas trying to dig one of their trucks out of a rut. There was an exchange of fire that forced the soldiers back into the schoolhouse, with the guerrillas in pursuit. By then, seven other soldiers working in the area were alerted and hurried to their comrades' relief. Heavy fire forced them to take cover in a ditch. Then another army truck came up the road, and its five occupants had to dive for cover. As the battle raged on all sides, Iruzún began to fear that the soldiers may have radioed Famaillá for reinforcements. Suddenly he ordered a retreat, leaving behind four dead, two wounded, two heavy trucks, three pickup trucks, a large quantity of arms and munitions, and an ERP flag. *El Combatiente* called Manchalá a victory because more soldiers than guerrillas died, but Santucho demoted Iruzún because he had to abandon his plan.[24]

Following Manchalá, Santucho ordered reinforcements from Buenos Aires and Córdoba because local recruitment had dried up. Ever confident, Santucho assured his men that the *tucumaños* would come flocking back in once ERP had demonstrated its fighting power with a few victories. His new replacements were city-bred men and women, however, who were not used to the rigors of jungle camp life. Also, the mixing of the sexes led to sexual jealousies and quarrels. The women were often couriers between the Companía del Monte, the underground network in San Miguel de Tucumán, and activists in the neighboring provinces, where ERP had made considerable headway among students and sugar workers. Many of them fell prisoner as the army tightened its grip on Tucumán. Although they were trained to give false information and stall their interrogators, they quickly broke down under torture. Most of them "disappeared," after being raped by the soldiers. Information gained from them led to some important raids by army and police units in those neighboring provinces, despite the fact that Isabel's enabling decree expressly limited army operations to Tucumán. Much of ERP's mass front in the northwest region was smashed in a few weeks, with those lucky enough to escape fleeing for safety to Córdoba or Buenos Aires.[25]

Throughout July Vilas tightened the pressure on the Companía del Monte, stationing more soldiers in the villages at the jungle's edge and sending in commando patrols more frequently on search-and-destroy missions. By this time they were better acquainted with the *monte* than were most of the guerrillas, who had been brought in from the cities. Jungle war, fought in thick vegetation and semidarkness, was typified by sudden skirmishes and surprise ambushes. "The normal distance between combatants was very short, no more than two or three meters—ten at the most," one army officer recalled. "That's why there were so few prisoners. You beat the enemy by knowing the terrain better and taking advantage of the darkness." "Little by little," Mattini recalled, "various parts of the guerrilla organization fell victim to army ambushes. . . . The losses were neither serious nor heavy in immediate terms, but over time they effectively bled the guerrillas." Occasionally ERP counterattacked, as when it sent 40 guerrillas to take an army outpost at Río Seco, which had 1 officer, 3 sergeants, and 25 conscripts. The attempt failed, and two guerrillas were killed because the attackers were poorly trained, according to the army's report. By the end of July, additional important changes had taken place on both sides. A crisis in the government led to the fall of López Rega from power. General Jorge Rafael Videla would replace General Numa Laplane and prosecute "Operación Independencia" even more vigorously. Meanwhile, the weakening of ERP's urban network had forced it to ask for help from the previously despised Montoneros, whose Tucumán organization numbered around 30 combatants, 200 mass front activists, and a sizable network of sympathizers, many of whom worked for the provincial government.[26]

Near the end of August the Montoneros carried out two impressive acts of sabotage that were intended to distract the military. On 24 August their frogmen mined the navy's 3,500-ton frigate, *Santissima Trinidad*, as it lay in dry dock at Río Santiago. The explosion caused considerable damage. Closer to home, the Montoneros blew up a transport plane at the Tucumán airport as it was taking off. A squadron of gendarms was aboard, of whom 34 were killed. The explosives had been placed in a drainage canal that ran underneath the airfield and were set off by remote control. Nevertheless, the army continued to pressure the guerrillas with ever widening commando patrols in the jungle and intense block-by-block, house-by-house searches in the towns. About the same time that the Montoneros were blowing up ships and planes, an army commando patrol discovered Santucho's mountain headquarters. It was late in the afternoon and Santucho, his general staff, and some of the PRT politiburu were holding a meeting when the soldiers stumbled on the camp. They had been helicoptered in and worked their way down from the top, instead of coming up from the jungle floor as the ERP sentinels expected. The guerrilla leaders quickly scrambled out of the area without losing any of their men, but they left behind all their papers. On 19 September the police finally located ERP's urban headquarters, and a tremendous shootout followed. Soldiers surrounded the entire block and closed in as the guerrillas, using the residents as shields, retreated from one house to the next until they finally were cornered. Five of them were killed, and many important documents were seized.

On 5 October the Montoneros again tried to relieve the pressure on the embattled Companía del Monte by a spectacular operation against the 29th Infantry Regiment in Formosa Province. It was an intricate plan that involved the hijacking of a Boeing jet and the takeover of the airport at Resistencia, the provincial capital. The Montoneros also had the help of a conscript, Roberto Mayol, who let them onto the base. The entry did not go smoothly, however. There was a scuffle at the guard box, Mayol was shot, and the alarm was given. The soldiers, who had been napping or listening to a soccer game on the radio, rallied just in time to avoid being overrun. Still, the guerrillas, having been given a map of the base by Mayol, moved quickly according to a prearranged plan, attacking the barracks, noncommissioned officers quarters, and the recreation room. Their main target was the arsenal, but to reach it they had to cross a courtyard that was guarded at one end by a MAG heavy machine gun. The Montoneros made a charge for this, but the soldiers got there first. "From that point on the exchange of fire was impressive," according to the version published in *Evita Montonera*. "To get some idea of its intensity you have to figure that something like sixty people, on both sides, were firing simultaneously with FAL rifles, machine gun pistols, a MAG heavy machine gun, grenades, and small arms. . . . One had no exact notion of where it was coming from, how many [were firing,] or what type of arms were being used." This counterattack cut short the operation. Still, the Montoneros claimed success in opening the arsenal and hauling away more than 50 automatic rifles, and indeed eyewitnesses at the airport claimed to have seen weapons being loaded on the waiting airplane. The guerrillas admitted to losing 11 men in the attack but claimed to have killed 40 soldiers. The army's figures put its own losses at 12 dead and 17 wounded, insisting that 16 Montoneros were killed. Arriving at the airport ahead of their pursuers, the Montoneros took off and landed safely about an hour later at a ranch in Santa Fe Province, where several vehicles were waiting to rush them to hideouts.[27]

Impressive as this intricate operation was, it did nothing to alleviate ERP's desperate situation in the Tucumán *monte*. On 10 October, just five days after the Formosa operation, Vilas's commandos caught a group of guerrillas trying to pass through a cane field near the village of Acheral. Supported by helicopters, they killed 12 of the band, including Santucho's brother, Asdrubal, and most of the Companía del Monte's general staff. Those who managed to escape were hotly pursued, and over the next two days five more were killed. This was a real turning point. Since "Operación Independencia" began in February, ERP had lost more than 160 people in Tucumán, compared to 53 for the army, police, and gendarmerie. This was a bloodletting that it could not sustain. It made one last serious attack, on 8 November, when it ambushed an army patrol, killing five. However, it lost six guerrillas in that clash, and unlike the army, the ERP had no easy way to replace them. Santucho already had left Tucumán to plan a major attack that would, possibly, draw the army away from the province. While he planned, the Companía del Monte broke up into little bands of two or three, the better to escape the relentless commando patrols. Too weak now to mount any more attacks, their only concern was to evade their hunters.

NOTES

1. Berger, *Historia* 59–65, 128–56; Bra, "La 'P-2,' " 10, 14, 16, 19; Pino Buongiorno, "La internacional del Venerable Licio," *Todo es Historia*, no. 214 (February 1985), 32–33, 35.

2. FAMUS, *Operación Independencia*, 58–61, 168; Héctor R. Simeoni, *¡Aniquelen al ERP! La "guerra sucia" en el monte tucumaño* (Buenos Aires: Ediciones Cosmos, 1985), 16–17.

3. FAMUS, *Operación Independencia*, 63–64; Pineiro, *Crónica*, 90–92; Seoane, *Todo o nada*, 243.

4. Seoane, *Todo o nada*, 240; Fraga, *Ejército*, 128, 133.

5. Landivar, *La universidad*, 151–67.

6. Guido Di Tella, *Argentina Under Perón, 1973–1976* (New York: St. Martin's Press, 1983), 125; Juan Carlos De Pablo, *Economía política del peronismo* (Buenos Aires: Editorial El Cid, 1980), 139–41, 146–47, 150, 152.

7. Elizabeth Jelin, *Conflictos laborales en la Argentina, 1973–1976* (Buenos Aires: Centro de Estudios de Estado y Sociedad, 1977), 16–17, 21–22, 29–30; Juan Carlos Torre, *Los sindicatos en el gobierno, 1973–1976* (Buenos Aires: Centro Editor de América Latina, 1983), 87–89, 92–94; García, *Patria sindical*, 49, 50, 52, 55–60; Calello and Parcero, *De Vandor*, vol. 2, 147–48; Paoletti, *Como los nazis*, 44–46.

8. Fraga, *Ejército*, 122, 129–31, 138–39, 141, 143–46, 159; Díaz Bessone, *Guerra revolucionaria*, 212, 238–39.

9. Fraga, *Ejército*, 127–28, 132; Díaz Bessone, *Guerra revolucionaria*, 240.

10. Argentine Republic, *Evolution of Terrorist Delinquency in Argentina* (Buenos Aires: Poder Ejecutivo Nacional, 1980), 199–205; Pineiro, *Crónica*, 36–38.

11. Simeoni, *¡Aniquilen al ERP!*, 19–20; Argentine Republic, *Evolution*, 163–66; Seoane, *Todo o nada*, 249.

12. FAMUS, *Operación Independencia*, 43–44, 52–56; Mattini, *Hombres y mujeres* 323, 419–420.

13. FAMUS, *Operación Independencia*, 67–68, 72–73; Fraga, *Ejército*, 152, 157, 164, 172, n. 40; Seoane, *Todo o nada*, 262; Hernán López Echagüe, *El enigma de General Bussi* (Buenos Aires: Editorial Sudamericana, 1991), 170.

14. FAMUS, *Operación Independencia*, 75–78.

15. Simeoni, *¡Aniquelen al ERP!*, 132–36.

16. Ricardo Burzaco, *Infierno*, 100–2, 110–13.

17. Burzaco, *Infierno*, 60–61; López Echagüe, *El enigma*, 164; FAMUS, *Operación Independencia*, 91.

18. Seoane, *Todo o nada*, 261; López Echagüe, *El enigma*, 172; Mattini, *Hombres y mujeres*, 420; *Nuevo Confirmado* (18 December 1975), 23.

19. Mattini, *Hombres y mujeres*, 421, 461. See also Burzaco, *Infierno*, 62–64, 103; FAMUS, *Operación Independencia*, 94; Simeoni, *¡Aniquelen al ERP!*, 37, 45–46, 121.

20. FAMUS, *Operación Independencia*, 95, 120, 190–91; Simeoni, *¡Aniquelen al ERP!*, 118–21.

21. Simeoni, *¡Aniquelen al ERP!*, 37, 45–46, 118.

22. Mattini, *Hombres y mujeres*, 421; Simeoni, *¡Aniquelen al ERP!*, 83; Burzaco, *Infierno*, 64–66.

23. Mattini, *Hombres y mujeres*, 423; FAMUS, *Operación Independencia*, 106, 109.

24. FAMUS, *Operación Independencia*, 107–15; Simeoni, *¡Aniquelen al ERP!*, 59–63; Mattini, *Hombres y mujeres*, 423–24; Seoane, *Todo o nada*, 264–65.

25. Mattini, *Hombres y mujeres*, 431, 433–34; FAMUS, *Operación Independencia*, 116–21.

26. Simeoni, *¡Aniquelen al ERP!*, 119; Mattini, *Hombres y mujeres*, 473; FAMUS, *Operación Independencia*, 120, 123.

27. Díaz Bessone, *Guerra revolucionaria*, 333–37; *Evita Montonera*, no. 8 (October 1975), 2–8; Gillespie, *Soldiers of Perón* 197–200, esp. n. 106. The army claimed that they failed to haul off any large store of weapons, but Gillespie sides with the guerrillas' version. Méndez, *Confesiones* 126–35, claims that the Formosa operation, while it shocked Argentine society, had mostly propaganda value. He puts the guerrillas' losses at 20 and says that only the four leaders of the operation escaped.

EIGHT

The Coup

By June 1975 José López Rega, éminence grise behind the presidential throne, minister of social welfare, master of the P-2 clone called "Logia Pro-Patria," chief spiritualist of the ANAEL Lodge, and boss of the feared AAA, had reached the zenith of his power. He had secured his position with the army by getting his friend, General Numa Laplane, named as commander. Now he aimed to control economic policy and the unruly labor movement by convincing Isabel to appoint his fellow spiritualist, Celestino Rodrigo, as economic minister. There were good reasons to want to control labor. Prices were rising at the rate of 20 percent a month and would reach 35 percent by July. The unions' irresponsible behavior, reflected in lower productivity, more absenteeism, and big wage increases, was a major factor. Their reiterated response to inflation was to demand price controls and just one more boost in wages to get them slightly ahead. They rejected the idea that prices were largely beyond the government's control and that big wage increases only fuelled inflation's fires. Labor leaders were also caught in a squeeze. Their control over the rank and file was rapidly eroding as runaway inflation wiped out the monthly paycheck. The CGT demanded "an active and genuine" role in formulating the government's economic policies. What it got from Rodrigo instead was an anti-inflation package, unveiled on 5 June, that limited wage increases and lifted price controls.[1]

For the first time in Peronism's history, its labor branch was openly defiant and threatening. Casildo Herreras, the CGT's general secretary, flatly announced that no union would sign a labor contract under the present terms. Spontaneous strikes and street demonstrations broke out in Buenos Aires and all other major industrial cities. A protest march by one group of workers was usually enough to empty the shops and factories of other workers. In Congress, Peronist deputies representing the labor wing demanded that Rodrigo appear before them to defend his program. By 12 June the government signaled a willingness to compromise on wage increases. Having won their point and demonstrated their power to the rank and file, Lorenzo Miguel and Casildo Herreras decided that it was time to mend fences with the government. So on 24 June, crowds of workers filled the Plaza de Mayo, holding up placards reading *"Gracias, Isabel."*

The president appeared on the balcony of the Casa Rosada to receive their applause, and later she graciously appeared at UOM headquarters, where a party was being held to celebrate the signing of the contracts. However, the contracts had not been formally ratified by the government, nor was ratification announced the following day or the day after that. Rumors circulated that Isabel was going to renege. Caught between their expectant workers and a slippery government no longer supportive of their authority, Miguel and Herreras called for another demonstration in the Plaza de Mayo for 27 June. This time the theme was to "demonstrate unconditional support" for Isabel for "having decided to ratify the labor agreements." On the day of the demonstration, strikes closed down government offices, private shops, radio and television stations, public transportation—practically all economic life in downtown Buenos Aires. Workers packed the Plaza de Mayo shouting insults about López Rega and Celestino Rodrigo.[2]

The next day Isabel went on television and told the nation that Argentina was facing an economic "zero hour." Unless drastic measures were taken, the country would be swept up in a cyclone of hyperinflation, and therefore she would not ratify the recent labor contracts. It was not she who had broken her promise, she insisted. The labor leaders had broken their promise to General Perón that they would act responsibly. Having stated her case, she, López Rega, and Rodrigo dug in. CGT negotiators who contacted the three could only report that the government was inflexible. Ricardo Otero, the labor minister, resigned after nearly coming to blows with López Rega. Finally, Miguel and Herreras called another mass demonstration, for 7 July.

This time CGT gunmen, armed and bearing walkie-talkies, led the mob in attacking the Economics Ministry, overpowering the AAA gunmen sent by López Rega to guard the building. Rodrigo made his escape through a secret underground passage that led to the Casa Rosada while the invaders sacked the ministry's offices.[3] The shock of an angry proletarian mob storming a Peronist government broke the Sorcerer's spell. On 11 July there was a complete cabinet shake-up in which López Rega resigned all of his official posts. He continued to live at the Presidential Residence in Olivos, however, where Isabel remained incommunicado. When her new ministers of interior, defense, justice, and education went to see her, they were stopped at the door by López Rega himself. Isabel would see no one. Jorge Garrido, the new defense minister, then called a meeting of the three armed forces commanders. On Friday afternoon, 18 July, when the four ministers were again refused admittance to the Presidential Residence, units of the Mounted Grenadiers Regiment arrived and began clearing the grounds of the AAA bodyguards. This news was relayed upstairs, and Isabel soon appeared, distraught and hysterical. Eventually she got control of herself and asked for a day's respite: she would meet tomorrow with her cabinet.

Lights were on in the Presidential Residence all through the night. In the morning Isabel called her ministers and demanded two concessions: López Rega would go abroad on an "official mission," and he would leave in the presidential airplane. The ministers and the armed forces chiefs all agreed. That evening López Rega drove to the downtown airport with his daughter, Norma, and Raúl Lastiri, while Isabel stayed behind in Olivos. Accompanied by half a dozen bodyguards, he boarded the presidential plane and took off.[4] Lorenzo Miguel congratulated the president for having shown "great sensibility," but rebellious elements in the Peronist movement, now calling themselves "antiverticalists," demanded a complete housecleaning of *lopezreguistas* from the cabinet. One by one they fell, including Rodrigo, over the next two weeks. Meanwhile, the antiverticalists in the Chamber of Deputies forced Lastiri's resignation as president of that body on 25 July, despite strenuous lobbying by Lorenzo Miguel to save him.[5] Isabel's health collapsed. She was in a state of extreme fatigue and remained secluded at the Presidential Residence, seeing no one except for matters of special urgency. Even the normally robust Lorenzo Miguel was so worn out and depressed that he took a leave of absence in early September.

UPHEAVAL IN THE ARMY

The *rodrigazo*'s shock waves affected the army as well as the government. General Numa Laplane's Peronism was a minority position among his military colleagues. He had first sought allies against the anti-Peronists by recommending General Jorge Videla, a leading professionalist, to head the First Army Corps and General Roberto Viola to head the Second Army Corps. The *lopezreguista* defense minister, Adolfo Savino, refused to ratify Videla's appointment, however, because the letter had carried out an investigation of the AAA's activities that linked the death squads to the Casa Rosada. Videla was to get no assignment at all but was to be eased into retirement.[6] That sort of political interference with the army's professional recommendations was widely resented by the officers, and Laplane's acceptance of it hurt him. It also resulted in a new alliance of army factions between the "professionalist" and the "anti-Peronist interventionist" officers. Meanwhile, as the government's battle with the CGT approached its climax, Defense Minister Savino, thinking it would be well to ensure the army's full support, reversed himself and appointed Videla as chairman of the Joint Chiefs of Staff, a largely honorific post.

As Isabel tried to surround herself with trusted men in the confusion that followed López Rega's departure, she and General Laplane made a fatal mistake by choosing Colonel Vicente Damasco, an active duty officer and a friend of Raúl Lastiri's, for the post of minister of interior. The appointment broke an old rule of the armed services that an active-duty officer could not hold a political office. There was an immediate outcry from many senior officers, who demanded that Colonel Damasco either retire from the army or resign as minister. Isabel was opposed to his doing either because she wanted Damasco to connect her government with officers in command of troops. Lorenzo Miguel and Casildo Herreras backed her, assuming that Colonel Damasco would use troops to protect labor's traditional leadership from rebellion from below.[7]

On 14 August, General Laplane met with the senior generals in his office, having first warned his adjutants to arm themselves with pistols and wait just outside, in the event that any of the officers got too belligerent. The meeting was bitter and indecisive. Five of the generals voted to demand Damasco's resignation from the cabinet, and five voted to keep him there. However, the anti-Damasco faction included three of the four corps commanders, so a coup was likely. During the next week, commanders negotiated with one another and lined up their subordinates. The only loyal corps commander, General Alberto Cáceres, of the First Army, found that his subordinates would not obey him, which made it impossible for Laplane to hold out. He had the support of Lorenzo Miguel, who expended more of his shrinking political capital in another losing cause, but the antiverticalists demanded Damasco's ouster. Cross-pressured, the CGT stayed on the sidelines. Perceiving his position to be untenable, Colonel Damasco resigned on 21 August, but now that was not enough to satisfy the army opposition, which demanded General Laplane's resignation as well.

This time the CGT, perceiving the danger of an anti-Peronist takeover of the army, declared a "state of alert in defense of the institutional order" while Laplane made a last effort to salvage his authority. In the meantime, the body of Major Julio Argentino Larrabure, the engineer who had been kidnapped by ERP during the raid on the Villa María munitions factory, was discovered, emaciated and bearing marks of torture and strangulation. The funeral was another of those emotional events in which soldiers identified with their dead comrade and swore to avenge him; but in this case Laplane used the occasion to make a partisan defense of the government. That was his last mistake. On the following day, 27 August, General Videla was commissioned by his fellow generals to issue an ultimatum to Isabel, while General Viola met with Laplane to convince him to avert a coup by resigning. Late that evening Laplane told Isabel that he could not continue. On his advice, and with Lorenzo Miguel's blessing, the top army post was then offered to General Alberto Cáceres. Cáceres refused it, however, on the grounds that it was Videla, not he, who was the popular choice and natural leader of the army chiefs. Blocked at every turn, Isabel gave in and appointed Videla to be the new army commander in chief.[8]

Videla's career had been remarkably uneventful, considering the upheavals that marked his era. After graduating near the top of his class from the Military Academy in 1945 and spending a couple of years in the field, he had devoted much of his time to teaching at the Military Academy and the Superior War School. He came out unscathed from the factional battles that divided the army after overthrowing Perón because he was a junior staff officer, not a line officer, and he kept his opinions to himself. Videla moved quietly up the career ladder, interspersing stints as a representative to the Inter-American Defense Board, military attaché in Washington, liaison between the War Ministry and the General Staff, and head of the Cadet Corps, with his teaching duties. After a year of training in antiguerrilla warfare at the School of the Americas, he became a full colonel at the end of 1965. Late in 1968 he was posted to Tucumán as second in command and chief of staff of the Fifth Infantry Brigade, and he would return to Tucumán in 1970 as interim governor of the province. When popular riots led to the burning of much of downtown San Miguel de Tucumán, he put them down with exemplary severity. Lanusse promoted Videla to brigadier general in December 1971 and made him commandant of the Military Academy, where he would remain until General Carcagno appointed him Anaya's second in command of the Second Army Corps. When Anaya succeeded Carcagno, he selected Videla to be the chief of the Army General Staff.[9]

Until then Videla had been considered "inoffensive" by the Peronists. He had no public record of anti-Peronist activity and had not been particularly close to Lanusse. Indeed, Videla was originally offered the opportunity to accompany Perón on his return to Argentina but turned it down, after which it was offered to Laplane. That refusal, and his subsequent coolness toward the Montoneros during Operation Dorrego, would be noted; but his known opposition to the national security doctrine and his professionalist stance against army intervention still made him appear innocuous. Only after his investigation of the AAA did his professionalism suddenly appear dangerous to the government. Now, as commander in chief of the army, Videla began a systematic purge of his own against all pro-Peronist officers. Furthermore, he had no hesitation at intervening in political matters. When Lorenzo Miguel mounted a campaign to oust the antiverticalist Victorio Calabró as governor of Buenos Aires Province, Videla made it clear that the army would not tolerate it. And at the 11th Conference of American Armies, held in Montevideo, he announced that the Argentine army had accepted the doctrine that Marxism-Leninism was involved in the equivalent of "internal war" against the Latin American republics. While Isabel was resting after another nervous collapse, Senator Italo Luder, the provisional president, signed three more fateful decrees that expanded the army's antiguerrilla role. Essentially, they extended the military's authority to "annihilate the activities of subversive elements" to include the entire national territory, not just Tucumán Province, and placed at their disposal all police and penal institutions to carry out this task. Thus, Videla could assure his counterparts at the Montevideo conference, "The present effort of the armed forces is being conducted, at great sacrifice, in accordance with the constitutional government of my country."

What Videla did not tell the other delegates at Montevideo was that, in the meeting with Luder that led to the army's expanded powers, he had offered the provisional president four strategic options, which ranged from a restrained response to terrorism that would be hedged in with legal restrictions to a radical response of the sort that General Vilas had applied in Tucumán. Videla argued for the radical option, on the grounds that anything less would drag out the war against subversion with no certainty of victory, whereas radical measures would bring it to a quick, decisive end. Luder bought the argument and signed the decrees, giving the armed forces essentially a blank check. At Montevideo, Videla hinted at what that would mean in practice when he argued, in a strong speech, that each country should decide for itself what methods to use in fighting subversion. He also drew a more explicit picture when he told the delegates, "As many people will die in Argentina as are necessary to achieve peace in our country."[10] This was an astonishing turnaround for a man who had been a legalist, a noninterventionist, and an opponent of "Dirty War" tactics; but for many Argentine officers, including Videla, the promise of a quick end to the war by the use of overwhelming force seemed to seduce them. Nor did they, at first, equate the rapid prosecution of the war with the overthrow of civilian rule. That would come later.

MONTE CHINGOLO

The guerrillas' power to inflict damage reached its apogee in December 1975. The month began with another assassination of a high-ranking army officer. Brigadier General Jorge Cáceres Monie, former Federal Police chief, was traveling with his wife, Beatriz, in a pickup truck along the back roads of Santa Fe Province. It was 7:00 P.M. and they were heading back to Second Corps headquarters. They came to the banks of the Las Conchas River and had just driven onto a raft that would ferry them across the river. As the ferryman was about to cast off, four Montoneros in a Ford Falcon rushed aboard and slammed into the back of the pickup. Then the guerrillas ran up to the truck and began firing through the windows at the dazed couple. One guerrilla named Julia opened the cab door and finished off the general with her revolver. As one of the guerrillas proceeded to guide the raft to the opposite shore, the others pushed the smashed Ford Falcon into the water. Once on the other side, the guerrillas proceeded in the pickup truck, carrying with them the general's badly wounded wife. A little farther down the road they threw her into a ditch, where she bled to death.[11]

On 23 December ERP guerrillas attacked the Domingo Viejobueno arsenal at Monte Chingolo, in the Buenos Aires industrial suburb of Lanús. This heavily guarded military base was the country's largest arsenal, and the guerrillas' operation employed the largest number of combatants and support troops ever assembled by them. Exact figures on the number that took part vary greatly, but an estimate of around 120 heavily armed combatants, supported by about 200 more lightly armed ERP and PRT mass front auxiliaries, would probably not be far off.[12] Juan Ledesma, who had planned the successful attack on the Villa María explosives factory, was put in charge of working out the operational plan. His general idea was to launch simultaneous attacks on the front and rear entrances, using as battering rams some heavy gasoline trucks whose empty containers could then be filled with captured weapons. They would also be helped by the fact that one of the conscripts at Monte Chingolo was an ERP sympathizer. Meanwhile, at the same time that the combatants were forcing their entry, the support troops would encircle the base and cut off all access to it so as to stall any reinforcements. Ledesma was captured by a military patrol on 7 December, however, and taken to Campo de Mayo to be interrogated, after which he "disappeared." That should have been a signal to abandon the whole plan, but instead Santucho insisted on going ahead and appointed Benito Urteaga to take Ledesma's place. Santucho was desperate for a triumph over the army after Tucumán, so he told the PRT politburo that he had made a careful investigation of Ledesma's capture and was convinced that the army was still ignorant of the Monte Chingolo operation.[13]

Had Santucho's investigation really been as careful as he pretended it was, he would have discovered that army intelligence had penetrated ERP in the person of Jesús Rames ("El Oso") Ranier, an unemployed worker who lived in a slum near Monte Chingolo. Because of him, the army was now aware that ERP was assembling people, weapons, trucks, and supplies for an attack on some military base in the Lanús area, which made Monte Chingolo a likely target. This was confirmed on 21 December, when Santucho called his lieutenants to a meeting and tried to fire their enthusiasm by telling them that this was to be the biggest guerrilla operation ever seen in Latin America. One of those present criticized the plan, however, by pointing out that no mention was made in it of eliminating the guards on top of the base's two water towers. Wouldn't the attackers be exposed? Santucho silenced him by explaining, with withering scorn, that all the angles of fire had already been studied carefully and there was no need to be concerned about the water towers. What is more, he assured the assembly, "there is no possibility of our being defeated."

Ranier was present at that meeting and had plenty of time to tip off the military as to exactly where and when the attack would happen. To lure the guerrillas into the trap, the army gave several of the soldiers on the base Christmas holiday passes, in order to make it seem that Monte Chingolo was lightly defended. After they departed, however, the remainder were heavily armed and put on alert. Also, the Third Infantry Regiment and the Buenos Aires provincial police were readied for action. Instead of establishing a strong defense perimeter immediately outside the arsenal, they stationed their camouflaged troops farther away.

The attack began at 7:00 P.M. on 23 December, when a guard at the front entrance opened the gate to allow a delivery truck to leave. Before he could close it, the guerrillas smashed through with one of their big tankers, followed by a line of cars. Guerrillas also broke through the rear entrance. The attackers sang victoriously as they poured out of their vehicles and headed for the warehouses and the radio station. One woman outside the base backed up the attack with a bazooka, while other support troops, many of whom were women, began setting up barricades. Suddenly, however, the entire operation went awry. As the invaders at the rear of the base broke through the gate, they were met by withering fire from a guard box farther inside. Every one of them was killed. Those at the front were also coming under heavy fire—especially from atop the water towers. Their heavy truck was disabled before it could ram the base's radio antenna, and they were driven back from the warehouses by a hailstorm of bullets. Trying to avoid a retreat, they were now forced to fight hand to hand with the soldiers who pressed in on them. Meanwhile, the auxiliaries outside found themselves encircled by the Third Infantry Regiment and the Buenos Aires provincial police, who began picking them off with their superior fire-power. The woman with the bazooka was blown to bits, as were many of her comrades, while the others fled in panic to an adjacent shantytown, where they hoped to find refuge. Air force helicopters kept them spotted, however, allowing the police and soldiers to hunt them down. Only a few guerrillas escaped. The government's security forces lost seven men: two officers, a sergeant, and four conscripts. Estimates of the guerrillas' losses vary, but were probably between 50 and 60.[14]

Santucho was stunned by the defeat. Nevertheless, when the PRT leaders met two days later at a hideout in Villa Martelli, Santucho dismissed their angry criticism by insisting that Monte Chingolo was a political triumph, even if ERP had suffered a military defeat. He adopted this same line in a testy exchange with the Montoneros, who criticized him for squandering the lives of so many veteran combatants in a poorly conceived battle with the army, especially when there was evidence that the enemy might have been alerted beforehand. Still, Benito Urteaga began to reconstruct events over the past month, from the arrest of Ledesma to the Monte Chingolo disaster. The trails all led back to Jesús Rames Ranier, who was hauled before a revolutionary tribunal, where he confessed to being an agent of the army's intelligence service. On 14 January his body was found in the Buenos Aires suburb of Floresta.

THE ARMY CLOSES IN

Hours after the fighting stopped at Monte Chingolo, a triumphant General Videla flew to Tucumán to be with the soldiers on Christmas Eve. While there, he shuffled commands as well. General Vilas, although he had piloted Operation Independence to success, was a Peronist officer, so Videla replaced him with General Domingo Bussi, a fellow infantry officer with experience as an observer of U.S. counterinsurgent operations in Vietnam. Vilas's chief subordinate, General Luciano Benjamín Menéndez, was moved up from the command of the Fifth Infantry Brigade to commander of the Third Army Corps, headquartered in Córdoba. On taking over, Bussi warned that the military campaign against the guerrillas would not end the war on subversion.

We still must uncover and destroy those who are largely responsible for unleashing subversion: those who attempt day and night, through deed or omission, while taking advantage of their high leadership positions and functions, to hide and protect those delinquents we are fighting today. On those ideologues who instruct and encourage delinquency . . . corrupting and encouraging corruption, justifying, facilitating, or favoring subversion in all its aspects—on them, sooner or later, we will make the power of our arms and the force of our cause felt, regardless of how deeply they have burrowed.[15]

Bussi's warning pointed to Isabel Perón and the regime she symbolized. There was evidence that the guerrillas still had many supporters inside the government. Catamarca's Peronist governor, Hugo Mott, had released six alleged terrorists whom the army had arrested. In San Luis, the head of the provincial police denied the existence of a guerrilla base that the army had discovered, and in Buenos Aires a judge released the members of a guerrilla cell that the soldiers had uncovered. Isabel herself helped to undermine her position by touching off a scandal and a congressional investigation over 3.1 billion *pesos* (about half a million dollars) that she drew from a disaster relief fund in the Ministry of Social Welfare for her personal use. The investigation soon uncovered other financial abuses: raids on the National Pension Fund and "loans" to cabinet ministers and other prominent Peronists from the National Mortgage Bank. Though dismissed by a federal judge in January, the case stripped her of any remaining authority and rendered her useless even as a figurehead. Nevertheless, there seemed to be no alternative. On the Left, the Montonero-backed Authentic Peronist Party (PPA) claimed 98,000 registered members in December 1975, and it was growing. Led by Héctor Cámpora and Oscar Bidegain, the PPA might very well slip into power behind a fusion ticket headed by some fellow traveler like Oscar Alende of the Intransigent Party, or Horacio Sueldo, the head of the Partido Revolucionario Cristiano.

By Christmas there was widespread support in the military, among businessmen, and even among politicians for removing Isabel from office. The economy was in chaos, with runaway inflation reaching nearly 1,000 percent, which touched off widespread black marketeering, smuggling, farmers' boycotts, labor strikes, and employers' lockouts. Only a few days before the Monte Chingolo attack, there had been a revolt of air force officers at the Morón air base and at the downtown Aereoparque airport. Planes had flown over the capital, dropping leaflets that called for the removal of the corrupt administration and for General Videla to assume control of the country. Videla rejected any call to oust the government, for the present, but now in Tucumán he used his Christmas message to the troops to issue a warning to Isabel and her entourage. "Subversive delinquency . . . has been encouraged by a supportive passivity," he alleged. Moreover, the government had sown chaos and insecurity by its opportunism, immorality, and corruption. Only by immediately taking a firm stand, cleaning its house, and acting decisively to restore public confidence could it salvage itself. The army did not wish to act with "unjustifiable impatience," but neither could it accept with infinite resignation the collapse of order.[16]

Moderate union leaders like Victorio Calabró and Juan José Taccone, the longtime head of the Power & Light Union, were urging the military to step in and impose order before the ERP and Montoneros took over the labor movement or profited from Peronism's internal chaos by gaining control of the party and possibly the government. Ricardo Balbín had long been in touch with Videla and other army chiefs, urging a "legalist coup" that would replace Isabel with a coalition government based on representatives of all the democratic parties. Business and *estanciero* support for a coup was there for the asking. Even the Catholic Church, though ostensibly on the sidelines, was sympathetic toward military intervention. Monseñor Victorio Bonamín, of the military vicarate, called upon the armed forces, "purified in a Jordan River of blood," to do their duty and bring order back to the nation. By the end of the year it was evident that the military was heading for a confrontation with Isabel. The officers were not enthusiastic about taking over, but they had come to believe that the current situation was intolerable and that any alternative to military rule would be inadequate.[17]

Ironically, the decision to intervene came just as the guerrilla threat had abated somewhat, although it still was serious. The Monte Chingolo disaster severely crippled ERP's remaining military capacity, and the Montoneros were unable to mount any more large-scale attacks after their brilliant but costly operation in Formosa. Moreover, the Montoneros were badly damaged when their second in command, Roberto Quieto, was arrested on 28 December by the police while picnicking with his family on a beach outside of Buenos Aires. Tortured for information, Quieto talked plenty, with the result that over the next few weeks several other Montoneros were picked up and the police began uncovering hideouts and arms caches. Quieto's capture set off riots and bombings by Montonero *milicianos* in downtown Buenos Aires, while Quieto's wife and mother were busy obtaining telegrams from international socialist figures like François Mitterand, Jean-Paul Sartre, and Simone de Beauvoir, exhorting the Argentine government to respect his human rights. The campaign was cut short, however, because a Montonero revolutionary tribunal, surmising that the increasingly successful police raids on their operations could only mean that Quieto was providing information, sentenced him to death.

Although ERP had received major setbacks during 1975, it was by no means destroyed. María Seoane, whose study of Santucho and his movement is the most thorough to date, estimated ERP's peak strength at between six hundred and one thousand combatants, with another estimated two thousand to five thousand front organization activists. Official figures state that during the course of 1975, ERP lost 106 guerrillas in Tucumán, and if we take the highest estimate (Burzaco's) of its losses at Monte Chingolo, Santucho would still have had three hundred to seven hundred combatants at his disposal, with probably another 1,500 to 4,500 active militants to support them.[18] As for the Montoneros, they had suffered perhaps as many as five hundred combatants and militants killed or "disappeared" since the beginning of 1975. Nevertheless, in the three months from their 5 October attack in Formosa until the end of the year, they assassinated 18 people, including an army general and his wife, an air force major,

Córdoba's police chief, two business executives, three guards at the Presidential Residence, five policemen, and four enlisted men. They also attacked four police stations, carried out several bombings, and made two kidnapping attempts, one of which was successful.[19]

The Montoneros also tried to succeed where ERP had failed by sending their own *Fuerza de Monte del Ejército Montonero* (Montonero Mountain Troops) to Tucumán. Its commander, Juan Carlos ("El Hippie") Alsogaray, a sociologist and son of a former army commander in chief, soon proved that military skills are not inherited. General Bussi's counterguerrilla forces caught up with the Montonero "jungle fighters" on 13 February and wiped them out. Nevertheless, the Montoneros were stepping up their urban tactics, trying to take advantage of an enormous outbreak of strikes. Everywhere they could, the Montoneros involved themselves in the tumult, bombing and burning business establishments, shooting policemen, and "executing" an army colonel. Thus, the guerrilla threat was still formidable. In the week preceding the coup, the Montoneros killed 16 people, including 13 policemen, as part of its "Third National Military Campaign." Meanwhile, they continued to seek alliances that would allow them to influence the next election and took whatever advantage they could to extend their "Authentic Trade Union Bloc." Given the collapsing economy, the erosion of the traditional union leaders' authority, and the escalation of labor protest, both the Montoneros and ERP had more possibilities for winning over greater numbers of workers to the revolutionary cause. Under a sympathetic government, or just a weak one, the guerrilla organizations would have quickly recovered from their recent defeats.

THE TAKEOVER

General Videla later claimed that he was not certain that Isabel would have to go until very near the end, and pointed to his refusal to back the December 1975 air force revolt as proof. Even as late as the beginning of March, he said, there were no concrete plans for a coup. About that time, Ricardo Balbín met with him to ask whether the army was about to take over and was given the somewhat evasive answer that nothing was definite about either a coup agenda or the allocation of government posts afterwards. Balbín urged Videla to move as soon as possible and restore order. When asked whether, in retrospect, it was a mistake to have overthrown the constitutional order, Videla admitted that the military might have forced Isabel, or some provisional president, to call early elections and install a new civilian government. Nevertheless, he insisted, at that time the country was in chaos—and, indeed, the guerrilla threat was only one aspect. Corruption was rife, political institutions had broken down, and there was only enough foreign exchange in the Treasury to last for a week. Argentina was in shambles, and it seemed, in mid-March, that it was urgent for the armed forces to act. On the other hand, Videla confessed that General Julio Alsogaray, the retired former commander in chief, advised him to wait even longer, until things got much worse ("until the country touches rock bottom," was the way Alsogaray put it) and the public clamored for a coup. That was good advice, but at the moment Videla did not think the armed forces could wait any longer.[20]

In fact, others were already proceeding with the "Dirty War" against subversion. Between 1 January and the coup, some 45 militant labor leaders, leftist politicians, and human rights lawyers "disappeared." Another 149 deaths were recorded in that same period, mostly of Montoneros. In Tucumán, General Bussi pursued the guerrillas with even greater zeal than Vilas had. During January the army scoured the mountains, destroying guerrilla camps and depots. When the Montoneros sent in their "jungle troops" in February, ERP backed them up with a company of guerrillas from Córdoba, but neither of these reinforcements was familiar with the terrain. Both were used to urban guerrilla warfare and were quickly mauled by the army. Throughout April and May, the Companía de Monte tried to regain the initiative by shooting down a helicopter, blowing up an army ambulance, executing an army scout, and raking with gunfire a squad of soldiers in a truck, but the army's pressure was inexorable. By the end of 1976, the guerrillas and their underground supporters had lost 304, as compared to only 106 the year before. Most of those were people arrested in the provincial capital while trying to provide supplies and information to the guerrillas. A large percentage of them were students, professors, or recent graduates of the local university. These were the "instructors," "instigators," and "infiltrators" to whom Bussi had referred in his speech. The campaign of annihilation against the guerrillas was only the beginning of a profound restructuring of Argentine society that would uproot the sources of subversion.[21]

With the value of hindsight, we now know that the military takeover was a grave mistake. Although it eliminated very efficiently the guerrilla and terrorist organizations, it made all the other problems—corruption, institutional breakdown, and economic chaos—a great deal worse. Nevertheless, when it came, on 24 March 1976, it had wide support among just about all the major interest groups and political parties, from the UCR to the Communist Party. The last days of Isabel's government were chaotic. Everyone knew that the coup was coming. By Monday, 22 March, Buenos Aires's leading newspapers, *La Nación, La Opinión, La Prensa*, and *Clarín* were openly predicting it. There was only scanty attendance on the floor of Congress because most legislators were in their offices, packing their belongings. Isabel's ministers were frantically trying to stave off the inevitable. Interior minister Roberto Ares was trying to get her to agree to a compromise plan by which she would stay on as president but surrender the management of the government to a prime minister, but Isabel was too apathetic to listen. Labor minister Miguel Unamuno was meeting with union leaders throughout Tuesday and into the early morning hours of Wednesday, the day of the coup, trying to organize a defense of the regime; but Casildo Herreras, the CGT's general secretary, had already left the country, announcing to reporters in Montevideo: "I don't know anything. I'm out of touch with it all. I've taken myself out of the picture (*me borré*)." Defense minister José

Deheza met several times on Tuesday, March 23, with the armed forces commanders, who listened in silence to his various proposals. He handed them a written promise from Isabel to form a new cabinet composed of all the democratic parties, stop government corruption, halt inflation, eliminate the remnants of the AAA, root out subversives in the trade unions, and adopt a more pro-Western foreign policy. It was too late—and, besides, they didn't believe her. Then Deheza requested permission for Isabel and about 79 leading government officials to leave the country and was refused. That was it: the government's fate was already sealed. Even as Deheza was talking to the officers, there were large troop movements taking place around the country. Tuesday evening, *La Razón* announced in its headlines: "The end is imminent. Everything is arranged."[22]

At the Casa Rosada, Isabel held a birthday party Tuesday evening for Beatriz Galán, her chief of staff for legal affairs. There were drinks and sandwiches. Her presidential secretary, Julio González, was in attendance. So was Lorenzo Miguel, who, despite their recent conflicts, was a loyalist to the end. So was Deolindo Felipe Bittel, the Justicialist Party's secretary, along with Isabel's bodyguards and other members of the presidential staff. Outside, in the Plaza de Mayo, about 50 of the party faithful, most of them women, were chanting their support for Isabel and promising to die fighting for the government. At around 11:30 P.M. Deheza showed up, sweaty, bedraggled, and dejected, to warn the president that the blow was about to fall. As he walked into the party, Isabel cut him short before he could speak. "Señor minister," she snapped, "I told you before not to smoke in my presence. Smoke makes me sick." When Deheza finally got to speak, she would not believe him. Others in the room dismissed the news as well: the military wouldn't dare. Still, the news—or rumor, as some preferred to call it—cast a pall on the party, so it was decided that it was best for Isabel to go back to the Presidential Residence in Olivos. Shortly after midnight, accompanied by Julio González and three bodyguards, she went to the roof of the Casa Rosada and boarded the presidential helicopter. Instead of taking her home, however, the helicopter landed at the Aereoparque. There she was met by a high-ranking air force officer, Brigadier Basilio Arturo Lami Dozo, who told her that she was no longer president of the nation, and placed her under arrest.

Shortly after 3:00 A.M. on Wednesday, the new junta, composed of the three armed services' heads—General Videla, Admiral Massera, and Brigadier Orlando Agosti—informed the nation that it had a new government. Other communiqués issued throughout the night warned against street demonstrations, strikes, antigovernment posters or propaganda, absenteeism in the public services, and the use of private planes or boats without official permission. At dawn the junta declared a bank holiday, during which all accounts were frozen. The stock exchange was closed as well. Congress was declared to be dissolved and soldiers occupied the building. Intervenors took over the CGT and CGE, the federal government's ministries, the provincial and municipal governments, and the labor unions. Leading Peronists were arrested: Lorenzo Miguel, Juan Manuel Abal Medina, Raúl Lastiri, Julio Broner (Gelbard's successor as head of the CGE), Julio González, and all of Isabel's cabinet ministers, both current and former. So were many former Peronist governors and lieutenant governors, while former President Cámpora took refuge in the Mexican Embassy. The Peronist restoration was over.[23]

NOTES

1. Juan Carlos De Pablo, *Economía política del peronismo* (Buenos Aires: El Cid Editorial, 1980), 181–83.

2. Callelo and Parcero, *De Vandor*, vol. 2, 159–60; Andrew Graham-Yool, *De Perón a Videla* (Buenos Aires: Editorial Legasa, 1989), 353–54; Álvaro Abós, *La columna vertebral: sindicatos y peronismo* (Buenos Aires: Hyspamerica Ediciones, 1986), 183.

3. Revista Somos, *Historias y personajes*, 35.

4. Kandel and Monteverde, *Entorno y caída*, 79–83.

5. Graham-Yool, *De Perón a Videla*, 355–56; *Review of the River Plate* (8 July 1975), 25; (22 July 1975), 79, 82, 88, 90; (13 August 1975), 203; (29 August 1975), 327–28.

6. García, *La doctrina*, 43–44, 153–57; Fraga, *Ejército*, 168, 196–97, 205.

7. *Review of the River Plate* (21 August 1975), 253–55; (21 August 1975), 264.

8. Fraga, *Ejército*, 211–15; *Review of the River Plate* (29 August 1975), 311; (10 September 1975), 367; (19 September 1975), 421.

9. On Videla's career, see *La Nación* (25 March 1976), 12; *Clarín* (28 March 1976), 4; *New York Times* (24 March 1976), 3; *Current Biography*, 1978, 438–41.

10. Author's interview with General Videla, Buenos Aires, 27 May 1992. General Videla was very firm in insisting that he drew Luder a clear picture of exactly what the radical strategy would entail and that Luder gave his assent, even overruling objections on the part of some of his cabinet ministers present at the meeting. Called to the witness stand at the 1985 military trials, Luder denied that calling for the "annihilation of the activities of subversive elements" was meant to justify "Dirty War" tactics. See also García, *La doctrina*, 44; *Nueva Confirmado* (3 December 1975), 23.

11. Díaz Bessone, *Guerra revolucionaria*, 339.

12. *Review of the River Plate* (30 December 1975), 1021, put the total guerrilla force at 1,000, of whom 200 were combatants. These are far higher than any other estimates. At the other extreme, Andersen, *Dossier Secreto*, 163, claims that only 100 guerrillas took part. That would not have been sufficient to attack such a large base. Ranging between those estimates, Díaz Bessone, *Guerra revolucionaria*, 340, puts the number at 70 combatants and 200 auxiliaries; Burzaco, *Infierno*, 123, gives figures of 120 and 200; whereas Seoane, *Todo o nada*, 281, says there were 130 and 120, respectively.

13. Burzaco, *Infierno*, 124; Mattini, *Hombres y mujeres*, 477; Seoane, *Todo o nada*, 276, 280–82.

14. Mattini, *Hombres y mujeres*, 477–78, claims that 60 combatants died, which closely accords with Díaz Bessone's figure in *Guerra revolucionaria*, 340–41, of 58. Andersen, *Dossier Secreto*, 163, gives a lower estimate of 45, which is similar to Seoane's 49, in *Todo o nada*, 283–85. Later official figures, cited by Burzaco, *Infierno*, 125–

26, put the total number of guerrillas killed at 211, a discrepancy that is either due to exaggeration or accounted for by including dead auxiliaries with the combatants.

15. Hernán López Echagüe, *El enigma*, 189–90.

16. Kandel and Monteverde, *Entorno y caída*, 139–52.

17. Fraga, *Ejército*, 156, 161–62, 164, 258–59; Kandel and Monteverde, *Entorno y caída*, 121; García, *La doctrina*, 158; De Riz, *Retorno y derrumbe*, 142.

18. López Echagüe, *El enigma*, 198; Gisela Zaremberg and Pablo Larrea, "El General ha vuelto: un análisis del discurso bussista," in Pablo Lacoste, ed., *Militares y política, 1983–1991* (Buenos Aires: Centro Editor de América Latina, 1993) 47.

19. Details on these actions are from *Evita Montonera*, vol. 1, no. 9 (November 1975), 27–31; vol. 1, no. 10 (December 1975), 28–31; vol. 2, no. 11 (January 1976), 13–15. On estimated Montonero losses in 1975, see Gillespie, *Soldiers of Perón*, 215–16.

20. Interview with Lieutenant General Jorge Rafael Videla, Buenos Aires, 27 May 1992. Fraga, *Ejército*, 259, says that the armed forces had decided on a coup by early February but had not worked out the details.

21. Burzaco, *Infierno*, 120–21; López Echagüe, *El enigma*, 198; Zaremberg and Larrea, "El General ha vuelto," 47–48.

22. Oscar Troncoso, *El Proceso de Reorganización Nacional* (Buenos Aires: Centro Editor de América Latina, 1984) vol. 1, 11; Kandel and Monteverde, *Entorno y caída*, 209–212; De Riz, *Retorno y derrumbe*, 143–44; *Review of the River Plate* (31 March 1976), 403.

23. Troncoso, *El Proceso*, vol. 1, 18, 27, 29, 40–41, 51; García, *La doctrina*, 47, 171; Kandel and Monteverde, *Entorno y caída*, 209–21; Revista Somos, *Historias y personajes*, 7, 37–42; *Review of the River Plate* (31 March 1976), 404; (20 December 1978), 990–91; (30 November 1979), 858–59; (30 April 1980), 611; (31 March 1981), 390; (10 July 1981), 10, 19. Isabel was finally put on trial for embezzlement of government funds and found guilty. She was ordered to reimburse the Social Welfare Ministry 3.25 million pesos and was sentenced to eight years. She eventually was allowed to return to Spain, however. Cámpora, found to be suffering from incurable cancer, was permitted to go to Mexico in November 1979 and died there. Lastiri died while under house arrest in December 1978. Lorenzo Miguel stayed in prison until September 1978 and then was allowed to return home under arrest. He finally was released from that in April 1980. He is still active in politics today.

NINE

The Ideology of Repression

In the early morning hours of 24 March 1976, the new military junta issued its manifesto justifying the coup. Videla, Massera, and Agosti asserted that the Peronist government had lost all of its ethical and moral standing and could no longer lead the nation. Its economic policies had led to the collapse of production, its corruption and mismanagement had created a power vacuum that invited anarchy, and it had no strategy for combating subversion. Looking back upon the past 20 years, the junta concluded that all constitutional mechanisms for solving the ongoing national crisis had failed, so now the armed forces had to take power and make the hard decisions that others had avoided. They would restore the "basic values"—such as morality, competence, and efficiency—on which the state must rest. They would uproot subversion and promote economic development so as to eliminate its causes. Argentina would gain a larger role in the world order, adopt a clear commitment to the Western and Christian camp in the Cold War, and achieve a harmonious cooperation between capital, labor, and the state. Eventually there would be a return to democracy, but no definite timetable was offered.[1]

A hint of the terror to come followed these general statements of purpose. The new government would proceed "with absolute firmness and devotion to service," the proclamation continued. "From this moment on, the responsibility assumed [by the armed forces] requires the severe exercise of authority in order to *definitively eradicate the vices affecting our country*," it emphasized. Specifically, the armed forces would continue the fight against "subversive criminality, whether overt or covert, and will suppress all demagoguery." Moreover, "it will not tolerate corruption or venality in any form or under any circumstances, nor any breaking of the law or opposition to the process of reform being initiated."

The 1853 Constitution remained formally in effect, but the governmental structure was modified by an Enabling Act. Moreover, the Constitution could be suspended whenever it conflicted with acts of the "Process of National Reorganization." A Junta Militar, composed of the heads of the army, navy, and air force, would be the highest political authority, with the power to supervise all other state bodies. It would designate a president of the nation and could remove him or any of his cabinet ministers "for reasons of state." It would review the president's actions and act in the place of the now dissolved Congress. Three representatives from each of the three branches of the armed forces would constitute a Legislative Advisory Committee. Beneath those nine high-ranking officers, chosen from the General Staffs, were eight subcommittees, one for each cabinet ministry, composed of officers with the rank of full colonel or its equivalent. Their task was to study all policy proposals and report their opinions to the Legislative Advisory Committee, which could then approve, reject, or modify them. In the event of a rejection, the matter would go to the junta, which had the last word. The junta's power to promulgate special laws, take arbitrary measures, and assume discretionary powers was greatly enhanced by an Institutional Act, issued by decree on 18 June 1976, that allowed it to "judge the conduct of those who have caused harm to the vital interests of the Nation." The junta could also remove and replace Supreme Court justices, the attorney general, and provincial governors. All governments, national, provincial, or municipal, had to make their policies conform to the basic objectives of the *proceso*, as interpreted by the Junta Militar.[2]

The armed forces wanted to avoid a personalistic dictatorship like the one in Chile under General Augusto Pinochet. Argentine junta representatives had fixed terms, and their control over field commanders was strictly limited. To further ensure against any individual junta member expanding his power, each service branch was allocated one-third of all government posts, including cabinet ministries and subcabinet positions, the presidential secretariat, and the state enterprises. All junta decisions had to be unanimous.[3]

The Junta Militar, while supposedly the supreme organ of the state, was actually without real authority. It could set general government policy, appoint government personnel, and deal with routine matters, but the conduct of the "war against subversion" was vested in the regional commanders. The navy became responsible for much of the federal capital, because of the port of Buenos Aires. It also controlled areas around other naval bases and shipyards. Within the government, it tended to dominate the Ministry of Foreign Affairs. The air force's "war zones" were in the Buenos Aires suburbs of Morón, Merlo, and Moreno, where its main bases were located. The rest of the country, including part of the federal capital, fell under army control. There were four army regional commands. The First Army Corps, headquartered in the *barrio* of the federal capital known as Palermo, was composed of the First Armored Cavalry (tank corps) at Tandil, the First and Seventh Airborne Brigades at Azul and Tandil, the Tenth Infantry (Patricios) Brigade in Palermo, and the Mounted Grenadiers. Consequently, most of Buenos Aires Province fell under its jurisdiction. Also connected to the First Army Corps, but functionally separate, was the Military Institutes Command, which was in charge of the Military Academy, the Superior War School, and the Campo de Mayo base. The Second Army Corps, headquartered in Rosario, was also in charge of the Seventh Infantry Brigade in Corrientes, the Third Infantry Brigade in Curuzú Cuatiá, the Second Armored Cavalry and the Second Airborne Brigade in Paraná. Its war zone comprised the entire northeastern region. The northwest fell under the Third Army Corps, headquartered in Córdoba. Its subunits included the Fourth Infantry Brigade in Córdoba, the Fifth Infantry Brigade in Tucumán, the Fourth Airborne Brigade and the Eighth Mountain Infantry Brigade in Mendoza, and the Fifth Airborne Brigade in San Luis. The Fifth Army Corps (there was no Fourth) covered the Patagonian region, with the Sixth Mountain Brigade in Neuquén, the Ninth Infantry Brigade in Comodoro Rivadavia, and headquarters at Bahía Blanca.

Those were only the main units and subunits. The chain of command spread out like a fine net to smaller bases that dotted the interior, allowing the army, in collaboration with the National Gendarmerie and the police, to penetrate every corner of the country. Each unit, subunit, and sub-subunit was responsible for a particular "security zone," and its commanding officer had much discretion in determining how to root out subversion. "Each in his own fiefdom was supreme," Eduardo Crawley noted, "reporting only to his superiors in his own branch of the service." Furthermore, this highly decentralized repressive apparatus resulted in "a tangled, overlapping network that led upwards, not to a single national authority, but to three separate authorities—the commanders in chief of each of the three separate services who made up the ruling Junta. This decentralization and autonomy, at the other end of the scale, meant enormous power in the hands of very junior officers, each secure in the knowledge that no one could really tell under whose instructions he was acting."[4]

Under such a loose chain of command, it was impossible to keep atrocities from happening, or even to minimize their occurrences; yet the Argentine commanders had decided upon this approach far in advance of the coup against Isabel Perón, despite warnings from French advisors about the probable consequences for human rights. In September 1975, even before Videla went to Provisional President Italo Luder with his radical plans for annihilating subversion, the army chiefs had decided that the enemy was not to be merely defeated but exterminated, so that no future civilian government could release the guerrillas to fight again, as Cámpora's had. Moreover, the guerrillas' front organizations and clandestine support networks were to be wiped out, root and branch. This was all to be done in such a way as to avoid the international protests and pressures that Pinochet's government had faced after the coup in Chile. General Cesareo Cardozo, the future Federal Police chief, was charged with elaborating a plan of operations, but the general outlines were clear: the war was to be conducted through small, local operations much like those that General Vilas had used against the guerrillas and their supporters in Tucumán. Everyone present, including Videla and Viola, knew that Vilas's methods included torture and disappearances and that a decentralized repressive apparatus might unleash uncontrolled terror on the population. For many years the Superior War School had invited French advisors and instructors with experience in Vietnam and Algeria to offer courses and lectures on counterguerrilla strategy and tactics. Many of them had related how, when clandestine methods of repression were used in Algeria, the normal chain of command had been disrupted, making it hard for those at the top to control their subordinates. In fact, the clandestine "task forces" had gotten so out of control that they began to act as bandits, killing, kidnapping, robbing, and extorting for their personal profit. The same was to happen later in Argentina, but at the September 1975 meeting the army chiefs were convinced that the risk was worth taking.[5]

After the armed forces took power, Videla, as head of the state, tried to reassure both domestic and foreign opinion of his government's good intentions. Speaking to a group of Argentine journalists in May, he insisted that the *proceso* aimed at restoring "a representative, republican, and federal democracy"; at the World Congress of Advertising that same month, he told an audience of 1,200 that the *proceso* aimed at a society of liberty and responsibility, rights and duties. Even some people who were victims of the *proceso* believed that he was sincere. For instance, Jacobo Timerman wrote:

General Videla's government strove to accomplish peaceful acts. It spoke of peace and understanding, maintaining that the revolution was not aimed against anyone in particular or any special sector. But military leaders hastily organized their personal domains, each one becoming a warlord in the zone under his control, whereupon the chaotic, anarchistic, irrational terrorism of the Left and of the Fascist death squads gave way to intrinsic, systematized, rationally planned terrorism. Each officer of a military region had his own prisoners, prisons, and form of justice, and even the central power was unable to request the freedom of an individual when importuned by international pressure.[6]

SAVIORS OF THE NATION

The armed forces were not monolithic. There were rivalries between the army, navy, and air force and within each of those there were divisions along functional lines. Then there were factions based on personal loyalties. Subordinates attached themselves to a leader and worked for his advancement, in return for which he guided their careers upward as he rose. Most officers were professionals with little interest in politics, but among the minority of officers who did take an interest in politics, there were ideological divisions: liberals, populist nationalists (Peronists) and the more elitist Catholic nationalists.

Despite these internal divisions, the armed forces' education and professional training taught them to think of themselves as a special group set apart as guardians of the nation. A belief in national unity, authority, and inequality as inescapable aspects of life usually made the officers hostile to Marxists and radicals, resentful of the disruptions caused by strikes, and impatient with the demagoguery and backroom deals that frequently characterized the democratic process. Indeed, there was a notable disdain for mass politics that inclined them toward antidemocratic corporatist schemes that would tame and channel mass action. The officers' elitism was heightened also by the extensive role that the military played in Argentina's economy. All three service branches had developed their own military and ancillary industries and frequently headed other state enterprises as well. So wide was the military's influence that Alain Rouquie felt justified in characterizing the Argentine economy as being essentially "militarized."[7]

Small wonder, then, that the military considered itself uniquely qualified to lead the country. In its own view, it had the skills to run Argentina as well as the patriotism to rise above the petty interests of class or party. As Kenneth Johnson noted, "Argentine military elites are proud, and theirs is a smug pride— a pride born of de facto status as the dominant elite." He also noted that "it is a fragile and transparent pride, one that is easily threatened by the prospect of an adverse popular judgment." Therein was the dilemma that made military interventions both frequent and short-lived, at least until the 1976 coup: the armed forces were reluctant to face public hostility. Their self-image as guardians of the nation shrank from the possibility of being hated and opposed by that very nation. In the meantime, however, the Argentine military was drawn into the Cold War, became part of the Western Hemisphere's defense system, accepted the U.S. concept of a bipolar struggle, and began to focus its attention on internal enemies of the state. Brought to the United States to study at the military academies or to the School of the Americas in Panama for counterinsurgency training, Argentine officers developed a wider interest in economic, social, and political issues. Their own intelligence services already were aware, of course, that Trotskyite and *fidelista* communists had infiltrated the Resistance, the Peronist movement, and many labor unions. Now they began to weave that information into a broader vision of a titanic world struggle in which Argentina was an important battleground. Resistance and sabotage were not merely the result of workingmen's misplaced loyalty to Perón but were caused by the machinations of subversive forces directed from Cuba and the Soviet Union, using the ignorance and resentments of the lower classes to turn them against their own *patria*.[8]

The National Security Doctrine that grew out of this social analysis linked politics, economics, sociology, and culture into a more or less coherent nationalist ideology justifying a new kind of military intervention that would be both broader in scope and more intensive in its methods. Ironically, it was in many ways a mirror image of Perón's "organized community," in which every facet of society would be mobilized by the state for the purposes of military efficiency and national power. As for the charge that this subordinated Argentine security to U.S. strategy, even critics like Ernesto López admit, "The military are not instruments of the Pentagon, nor of the Oligarchy, nor of the State, regardless of how it is constituted, nor of the middle classes. . . . The military are social and political actors and not mere instruments." Specifically, with regard to the United States, he concedes that military aid and training could not have had an effect unless it had corresponded to local military demands. The U.S. Mutual Assistance Programs of the 1950s and 1960s accentuated an already existing predilection on the part of the Argentine military to intervene and facilitated its ability to do so. The Cuban Revolution, which brought Soviet power directly into the hemisphere, tightened U.S.-Argentine military relations.[9]

In the formulation of the strategy and tactics that would later characterize the "Dirty War," U.S. influence was much less than the contributions of French counterinsurgency doctrine or even of Argentina's own military thinkers. Alicia García, in her study of the National Security Doctrine in Argentina, points to the use of paramilitary squads to smash labor unions during the 1919 Semana Trágica and the mass executions ("disappearances") employed by the Argentine army in 1920 against the anarchist strikers in Patagonia as examples of Argentina's own traditional way of dealing with "subversives." General Osiris Villegas, one of the chief theorists of counterguerrilla strategy, acknowledged the importance of the United States as a source of equipment but not of strategic doctrine, which he claimed was developed from many sources, including purely domestic ones. Indeed, U.S. influence on Argentina's version of the National Security Doctrine was, according to him, about nil: the Argentine military had little to learn from an army that had just lost Vietnam. General José T. Goyret was even more specific. Although the Americans published a great deal on the subject of counterguerrilla warfare after 1961, they deliberately ignored the French experience in Vietnam and Algeria. Consequently, they emphasized the military aspects while mostly ignoring the political side of revolutionary warfare. At their most ludicrous, Goyret added, the Americans tried to apply behaviorist theories to the subject, trying to encompass it in "scientific" formulas that contributed nothing to understanding how to deal with wars of national liberation. Thus, their influence was slight, at best. General Ramón Camps framed the matter somewhat more kindly:

In Argentina we first received French influence and then North American, and we tried them out separately as well as in combination, drawing out ideas from both. . . . The French approach was better than the North American. It pointed to an all-around conception of the problem of subversion whereas the latter focused exclusively, or almost exclusively, on its military aspects. . . . So it went until the moment arrived in which we reached our maturity and applied our own doctrine, which definitely permitted us to win the victory in Argentina against armed subversion.[10]

On the other hand, the frequent military coups that plagued Latin America throughout the 1960s and 1970s were certainly facilitated, if not encouraged, by

U.S. military aid and diplomacy. By spreading a vision of Cold War bipolarity, the United States also encouraged a rigid polarization that easily confused communist subversion with popular reform. For a military that had not fought in a war since 1870, the Argentine armed forces were charmed by the thought that they were part of a grand crusade to save the Christian West from communism and that Argentina might figure as one of the principal theaters of the Cold War. As Colonel Romulo Menéndez, one of the directors of the Círculo Militar and editor of its *Revista Militar*, summarized it in October 1961: "It is worth mentioning that Khruschev recently said that Argentina will be the next country to go communist. . . . The United States is the anti-communist bastion, the only country in the noncommunist world that . . . has enough power to stand up to the USSR."[11]

Although Argentina was not likely to "go communist," Colonel Menéndez had put his finger on a military fact of life: that in the nuclear age Argentina was indeed dependent on the United States for security against an attack by the Soviet Union. On the other hand, given the nuclear stalemate that existed between the world's two superpowers, such an attack was not likely. Instead, it was more plausible to suppose that the United States and Russia would resort to "low intensity" conflicts using surrogate forces. Terrorism, not an overt attack, was the likeliest danger to Argentina from the communist world. That was where French doctrine provided a "superior" blueprint.

THE IDEOLOGY OF REPRESSION

French influence extended back as far as 1956, when Colonel Carlos J. Rosas, recently returned from a tour of duty as a military attaché in France, took over the editorship of the *Revista de la Escuela Superior de Guerra*. Rosas knew many French officers who had fought in Vietnam and Algeria. Their writings began to appear in the *Revista* and met with great interest on the part of the Argentine army, which was trying to grapple with the Peronist Resistance. Some of the Frenchmen were invited to teach and act as advisors to the Superior War School (ESG). Rosas himself eventually moved on to become chief of operations at the army's General Staff headquarters, but he left behind a new curriculum at the ESG that put more emphasis on the study of guerrilla warfare and how to combat it. The revised curriculum taught army officers that there was a new kind of warfare, "revolutionary warfare," which differed from the traditional kind. To understand it, it was necessary to learn about politics, and even to read the main works of Marx, Lenin, and Mao. With Fidel Castro's triumph in Cuba, the Cold War finally reached Latin America, and interest in the French doctrine reached new heights. More French officers were brought to the ESG, and an increasing number of Argentine officers went to France to pursue their counterrevolutionary war studies at the French Superior War School. By October 1961, the Argentine ESG was able to host the first inter-American course in counterrevolutionary warfare, with a text based on the lectures of the visiting French officers.[12]

In the meantime, French counterrevolutionary war doctrine had been developing as the Algerian war provided more experience. In December 1956 Jacques Hogard wrote, in the *Revue de Defense Nationale*, that "we are in the presence of a transformation even more radical than the one brought about by the French Revolution with respect to the political and military concepts of an age." In July 1957, Colonel Charles Lacheroy organized a conference on revolutionary war, which, in the opinion of General José T. Goyret, proved to be "the most original and profound of all the many conferences held on the subject over the next two decades." During the conference someone asked Colonel Lacheroy why the so-called new revolutionary war was different from any other. He answered that it was not just a new phase of warfare but an immense step in the direction of total war, and that it was destined to spread worldwide. It was total because "it not only mobilizes all of the industrial, commercial, and agricultural power of a country for the purpose of war, but because it also seizes and directs for the purpose of war all the children, all the women, all the old people, everyone who thinks, all who live and breathe—with all their power to love, all their power of enthusiasm, and all their power to hate." Revolutionary war not only takes possession of people physically, Col. Lacheroy, a Vietnam veteran, continued, "it also takes possession of their souls." Revolutionary war is not waged with an army organized in traditional divisions, he concluded, and you cannot win it with a government organized for times of peace, or with the Napoleonic Code.[13]

General Andre Beaufre was perhaps the leading ideologue of the French school, and his book, *La guerra revolucionaria*, became obligatory for those officers engaged in the subject. The first distinguishing feature of revolutionary warfare, for General Beaufre, was the importance it gave to ideology. In the modern world, revolutionary ideas easily cross national boundaries, creating fifth columns of sympathizers. Because public opinion now has international dimensions and influence, ideology can soften up a target country and also bring international pressure to bear against governments trying to fight subversion. A second distinguishing feature of revolutionary warfare is that it consists of skirmishes and ambushes rather than set battles between organized armed contingents. This is because the nuclear stalemate forbids direct confrontation between the superpowers; therefore, limited wars, fought with surrogates, have become the means for gaining advantage. This commonly takes the form of a guerrilla movement, backed by the Soviet Union, launching an attack on a target government in the name of social justice or national liberation from imperialism. Frequently, the target government may, in an imperfect world, be guilty of economic mismanagement, corruption, and indifference to social problems, all of which offer the rebels a potentially sympathetic population as well as broad international support from neutral and even allied countries. Beaufre was vague as to how a target government should act, but his brief discussion of Israel's dealings with its Palestinian population suggested that counterterror and real full-scale repression might be the most effective responses. Half measures are worse than none; repression must not be a bluff. At the same time, the government should be aware that by escalating the war it risks condemnation by "world public opinion," international isolation, and more internal disruption.[14]

Beaufre was invited to give a series of lectures at Argentina's Superior War School in November 1971, which were published in the ESG's *Revista*.[15] They added to his basic argument an emphasis on the need for the military to develop a "grand politics," or counterrevolutionary ideology, as the first step toward a strategy to combat revolutionary warfare. It would be a mirror image of the Marxist-Leninist "grand politics" that it seeks to destroy, and he admitted that its adoption would involve a fundamental change in a country's politics. In contrast to ordinary civilian politics, which lacks any long-range goals, "grand politics" sees every move as part of a total strategy. In countries like Argentina, which are in the middle stages of modernization, it involves adopting a development model that will promote rapid economic and social progress, regardless of any internal or external obstacles. Unless this route is taken, Beaufre insisted, "there is no salvation in our era." Both in his book and his lectures, General Beaufre advanced his argument in rather general terms, although its dangerous implications were fairly easy to spot. Nevertheless, it was up to other French theorists of counterrevolutionary warfare to make these specific.

One of these was Colonel Patrice de Naurois, another veteran of Vietnam who came to lecture at the ESG. In an article published by the *Revista* in 1958, Naurois emphasized the dual strategy employed by guerrillas to subvert the state: propaganda, on the one hand, to undermine the masses' loyalty to the existing order, and terrorist violence aimed at undermining the state's morale. To combat this, he argued, the state needs information as to who the subversives are, where their bases and hideouts are located, and who is helping them. Then the army must centralize and collate its information. The best way to gather it is to divide the national territory into zones, each under the authority of some military or police unit. The more finely divided the territory, the easier it will be for each unit to gather information, because it will have a more intimate knowledge of the inhabitants and physical layout of the zone.[16]

None of the writers on counterrevolutionary warfare was quite so frank as Colonel Roger Trinquier, however. A marine paratrooper with long service in Asia, survivor of a Japanese prison camp, and veteran of both Vietnam and Algeria, he was the most experienced of all in antiguerrilla tactics. In Vietnam his specialty was the training of anticommunist irregular forces, some 20,000 strong, recruited mainly from the native mountain tribes. After the French evacuated Vietnam, Trinquier went to Algeria to organize paratroop units whose task was to close off the frontier with Tunisia. His other task was to eliminate urban terrorists from the city of Algiers. In 1963, Trinquier, now retired, wrote about his experiences in a book entitled *La guerre moderne*. After covering much the same ground as Beaufre, describing the new revolutionary warfare's unique character, he then drew a sharper picture of a typical urban guerrilla operation, with its cells, front organizations, intelligence network, hideouts, terrorist squads, and propaganda apparatus. Its terrorists tend to be drawn from two classes of the population: idealists and criminals. Their violence is a form of psychological warfare that aims to drain the state's morale and make the ordinary citizen feel that the government is unable to protect him. Thus, citizens collaborate with the terrorists even though they may hate them, because they feel defenseless. A small number of terrorists can cow a whole population, Trinquier observed, and that is why terrorism has become the main weapon of modern revolutionary warfare. This is not to condemn the terrorist, Trinquier maintained, because terrorism and guerrilla tactics are logical responses to the technological superiority of the regular army. The terrorist considers himself a soldier engaged in a war. His conscience does not bother him when he shoots at civilians from ambush or throws a bomb into a cafe, because he is using the only weapons available to him. On the other hand, the terrorist, striking from ambush with his escape route already prepared, does not take the same risks that a soldier takes in conventional warfare. Thus, the terrorist is a bit more like a criminal. Nevertheless, Trinquier did not think that the terrorist ought to be treated as a criminal; rather, he should be treated as an enemy soldier whose army has to be destroyed so that it will be unable to continue fighting.[17]

Uprooting terrorism requires, for Trinquier as for Naurois, dividing the country into fairly small military zones, each with counterrevolutionary organizations capable of disrupting the flow of information, food, medical supplies, and arms to the guerrillas. This should start with the major cities, where the counterrevolutionary network, like a mirror image of the guerrillas, will extend to every block and even to each building on each block. The population should be censused, identity cards issued, and family heads held responsible for the whereabouts of their family members. It is essential to know each inhabitant of a district and where he lives. Surveillance should also be extended to the workplace. Sooner or later, people will be discovered coming and going where they have no business to be; then they will be arrested and interrogated. As the terrorist organization is uprooted, and ordinary people in those places gain a greater sense of security, they should be recruited into the surveillance network. Next will come the crucial struggle for the "intermediate zones," those areas that surround the cities, from which food, information, and arms are channeled to the guerrilla underground. Those will have to be secured one by one, using the same methods. The aim is to drive the guerrillas out to the country's peripheral zones, where they have more difficulty supplying themselves.[18]

Trinquier believed that torture is a necessary weapon in the counterrevolutionary arsenal. In his introduction to *La guerra moderna*, Bernard Fall, a journalist veteran of Vietnam, recalled with regret that Trinquier was denied permission by the French commanders to use torture in his operations. "Torture is the particular poison for the terrorist," Fall argued, "just as anti-aircraft artillery is for the pilot and the machine gun is for the soldier." Uprooting an underground organization requires specially trained interrogators who can get information quickly and who know precisely what sort of information a given victim might possess. Because of the terrorist organization's mobility, it is essential to make the victim talk quickly, and that means that torture must be used. "Otherwise, the others will have time to escape, the thread will be broken, and all the effort expended in uncovering the organization will be for naught." The interrogator should have good knowledge of terrorist organizations in general and the one at hand in particular, because that allows him to place the victim within its organizational system and to be more efficient in getting the necessary information. A skilled interrogator will not be so excessive as to permanently damage his victim, physically or morally, because that will often delay the process of extracting information. Each victim should be interrogated separately. Experience shows that intellectuals are more likely to confess to an interrogator than are people from the lower classes. The interrogator should remember, too, that some members of the subversive organization were forced by threats into collaborating, and now they can be turned against their former companions. Once a victim confesses, giving names and places, he has no recourse but to continue collaborating. Therefore, a practiced interrogator will treat his victims with flexibility.[19]

Given the importance of propaganda in revolutionary warfare, Trinquier warned, the state must expect that the terrorists will use all the opportunities offered by the criminal laws of procedure to slow down or thwart counterrevolutionary strategy. What they most fear is the suspension of legal guarantees. Terrorists will also try appealing to public sympathy and will certainly enlist the support of their ideological sympathizers abroad to bring international pressure on the authorities to relent. The state and the army must be prepared, therefore, for a propaganda duel in which they constantly remind the people that their measures have only one purpose: "to pursue and wipe out the band of terrorists that are flagellating it." At the same time, protests can be kept to a minimum by arresting suspected terrorists at night, in their homes, and taking them to special, secret detention centers where torture will take place out of sight. Trinquier followed this advice with another warning, however: "Although an occasional excess is inevitable, we nevertheless should avoid abuses of power, and consequently our operations have to be closely watched by our own chiefs so that no mistakes are incurred through a loss of temper. The army should never forget that it is defending the people by applying the law. Therefore, that very same army must take care that at no time are excesses, crimes, and injustices committed in the name of that law."[20] Although Trinquier's choice of words betrays a poor understanding of law, since the laws of no modern state condone torture, his advice about the top authorities supervising the operations was correct. By ignoring it, the Argentine armed forces got out of control and marched themselves toward disaster.

THE ARGENTINE SYNTHESIS

U.S. Cold War concepts and French counterrevolutionary doctrine provided the Argentine officers with tools of analysis, but their application to Argentina's politics was filtered through different ideological prisms. For Catholic nationalists, the Cold War was a struggle between Western Christianity and atheistic communism, in which secular liberalism was but an opening wedge for subversion to enter. Colonel Horacio E. Querol, in a speech given at the ESG in October 1961, blamed the Argentine educational system for failing to teach the principles that God is the essence of truth and that the truth about God is to be found in the eternal church He created: the Roman Catholic Church. In fact, Colonel Querol asserted, the modern world's troubles began with the Protestant Reformation, which replaced the unity of truth with individual, subjective interpretations. Then Descartes made it worse by elevating reason over faith, and the French Revolution deepened the crisis by freeing humanity from its sense of duty and making it the repository of all sorts of "rights." This whole trend is summarized in the ideology of liberalism, a querulous, carping doctrine that holds everything traditional and sacred up to criticism and finally ends by spreading cynicism, atheism, and nihilism. Colonel Querol's was not an isolated voice. In the *Revista del Círculo Militar*, one of the most prestigious military publications in Argentina, articles appeared throughout the 1960s echoing the same sentiments: that Christianity was the only effective antidote to communism, that Protestantism and philosophical rationalism were sources of decadence and anarchy, and that liberalism was the antechamber of Marxism-Leninism.[21]

Conservative liberals, on the other hand, tended to emphasize economic reform as the proper answer to communism and to make distinctions among critics of the status quo. General Jean Nogués was particularly restrained in his approach to the "communist threat." In his opinion, given Argentina's racial, linguistic, and religious homogeneity; its relatively high living standards and literacy rates; and its relatively large middle class, the threat of a communist takeover was rather remote. Moreover, the country's geography was not conducive to guerrilla warfare. Only the northwestern corner had high enough mountains or sufficient jungle to provide cover; the rest was flat and open. It was empty, too, because three-fourths of the population lived in cities. Thus, except for a few places like Tucumán, there was no rural peasantry large enough to support guerrillas. Finally, communism was unpopular in Argentina, not just among the middle classes but in the working class as well. The only way that communists could make headway in Argentina, Nogués insisted, was by pretending to be nationalists and trying to infiltrate the Peronist movement, whose masses were still imperfectly integrated into the society. Communist intellectuals, by playing on Argentina's traditional anti–North American sentiments and waving the anti-imperialist banner, might be able to seduce the Peronists but unlike Cuba they would have to concentrate on the cities, and their tactics would therefore involve mass demonstrations, sabotage, and terrorism. That was the kind of communist attack for which the Argentine military should prepare. Like other liberals, Gen. Nogués emphasized the need to eliminate pockets of poverty and to fully integrate the working class into society. Unlike many liberals, however, he warned against orthodox economic austerity plans that force painful sacrifices on the workers.[22]

Not many military intellectuals were as careful and moderate as General Nogués. Whether Catholic nationalists or conservative liberals, most of them came to view the fight against communism as an all-out war requiring total solutions. As Brigadier General Carlos Túrolo told his audience at the inauguration of the ESG's first Inter-American Course on Counter-Revolutionary War, in October 1961, war had become increasingly total, as World Wars I and II had targeted civilians as well as soldiers. However, revolutionary warfare went further: it actually *focused* on civilians. It was a struggle for civilian minds and souls. Consequently, counterrevolutionary warfare would also require concentrating on civilians, in all fields, starting with the school and the home. In combating communism's internal forces, "he who is able to fight against Communism with all the authority and means of his specialty, profession, function, or occupation but fails to do it—whether from indifference, ignorance, or selfish personal interest—permits, directly or indirectly, the progress of Communism. And, as a result, he cooperates with it." Fifteen years later General Ibérico Saint-Jean, General Videla's appointed governor of Buenos Aires Province, announced his agenda in similar, but more brutal, terms: "First we will kill all the subversives; then we will kill all their collaborators; then their sympathizers; then those who remained indifferent; and finally we'll kill the undecided."[23]

As early as 1962, Lieutenant Colonel Mario Orsolini predicted the path that would take the army from Túrolo's preliminary observations to Saint-Jean's grisly blueprint. Cold War crusaderism allied to extralegal tactics taught that morality could be suspended in the "higher cause" of defending the nation, the West, or Christianity. As the National Security Doctrine became diffused throughout the military, even down to the common soldier, it produced a psychological imbalance, a hypersensitivity to communism, impatience, intolerance, and an urge to snap judgments and drastic actions. Having defined its ideology as a cause, the military had become "easily led to a holy war, with all the characteristic ferocity peculiar to that." It also bred suspicion of the people, viewing them as potentially hostile and subversive. Therein lay an error in the Argentine army's adoption of French doctrine. The French carried out their operations against hostile, non-French populations—Vietnamese and Algerians—not against the French people themselves.[24] What the Argentine military was preparing to do was to declare war on its own nation in the name of saving it.

NOTES

1. García, *La doctrina*, 169–70; Troncoso, *El Proceso*, vol. 1, 107–8, 110–11.

2. Troncoso, *El Proceso*, 109–10, 112–14; Marta Castiglione, *La militarización del Estado en la Argentina (1976–1981)* (Buenos Aires: Centro Editor de América Latina, 1992), 35–37; Organization of American States, Inter American Commission on Human Rights *Report on the Situation of Human Rights in Argentina* (Washington: the General Secretariat of the O.A.S., 1980), 26–27, 30.

3. Carlos H. Acuña and Catalina Smulovitz, "Militares en la transición argentina: del gobierno a la subordinación constitucional," *Revista Paraguaya de Sociología*, vol. 31 (January–April, 1994), 100; Castiglione, *La militarización*, 55, 58.

4. Eduardo Crawley, *A House Divided*, 427.

5. Acuña and Smulovitz, "Militares en la transición," 100–1, n.11; and 104, n. 25, based on an article by General Ramón Camps in *La Prensa* (4 January 1981), Section 2, 2.

6. Troncoso, *El Proceso*, vol. 1, 23, 26; Jacobo Timerman, *Prisoner Without a Name, Cell Without a Number* (New York: Vintage Books, 1988), 26.

7. Rouquie, *Poder militar*, vol. 2, 316, 319–20, 322–23, 325, 327–30, 346; Castiglione, *La militarización*, 16–17.

8. Castiglione, *La militarización*, 19–20; Carlos A. Florit, *Las fuerzas armadas y la guerra psicológica* (Buenos Aires: Editorial Arayú, 1963), 61–63.

9. Ernesto López, *Seguridad nacional y sedición militar* (Buenos Aires: Editorial Legasa, 1987), 14, 16, 68, 70–71.

10. García, *La doctrina*, 18; Osiris G. Villegas, *Testimonio de un alegato* (Buenos Aires: Author, 1990), 86–87; José Teofilo Goyret, *Geopolítica y subversión* (Buenos Aires: Ediciones Depalma, 1980), 136–37; Camps, as quoted in Gasparini, *Montoneros*, 93; J. Patrice McSherry, *Incomplete Transition* (New York: St. Martin's Press, 1997), 47–55.

11. Quoted in Ollier, *Orden*, vol. 1, 20. On the influence of U.S. Cold War views, see also López, *Seguridad nacional*, 50–51; García, *La doctrina*, 13.

12. López, *Seguridad nacional*, 158; Rouquie, *Poder militar*, vol. 2, 158; García, *La doctrina*, 22.

13. Goyret, *Geopolítica*, 134–35.

14. Andre Beaufre, *La guerra revolucionaria* (Buenos Aires: Editorial Almena, 1979), 53–54, 56, 65, 68, 80, 83–85, 87–89, 92, 96–98, 110. Beaufre was chief of operations of the Free French General Staff during World War II, a veteran of both Vietnam and Algeria, commander of the French forces during the 1956 Suez crisis, and the French representative to NATO in Washington in the early 1960s.

15. Andre Beaufre, "Política, estrategia, y sus relaciones recíprocas," *Revista de la Escuela Nacional de Guerra* (September 1973), 31–38; Beaufre, "Bases de elaboración de la estrategia total de un país en vías de desarrollo," *Revista* (December 1973), 17–25; Beaufre, "La estrategia de las grandes potencias y las dinámica de los bloques," *Revista* (June 1974), 107–16); Beaufre, "Perspectivas estratégicas de los años 1970," *Revista* (September 1974), 95–106.

16. Patrice de Naurois, "Algunas aspectos de la estrategia y de la táctica aplicadas por el Viet-minh durante la campaña de Indochina," *Revista de la Escuela Superior de Guerra* (January–March 1958, cited in López, *Seguridad nacional*, 146–50.

17. Roger Trinquier, *La guerra moderna* (Buenos Aires: Editorial Rioplatense, n.d.), 22–24, 29–31, 33, 35–37, 41. Trinquier's biography is from Bernard Fall's introduction to *La guerra moderna*, 7–18.

18. Trinquier, *La guerra moderna*, 44–46, 50, 58, 65–73, 76–78, 84–87, 90.

19. Trinquier, *La guerra moderna*, 15, 38–39, 53, 59

20. Trinquier, *La guerra moderna*, 60–63.

21. Horacio E. Querol, "Acción comunista en el campo educacional," *Revista del Círculo Militar* (January–March 1962), 59–69; Major Julio Mendioróz, "Como se ve y como debe verse al comunismo," *Revista* (October–December 1962), 52–77; Sergeant Eulogio D. Carrizo, "El objectivo fundamental de la revolución mundial," *Revista* (April–June 1963), 122–45; Major Florencio Díaz Loza, "La guerra ideológica," *Revista* (July–September 1963), 80–87.

22. General Jean Nogués, article in the January–March 1962 edition of the *Revista*, quoted in López, *Seguridad nacional*, 153–55.

23. Brigadier General Túrolo is quoted in García, *La doctrina*, 69–72; General Saint-Jean in Veiga, *Las organizaciones*, 43.

24. Lieutenant Colonel Mario Horacio Orsolini, *La crisis del ejército* (Buenos Aires: Ediciones Arayú, 1964), 45–49, 52–53, 59.

TEN

The Inferno

As the military took power, General Luciano Benjamín Menéndez warned, "We are going to have to kill 50,000 people: 25,000 subversives, 20,000 sympathizers, and we will make 5,000 mistakes." According to some investigators, his prediction proved to be very accurate. After civilian rule was restored in 1983, a National Commission on Disappeared Persons (CONADEP) prepared a report that charged the former regime leaders with the permanent disappearance of an estimated 8,961 people, but the report added that in the absence of records or other documentation it was impossible to give a definite figure and the actual number might be much higher. Thus, estimates have ranged widely, from the rather conservative 6,000 by the Organization of American States Human Rights Commission to Amnesty International's 20,000. The São Paulo–based Commission for the Defense of Human Rights in the Southern Cone estimated the total at 7,500, two-thirds of which happened in the *proceso*'s first two years. General Ramón Camps, former police chief of Buenos Aires Province, admitted to "disappearing" 5,000 just by himself. Whatever the true number may be, Daniel Lutzky is right in saying that this was "the most terrible repression ever known in Argentina in its entire history."[1]

As to the relative innocence of the victims, the military, when pressed, might admit that perhaps 10 or 15 percent might have been innocent or only marginally connected to the subversives. Human rights groups, however, preferred to believe that a majority were completely innocent, that their only "crimes" had been to express progressive ideas or to join an occasional protest to demand social reforms. They accused the military of targeting students, shop stewards, psychiatrists, social workers, journalists, and professors (especially social scientists) because they represented modernity, rationality, social justice, secularism, and youthful idealism.

Some left-wing critics claimed that the *proceso*'s terror was intended to prevent the Argentine people from resisting a capitalist restructuring of the economy. Indeed, the military's crackdown on labor was aimed at more than cleaning out the Trotskyites and Maoists. Oscar Smith, the leader of the National Power & Light Union, originally supported the military coup because ERP and the Montoneros had assassinated so many trade union moderates. However, when the junta installed a new management at the Greater Buenos Aires Electrical Services (SEGBA) that announced payroll cuts and raised the work week from 32 to 42 hours, the union fought back with a slowdown strike and sabotage. After four months of disrupted electrical service in the Greater Buenos Aires metropolitan area, the military kidnapped Smith, and he was never seen again. The National Power & Light Union dropped its strike and accepted defeat. Even before that, the government intervened in the CGT, arrested its officers, and seized all its property and bank accounts. Labor leaders in factories that suffered frequent strikes were targeted by their employers, after which army or navy personnel would burst in to arrest the shop committees. On the day after the coup, the union stewards at the Ford automobile plant in Buenos Aires Province were wrangling with the director of labor relations. "Give my regards to my friend Camps," he told them, sarcastically. Who was he? they asked. "You'll find out. Don't worry, you'll find out," was the answer. Three days later eight heavily armed men came to the factory and took them all to Buenos Aires Province police headquarters. A few survived, but most of them didn't.[2]

As with labor, so with youth. Videla's education minister, Ricardo Pedro Bruera, made it clear that he intended to maintain order in the schools and colleges and would punish any student or teacher who opposed him. Teachers with leftist sympathies were dismissed; students had to carry identification cards and wear their uniforms properly. Those who failed to conform to the norms of conduct could be suspended or expelled without any right of appeal. Students or teachers who were expelled from the schools had their names turned over to the police. Dr. Alberto Remus Tetu, rector of the University of the South, in Bahía Blanca, provided the police with the names of all the professors and student activists who were "agitators." Scores of his enemies were arrested immediately after the coup, and others hurried into exile. The same happened in Córdoba, where professors denounced student activists to the Federal Police. Those students, and the faculty who encouraged them, were rounded up and sent to "La Perla," a secret detention camp. In La Plata, where university and high schools had been scenes of some of the worst student disruptions, the rector, deans, principals, teachers, and preceptors (many of whom were from the right-wing Concentración Nacional Universitaria), gladly pointed out the chief agitators to the police. Taken to clandestine torture centers, they soon helped to uproot the guerrillas' vaunted cell system by naming names and even going in police cars to identify guerrilla hideouts and people involved in the underground.[3]

Because the police and military intelligence had been drawing up lists for many years of left-wing labor and student activists, as well as left-wing priests, journalists, lawyers, and professors, many Argentines were convinced that mistakes were almost never made. Hernán López Echagüe interviewed Juan Manuel Avellaneda, a distinguished *tucumaño* whose son was arrested after the coup. Soldiers came to the house and took him away for questioning, but he returned five hours later, unharmed. Someone had accused him of being a guerrilla as a "joke." Dr. Avellaneda told López Echagüe: "Since I knew about the incident, I told myself: if my son is innocent, he'll be back. And in fact he did return in five hours. I didn't even try to use my influence." "Suppose he hadn't come back?" López Echagüe asked. Avellaneda was nonplussed: "You mean, if he had been guilty?" "No," López Echagüe repeated, "I mean, what if he hadn't come back?" "You're saying, if he was guilty?" Avellaneda insisted. "If he had been guilty?" Obviously, it was a dialogue of the deaf.[4]

Nevertheless, innocent people were "sucked up" (*chupado*) in those dragnets. Antonio Horacio Miño Retamozo was arrested because someone undergoing torture had screamed out his name, along with many others, in a delirium of pain. He had known Mirta Insfrán back in 1975, as a casual acquaintance and classmate in a university course on forestry technology, but he had no connection at all to the Montoneros. Still, her mention of him was enough to get him "sucked up." Brought at first to a police station, his captors demanded to know his Montonero alias and his rank. He had no idea of what they meant, so he couldn't answer; whereupon they beat him up and passed him on to the Federal Police. They, in turn, tortured him unmercifully with electric shocks, but no matter what they did to him, he never gave them any information. Frustrated, the Federal Police then turned him over to the army, where his tortures were even more gruesome. Eventually his captors decided Miño Retamozo was innocent after all and released him.[5]

Family members were another kind of innocent often "sucked up" in the repressive apparatus. They might be held as hostages, and even tortured in front of their relatives in order to make the latter talk. Martha García de Candeloro was kidnapped with her husband, Jorge, in June 1977 and taken to an air force base in Mar del Plata, where they were tortured. Ordinarily they would torture him first, then her; but one day they reversed the process.

In the middle of my interrogation they brought my husband in and told him that if he didn't talk they would kill me. They began applying the *picana* (electric prod) to me so he would hear my screams. He shouted out to me: 'Darling, I love you. I never thought they would do this to you.' His words infuriated them and they began torturing him. . . . Me, they threw into a cell. They were enraged at him. His interrogation was interminable. Suddenly I heard an earsplitting scream—I'll never forget it. It was his last cry, and then came silence.

She was later released, but her husband, according to the official report, was "killed while trying to escape."[6]

KIDNAPPING

The "sucking up" process involved *grupos de tarea* ("task forces") of any-where from 6 to 20 heavily armed men recruited from several sources. The navy's first groups were formed at the Naval Mechanics School (ESMA) in October 1975, after ERP had assassinated several officers in retaliation for the Trelew airport massacre (see chapter 5). Composed of officers, NCO, and retired navy and police personnel, they were coordinated through ESMA's chief officer, Capt. Rubén Chamorro, who reported directly to Admiral Massera. In the army, the dirty work was turned over to a special unit known as Battalion 601, head-quartered at the Domingo Viejobueno Arsenal in Monte Chingolo. Its com-manding officer, Colonel Alberto Valín, and his immediate subordinates were soldiers, but the task forces were usually formed by men on loan from SIDE or the Federal Police, both of which were headed by army officers. They, in turn, often used former AAA terrorists, as well as known criminals with convictions for murder, smuggling, and bank robbery who, in return for leniency, would collaborate with the security forces. The army officers, while willing to order "Dirty War" tactics, were unwilling to soil their own hands. As with the navy, these task forces were divided into those who kidnapped, those who tortured, and those who collated information and kept records. Sometimes they switched duties, but only infrequently.[7]

A kidnapping usually started by cutting off the street and sometimes the electricity in the immediate neighborhood. The nearest police station was usually informed ahead of time so that the police would not respond to any calls to interfere. If a policeman happened to be in the vicinity when a kidnapping occurred, he would quickly leave after a talk with the task force leader. So would bystanders: the kidnappers, wearing masks and carrying walkie-talkies, were well-armed and tough. Kidnappings made on the street or at a workplace lasted only a matter of minutes; the victim was quickly overpowered, hand-cuffed, dragged to a waiting car, and forced inside, blindfolded or hooded. Kid-nappings of people at their homes usually took place at night. The task force would surround the building and force its way into the victim's apartment. Once inside, the kidnappers handcuffed or tied anyone they found: the victim, his family, friends, or neighbors. Then they turned the place upside down, looking for incriminating evidence. Anything of value—money, jewelry, appliances, art objects, rare books, wine, liquor—was hauled away as booty and never returned. If the victim wasn't at home, they shoved his family and friends into back rooms and waited for him to return. If he didn't show up, his family might be taken into custody as hostages. If he did show up with a friend, the friend would be seized as well, on the principle of guilt by association.[8]

Task forces sometimes encountered bullets from well-armed guerrillas, so they were inclined to shoot first, before assessing the situation. Juan Gasparini, a former Montonero, saw his wife and a neighbor killed when a task force burst through the door without warning, firing indiscriminately. His two children were saved by hiding under a bed. One of the most controversial and well-publicized cases of this sort was that of 17-year-old Dagmar Hagelin. She had gone to the home of an older friend, Norma Susana Burgos, but she fled when two men with pistols appeared from the side and a third stranger flung open the door. Neighbors, hearing a shot, went out into the street and witnessed a blond, athletic-looking man stopping a taxi and getting inside with a wounded girl. Later, Dagmar's father traced her to ESMA and learned that the man who shot her was Captain Alfredo Astiz, but he was never to find his daughter. However, because Hagelin was of Swedish descent, the Swedish government became involved in the matter, and the case soon became an international affair. The Swedish authorities saw Dagmar as the innocent victim of a trigger-happy naval officer, but the Argentine authorities showed that Norma Burgos was the wife of Carlos Caride, one of the original Montoneros. She had been arrested the evening before as a member of the Montoneros, and the navy officers were waiting to see who contacted her. Apparently Dagmar was mistaken for another Montonera, María Antonia Berger. The Argentine authorities insisted that Dagmar had been living with Berger, posing as her cousin "Gladys," at the time of the shooting. Moreover, she had been introduced to both Burgos and Berger by her mother's boyfriend, Edgardo Waisman, a Montonero who once had been Carlos Caride's defense lawyer.[9]

Some arrests and "disappearances" were acts of revenge. Mario Abel Amaya, the human rights activist and UCR deputy from Chubut, was kidnapped by an army task force in August 1976, along with the UCR's senator, Hipólito Solari Yrigoyen. Amaya was suspected of helping captured guerrillas to escape from Rawson Prison in August 1972, while Solari Yrigoyen had been one of the loudest voices in demanding that Cámpora grant amnesty to the political prisoners at Villa Devoto. Both were taken to an army base in Bahía Blanca and there savagely beaten—in Amaya's case, so badly that he died. Responding to an OAS investigation, the Argentine government concocted a fantastic tale about the two men having been kidnapped by a gang of common criminals, but Solari Yrigoyen survived to tell a different story.[10]

TORTURE

Guilty or innocent, those who were "sucked up" in the dragnets were dumped into *pozos*, or secret detention centers, where they were subjected to torture. CONADEP estimated that there were approximately 340 of these centers throughout the country, each one under the supervision of a high-level military or police officer. Some of them were located on military bases, some were behind the façades of respectable mansions, and still others were in converted farmhouses or abandoned office buildings. Whatever their setup, what went on inside was depressingly similar. Prisoners arrived handcuffed and hooded, and they were kept that way. Often they had been beaten by their kidnappers on the way there. On being led inside, the prisoners were stripped of all their belongings and then conducted to a small room, where each would be asked about his activities and associations. If the prisoner was innocent—and lucky—the interrogator might decide to release him; but if the interrogator suspected any connections to the guerrillas, he would demand the victim's code name, rank in the underground organization, activities participated in, and the names of other known active subversives.[11]

One was lucky to escape torture. In a few cases, where doubt still prevailed, a prisoner might be held for several hours or days in a holding pen with others awaiting interrogation, while the screams of those being tortured rose above the blaring music. The guards were often young toughs between 15 and 20, who bragged about their karate skills and were often drunk and violent with the prisoners. Food was adequate (usually stew), and medical attention was regular, if perfunctory. Thirst was always a problem, bathing was infrequent, and prisoners had to wait long intervals before being allowed to use the bathroom, and then they were always accompanied by one of the guards. Those who were finally released unharmed were cleaned up, given clothes that made them presentable, and warned to speak to no one about their experience.[12]

The less fortunate were taken to "operating rooms" for torture. Methods ranged from simple beatings to more complex torments with electric prods. Beatings could be applied with the fists, rubber truncheons, boots, wooden clubs, or even metal bars. Burning with cigarettes and the insertion of sharp instruments under fingernails and toenails were other crude methods. Another common torture was to hang prisoners upside down from a bar and lower them into a vat of water, keeping them there almost to the point of drowning. That was called "the submarine." Alternatively, prisoners could be lowered into feces. There was also the "dry submarine," in which a victim's head was covered with a plastic bag until suffocation occurred. Female prisoners were almost certain to be raped at some point in their incarceration, usually frequently. Although it was much less common, men were sometimes raped, too. Psychological torture was common. There were mock executions, and sometimes prisoners were forced to watch real executions. Sometimes the victims would see their spouses or children brought in and threatened with rape and torture unless they talked.[13]

The most common torture was the application of the electric prod (*picana eléctrica*) to the most sensitive parts of the body. Usually the prisoner was tied to a metal bed frame (the *parrilla*, or "grill") and wetted so as to facilitate the passage of electricity all over the body. A doctor was present to periodically examine victims and determine how much they could take. As the electric current passed through the body, the metal frame became burning hot. The *picana* was applied all over the body—to the genitals, the anus, the nipples, and, perhaps worst of all, the teeth. "It felt as if lightning was blowing your head apart!" Miño Retamozo recalled. In his case, too, he was made to swallow a narrow string of beads, despite retching and vomiting, that turned out to be electrodes. When activated by the *picana* they "seemed like a thousand crystals were shattering and splintering inside of you" and left the victim with convulsions. Those who survived such torture were left in a state of serious physical and psychological breakdown, haunted by pereptual fear.[14]

As for the torturers, General Vilas, the head of "Operation Independence," denied that his interrogators were either brutal or that they took any morbid pleasure in their work. He insisted that the prisoners were carefully classified and that the least important or dangerous were not tortured. Thus, the interrogator could be certain that the person he was working on was guilty of subversion. This was a widespread myth that the *proceso* leaders encouraged in order to create the moral ambiguity that would make a possibly hesitant soldier willing to obey an order that his conscience told him was wrong. Torture was justified on the grounds that, in the new kind of revolutionary war being fought, it was necessary to get information quickly from the prisoners so as to prevent the guerrillas from changing their hideouts.

As a rule, the upper echelons preferred not to know about torture, but there were exceptions. Certainly, General Camps had no qualms about admitting to the use of torture or of applying the *picana* himself. Admiral Massera was another such "hands-on" type. He accompanied his task forces on their search-and-destroy operations and, back at ESMA, would apply the *picana* to those who had been kidnapped. "We're all a solid unit," he would tell his men, "and I'm not going to ask you to do anything that I wouldn't do myself." Such leaders were rare, however. Ordinarily torture was left to lower-level people, often recruited from the police. Arbitrary arrest, brutality, and even torture had long been standard police procedures in Argentina and had been widely accepted, and even applauded, by every class in society as the most direct way to deal with lawbreakers.[15]

Under the *proceso* the volume of political prisoners became so great that young, lower-ranking soldiers were pressed into service as torturers. "They were given authority over the subversives and they made it a power over life and death," an officer told Andrew Graham-Yool. Barely out of adolescence, the soldiers were "conscription-age boys" who had signed on as regulars, young corporals. These were the ones who stripped the incoming victims, pushed them onto a metal table, and turned on the electricity. "It was enough to tell them, 'That is your enemy, a communist' and for them it was just like a football match. They had to beat the other side." This officer also applied torture, and to him too there was something of a contest going on: the soldier aimed at breaking the enemy as quickly as possible, whereas the guerrilla's strategy was to hold out. "You feel sorry to cause pain," the officer reflected, "but you work quickly. You don't look at the face, even when you put the prods in the mouth; you keep their eyes covered. The secret is not to look at their eyes. The other secret is do not draw blood; leave that for the sick bastards or the young brutes." "During the 'session,' the fact of a naked body entirely at one's mercy causes excitement, which leads to 'excesses'—too much electricity, too prolonged a dose, rape," the officer added. Afterwards, the effect is like a hangover. You feel sheer physical disgust. "But life goes on—you live or you break down."[16] Some men could not bring themselves to torture. Some refused outright; others tried but could not bear the psychological stress. Many came down with severe psychological and even physical problems. They secured transfers. However, soldiers and policemen who opposed "Dirty War" tactics had to be careful. Those who were too outspoken sometimes "disappeared," after being listed as "deserters."[17]

Psychologists who have studied cases of torture and sadism seem to concur that true, natural-born sadists are relatively rare. For someone to intentionally inflict pain or death on a stranger requires certain psychological changes that allow the perpetrator to "distance" himself from the victim and the deed. The young corporals described above had to perceive the victim as an enemy agent first, because in wartime some acts that ordinarily are crimes become acts of "patriotism." Moreover, when acting under orders within a military hierarchy, the onus can be transferred upwards; in any case, the obligation of "due obedience" to orders helps to make the act of torture or killing somewhat morally ambiguous (i.e., Who am I to question the wisdom of my superiors?). Finally, one is acting as a member of a corps in which loyalty to the group is a paramount value. One is continually reminded of comrades who have fallen to enemy violence and is urged to revenge them. Furthermore, the infliction of pain seems to get easier as the act is repeated. Even so, participating in torture took its toll on the perpetrators. It tended to separate them from their other military peers, so that their contacts were limited to other torturers, whose approval they needed. Doubts and repressed self-loathing often took the form of rage against new prisoners. Torturing became an act of self-affirmation. This rage was often directed against the torturers' families, too: wifebeating and childbeating were common among them. Some torturers developed symptoms of delirium and hysteria, which might include hallucinating about half-decomposed cadavers or engaging in melodramatic acts of mysticism. Other torturers displayed a desire to befriend their victims after tormenting them, to convince them of their errors.[18]

Many victims who survived the torture centers described their tormentors as sadistic psychopaths. At the air force's Mansión Seré, one of the torturers, nicknamed *El Raviol*, "tortured with fury, with rage, as only a psychopath could." He worked over Jorge Oscar Cardozo, a journalist who had criticized the regime's neoliberal economic policies. "But he was no anti-Peronist nor anything like that," Cardozo hastened to add, "just anti-everything. He beat and shocked because he liked to, sometimes without any interrogation." Another survivor of the Mansión Seré recalled *El Tano*: "He hit hard, *El Tano*. One day he started shouting 'sons of the devil, sons of the devil!' and picked up a whip and began to beat us. 'You're all Jews,' he said, 'I've got to kill you!' He was very devout and made us pray the Our Father." Another torturer, *Chiche*, suffered from acne so badly that his face was all pockmarked. "One day, to calm his nerves, he let go a machine gun blast at the windows," another victim reported. Federal Police Sergeant Héctor Julio Simón (alias *El Turco Julián*) was a furious anti-Semite who wore a swastika pendant on his chest. He preferred beating his victims with a stick or a chain to giving them electric shocks. One of his victims, Isabel Blanco de Chezzan, recalled that "he felt more affinity to someone he had personally tortured. He tortured me until I was left deformed by his blows. He threw me on the floor and kicked me. I got up and he beat me and threw me back on the floor. At some point I couldn't stand the pain and my weakness anymore and I began to weep. Then he came up to me and said 'How lucky you are to be able to cry. . . . Would you like a cigarette?' After that he would come to my cell and talk to me."[19]

Although the military justified torture on the grounds that it was necessary to get information quickly and prevent incipient terrorist acts, in most cases it did not elicit information of any immediate value. However, state terror did serve to break the morale of the guerrillas and their supporters. "Disappearances" had a horrifying effect that made people afraid to aid the guerrillas in any way, even indirectly. Furthermore, a prisoner who had been broken by torture could be used in a number of ways that would help to unearth the guerrillas: identifying other subversives, preparing lists of questions for other prisoners, and even participating in the interrogations. Naturally, the Montoneros exhorted their members to resist at all costs; one of the main purposes of political indoctrination was to give the members the strength to endure. According to *Evita Montonera*, of the estimated eight hundred to one thousand *compañeros* who had been arrested and tortured over the years, 95 percent had survived without revealing information of any use to the authorities. Of the remainder, 4 percent had given some information, but not much, and only 1 percent had really opened up— like the "traitorous" Roberto Quieto, who was sentenced to death in absentia by a Montonero tribunal. From those statistics *Evita Montonera* concluded that "torture is quite tolerable and . . . resistance is no problem if there is ideological certainty."[20]

The Montoneros's cocksureness was as off-base as their statistics. Juan Carlos Scarpati and his wife, Nilda Haydeé Orazi, two Montoneros held prisoner at ESMA, told Juan Gasparini, another *compañero* who survived in that prison, that approximately 95 percent of the captured guerrillas of all ranks spilled their guts of everything they knew. Not only that, but they helped to suggest strategies for uprooting the rest of the organization. Scarpati and his wife calculated that between 1976 and 1978 some six thousand guerrillas and activist supporters passed through clandestine prisons; they also estimated that only 5 percent were captured through police work, whereas the vast majority were arrested as a result of prisoners cruising the streets with their captors, pointing out subversives and hideouts. Collaboration was the real cause for the total collapse of the guerrilla movements after the coup. Perhaps before the coup a captured guerrilla might hold out under torture, knowing that within a few days a human rights lawyer would bring a habeas corpus petition before a judge and get him transferred to a regular jail. Moreover, he could be morally sustained in the knowledge that the *compañeros* on the outside were keeping up the good fight and were counting on him to hold out for at least 48 hours until they could adjust their operations. The coup, and the tidal wave of repression that followed, changed all that. Now there was no limit to the torture, no judge to intervene, no press to publicize the case. One's *compañeros* were cowering with terror; throughout the guerrilla movement there was a sense of defeat, and that lowered the will to resist.[21]

Indeed, some of the prisoners became avid collaborators. Federico Ramón Ibañez was kidnapped by an ESMA task force in December 1976. ESMA was looking for his wife as well, so he struck a bargain with his kidnappers: in return for sparing her, he would divulge the whereabouts of another Montonero officer, Marcelo Kurlat. ESMA even allowed him to telephone his wife to warn her to leave the house without letting Kurlat, who was hiding there, know. Marines and soldiers then attacked the building, and Kurlat was killed when his ammunition ran out. The Montoneros considered his death a great loss, and a few days later they executed Ibañez's wife for failing to warn him of the impending attack. Ibañez himself remained at ESMA, actively helping the repression, and became something of a religious mystic.[22]

This was not an isolated case. Another notable example was Marta (*La Negra*) Bazán, a Montonera who was captured with her husband. He died at ESMA, but she collaborated and even became the mistress of Admiral Rubén Chamorro. She participated in antiguerrilla operations under the code name of "Sargenta Coca." Later, as the military's rule was nearing its end, she fled abroad with Chamorro and married him. There were other "love matches" at ESMA as well: Lieutenant Jorge Radice's marriage with Anita Dvatman, Lieutenant Antonio Pernía's long-standing affair with Lucy Changazzo, whose husband he had killed under torture. These were not simple matters of sexual exploitation (although that may have been involved, too): there was a kind of classificatory system among some military officers that allowed for the redemption of some prisoners. "Hard cases," hostile prisoners, and members of Marxist organizations like ERP that were considered hopelessly "antinational" were marked for death. Montoneros, on the other hand, were viewed as more nationalistic and therefore capable of salvation. Those who showed promise in that direction might be transferred to a legal jail, which was an intermediate step toward eventual release, or they might be freed directly, usually in the care of their family or close relatives. Often, in the latter cases, there would be follow-up visits by military officers or policemen to make certain that the former prisoner was "behaving."[23] Ana María Cossio, arrested in her apartment in Tucumán in 1977, received the following letter, accompanied by her wristwatch, from one of her torturers—a soldier nicknamed "Pepe," whose face she never saw:

How are you behaving, Ana María? I hope your behavior is very good and leaves no doubt about your change. Think back, as I too remember the night I took you from your apartment, and I assure you that they were ugly moments, although I am completely convinced of the action I engaged in. As you must realize, I belong to this unit and I believe that we are doing something good for our homeland, because there are times when our Army behaves in a very caring way. We are just toward everyone and all our actions are perfectly analyzed. We never judge anyone without having plenty evidence of his guilt. . . . In closing, let me say that you're a girl that I like a lot and that it's a shame that I cannot make myself known to you. I see you occasionally and feel a "pang" when you pass by. Good luck in all that you undertake to do. May your behavior always be for the good of our country and not influenced by ugly foreign ideas that do not suit you. Take care of your parents and don't give them any more unnecessary pain.[24]

DEATH

Besides direct release or removal to the legal judicial process, there was only one other way out of the military's underground penal system: to be "sent up" or "transferred"—that is, killed. Most prisoners were "transferred" when the interrogators became convinced that they had no more information to give, although some were sent to other detention centers for questioning first. There were to be no more amnesties like Cámpora's in the future. Killing the prisoners would protect those who ordered, or actually did, the dirty work; and it aimed to avoid international pressure, which surely would be aroused if tortured prisoners were released to tell their stories to the press.

Prisoners died in various ways. The simplest was to put a group of them before a firing squad and dump their bodies into an unmarked mass grave. The victims would be listed as having been "shot while trying to escape." As time went on and the volume of prisoners marked for death rose, the military became more inventive at disposing of the bodies. In the months immediately following the coup, there were daily reports in the newspapers of clashes between the security forces and the "subversives" in various parts of the country, replete with casualty figures: so many guerrillas killed, so many policemen or soldiers. Gradually, however, a suspicious trend set in. Ever larger numbers of dead guerrillas resulted from these clashes, whereas government casualties were nil. In reality, as CONADEP later discovered, there had been no fighting: the dead guerrillas were prisoners who had been killed beforehand and simply strewn around.[25]

The most sinister method for prisoner disposal, however, was to drop them from airplanes over the South Atlantic Ocean. The hooded, shackled prisoners were called out by their case numbers, formed into a single file, and taken to ESMA's basement, where a nurse gave them an injection that knocked them out. Still alive, they were then hauled into trucks, driven out to a military airport, and dumped into transport planes. Once aboard, the sedated prisoners were stripped as the planes flew south, out to sea. Far out of sight of land, the prisoners were then thrown out. In 1995 a former naval commander, Adolfo Francisco Scilingo, admitted that he took part in two of those "death flights" and described the procedure. Scilingo confessed to throwing about 30 people into the South Atlantic, and estimated that ESMA killed between 1,500 and 2,000 in this manner. "At first it didn't bother me that I was dumping these bodies into the ocean because as far as I was concerned they were war prisoners," Scilingo recalled. He did not get too close to the intended victims, who were sedated, anyway, and told himself that he was only following orders. While Scilingo was throwing the prisoners out of the plane, a sergeant who had not been informed of the mission's purpose began to express reservations about what was going on. "I reached over to try to comfort him, and I slipped and nearly fell through the door," Scilingo said. "That's when it first hit me exactly what we were doing. We were killing human beings. But still we continued. When we finished dumping the bodies, we closed the door to the plane. It was quiet and all that was left was the clothing which was taken back and thrown away." Back at ESMA, Scilingo's superiors told him the Catholic Church's hierarchy approved of these missions as a "Christian form of death"; indeed, when he went to his confessor, the priest told him that the killings were necessary "to separate the wheat from the chaff."[26]

Not all executions were carried out in cold blood; some were done in the greatest heat of passion. When General Arturo Amador Corbetta, a legalist and a "soft-liner," became head of the Federal Police in June 1976, he emphasized in his first speech at headquarters the need to respect law and ethics as the only way to win the citizenry's respect. On 2 July, Corbetta's moral standards collided with reality when the Montoneros set off a powerful bomb that destroyed the building's dining hall at about 1:20 P.M., when it was packed with both policemen and civilians, men and women. Eighteen people died immediately, and 66 were injured (the death toll eventually reached 50). A security guard who hurried to the scene described "women screaming, pieces of bodies strewn around . . . hard-faced apes whom I wouldn't want to tangle with under any circumstances . . . standing there weeping and swearing to get even."[27]

Immediately a group of top police officers stormed into Corbetta's office, demanding the summary execution of 18 political prisoners being held at headquarters as a reprisal. Corbetta refused, and the argument became so heated that he was forced to draw his pistol and point it at one of the more excited officers. Twenty minutes later, however, General Albano Harguindeguy, the interior minister, showed up and let it be known that if he were head of the Federal Police, he would carry out the executions with the penal code under one arm and the Code of Procedures under the other. Later that evening, five Federal Police prisoners were taken from their cells, in violation of Corbetta's orders, and shot at the base of the obelisk in downtown Buenos Aires, with their bodies left for the public to see as a warning. Corbetta reacted by suspending his two top aides and sending in his resignation to Harguindeguy. The next night he went to a wake for the dead policemen, whose number had by then risen to 27. Upon his entering, all the other mourners left, leaving him alone with the coffins. In the morning a great number of Federal Police signed a petition to Harguindeguy, threatening to resign unless Corbetta was removed. Harguindeguy fired Corbetta that same day, and the dismissal was immediately followed by the execution of another 30 prisoners, whose bodies were dropped off on the outskirts of a distant village.[28]

VICTORY

The Montoneros and ERP, drawing upon historical experience, had expected to go through a period of repression and resistance similar to what had happened after Perón fell in 1955. *Evita Montonera*, in its January 1976 issue, gave advice on how to ride out the bad times that were coming: dress and behave normally, keep one's documents in order, avoid large meetings, hide weapons and propaganda away from one's living quarters, and cultivate good relations around the neighborhood. Don't either overestimate or underestimate the enemy. The next issue assured the membership that the Montonero army was qualitatively and quantitively stronger than ever: its finances were in excellent order and it was well stocked with arms. Nevertheless, it was time to adopt a defensive strategy, until the enemy exhausted himself and dispersed his energies fighting many little ambushes. Bombings and the "indiscriminate" execution of soldiers and policemen would gradually sap the government's morale and show the public that the revolutionary war was still on. Then would come the counteroffensive. In the April/May issue, the Montoneros claimed to have killed between 83 and 87 policemen and soldiers since the coup, and two business executives were "executed." In every issue, *Evita Montonera* carried a column called "Crónica de la Resistencia" that listed all guerrilla and labor actions that had been carried out during the previous month. At the end of 1976 it claimed that the Montoneros carried out some four hundred operations resulting in the death of more than three hundred soldiers, policemen, businessmen, and security guards. Besides blowing up the dining room of the Federal Police headquarters, they set off spectacular explosions, costing many lives, at the officers' quarters in the Campo de Mayo, the movie theater of the Círculo Militar, the headquarters of the Buenos Aires provincial police, and the Defense Ministry. In September, guerrillas set off a car bomb that blew up a passing police bus returning from a soccer game in Rosario, killing 11 and wounding 20. Nevertheless, by mid-1977 *Evita Montonera* ceased publishing. Although the Montoneros claimed to have carried out more than six hundred "actions" in 1977, only five could be called "major," and only 35 people were killed.[29]

The Montoneros's fighting capacity was in rapid decline. By the end of 1976 they had lost 80 percent of their combatants, and the losses were especially felt at the top: Dardo Cabo, Norma Arrostito, Hugo Vaca Narvaja, Jr., Marcos Osatinsky, Carlos Caride, Rodolfo Walsh, "Paco" Urondo, and Ana María González, General Cesareo Cardozo's assassin. Even more demoralizing was the flight into exile of many Montonero chiefs. Firmenich left Argentina just after Christmas 1976 and was soon followed by Rodolfo Galimberti, Horacio Mendizábal, Roberto Perdía, and Fernando Vaca Narvaja. Their first stop was Havana, where they had already deposited some $50 million for safekeeping. From there they scattered—some to Europe, others to Mexico or Central America.[30]

ERP's organization fell apart even faster. An army task force discovered a central committee meeting on 28 March, killing 12 guerrillas, including ERP's chief of intelligence and Susana Pujals, head of the Mesa de Solidaridad, which linked ERP to human rights groups. The army also seized many documents containing information about the organization's networks. Before the week was out, the army uprooted about 100 of ERP's 120 cells in Córdoba, including the headquarters, killing the regional chief, Eduardo Castels, and capturing more than 300 combatants. Similar blows befell ERP in Mendoza, La Rioja, Rosario, Entre Ríos, and the industrial suburb of Zarate, where hundreds of Guevarist Youth were rounded up and "disappeared." In May, Haroldo Conti, a well-known journalist who was ERP's equivalent of Rodolfo Walsh, was captured by an ESMA task force and died under torture a few hours later. About the same time, ERP's chief of the general staff, José Manuel Carrizo, also was taken prisoner. Soon afterwards, ERP's underground factories and printing presses were discovered, as were its training schools. By mid-July the organization was in a shambles and the leadership badly depleted. Santucho and the remnants of his politburo—Domingo Menna, Benito Urteaga, and Mauro Gómez—were on the run, forced to change hiding places every night. Safe places were rare, because the military's roundup of left-wing labor leaders depleted their support network and other former sympathizers were so terrorized that their loyalty couldn't be taken for granted.

Reluctantly, Santucho decided to go to Cuba; but before leaving the country he arranged to meet with Mario Firmenich to form a common guerrilla front. While he and his wife waited in Domingo Menna's apartment in the Villa Martelli suburb of Buenos Aires, the army was already closing in. At about 2:30 P.M. Captain Juan Carlos Leonetti arrived at the building with a task force and forced the janitor to knock at the apartment. When Santucho's wife opened the door, Leonetti pushed her aside and barged in. At that moment Benito Urteaga emerged from a back room and shot Leonetti in the stomach. Santucho also opened fire, wounding some of the soldiers, but the latter had machine guns and the battle was soon over. Santucho and Urteaga were killed, while Santucho's wife and Menna's eight-month-pregnant wife were taken into custody—and "disappeared." The PRT-ERP was devastated by these losses. An attempt to reorganize and continue the fight under the leadership of Luis Mattini and Enrique Gorriarán Merlo failed to reverse their losses. More central committee members were arrested, and in May 1977 the Regional Committee for Buenos Aires, PRT-ERP's last remaining combat organization, was destroyed. Mattini and Gorriarán Merlo fled to Cuba.[31]

ERP had ceased to function after mid-1977, but the Montoneros struggled on until late 1979. During 1978 they tried to prevent Argentina's hosting of the World Cup soccer tournament with a series of bomb attacks and assassinations. They exploded bombs at the homes of General Reynaldo Bignone, Colonel Adolfo Pandolfi, and Rear Admiral Armando Lambruschini. In the latter incident, they killed three people, including the admiral's 15-year-old daughter. They also launched rocket attacks against the Superior War School, Army Intelligence headquarters, Army General Staff headquarters, the Naval Engineering School, the Casa Rosada, and several police stations. Though failing to stop the World Cup, in 1979 they bombed the home of Guillermo Walter Klein, the secretary of planning; attacked with bazookas the home of Treasury Secretary Juan Alemann; and ambushed and assassinated industrialist Francisco Soldati and his chauffeur in the heart of downtown Buenos Aires. In reprisal, the military hunted down and killed more than five hundred Montoneros, including Horacio Mendizábal, their commander. By the end of 1979, the Montoneros had ceased functioning in Argentina. Moreover, the dreadful toll taken on the faithful comrades back home had split the exile organization, leaving only a shell called the Movimiento Peronista Montonero. Firmenich dissolved their army in 1980.[32]

NOTES

1. James W. McGuire, "Political Parties and Democracy in Argentina," in Scott Mainwaring and Timothy Scully, eds., *Building Democratic Institutions* (Stanford: Stanford University Press, 1995), 220, for Gen. Menéndez's quote; Crawley, *A House Divided*, 433; Camarasa et al., *El juicio*, 42, for the Camps quote; Daniel Lutzky, "La izquierda de los 60 en los años 80," in Hilb and Lutzky, *La nueva izquierda Argentina*, 74. Comisión Nacional sobre la Desaparición de Personas (CONADEP), *Nunca Más: Informe de CONADEP* (Buenos Aires: EUDEBA, 1986), 479. Hodges, *Argentina*, 199, has one of the highest estimates, at 30,000; Gillespie, *Soldiers of Perón*, 250–51, puts the number at between 10,000 and 20,000.

2. Mario Baizan and Silvia Mercado, *Oscar Smith: el sindicalismo peronista ante sus limites* (Buenos Aires: Editorial Puntosur, 1987); Andersen, *Dossier Secreto*, 179–80.

3. Paoletti, *Como los nazis*, 213, 249–50; María Seoane and Héctor Ruiz Nuñez, *La noche de los lápices* (Buenos Aires: Editorial Planeta, 1992), 40, 73–75, 87–89, 115–16, 136, 146–47; Moyano, *Argentina's Lost Patrol*, 126, 160.

4. López Echagüe, *El enigma* 41–42.

5. CONADEP, *Nunca Más*, 35.

6. Paoletti, *Como los nazis*, 300–304.

7. Claudio Uriarte, *Almirante Cero: biografía no autorizada de Emilio Eduardo Massera* (Buenos Aires: Editorial Planeta, 1991), 25–26, 96, 111; Juvenal, *Buenos muchachos*, 10–13, 217, n. 6, 253, 315, 318; Graham-Yool, *State of Fear*, 160–63.

8. CONADEP, *Nunca Más*, 16–26.

9. Gasparini, *Montoneros*, 102; OAS, *Report*, 79–80; Ragnar Hagelin, *Mi hija Dagmar* (Buenos Aires: Editorial Sudamericana/Planeta, 1984); *Somos*, no. 437 (1 February 1985), 6–11. Dagmar's mother was living at the time with Edgardo Waisman, a Montonero who was Carlos Caride's lawyer.

10. OAS, *Report*, 59–62, 104–6, 124–29.

11. CONADEP, *Nunca Más*, 45, 63.

12. OAS, *Report*, 89, 91–95.

13. OAS, *Report*, 219–20; CONADEP, *Nunca Más*, 28–54, 479–80.

14. CONADEP, *Nunca Más*, 35–38; OAS, *Report*, 56.

15. Alejandro Garro, "Nine Years of Transition to Democracy in Argentina: Partial Failure or Qualified Success?" *Columbia Journal of Transnational Law*, vol. 31, no. 1 (1993), 24–25, 34–41.

16. Graham-Yool, *State of Fear*, 161–65.

17. Paoletti, *Como los nazis*, 261–62, 306, 313, n. 8, 383; Pablo Larrea, "Mittelbach: una visión particular," in Pablo Lacoste, ed., *Militares y política, 1983–1991* (Buenos Aires: Centro Editor de América Latina, 1993), 141.

18. Roy F. Baumeister, *Evil: Inside Human Violence and Cruelty* (W. H. Freeman & Co., 1997), 10–11, 40, 47, 85–86, 168, 174, 181, 186, 194–97, 232–37, 251–81, 285, 299; Ervin Staub, *The Roots of Evil: The Origins of Genocide and other Group Violence* (New York: Cambridge University Press, 1989), 13, 15, 17, 29; Uriarte, *Almirante Cero*, 135–38.

19. Paoletti, *Como los nazis*, 285, 288–89, 392.

20. "Juicio revolucionario a un delator," *Evita Montonera*, vol. 1, no. 7 (September 1975), 21; and "Juicio revolucionario a Roberto Quieto," *Evita Montonera*, vol. 2, no. 12 (February/March 1976), 13–14.

21. Gasparini, *Montoneros*, 147, 153.

22. Gasparini, *Montoneros*, 73n.

23. Uriarte, *Almirante Cero*, 118–20; Andersen, *Dossier Secreto*, 266.

24. López Echagüe, *El enigma* 198–99.

25. CONADEP, *Nunca Más*, 223–47. For a list of daily reports of clashes between guerrillas and the government's security forces, see Oscar Troncoso, *El Proceso*, vols. 1 and 2.

26. Horacio Verbitsky, *The Flight: Confessions of an Argentine Dirty Warrior* (New York: New Press, 1996).

27. Quoted in Kalev Pehme, *Argentina's Days of Rage: The Genesis of Argentine Terrorism* (New York: Argentine Independent Review, 1980), 59.

28. Paoletti, *Como los nazis*, 342–45, 366. The explosion was set off by José M. Salgado, a former police officer who joined the Montoneros. He was caught, tortured, and executed. See Andersen, *Dossier Secreto*, 256.

29. *Evita Montonera*, September 1975–April 1977; Gillespie, *Soldiers of Perón*, 236; Gasparini, *Montoneros*, 133–34. The Defense Ministry bombing was perpetrated by a Montonero employee who also worked for CONASE. The bomb went off at an evening conference attended by officers, civilians, and diplomatic representatives. It killed 14 people. See Pineiro, *Crónica*, 50–51.

30. Gasparini, *Montoneros*, 168; Gillespie, *Soldiers of Perón*, 238, 245–46, 251–53.

31. Mattini, *Hombres y mujeres*, 490–98, 511–13, 516–23; Seoane, *Todo o nada*, 298–308.

32. Gasparini, *Montoneros*, 129, 153, 159, 166, 173, 181, 190–91; Gillespie, *Soldiers of Perón*, 264–68; Pineiro, *Crónica*, 49–50, 56–61. Andersen, *Dossier Secreto*, 279–80, 285–86, claims that the armed forces themselves planted the bombs at the homes of Juan Alemann and Guillermo Walter Klein. Gasparini is certain, however, that Mendizábal planned and carried out those attacks.

ELEVEN

Power Struggles

Admiral Emilio Massera was a handsome, backslapping extrovert who had his eye fixed on the presidency. General Videla blocked him, however, by acting as both the president of the junta and the representative of the army. Videla intended to last the full six-year presidential term in order to oversee the process of economic reform, and he had the support of his generals. His austere manner and apparent sincerity made Argentines place their trust in him. Because Videla was the most popular man in the junta, Massera reluctantly accepted this arrangement for the time being. The army was by far the largest of the three armed services, and unity was required to win the war against subversion. However, when by late 1977 the war seemed won, Massera demanded that the presidency and the top army command be separated and a "fourth man" appointed to the junta. If Videla wanted to stay as head of the army, Massera would demand the presidency and pick a new navy chief. As president he could then call for elections and run as the official candidate.[1]

Massera might have sought allies among soft-liners like General Viola, the chief of the army's General Staff, because they, like him, wanted a quick return to civilian rule. However, they were suspicious of his character and hoped to turn over power to a moderate civilian, like Ricardo Balbín. Hard-line generals like Carlos Suárez Masón and Luciano Benjamín Menéndez also stood in Massera's way, with their plans for indefinite military rule, but he sided with them, hoping to deepen the army's internal divisions. He joined in their attacks on the current neoliberal economic policies, supporting the planning minister, General Ramón Genaro Díaz Bessone, over Videla's economics minister, José Martínez de Hoz. Díaz Bessone wanted to replace political parties and interest groups with corporatist councils and retain state control of industries that the military considered essential for national defense. When Videla made it clear that corporatist schemes had no place in Argentina's future, Díaz Bessone resigned, after a stormy cabinet session. Massera then tried to drive in his wedge, attacking Martínez de Hoz for failing to control inflation, protect national industry, or maintain the workers' purchasing power. The "hard-line" army corps commanders agreed, but they were not willing to split the army over Díaz Bessone's departure. However, they let Videla understand that he eventually would have to give up one of his two posts, and that they, not he, would fill the vacancy.[2]

Economic quarrels were soon overshadowed by a dispute with Chile over three islands in the Beagle Channel, one of the passages around the tip of the continent. International arbitration reached a decision favorable to Chile in February 1977, but Argentina rejected it, whereupon the two countries were on the verge of war. Fortunately, Argentina was hosting the World Cup soccer championship matches, scheduled for May and June, which would certainly be cancelled in the event of fighting. So instead, the military turned to constructing airports, television networks, and stadiums. Once the World Cup was over, the hard-liners seriously began gearing up for war, spending around $13 billion for armaments, purchased on short-term credit and at high interest rates, in the biggest military buildup in the country's history. Plans were laid for a Christmas Eve attack by land, sea, and air. Although Videla and Viola continued to press for negotiations, the hard-liners insisted that a successful military campaign against Chile would solidify their hold on power. Then, on the morning of 24 December, Pope John Paul II, at Videla's urging, offered the Vatican's offices to mediate the dispute. Videla quickly accepted the offer and ordered all military operations suspended. The warhawks were furious but wouldn't oppose the pope.[3]

Although the hard-liners had been "cheated" of their war, they were quite successful in blocking Martínez de Hoz's liberalizing reforms. Military-run industries were not subject to privatization, nor were state industries like oil, coal, steel, electricity, gas, telephone, telegraph, water, hydroelectric power, airlines, railroads, subways, ports, or the merchant fleet, which were said to have military significance. Social welfare programs could not be trimmed, and workers in state industries could not be laid off. Meanwhile, the military added other large private firms, like the Swiss-owned Companía Italo-Argentina de Electricidad, to the state sector, at a cost of $93 million. The military men and their circle of friends now heading state enterprises paid themselves big salaries and large bonuses, but Martínez de Hoz was not allowed to raise prices for public services, on the grounds that it would be inflationary.[4]

The military spent heavily on massive public works projects. The World Cup preparations alone cost $520 million. Treasury Secretary Juan Alemann warned that hosting the World Cup championships was a huge expense that was bound to be inflationary. In reply, the hard-liners set off a bomb at his house. Worse

still, General Omar Actis, chairman of the local World Cup arrangements committee, paid with his life for attempting to hold down the megalomaniacal spending schemes. Actis was gunned down by a band that left behind a shower of leaflets proclaiming itself to be "the Revolutionary Montonero Army." Only Videla and a few others showed up for his funeral; Admiral Carlos Alberto Lacoste, who succeeded him as committee head, was conspicuously absent. Rumor and circumstantial evidence pointed to Massera and his ESMA task forces as the authors of the assassination, but nothing was ever proven. Meanwhile, public expenditure as a portion of the GNP more than doubled. Argentina's money supply expanded from 5.2 to 15 million pesos from the end of 1977 to the end of 1978, then rose to 44.3 million during 1979, to 84 million during 1980, and finally reached 222 million by the end of 1981. In the meantime, the peso depreciated, but Martínez de Hoz refused to devalue it because it would add to the burden of paying back the $40 billion of foreign debt accumulated so far by the military regime. Thus began the era of "sweet money" (*plata dulce*), when foreign exchange could be bought at low cost, because the peso was greatly overvalued. Some Argentines went into a frenzy of buying foreign goods and taking expensive overseas vacations; others, clever at currency speculation, rode "the bicycle" (*bicicleta*), in which they obtained dollars with their overvalued pesos at the bank, exchanged them for many more pesos at their real value on the black market, and then went back to the bank to get more dollars at government-subsidized rates.[5]

Martínez de Hoz tried to tackle inflation by raising interest rates and opening the economy to foreign competition. Many weak companies quickly went bankrupt; others stayed afloat temporarily by heavy foreign borrowing. From the beginning of 1976 to the end of 1983, the private foreign debt rose from $3 billion to nearly $13 billion, while the public debt went from $4 billion to more than $33 billion.[6] By 1981 business failures were sharply on the rise, threatening the banks that had extended them credit. Argentina's fragile hothouse economy teetered on the edge of a dreadful collapse that would help to bring down the regime.

SOFT-LINE UNDER SIEGE

In the struggle for power, the hard-liners sought to cut off the junta's moderates from their civilian allies in the Radical Party. Human rights lawers for the UCR, like Mario Abel Amaya, Hipólito Solari Yrigoyen, and Sergio Karacachoff, made convenient targets. Massera took a special interest in Héctor Hidalgo Solá, the ambassador to Venezuela. Hidalgo Solá was urging exiled Radicals and Peronists to form an alliance that would force the military to restore civilian rule. He also had been observing Massera's frequent visits to Venezuela and Europe and had learned that he was meeting with both Montoneros and shady Italian businessmen who belonged to P-2, the masonic lodge discussed in chapter 5.[7]

Massera saw that the "Dirty War" was rapidly coming to an end and would be followed by civilian pressure to restore elections, so he was preparing for the transition. Financed partly through plundered funds and partly by P-2, he had bought two newspapers, *Convicción* and *Nueva Provincia*, and had rented offices for his future Party for Social Democracy in downtown Buenos Aires. These were staffed by his followers and by Montonero "slaves" on loan from the clandestine prison at ESMA. In return for their forced labor, the "slaves" were treated more leniently than other prisoners, were given better food, and were even allowed to visit their families, on the understanding that they continue rendering service to Massera. In some cases, part of their service was to facilitate contacts with their fellow Montoneros overseas, whom Massera hoped to entice into supporting his presidential ambitions.[8]

Having guessed at Massera's intentions, Hidalgo Solá moved quickly to frustrate them by convincing Venezuela's president, Carlos Andrés Pérez, to invite Videla there for a goodwill visit. If Pérez could persuade Videla to issue a public promise to call immediate elections, Massera would be caught unprepared. Unable to block the invitation in the junta, Massera now turned on Hidalgo Solá as a dangerous enemy. When the ambassador returned briefly to Argentina to attend his daughter's wedding, which was to be squeezed in before Videla's scheduled visit, an ESMA task force kidnapped him, and he was never seen again. His replacement as ambassador, appointed three days later at Massera's insistence, was Federico Bartfield, whose name later appeared on a P-2 membership list.[9]

Hard-liners kept up the pressure on the Radicals by arresting Ricardo Balbín and other leaders for criticizing the regime's economic program. While the Radicals gradually distanced themselves from the *proceso*, the hard-liners turned to another target: former President Lanusse, the quintessential symbol of military "liberalism" and a possible "fourth man" to whom Videla could turn over the presidency. He was known to favor a quick return to civilian rule. First they attacked his friends. An ESMA task force kidnapped Mónica Mignone, the daughter of Lanusse's former education minister, Emilio Mignone, on 14 May 1976. She had been doing Catholic charity work in one of Buenos Aires's slums and also holding consciousness-raising classes for the poor. On the same day, another task force picked up María Marta Vázquez Ocampo, the daughter of a diplomat and one of Mónica's coworkers, as well as her husband, Cesar Amadeo Lugones. A week and a half later, about a hundred marines swept through the Bajo Flores slum and arrested two Jesuits and a novice nun, Mónica Quintero, the daughter of a retired naval captain. All attempts by the fathers of these women to locate their daughters were frustrated. Then, on 7 June, Massera's men kidnapped Adriana Landaburu, a Peronist University Youth activist and the daughter of Lanusse's former air force secretary. Landaburu's father went to Videla, who promised an investigation, and then to Massera. The admiral was emphatic: "There are not, nor ever have been, prisoners held at ESMA." Yet

survivors later testified that Landaburu had been a prisoner there and was disposed of by being thrown into the sea.[10]

General Acdel Vilas, second in command of the Fifth Army Corps in Bahía Blanca, launched the next attack by ordering 17 professors arrested in a campaign to "cleanse" the University of the South. One of the accused, Gustavo Malek, who had served as Lanusse's education minister, was out of the country at a UNESCO conference. Lanusse promptly published an open letter defending Malek and questioning whether Vilas had any proof to back up his charges. Two days later Lanusse was arrested and sentenced by a military court to five days of confinement at the Army Engineering School for insulting a commanding officer. Meanwhile, a court in Bahía Blanca dismissed the charges against Malek, after which General Viola, as army chief of staff, put Vilas on the "disposable" list, along with two other hard-line generals. Vilas declared himself to be in revolt, and he even accepted refuge from Massera at the Puerto Belgrano Naval Base, but the army would not allow naval interference in its affairs. Vilas was thus forced to accept his removal from active duty.

Nevertheless, the attacks on Lanusse did not stop. At the beginning of April 1977, his former press secretary, Edgardo Sajón, disappeared. He had been working as production manager for *La Opinión*, a prestigious Buenos Aires daily run by Jacobo Timerman, another friend of Lanusse's. Lanusse went to Videla to demand his help in getting Sajón freed, but he found the president nervous and indecisive. Videla already knew enough to suspect that something big was about to burst, and he blurted out to Lanusse that Suárez Masón, Saint-Jean, and Camps were behind it. Almost immediately, however, he denied any certain knowledge and refused to call First Army Corps headquarters or take any other decisive action. A disgusted Lanusse told Timerman: "What can you do with an army in which the officers ride around in stolen cars and their wives serve tea from sets seized during raids?" Timerman, meanwhile, had been publishing a daily page in his paper devoted entirely to demanding the whereabouts of Sajón. Within a few days he was putting out a second page, this time about his assistant editor, Enrique Jara, who also had "disappeared." Then, a few days after that, on 22 April, Timerman himself was arrested. Lanusse's turn came on 4 May, when he was arrested and charged with corruption involving the building of the Aluar aluminum plant.

A month later Lanusse was out of prison, having been found innocent by an appeals court, but Sajón, Jara, and Timerman were only beginning their suffering. Sajón would not survive it. According to a police officer who witnessed his end, he died under torture on 27 September 1978. Strapped to a billiard table soaked with water at the casino of the Buenos Aires Police School, he was given electric shocks until he died.[11] Nor was Lanusse's suffering finished, either. The next victim in his circle would be his sister-in-law, Elena Holmberg. She, like Ambassador Hidalgo Solá, made the mistake of learning too much about Admiral Massera.

THE HOLMBERG AFFAIR

Elena Holmberg was an educated, strong-minded career woman from the *porteño* upper class who worked at the Paris embassy as First Secretary. Her principal job was to run a public relations department called the Centro Piloto, which had been set up to counter the growing hostility in the European press toward Argentina because of its human rights violations. The usual source of this bad publicity was the Argentine exiles, so Holmberg expanded her duties to include gathering information on them. Ambassador Tomás de Anchorena found the reports both informative and fascinating because they described strange meetings between the exiles and Argentine naval officers. What neither Anchorena nor Holmberg realized at first, however, was that Massera was taking steps toward enlisting the Montoneros and other Peronist exiles in his forthcoming presidential bid. Holmberg decided to dig deeper, and to do so she enlisted the support of Silvia Agulla, whose brother Horacio edited a weekly Argentine magazine called *Confirmado*. Agulla had been living in Paris for nearly 25 years and had good contacts with the French press.[12]

The Foreign Ministry, headed by Massera's designee, Admiral Oscar Montes, was much less pleased with Holmberg's work. In January 1978 two naval officers arrived at the embassy and began to interfere in her operations. Ambassador Anchorena, who had started the Centro Piloto as his own idea, defended her, which led to a series of battles with Massera himself. Finally, Videla intervened and forbade Admiral Montes to remove Holmberg. Meanwhile, in April 1978 Massera flew to Europe and soon established a network of contacts between his naval representatives and the Peronist exiles. He even managed, by working through Licio Gelli, to meet Mario Firmenich at Gelli's estate. Follow-up meetings were held at the Hotel Intercontinental in Paris. No one knows, except the principal parties, exactly what transpired between Massera and Firmenich at those meetings, but Elena Holmberg was following Massera's moves with interest and disgust. At a reception held at the Paris Embassy on the eve of Massera's departure, she displayed her anger very undiplomatically. Approaching Massera's wife, who was wearing a large diamond pendant, she took the jewel between her fingers and asked loudly if it was a gift from Firmenich. Lily Massera didn't know what to answer, so Holmberg repeated the question twice, generating nervous laughter all around. Not long afterwards, according to Silvia Agulla's testimony at the trial, she and Elena were nearly killed in a mysterious accident as they were driving to the south of France. The car went out of control, but fortunately they came to a safe stop on the outskirts of a small town. The mechanic who inspected the car showed them that the accelerator cable had been cut.

Then, on the night of 28 August, Massera sent another warning from Buenos Aires. Horacio Agulla was shot to death while trying to park his car in front of a friend's house on Posadas Street at around 9:30 P.M. As a taxi pulled up alongside him, a man jumped out of the back and approached. Apparently re-

alizing the danger, Agulla tried to back his car out but slammed into the vehicle behind. The gunman pumped five bullets into him before he could do anything more. A witness got the "taxi's" license plate number, which turned out to belong to a car owned by the navy. According to Silvia Agulla, her brother had been completely informed by Elena Holmberg about what was going on in Paris, even down to the name of the naval attaché who drove Firmenich to the meeting with Massera at the Hotel Intercontinental. He knew too much.

Meanwhile, there had been more clashes with naval officers at the Centro Piloto, which resulted in Holmberg's gradually being dislodged. Admiral Montes again demanded that she return to Argentina. Holmberg apparently suspected a plot to murder her and therefore waited until Massera had retired from the junta, in August, before making her plans to go back. In early December, Gregorio Dupont, a former Foreign Ministry official, met with Holmberg at a Buenos Aires *confitería* in the fashionable Recoleta district. Dupont was an old friend who shared her distaste for Massera, having been dismissed from the diplomatic service for having made disparaging remarks about the admiral. At that meeting she told Dupont that she could prove not only that Massera met with Firmenich but also that he had given the Montonero leader over a million dollars. On 20 December, shortly before she was to meet with a group of reporters from *Paris Match*, whom she herself had invited to Argentina, she was kidnapped in a parking garage by two naval officers. Despite her cries for help, they threw her into a car and drove off.

Upon learning of her kidnapping, Elena's four brothers and General Lanusse went directly to Interior Minister Albano Harguindeguy. He immediately saw the connection between her activities at the Centro Piloto and her disappearance: "It's the work of that son of a whore, Massera," he said. The Federal Police and Army Intelligence's infamous Battalion 601 had already been investigating Hidalgo Solá's disappearance and were now convinced that both it and Elena Holmberg's kidnapping were the navy's doing. "You think that our war is with Chile?" Harguindeguy asked Lanusse and the Holmbergs. "No, the war is with them—with [Rubén] Chamorro and ESMA." The next step was to see President Videla, but Videla would do no more than send a radiogram to all army units saying that Holmberg's kidnapping should be treated as seriously as if a high-ranking army officer had been seized. It was an exercise in futility. She was not at an army base, and there was no way to free her from ESMA short of sending a large contingent of soldiers there to invade the place. Videla was not willing to issue that order, and now that he was no longer the army's commander in chief (having been forced to give up that post at the end of July), he was not sure that he would be obeyed by the hard-line troop commanders, anyway. In addition the Argentine armed forces were scheduled to go to war with Chile in four days. For Lanusse, it was another instance of Videla's weak will.

A few days later Elena Holmberg's badly decomposed body was found floating in the Río Lujan a few kilometers north of Buenos Aires. It was turned over to her family at the Benavídez Cemetery on 11 January 1979, but only after a grotesque twist in the case. Enrique and Ezequiel Holmberg, representing the family, went with Lanusse. They were met by the army officer who was in charge of the body and by Judge Enrique Marquardt, who had ordered Lanusse jailed a short time before in connection with the Aluar case. Judge Marquardt was said to be "investigating" the murder. As they were signing the papers, Enrique Holmberg, who was a doctor, asked to see the corpse. The army officer protested, but Lanusse shouted him down. A quick examination of the body revealed that it was a man! Lanusse, meanwhile, had noticed a new grave nearby and demanded that it be reopened. Inside the disinterred coffin they found a woman's skeleton bearing the remains of a dress that the Holmberg's recognized as Elena's. A subsequent X-ray of the skeleton also coincided with X-rays in the medical archives of the Foreign Ministry. Apparently, her corpse had been treated with acid.

THE WHIZ KID

The horrors that befell Edgardo Sajón, Enrique Jara, and Jacobo Timerman were linked to a dead banker, David Graiver. While Massera and the navy were weaving the web that entangled Elena Holmberg, Horacio Agulla, and Héctor Hidalgo Solá, Generals Carlos Suárez Masón, Ibérico Saint-Jean, and Ramón Camps inadvertently came upon information so bizarre that it tied together the seemingly respectable international banking community, the most brilliant names in Argentine journalism, and former President Lanusse with the guerrilla underworld and a missing fortune amounting to millions of dollars.

Graiver's family were Jewish immigrants from Poland who settled as merchants in the city of La Plata. They bought real estate, lent out money on mortgages, and made other kinds of loans. David was an especially precocious capitalist, having made enough money through lending at black market rates to marry into a prosperous Jewish family by the time he was 26. Two years later, with the help of his wife's family and a loan from the Banco Tornquist, he acquired a small bank, the Banco Comercial de La Plata. During the next few years he bought a second bank, the Banco de Hurlingham, and started a construction company called Fundar. He also had acquired a powerful friend in José Ber Gelbard, another offspring of Polish-Jewish immigrants and head of the CGE, whose influence was on the rise in official circles as the Lanusse government sought to make peace with the more conservative elements in the Peronist movement. Graiver joined the CGE and used his influence to get other La Plata businessmen to do the same. In return, Gelbard saw to it that the Banco Comercial de La Plata prospered. It soon rose from a small bank to one of the most important in Buenos Aires Province. Gelbard also introduced Graiver to General Lanusse, who had already become a business partner in the questionable deal to build the state-operated aluminum plant, Aluar. Through Gelbard, Graiver became undersecretary of Social Welfare, in charge of housing.[13]

When the Peronists came to power and Gelbard was named economics minister, the Banco Comercial was specially favored by the Central Bank for placing its deposits and soon became the area's leading lending institution. Graiver was aiming even higher, however. Using Gelbard as a reference to New York banking circles, in 1973 he acquired the Century National Bank. In the following year he bought the Banque pour l'Amerique du Sud in Brussels and in 1975 he took over the Swiss-Israel Bank in Tel Aviv. Also in 1975, Graiver took initial steps to acquire the American Bank and Trust Company in New York.[14]

By May 1975, Graiver had established the headquarters of his $200 million empire at 998 Fifth Avenue, New York. In addition to the banks he had already acquired, he was negotiating with José Klein, a Chilean financier, to take over the Continental Trade Bank in Geneva. He also owned several Argentine businesses: a newsprint plant, a television station, apartment complexes, an insurance company, a downtown shopping arcade, construction companies, factories, import and export firms, publishing houses, and a chain of newspapers that included the very influential *La Opinión*, owned in partnership with Jacobo Timerman. Graiver also owned controlling interest in Editorial Gustavo, the modern printing plant that turned out *La Opinión*, whose board members included Timerman, Sajón, and Marcos Lanusse, son of the ex-president who also sat on the board of another of Graiver's companies, Electro Erosión, which made disposable syringes. The Lanusse connection didn't stop there. The general's daughter, Virginia, served as Graiver's private secretary at his downtown Buenos Aires branch of the Banco Comercial, and her husband, a former official in the Federal Police, headed Graiver's bodyguard in the city. He needed one: early in 1975 his brother-in-law, Osvaldo Papaleo, who was Isabel Perón's press secretary, told him that he had seen his name on an AAA hit list. After Gelbard's fall from power, Graiver was out of favor at the Casa Rosada, as indicated by Isabel's moving some $5.3 million out of the Banco Comercial. He decided to move to New York. To manage his Argentine properties, he set up a holding company, Empresas Graiver Asociadas (EGASA), and placed it in charge of his lawyer, Jorge Rubenstein. Another holding company, Santa Fe Management, housed in New York, oversaw his foreign banks.[15]

Graiver's meteoric rise to international prominence was partly due to Gelbard's help, but he also had another backer: the Montoneros. No one is sure when Graiver first made his deal with the guerrillas to launder their money. It may have been as early as August 1972, when FAL kidnapped his brother, Isidoro, for ransom. Evading the police, David dealt with the guerrillas directly and secured his brother's release. Some people think that it was then that he offered to use his bank as a repository for ransom money, acting through decoys, and to launder it out of the country. Some suggest that Gelbard, his mentor, was already doing a similar service for FAR. Other stories link Graiver to the Montoneros through his mistress (later his second wife), Lidia Papaleo. Lidia's brother, Osvaldo, not only became Isabel Peron's press secretary but also was married to a relative of Carlos Maguid, who was famous for his part in the Aramburu assassination. It was possibly through that connection that Graiver and the Montoneros got together. On the other hand, Juan Gasparini asserts that the real contact with the Montoneros came through Enrique Walker, Lidia Papaleo's ex-husband, who wrote for the Montoneros's *El Descamisado*. The agreement between the Montoneros and Graiver had advantages for both sides. They had $60 million or more from their various kidnappings and needed to get it out of the country. He convinced them that their money was doing them no good unless it was put to work, and he offered them 9.5 percent interest. They are said to have turned over $16,825,000 to him, from which they got a monthly income of around $133,000. On his side, Graiver got a large boost in his drive to become an international banker. Through his foreign banks and "dummy" companies in Andorra, the Bahamas, Panama, Liechtenstein, and Luxembourg, he had many conduits through which to launder money.[16]

Then, on the night of 6 August 1976, David Graiver died (or is presumed to have died) in a mysterious private airplane accident in Mexico. The next day the crash was located on a mountainside about 50 miles from Acapulco, and a military patrol was sent out. At nightfall, the "remains" of the pilot, copilot, and Graiver were brought to a funeral home in Acapulco, where Isidoro went to identify his brother. Although the corpse had no head and consisted only of the trunk with some skin fragments, Isidoro agreed that it was his brother, based on the skin color and thickness and other information from the soldiers who brought in the few body parts they found. The airplane's "black box" was never found, and the Acapulco control tower's tape was accidentally erased. Two days after the accident, Graiver's remains were cremated, so that no further investigation of them would be possible that might put the inheritance in doubt. Many people, including Generals Suárez Masón, Saint-Jean, and Camps—and the Montoneros, too—would later suspect that the accident was a fake and that Graiver was hiding underground, under an assumed name, with as much as $60 million bilked from his various clients and partners. Because more than 25 years have passed without a shred of evidence that Graiver survived his crash, it seems reasonable to conclude that he indeed was killed that night. That he had stolen a considerable fortune from his depositors and creditors and squirreled it away in places still undiscovered is certainly indisputable, however. News of his death caused bank failures on four continents. Loans to Graiver's dummy companies were to blame.[17]

During the weeks after David Graiver's death, his family struggled to keep his empire intact. They had been living in Mexico to avoid the AAA on the one hand and the U.S. Internal Revenue Service on the other. When they learned that U.S. authorities were preparing to call for the Graiver family's extradition, they fled to Argentina. On arriving in Buenos Aires, Isidoro went to the Banco de Hurlingham, of which he was the president, and found inspectors from the Central Bank going through the books. The same was true when he visited the Banco Comercial de La Plata. His next stop was at Jorge Rubenstein's office at EGASA headquarters, situated on the corner of Suipacha and Santa Fe. Rubenstein counseled him not to pay any debts, except one to himself for $240,000 for his services and another of $17 million to the Montoneros.

The Montoneros had already been in touch with the Graivers. While still in Mexico, Lidia Papaleo received an anonymous call from a stranger with an Argentine accent. The message was simple: pay $30 million or the whole Graiver family would die. Further calls gradually lowered the demand, first to $20 million and then to $17 million. After returning to Argentina, Lidia took over Rubenstein's office at EGASA and, with Isidoro's help, tried to keep the business intact. The Montoneros soon paid a call and demanded the return of their $17 million, whether in dollars, pesos, or negotiable paper. When Lidia and Isidoro insisted that they were broke, they were told that they had better find the money somehow, because the lives of their loved ones depended on it. Finally, the two sides agreed that the Montoneros would wait until the Graivers liquidated all their holdings.[18]

One of the first properties sold was Papel Prensa, the newsprint company. Through the intercession of President Videla and General Viola, the newspapers *Clarín, La Razón*, and *La Nación* got an $8 million loan to buy out the Graivers. Next, the printing plant, Editorial Gustavo, was put up for sale. The syndicate that approached the Graivers to buy it consisted of a former foreign minister under Arturo Frondizi, a Cuban exile, and the Besrodnik family, which controls the Buenos Aires Building Society, a financial front for the Communist Party. This strange combination excited the suspicions of Buenos Aires's governor, General Ibérico Saint-Jean. He ordered General Camps, the chief of police, to begin an investigation on 28 March 1977. Four days later, Edgardo Sajón, the manager of Editorial Gustavo, was arrested.

Even before this, however, the army was on the trail of the Graiver-Montonero connection. In early December 1976, Marisa Gierme, a Montonera lawyer from Mar del Plata, was captured. She had been involved in the killing of a policeman during an attack on a commissary in May 1975. In return for her life, she offered to collaborate fully (she eventually married an army captain) and fingered a Montonero courier named Ramón Ñeziba. Arrested soon afterward and tortured, Ñeziba told everything he knew about the Montoneros's finances. He did not know Graiver, having dealt only with Rubenstein, but he pointed the army in the right direction. Also in December, Roberto Quieto fell into the army's hands, and through him, Enrique Walker, Lidia Papaleo's ex-husband, was arrested, too. Through these interrogations the police began to piece together an intriguing but complex story. They learned that the Montoneros had appointed two contact men, Carlos ("Ignacio") Torres and Jorge ("Antonio") Salazar, to deliver cash to Graiver and collect interest payments. Then, on 15 January 1977, "Ignacio" Torres was arrested—but by ESMA, not by the army.[19]

This was dangerous for the Graivers and for Suárez Masón, Saint-Jean, and Camps. With Torres now in his hands, Massera would soon be after the Montoneros's millions and closing in on the Graivers. The Graivers sought General

Videla's protection, approaching him through Francisco Manrique, Lanusse's social welfare minister and David Graiver's former boss. Another family friend, Bernardo Neustadt, a popular television talk show host, went to Suárez Masón and Saint-Jean. They, in turn, ordered Camps to make a sweep of the whole Graiver operation, 24 people in all, including Graiver's father, Juan; his brother, Isidoro; Lidia Papaleo; Jorge Rubenstein; Edgardo Sajón, and, finally, Jacobo Timerman.

THE TIMERMAN AFFAIR

In the entire 164 pages of Timerman's celebrated book, *Prisoner Without a Name, Cell Without a Number*, there is not a single mention of David Graiver. Timerman insisted repeatedly that he was arrested and tortured only because the army hard-liners were Nazis and he was a Jew and a Zionist whose newspaper occasionally printed stories about people "disappearing" after being arrested. According to General Ramón Camps, who supervised the interrogations of all of Graiver's connections, including Timerman, the latter was arrested because he was Graiver's partner in both *La Opinión* and Editorial Gustavo. Timerman also was accused of deliberately staffing *La Opinión* with known Montoneros and *erpistas*, which amounted to "cultural subversion." "He was an obvious exponent of the Marxist strategy of infiltrating the cultural institutions and spreading subversive ideas, while proclaiming all the while that he was only being 'modern,' 'progressive,' 'humanistic,' 'democratic,' " Camps asserted in one of his own books on the subject.[20]

At the time of Timerman's arrest, in April 1977, *La Opinión* was considered by many *porteños* to be the best-written newspaper in Buenos Aires. Launched in 1971 with Graiver's money and Lanusse's moral support, it was modeled after *Le Monde*. Timerman apparently put up little or no money himself, but because of his already considerable fame as a journalist and editor he kept 45 percent of the shares; Graiver claimed an equal 45 percent, and the remaining 10 percent was held by Jorge Abraham Rotemberg, a lawyer who was Graiver's ex–father-in-law. Rotemberg had been the treasurer of an earlier Timerman publication called *Primera Plana*, and it was mainly through him that Timerman came to know David Graiver. Rotemberg also was a minor shareholder in Editorial Gustavo and Editorial Olta, the holding company for *La Opinión*, as well as other Graiver publishing enterprises. In each case, Graiver put up the money, Timerman contributed his journalistic skills and prestige, and Rotemberg was to take care of administration. Now Lidia Papaleo was liquidating David Graiver's publishing empire to pay off the family debts. *Papel Prensa* was the first to be sold; next she prepared to give Gelbard the Graivers' shares of *La Opinión*.

Upon hearing that, Timerman and Rotemberg moved to protect themselves. Rotemberg had no reason to be loyal to the Graivers, because David had divorced his daughter, Susana, to marry Papaleo. Furthermore, all but $50,000 of the half million Graiver paid Susana in alimony was lost when the American Bank and Trust Company failed. So on 5 November 1976, Rotemberg and Timerman placed announcements in the *Boletín Oficial* and the *Cronista Comercial* announcing a shareholders' meeting for Olta, Gustavo, and *La Opinión*. Three days later, they showed up, but none of the Graiver family did. The two men therefore passed a motion for a new emission of stock, which they then bought up themselves. As a result, the three companies' stock was now distributed as follows: 68 percent for Timerman, 30 percent for Rotemberg, and only 2 percent for the Graivers.[21]

Timerman's joy at gaining control of the Graiver publishing network turned to pain after his arrest. Under relentless questioning by General Camps, he admitted that Graiver had put up the money for *La Opinión*, but he insisted that he knew nothing of his contacts with the Montoneros or with Gelbard. Camps had more success at pursuing the question of guerrillas employed on the staff of *La Opinión*. There had been quite a few, and they had been in key places. Francisco Urondo, a poet and Montonero combatant, wrote for the cultural affairs section. Juan Gelman, another Montonero poet, edited the cultural section until 1973. Miguel Bonasso, the Montoneros's press secretary, had been on *La Opinión*'s editorial staff. Ernesto Alsina Bea, an Uruguayan exile who had been arrested in a hideout with other ERP guerrillas in 1972, was the leading general news commentator. Ted Córdoba-Claure, chief of *La Opinión*'s foreign news section, was a Bolivian exile who had been the press secretary for General Juan José Torres' Marxist government before becoming a Montonero. He, in return, recruited Augusto Montesinos Hurtado, another Bolivian refugee with guerrilla contacts throughout the region, to help him with the newswires. Other reporters and columnists recruited from the far Left included María Victoria Walsh, Rodolfo Walsh's daughter, a Montonera who killed herself rather than surrender to the security forces; Roberto Reyna, the Córdoba correspondent, who was arrested during a raid on a guerrilla cell; Juan Carlos Portantiero and Juan José Real, who were both communists; Jorge Abelardo Ramos and Tomás Eloy Martínez, who were both Peronists of the far Left. The latter took over the editing of the cultural section after Gelman left, and when he himself finally fled the country in early 1975, his place was taken by Adolfo Spunberg, a militant in the left-wing Peronist journalists' union.[22]

Timerman was also forced to listen to a long list of supposedly incriminating articles praising Castro's Cuba, Allende's Chile, Mao Zedong's Cultural Revolution, and Ho Chi Minh. Other articles attacked the family as an obsolete institution; called for "children's liberation" from their parents; and approved the assassination of military officers connected to Trelew or to "Ché" Guevara's death. Pressed about *La Opinión*'s ideological orientation, Timerman finally admitted that the articles reflected his own Marxism and "formed part of the paper's policy of seeking leftist themes that would allow it to penetrate leftist and youth circles."

Camps had the advantage of holding all the principal suspects and witnesses in his jail, and he showed himself extremely adept at bringing them face to face with Timerman to pry admissions out of him. Enrique Jara and Ramiro Casabellas, *La Opinión*'s associate editors, accused Timerman of lying to them about being sole owner of the paper and of going back on his word to get rid of the Marxists on the staff. Lidia Papaleo charged that the family had never been informed of the stockholders' meeting at which Timerman and Rotemberg had taken over *La Opinión*, Editorial Olta, and Editorial Gustavo. No one ever bothered to telephone the Graivers, or to mention the forthcoming meeting during their frequent visits to Papaleo's office. Nor were the Graivers informed afterwards, although they continued to make large deposits to the account of Editorial Olta down to the end of December 1976. Then Papaleo completely confused Timerman by showing that Rotemberg could not have legally participated in a shareholders' meeting because, finding himself short of money late in 1973, he had sold his interest in Editorials Olta and Gustavo to David Graiver. She produced the shares, which had been deposited in the Banco Comercial de La Plata, with the transaction dated 15 January 1974. By then Timerman had given up trying to skirmish or evade. He admitted to using *La Opinión* to support Gelbard in the Aluar case and to receiving $250,000 deposited to his account in a Swiss bank. He also admitted that, while Fiat's Oberdán Sallustro was being held in an ERP hideout, one of *La Opinión*'s reporters told him where Sallustro was but instead of going to the police he only tipped off Fiat's public relations director.

Camps' investigation had two main objectives: to trace the Montonero money through Graiver's intricate financial empire, and to link Lanusse, Gelbard, the Graivers, Timerman, and the Montoneros in a conspiracy. In the process he did manage to learn many interesting facts, but his imagination tended to push connections much further than the facts really allowed. The financial side of the case petered out in the impenetrable thicket of the underground economy, and there was no evidence that Timerman was involved in money laundering for Graiver. On the political side, Timerman was exposed as a guerrilla sympathizer and a devious businessman, while Lanusse's connections to Gelbard and Graiver were only those of a desperate political leader trying to reach a compromise with his opposition.

Videla tried to get Timerman, Sajón, the Graivers, and their associates released, but Rubenstein and Sajón died under torture, and the Graiver family and other business associates went to jail for terms of various lengths. Videla was more successful with Timerman, who was backed by the Jimmy Carter administration and the World Jewish Congress.[23] Timerman secured a hearing before the Special War Council of the Armed Forces' Supreme Council on 14 October 1977. It concluded that there was insufficient evidence to convict him as a subversive; nevertheless, he should be kept in a regular prison, under the Ministry of Interior, pending further investigation. That got him out of the hands of Camps and Suárez Masón but left him for the next two years in a kind of limbo until April 1978, when he was released from jail and allowed to remain under house arrest. Finally, on 17 September 1979, the Supreme Court took up Timerman's case again, on a habeas corpus appeal, and ordered the state to set Timerman free altogether because it still had not found anything criminal with which to charge him.

Although the navy and the air force were willing to accept the court's decision, the army's top commanders rejected it by a 6 to 4 vote whereupon Videla announced that unless the court obeyed, the justices would resign in a body, and he would resign with them. The challenge worked. In a second vote, only Suárez Masón and Luciano Benjamín Menéndez held out for a confrontation. Timerman was released, quickly hustled aboard a plane, and sent to Tel Aviv. With all his property confiscated, all he had to his name was $1,000 with which to start a new life in Israel. That was not enough to mollify some hard-liners. On the morning of 29 September, General Menéndez raised a revolt in Córdoba, which received no support, however, and ended with his arrest and forced retirement.

NOTES

1. Carlos M. Túrolo, *De Isabel a Videla: los pliegues del poder* (Buenos Aires: Editorial Sudamericana, 1996), 73, 99; Uriarte, *Almirante Cero*, 123–24; Andrés Fontana, "Political Decisionmaking by a Military Corporation: Argentina, 1976–1983" (Ph.D diss., University of Texas, 1987), 45–48, 58.

2. Uriarte, *Almirante Cero*, 142, 230; Hugo Quiroga, *Estado, crisis económica, y poder militar (1880–1981)* (Buenos Aires: Centro Editor de América Latina, 1985), 63, 73, 84, 86–88, 92; Fontana, "Political Decisionmaking," 68.

3. Uriarte, *Almirante Cero*, 217–18; *Somos* (12 February 1982), 4–8; (27 August 1982), 40–41; (3 September 1982), 45; (10 September 1982), 8–12; *Latinamerica Press* (6 October 1983), 7.

4. Jorge Schvarzer, *Expansión económica del estado subsidiario, 1976–1981* (Buenos Aires: Centro de Investigaciones Sociales sobre el Estado y la Administración, 1981), 39–47, 52, 56, 58–59, 61–68, 99, 101, 103–5, 108, 112, 134.

5. Uriarte, *Almirante Cero*, 134–35, 206; Crawley, *A House Divided*, 435.

6. Schvarzer, *Expansión económica*, 16, 19–20, 22; L. Beccaria and R. Carciofi, "The Recent Experience of Stabilizing and Opening Up the Argentine Economy, 1976–1981," *Cambridge Journal of Economics*, vol. 6 (June 1982), 153–56; Argentine Republic, Banco Central, *Boletín estadístico*, 1979–82.

7. Uriarte, *Almirante Cero*, 161–62; Alfredo Leuco and José Antonio Díaz, *Los herederos de Alfonsín* (Buenos Aires: Editorial Sudamericana Planeta, 1987), 214–17.

8. Argentine Republic, Cámara Nacional de Apelaciones en lo Criminal y Correccional de la Capital Federal, *El Libro de El Diario del Juicio* (Buenos Aires: Editorial Perfil, 1985), 139–71; Uriarte, *Almirante Cero*, 191.

9. Uriarte, *Almirante Cero*, 162–66. Hidalgo Solá's wife was warned by General Videla's wife to beware of Massera, just before the ambassador was kidnapped. See Camarasa et al., *El juicio*, 174.

10. Mona Moncalvillo, Alberto A. Fernández, and Manuel Martín, *Juicio a la im-*

punidad (Buenos Aires: Ediciones Tarso, 1985), 242–44; Uriarte, *Almirante Cero*, 128–29; Paoletti, *Como los nazis*, 127.

11. Concerning Sajón, see the testimony of Carlos Hours, in Camarasa et al., *El juicio*, 133–34.

12. On the Holmberg case, see Sergio Ciancaglini and Martín Granovsky, *Crónicas del apocalipsis* (Buenos Aires: Editorial Contrapunto, 1986), 98–100, 108; Camarasa et al., *El juicio*, 177–78 180; Moncalvillo et al., *Juicio a la impunidad*, 222–23; Uriarte, *Almirante Cero*, 191, 198–200, 223, 225.

13. Revista Somos, *Historias y personajes*, 188–89.

14. Pehme, *Argentina's Days of Rage*, 88; Revista Somos, *Historias y personajes*, 189–90.

15. Irene Capdevilla, *El Caso Graiver, o la historia de los testaferros* (Buenos Aires: Editorial Agora, 1984), 9–10, 15–16; Juan Gasparini, *El crimen de Graiver* (Buenos Aires: Grupo Editorial Zeta, 1990), 12, 17, 29, 45, 154.

16. Gasparini, *El crimen*, 53–55, 31, 34, 104, 108, 149; Revista Somos, *Historias y personajes*, 191; Carlos Alberto Quinterno, *Militares y populismo: la crisis argentina de 1966 a 1976* (Buenos Aires: Editorial Temas Contemporáneas, n.d.), 234; Gillespie, *Soldiers of Perón*, 252. Gillespie states that the Montoneros sent another $50 million to Cuba, where it was kept safe but earned no interest.

17. Gasparini, *El crimen*, 140–41, 149–51, 167; Pehme, *Argentina's Days of Rage*, 88–89; Capdevila, *El Caso Graiver*, 40–41; Ramón J. A. Camps, *El poder en la sombra: el affaire Graiver* (Buenos Aires: Ro.Ca. Producciones, 1983), 28, 31–37, 40; Revista Somos, *Historias y personajes*, 197–98.

18. Camps, *El poder en la sombra*, 42, 64–72.

19. Gasparini, *El crimen*, 55–56, 108, 187–89; Quinterno, *Militares y populismo*, 233; Revista Somos, *Historias y personajes*, 192–93.

20. Timerman, *Prisoner*, viii, 30, 60–61, 64–80, 100–4, 109, 111–21, 124–28, 131–45, 154–58; Camps, *Caso Timerman*, 19.

21. On the complicated financial structure of the Graiver publishing empire, see the interrogation of accountants Carlos Ocana, Osvaldo Porteiro, and Jacinto Schuger by Camps on 26 April 1977, in Camps, *Caso Timerman*, 155–56, 173–75, 197–98, 202–3; Revista Somos, *Historia y personajes*, 198–99.

22. Camps, *Caso Timerman*, especially pages 42–45, 59–68, 71–83, 106–206, 209–27.

23. Pehme, *Argentina's Days of Rage*, 88; Camps, *Caso Timerman*, 67.

TWELVE

The Regime Crumbles

As March 1980 drew to a close, General Jorge Videla could look back on four fairly successful years as president. The *proceso* had so thoroughly uprooted the guerrillas and their supporters that even isolated acts of terrorism seldom disturbed the peace anymore. Videla had also avoided war with Chile by the brilliant stroke of involving the papacy in the Beagle Channel dispute. Economic reform was more difficult, although 1979 seemed promising as the economy swung out of its recession, the Gross Domestic Product grew by 10 percent, and there was full employment. Consumer spending reached unprecedented levels because an overvalued peso, with free convertibility, made imported goods cheap. It was the year of the *plata dulce*, when the man on the street suddenly felt rich and the phrase *deme dos* ("I'll buy two") became common. The government basked in popularity. Inside the junta, Videla succeeded in blocking Massera's pretensions to the presidency, although he had to give up command of the army in order to remain president. Still, he was able to get his close ally, General Roberto Viola, chosen to replace him as the head of the army. Stalemated, Massera retired from the navy and from the junta on 15 September. His replacement, Admiral Armando Lambruschini, was temperamentally no different, but he lacked Massera's strong character.[1]

Civilian politicians were optimistic that military rule was about to end. Political parties, though theoretically dissolved, were busy behind the scenes. It was widely rumored that Videla was preparing to announce the formation of a transition government, to be headed by Ricardo Balbín, the Radicals' leader. According to "inside-dopesters," Balbín would assume office as provisional president and would then call for a general election in six months.

Such were the sunny prospects on 26 March 1980, the fourth anniversary of Videla's coup, but the sunlight was all on the surface. Two days later, on 28 March, the *proceso*'s jerry-built economy was thrown into a profound crisis by the sudden collapse of the Banco de Intercambio Regional (BIR). With more than $3 billion in uncollectible loans, the BIR suffered a run on its deposits that forced the Central Bank to take it over and put it into liquidation. That set off a panic that swept through Argentina's financial community like a hurricane. Over the next 12 months, more than 40 banks and investment houses went bankrupt. There was plenty of room for finger-pointing in the aftermath. Orthodox economists blamed the military for not allowing Martínez de Hoz to drastically cut government spending and privatize the economy. Economic nationalists argued that the free market and free trade had destroyed Argentina's industrialists while benefiting only a handful of agricultural exporters. Meanwhile, the regime seemed blithely unaware of the public's growing dismay. Videla, whose popularity rapidly eroded, added fuel to the fire by announcing in September 1980 that the junta had picked General Roberto Viola, not Ricardo Balbín, to succeed him as president. It was a direct repudiation of his pledge, frequently given and reiterated only weeks before, to restore civilian rule at the end of his term. Surprise and consternation were succeeded by a sense of unease when it was learned that even Viola's nomination had been resisted by some elements in the military. That could only portend a weak administration riven by factional infighting. Coming on the heels of the economic crash, the psychological impact was devastating.[2]

Viola, sworn in as president on 29 March 1981, was in a weak position. The economy he inherited was in a shambles. The navy had opposed his nomination as president, and he had barely beaten General Suárez Masón as the army's choice. Worse, General Leopoldo Fortunato Galtieri, who had succeeded him as chief of the Army General Staff, had developed political ambitions.[3]

Viola sought to restore the *proceso*'s popularity by including more civilians in his administration. Ricardo Balbín was a close friend, and Viola was thought to be searching for some way to turn over power to him. As part of his strategy to restore civilian rule, Viola also made overtures to the Peronists by getting Isabel Perón and Lorenzo Miguel released from house arrest, but his ability to win over the unions was limited by the desperate state of the economy.

Viola's new finance minister, Lorenzo Sigaut, tried to reverse the economic situation by a 30 percent devaluation of the peso, which had been greatly overvalued under Martínez de Hoz. That undermined confidence in the peso and raised expectations of further devaluations, which indeed were borne out by another 30 percent devaluation in June. Now the peso would be undervalued, Sigaut announced triumphantly. Exports would rise and dollars would flow in, instead of being carried abroad by tourists. The industrialists expressed satisfaction that the new exchange rate would effectively shut off imports, but among the general public there was a panic selling of pesos and a frantic scramble to buy dollars. To keep the peso from a free fall, the Central Bank began selling off dollars, which were quickly snatched up. Concern began building up inside the cabinet. Just before the second devaluation, *La Nación* carried a front-page article quoting an unnamed "high cabinet source" (who turned out to be the commerce minister, Carlos García Martínez) to the effect that another devaluation would produce an economic collapse, for banks and businesses were heavily indebted in dollars to foreign lenders. Another devaluation would make it impossible for many of them to ever acquire the dollars to repay those loans. When the next devaluation did come, a few days later, the president and vice president of the Central Bank resigned in protest. The peso did go into free fall, from 3,380 to the dollar at the beginning of the year to 4,200 at the beginning of June, and to 7,800 at the beginning of July. In its futile attempts to cushion the peso by selling dollars, the Central Bank ran down its exchange reserves by some $2.5 billion.[4]

As Viola's economic problems mounted, his political strategy also unraveled when in September his old friend Balbín died. Raúl Alfonsín, leader of the party's youthful left wing and a vocal opponent of the military, became the new UCR head. With no popular support and unable to control the rapidly deteriorating economic situation, Viola was far more vulnerable to a coup than Videla had been, and when his health finally gave way under the strain, he was finished. After Viola suffered a heart attack in November, General Horacio Liendo, the interior minister, took over as provisional president; three weeks later the junta, headed by army commander in chief General Leopoldo Galtieri, removed Liendo from office and formally declared Viola to be deposed as well. A week later General Galtieri was sworn in as president, and the hard-liners were now in control.

CRIMINAL INTERESTS

The military hard-liners were free at last to perform deep surgery on Argentina's institutions. The Graiver case already had alerted them to the fact that seemingly respectable businessmen might be linked to the terrorists. Even before Videla stepped down from the presidency, some officers were investigating "economic subversion," as traditional Argentine business practices aimed at evading the laws were now called. Ironically, the arrests of businessmen allegedly involved in shady practices, or with suspected links to subversive groups, quickly evolved into shakedown rackets that ended by corrupting the military itself.

One typical investigation, launched in 1977 by Admiral Massera and ESMA, involved the arrest of a Mendoza land developer named Victorio Cerutti, whose son, now in exile, had been a lawyer for various left-wing unions. He, his son-in-law, and his accountant disappeared. Then followed a series of phony "sales" of Cerutti's land, worth $10 million, to dummy companies of Massera's, one of which was listed at the very same address as the admiral's "Party for Social Democracy." More notorious still was the kidnapping and torture of Luis Grassi, president of the Grassi Steel Company; Juan Claudio Chavanne, chairman of the board of directors of the Banco de Hurlingham; and some 30 other lawyers, businessmen, and their close relatives after Grassi purchased the bank from the Graiver estate. General Carlos Suárez Masón ordered the roundup when a federal judge began investigating the sale, after a complaint lodged by an officer of the Buenos Aires Stock Exchange. Juan Alfredo Etchebarne, who supervised the listing of companies on the exchange and knew something of the Grassi Steel Company's financial situation, wondered where it had gotten the $12 million to buy controlling interest in the Banco de Hurlingham. Because Chavanne had drawn $10 million out of the bank immediately after the purchase, it looked as though he had loaned Montonero money to Grassi and then laundered it back to the subversives. Etchebarne, Central Bank officials, and the judge were present at the interrogations. After one hundred days of starvation and subjection to electric shocks, freezing baths, and simulated executions, during which Chavanne's lawyer, Marcos Satanovsky, died, the prisoners "confessed." They were then transferred to Villa Devoto prison and held there until March 1980. Meanwhile, the Central Bank voided the sale to Grassi and liquidated the Banco de Hurlingham. Years later, Grassi and Chavanne repudiated their confessions.[5]

Bit by bit the pursuit of "economic subversion" turned into pure gangsterism, because the military had so corrupted itself by the incorporation of criminals into its operations that it no longer controlled its own task forces. At first, confiscated property taken from prisoners, such as clothes, furniture, money, or jewelry, was either given away to charity or turned over to agents who put the proceeds in secret accounts to pay for "special operations." They stockpiled seized weapons, cars, and fuel as well. Gradually, the task force leaders began keeping such plunder for themselves. That often led to quarrels over booty. Eventually, task forces were kidnapping, robbing, and extorting simply for economic gain. Anyone could be taken into custody and forced to sign over property.

Admiral Massera and General Suárez Masón, the most prominent of these gangsters in uniform, got bolder over time. Massera was accused of ordering the murder of Fernando Branca, one of his business partners, after Branca bragged that he had tricked Massera in a business deal. Mauricio Schoklender, who ran a front for the navy's secret arms purchases, was another business partner who fell victim to Massera's easily ignited temper. After a quarrel with Massera over payment on an arms shipment, he and his wife were found murdered.[6] Suárez Masón was less hot-blooded and more businesslike than Massera. Using Battalion 601, he made kidnapping and extortion into a regular and profitable activity. Desperate families paid hundreds of thousands of dollars—and in a couple of cases, more than a million—to free their loved ones. Some, like Rafael Perrotta, who recently had sold his newspaper, *Cronista Comercial*, remained "disappeared," although Jacobo Timerman and others claimed to have seen Perrotta at the Cotí Martínez detention center. Carlos David Koldobsky, son of a wealthy family, was ransomed for more than $600,000 and then was snatched a second time. His kidnappers then demanded $1.5 million, to be paid over in Switzerland. When they went to Switzerland to get the money, however, they were caught. "Lenny" Sánchez Reisse, Rubén Osvaldo Bufano, and Luis Alberto Martínez, all common criminals, admitted to working for Colonel Raúl Gática at Battalion 601 and for SIDE.[7]

At about the same time, Massera's and Suárez Masón's connections to the Masonic lodge P-2 were suddenly revealed. On the orders of an investigating magistrate, Italian police searched Licio Gelli's villa while he was out of the country and found a codebook containing the names of 953 persons, including three Italian cabinet members and several former prime ministers, members of Parliament, high-ranking bureaucrats and military officers, the president of the Banco Ambrosiano, and the head of the Vatican bank. It also contained several Argentine names: José López Rega and Raúl Lastiri, among many others of the past regime but the inclusion of Massera and Suárez Masón in the codebook was particularly shocking. Argentine officers are not supposed to belong to political organizations, especially not foreign ones. It was a serious setback for Massera, who was still hoping for a chance at the presidency and was calling for an end to military rule.[8]

CONSERVATIVES DESERT

With Galtieri leading the junta, there was little chance of a return to civilian rule. "The urns are well-guarded," Galtieri announced, as he complacently shrugged off calls for an election. There was no hope of appeal. From the Supreme Court to the justices of the peace, the judiciary was intimidated. Although the courts claimed to be independent and capable of upholding the law, in practice they were not and did not even dare to try. In a case brought early in the *proceso*, the Supreme Court ruled that "the institutional acts and the Statute of the Process of National Reorganization are norms compatible with the Constitution."[9]

Conservative organs of opinion like *La Nación, La Prensa*, and the weekly magazine *Somos* originally hailed such decisions as proving that Argentina, despite foreign criticism, still followed the rule of law. *La Opinión, Crónica, La Razón*, and *The Buenos Aires Herald* had originally supported the *proceso* as well. All of them eventually clashed with the government over censorship, however, and learned that the slightest deviation from the rules brought quick punishment. Ricardo Gangeme, the editor of *Crónica*, and Robert Cox, editor in chief of *The Buenos Aires Herald*, were jailed briefly for publishing stories about the "disappeared." Cox and his reporters began receiving death threats. His top political columnist, Andrew Graham-Yool, fled the country in September 1976. Cox himself endured constant anonymous threats until one day, in 1978, he was called to Admiral Massera's office about a news story. Massera, a big, athletic man, approached him with a broad smile, placed his hands on Cox's shoulders, and told him as he looked at him squarely in the face, "If you mention me in your newspaper one more time, I'm going to put you 'inside' for good." That was not the last threat that Cox received, either; he began to get calls saying that his children's school would be bombed. He finally left Argentina in 1979, after several prominent journalists had been murdered: Julián José Delgado, editor in chief of the monthly business magazine *Mercado* and of the daily *Cronista Comercial*; Rafael Perrotta, from whom Delgado had acquired *Cronista Comercial*; and Horacio Agulla, editor of the weekly *Confirmado*.[10]

The ultra conservative daily *La Prensa* was a feisty paper whose opinions were often quirky and unpopular, yet it was fearless about expressing them regardless of who was in power. Its publisher, Máximo Gainza, constantly received official complaints and anonymous death threats when the paper printed articles on the "disappeared" or advertisements from human rights organizations. Soon after the coup Gainza got a telephone call from a certain Captain Corti, who told him that *La Prensa* was to publish no more articles about the "subversives." Told that such an order would have to be in writing, Corti sent the letter, but not on official letterhead. Nevertheless, *La Prensa* published it on page 1. The government then tightened the screws by withdrawing all advertising by state agencies and companies. *La Prensa* countered by publishing figures showing how many column inches of official advertising had been withdrawn from the paper in the previous month and how many had been added to its rivals. Friends of the government then began to cancel their subscriptions. In 1978 *La Prensa* lost between 10,000 and 20,000 subscribers after publishing two pages containing the names of 2,700 "disappeared" and carrying three advertisements by the families of disappeared persons, including the family of Héctor Hidalgo Solá.[11]

Videla's government also tried to keep newspapers in line by controlling the supply of newsprint. To do so, it bought up a large portion of Papel Prensa's stock when David Graiver's empire was being liquidated, with the remainder going to *Clarín, La Nación,* and *La Razón.* To make sure that the operation was profitable, the government decreed that all newspapers had to buy at least 50 percent of their newsprint from Papel Prensa at $680 a ton, as compared to the $530 charged by importers of foreign newsprint. *La Prensa* then mobilized all the Argentine newspapers that were not partners in Papel Prensa to protest loudly, which forced the regime to back down. *Clarín, La Nación,* and *La Razón* then withdrew from the "unpatriotic" Argentine Press Association, but victory was costly and sometimes *La Prensa*'s staff suffered. On the night of 23 June 1981, thugs, probably from Battalion 601, tried to invade the pressroom. Although they were driven off by the staff, they compensated themselves by catching one of the reporters, Manfred Schoenfeld, and working him over with brass knuckles. A few weeks later, Iglesias Rouco was prosecuted for publishing a leak about the ongoing diplomatic negotiations over the Beagle Channel, in which he quoted the Vatican's arbitrator, Cardinal Samore, as being "exhausted and fatigued by Argentina's uncooperative attitude."[12]

As conservative journalists began criticizing the *proceso,* so opposition also grew inside the Catholic Church. Under past military regimes, provincial bishops had always been able to intercede on behalf of a political prisoner by a letter or telephone call, at least to the extent of getting some information and an explanation of the charges. Now, though importuned by hundreds of relatives of the "disappeared," they were told not to get involved in such matters. The bishops became alarmed by the scope and ferocity of the *proceso*'s "Dirty War" tactics, and so in July 1976 they sent the junta a note expressing their concern about the extreme measures being used against its enemies. They observed that government security forces acted with "total impunity and anonymity" and wondered "what guarantees, what rights does the ordinary citizen still have?" The government responded politely but vaguely. Videla frequently invited the executive committee members of the Bishops' Conference to the Casa Rosada for lunch and talks, during which both sides made every effort to be cordial.[13]

Some Argentine bishops were sympathetic to the *proceso*, including the two principal figures on the bishops' executive committee, Cardinal Juan Carlos Aramburu, the archbishop of Buenos Aires, and Cardinal Raúl Francisco Primatesta, the archbishop of Córdoba. Both defended the regime to the last. Cardinal Aramburu dismissed the whole subject of disappearances in a 1982 interview with the Roman newspaper *Il Messaggero* and assured the reporter that many so-called *desaparecidos* were actually living in Europe. The Church was not monolithic, however, and there were bishops and priests who opposed the regime. One of those was Monseñor Enrique Angelelli, the bishop of La Rioja, who was killed in a staged auto accident on 4 August 1976, as he was returning from the small town of El Chamical, where he had been investigating the disappearance of two priests. His car was run off the road and turned over. Afterwards, he apparently was pulled, unconscious, from the vehicle and his skull was smashed in with a blunt instrument, because an autopsy concluded that he could not have been thrown through either the windshield or the door. Despite that, Cardinal Aramburu dismissed the idea of murder as a rumor that lacked proof. Another Third World bishop, Carlos Ponce de León, of San Nicolás, was killed in a staged automobile accident in 1977.[14]

Liberal laymen and clerics battled the regime through two human rights organizations: the Servício Paz y Justicia (SERPAJ) and the Ecumenical Movement for Human Rights (MEDH). SERPAJ was organized throughout Latin America and included among its more notable members Brother Leonardo Boff, Brazil's "liberation theologian," and Father Ernesto Cardenal, the Sandinista priest. Its coordinator for Argentina was Adolfo Pérez Esquivel, who spent time in jail from April 1977 to May 1978 for his activism. His testimony before the OAS Interamerican Commission on Human Rights a year later would be influential in shaping its report on Argentina. MEDH was connected to the World Council of Churches, a Christian organization that supported sweeping economic and social reforms. Both groups' connections were useful for getting information about human rights abuses circulated abroad.[15]

Pérez Esquivel also belonged to an influential, nonreligious human rights organization called the Permanent Assembly for Human Rights (APDH), whose cofounders included Bishop Jaime de Nevares, of Neuquén Province; Alfredo Bravo, of the Confederation of Educational Workers; and Raúl Alfonsín, APDH was much more moderate in its approach than SERPAJ or MEDH. The latter groups, though sincere about human rights, were seldom objective. They could not usually bring themselves to condemn the guerrilla terrorists for causing the anarchy that led to the *proceso*; when they did, they hedged their criticism with excuses that the guerrillas had been driven to violence by Yankee imperialism or social injustice. APDH, by contrast, favored eliminating both state terror and guerrilla terror, which put it in the position of grudgingly accepting the 1976 coup but urging more central control over the task forces. Its main activities were collecting information about the "disappeared" and presenting habeas corpus petitions to the courts. It had no formal international ties, but its members often were well connected abroad. Those proved useful in getting Alfredo Bravo released from prison in 1977.

APDH's evenhandedness disappointed some activists who, whether for personal or ideological reasons, wanted a more aggressive approach. One of those was Emilio Mignone, who broke away in 1979 to found his own Center for Legal and Social Studies (CELS) after his daughter was kidnapped and disappeared. Like APDH, CELS built up an extensive archive of testimony and documentation about kidnappings, torture, and conditions in the secret detention camps. It also initiated habeas corpus cases and occasionally got a prisoner transferred from a secret detention center to the legal penal system. Mignone had excellent contacts in Washington, having worked for the OAS during the 1960s, and he also knew people on the International Committee of Jurists in Geneva and the International League for Human Rights in New York. His organization received advice and funding from the Washington Center for Law and Social Policy, the Agency for International Development, and the Ford Foundation.

Further to the Left were such communist groups as the Argentine League for the Rights of Man and the Families of the Disappeared and Detained for Political Reasons. The Argentine League's origins dated back to the 1930s, and its main function was defending the Communist Party. Families of the Disappeared was an offshoot, set up with the league's help in late 1976 to publicize the arrests of ERP and Montonero guerrillas. Originally very critical of the *proceso*, both groups became more tepid after 1979, when Argentina became a chief supplier of grain to the Soviet Union. Most other human rights groups kept them at arm's length.[16]

Also linked by blood and sympathy to the ERP and Montonero guerrillas, but independent of the communists, were the Madres de la Plaza de Mayo. Indeed, the Madres were probably the most effective of all the human rights organizations in focusing attention on the *proceso*'s abuses because of their ingenious talent for political theater. They made their first public appearance on Saturday, 30 April 1977, when 11 middle-aged women went to the Casa Rosada, secured an interview with Videla, and presented him with a letter demanding to know the whereabouts of their "disappeared" children. Receiving only a vague answer, they were back the next Friday in the Plaza de Mayo. This time there were 30 women. They came every week thereafter, their numbers gradually growing and their appearances becoming more ritualized and dramatic. They settled upon Thursdays, regardless of the weather, as the time to march silently around the Plaza de Mayo, carrying placards with enlarged photographs of their disappeared children. Each one wore a white kerchief tied under the chin, embroidered with the name, or names, of missing family members.[17]

The government never figured out how to deal with them. A student demonstration or a labor strike could be crushed, but how were soldiers and police to employ violence against a group of middle-age housewives who "look like Mom"? (Men were not allowed to participate in the marches, nor younger women, either, because the police were more likely to use violence against them.) If the police blocked them, they moved across the street; if some were arrested, others took their place. The Madres learned to infiltrate the plaza one by one, sitting on benches and pretending to sew, to evade police blockades. Nevertheless, participation in the Madres was not free of danger. On 8 December 1977 some of them, including a French nun named Alice Domón, who worked for MEDH, were abducted by an ESMA task force as they left a meeting just held in a neighborhood church. Two days later, the Madres' founder, Azunceña Villaflor de Devicenti, and another French nun, Leonie Duquet, were kidnapped. None of them was ever seen again.[18]

Bit by bit, as the *proceso* lost popularity, the Madres won over the public. *The Buenos Aires Herald* and *La Prensa* applauded them because they awakened the public to the atrocities being committed by the military, which the press could not report. By 1981 the Thursday marches in the Plaza de Mayo attracted more than two hundred women, and the Madres had become the focal point of the human rights movement's increasingly powerful offensive against the regime. They also had attracted attention overseas, having visited the United States, Canada, Mexico, and Europe. They had testified before the U.S. Congress, attended the Hemispheric Conference of the Catholic Church in Puebla, spoken before the OAS and the United Nations, and been received by François Mitterand, Felipe González, and the pope. A group of socialist members of the European Parliament proposed them for the Nobel Peace Prize in 1980, and although it went instead to a fellow Argentine activist, Adolfo Pérez Esquivel, the Madres had accomplished a political miracle by turning public opinion around, arousing the consciences of the timid and indifferent, and revealing the regime's utter arrogance toward the nation it claimed to be defending.

EXTERNAL PRESSURE

The *proceso* came under mounting pressure from abroad for its "Dirty War" tactics. Despite the clandestine interrogation centers and nighttime "death flights," stories leaked out. Most Argentines dismissed them at first, but in Western Europe and the United States there were growing denunciations of the regime. The guerrillas had planned on this. A couple of weeks before the 1976 coup, Mario Santucho contacted the artists, writers, and union activists in PRT-ERP and urged them to go into exile, where they would "carry out a laudable task of organizing protests against human rights violations and propagandizing the Argentine people's struggle."[19] Similarly, Montonero exiles, such as the poet Juan Gelman, used their literary connections in Europe with people like the exiled novelist Julio Cortázar, to mobilize opinion against the *proceso*.

Although they set up an Argentine Human Rights Commission in Madrid, the Argentine exiles found at first that Europeans applauded the military for throwing out the "fascist" Peronists. That attitude soon changed. On 20 June 1976, *Le Monde* carried a manifesto condemning the Argentine junta, signed by some of Europe's most prominent Social Democrats. Shortly afterwards, the United Nations passed a resolution condemning Argentina for violating international norms in the treatment of refugees and set up a "working group" to monitor "disappearances" there. Argentina's Paris embassy was constantly surrounded by hundreds of protesters, and there were frequent public petitions from French intellectuals for the release of Argentine leftist writers from prison. In 1977, the bishop of Paris refused to say a Mass at the embassy, in protest over the disappearance of the two French nuns who were connected to the Madres de la Plaza de Mayo. The human rights campaign against the *proceso* got an inadvertent boost from the government itself when it brought hundreds of foreign reporters to Argentina in 1978 for the World Cup soccer matches. For many patriotic Argentines, it seemed an opportunity to correct foreigners' mistaken ideas about their country and end the "anti-Argentine" campaign but the European reporters, who had kept their eyes and ears open during their stay, knew the extent of the *proceso*'s repression better than the Argentines and pitied them as victims of official propaganda.[20]

International pressure on Argentina continued throughout 1978. Videla met angry crowds of human rights protestors whenever he went abroad. Venezuela would invite him only after he secured the release of Senator Hipólito Solari Yrigoyen from prison, and the United States made him get Alfredo Bravo out of jail before he could visit. The Montoneros, by contrast, were enjoying a season of popularity among European intellectuals and politicians on the Left. Mario Firmenich was invited for interviews by Bruno Kreisky, the socialist prime minister of Austria; Willy Brandt, chancellor of West Germany; Felipe González, prime minister of Spain; Santiago Carrillo, general secretary of the Spanish Communist Party; François Mitterand, president of France; and Olof Palme, prime minister of Sweden. In April, Ricardo Obregón Cano, former Córdoba governor and prominent figure in the Montoneros's "Authentic Peronist Party," was entertained by the Yugoslavian trade unions, and Oscar Bidegain, former Buenos Aires governor, went with guerrilla leader Daniel Vaca Narvaja to Austria to meet with the leaders of the Socialist Party's youth, labor, and parliamentary branches. Vaca Narvaja and a group of Montonero writers and artists then went to the Netherlands at the invitation of the Dutch Labor Party. From there Vaca Narvaja went to Bremen, Germany, at the invitation of the local university for a meeting of European and Arab "socialist and progressive" parties. Meanwhile, Rodolfo Galimberti attended a socialist youth conference in Paris, and members of the Montoneros's "Bloque Sindical" and the "CGT in Resistance" attended the International Labor Office's 64th Annual Conference in Geneva, where they received pledges of support from the Scandinavian, Spanish, French, and Italian delegations. Miguel Bonasso, the Montoneros's press secretary, went to Tanzania as an official guest and Oscar Bidegain led a delegation of Montoneros to Algeria. Other Montonero representatives went to Lebanon and Mozambique.[21]

Pressure mounted from the United States as well. Patricia Derian, a crusading activist who worked closely with groups like Amnesty International and the Washington Office on Latin America (of the National Council of Churches), had direct access to President Carter. She used her influence to get Argentina turned down for two Export-Import Bank loans, to prevent the sale of U.S. military equipment to Argentina and to have Argentine officers excluded from U.S. military training programs. Argentine human rights activists were brought to the United States to testify before Congress during hearings on military aid, and Jacobo Timerman, upon his release from prison, was given a warm reception in the United States. Derian herself made three visits to Argentina in 1977, during which she met with human rights groups and criticized the regime.[22]

To try to turn the tide of American public opinion, Videla met with President Carter and assured him that the antiterrorist war was drawing to a close and that repression would be eased. Appearing at press conferences and on television, he admitted that "dirty acts" had been committed by the Argentine armed forces and blamed these on the "dispersed" character of the war, which made it difficult to exert discipline from the top. He also admitted that people had "disappeared" in Argentina as the result of "excesses" by the soldiers and police, but he also insisted that the lists of "disappeared" being circulated by human rights groups were exaggerated. He promised that the Argentine military would eventually restore democracy. In September 1978, Videla agreed to allow the OAS Interamerican Commission on Human Rights to conduct an on-site investigation of conditions in Argentina in exchange for the unblocking of certain Export-Import Bank loans. He assumed that other Latin American countries would support the Argentine government; instead, to his surprise and chagrin, the Interamerican Commission's report strongly condemned Argentina for abandoning the rule of law and embracing state terrorism. That was followed, in quick order, by Jacobo Timerman's *Prisoner Without a Name, Cell Without a Number* and the awarding of the Nobel Peace Prize to Adolfo Pérez Esquivel. A reviving CGT found international support in Europe's socialist trade unions and the AFL-CIO; the Movimiento Judio por los Derechos Humanos in Buenos Aires got the sympathetic ear of the World Jewish Congress and prominent Jewish citizens in the

United States; the World Council of Churches spread the claims of SERPAJ and MEDH: Dutch churches collected $20,000 for the Madres de la Plaza, and the Norwegian parliament gave them another $34,000; the governments of France, Denmark, and Switzerland also sent money to Argentine human rights groups and made publicity on their behalf. Argentina was more of an international pariah than ever.[23]

Opinion began to shift within the U.S. government in the last months of the Carter administration, however, as a result of growing concern over revolutions in Central America. In 1981 General Viola, treading Videla's well-worn path to foreign capitals after his inauguration, found a far warmer reception from official Washington. Ronald Reagan's administration was going to intervene in Central America to undermine the Sandinistas and smother the insurrection that was building up in El Salvador. Viola agreed that the Sandinistas endangered hemispheric security and pledged Argentina's full support in battling them; in return, Reagan agreed to request Congress to restore military aid to Argentina.[24]

Argentina's interest in Central America was not merely opportunistic. After escaping from the "Dirty War," some ERP and Montonero guerrillas had fought in the Sandinista rebellion and later were incorporated into the revolutionary government's security forces (Fifth Directorate) as a kind of death squad whose chief task was to hunt down and kill important survivors of the fallen regime. In September 1980 Enrique Gorriarán Merlo, Hugo Iruzún, and other *erpistas* slipped into Paraguay, where Nicaragua's Anastasio Somoza had taken asylum, and ambushed him with machine guns and a bazooka. Moreover, the Sandinista triumph led directly to the Montoneros's suicidal counter offensive in Argentina that same year. Believing that it signaled the beginning of a hemispheric wave of revolution that would sweep away the puppet regimes of U.S. imperialism, Firmenich sent guerrillas to carry out attacks against members of the Argentine government's economic team, businessmen, and the police. It was the Montoneros's last, desperate assault. After they failed to mobilize the factory workers for a mass uprising, they were hunted down and destroyed. After 1979 guerrillas were no longer a threat. Then the *proceso* proceeded to destroy itself.

SELF-DESTRUCTION

The Falkland Islands—or, as they are known in Argentina, the Malvinas—lie nine hundred miles southeast of Buenos Aires. Treeless, cold, damp, and buffeted by Antarctic winds, they are sparsely populated yet to Argentine nationalists they are of great symbolic importance. Argentina claimed them as a legacy from Spain, but in 1833 the British seized them. Since then the islands have been a source of diplomatic conflict. Upon taking office, General Galtieri announced that 1982 was to be "the year of the Malvinas," meaning that he intended to take back the islands, whether through diplomacy or force. Conditions inside Argentina were making it more imperative for the junta to do something to recover its popularity. The Madres were leading protest marches, and a newly revived CGT was calling for a general strike to protest falling wages, rising unemployment, and triple-digit inflation. Despite Galtieri's orders to cancel the rally, on 30 May some 15,000 demonstrators battled with the Federal Police in the Plaza, only to be driven off at last by clubs and tear gas.

Galtieri told the armed services to start working on invasion plans, but before they could, the conflict erupted over a trivial incident involving the raising of an Argentine flag by a construction crew on South Georgia Island, a dependency of the Falklands. An exchange of sharp diplomatic messages angered the Argentine junta.[25] On 1 April 1982—just two days after the confrontation with the CGT—Galtieri ordered the Third Army Brigade, stationed in the tropical province of Corrientes, to Buenos Aires to board a waiting fleet of ships. That night he telephoned Washington and informed President Reagan that the troops would sail for the Falklands the next day. Reagan implored him to change his mind, but Galtieri insisted that it was too late to call off the invasion.

When the invasion was announced, Argentines who had been demonstrating against the regime only a few days before poured out into the streets on 2 April to shout their approval. A formal rally of support packed the Plaza de Mayo on 10 April. People vied with one another in pledging money, jewelry, property, and works of art to the hastily devised "Patriotic Fund" to help defray the costs of the invasion. (The money disappeared, never to be recovered.) Little children ran around their neighborhoods collecting food and clothing for the soldiers, while their mothers baked *tartas malvinas* to send as well. Galtieri even got a cable from the Montoneros in Havana, asking permission to return home and join the fight for the Malvinas.[26]

Overseas, however, Argentina was all alone. The U.N. Security Council condemned the invasion by 15 to 1 (Panama), with 4 abstentions; a majority in the General Assembly was against Argentina, too, with even the Latin American nations willing to give no more than tepid support. Meanwhile, British Prime Minister Margaret Thatcher dispatched to the south Atlantic eight destroyers and frigates, two aircraft carriers with fighter planes and helicopters, and two nuclear-powered submarines. As the fleet approached, the junta began to realize its untenable situation. The British would have sea and air superiority, which meant that the Argentine troops occupying the Falklands would be cut off from any support. Those troops were not the best that Argentina had, anyway, because the most experienced units were posted along the Chilean border. The Third Army Brigade consisted mainly of recent conscripts and had been hastily brought up to full strength by calling up the reserves. Not only did the young men lack sufficient training, but they were poorly equipped as well. The original invasion plans had aimed for September, but the South Georgia incident had pushed the timetable forward to April, which meant that most details were not worked out. Consequently, the soldiers arrived lacking weapons, ammunition, vehicles, radios, and even simple equipment like shovels. Abandoned to their fate, and unequal to a war with crack British commandos, the Argentine forces finally surrendered on 14 June.[27]

The next day Galtieri spoke from the balcony of the Casa Rosada to a crowd gathered in the Plaza de Mayo and informed them of Argentina's defeat. Sprinkling his address with patriotic phrases to the effect that Argentina would never give up its claims to the Malvinas, he apparently hoped that anti-British sentiment would afford him another display of national unity. Instead, the crowd began to shout insults at him and the other junta members at his side. Soon the protests became a roar and were succeeded by a surge from the crowd toward the building. Before the police could drive them back, they broke several windows. Then, forced from the Plaza, the protesters went on a rampage in the nearby streets, turning over cars and buses and setting them afire. It was the final break between state and society, although the *proceso* would die a lingering death that would last another year and a half. Even then Galtieri was confident that he could ride out the crisis, so he was taken by surprise at a 17 June meeting of the top Argentine generals, when his colleagues demanded his resignation. The army's commander, General Cristino Nicolaides, then announced that a retired general, Reynaldo Bignone, would take over the Casa Rosada.[28]

THE RESTORATION OF DEMOCRACY

Bignone faced three major challenges. He had to bring some kind of relief to an economy that was suffering from runaway inflation, reaching nearly 200 percent, without resorting to painful austerity measures that would provoke violent reactions. He also had to find some way to get the military out of power without exposing it to the revenge of its enemies in the human rights groups. Finally, he had to schedule elections and supervise a smooth transition to civilian rule.

To halt inflation, Bignone imposed price controls, hoping they might stabilize things long enough to see the government through the transition period. But that simply meant that goods disappeared from the shelves and reappeared on the black market at prices that reflected the upward spiral of inflation. It was impossible to control inflation without drastically reducing government spending, and Bignone could make no headway against the government's swollen budget without tackling military expenditures. By 1982 those had reached $4.5 billion, more than the combined budgets of the Ministries of Public Health, Education & Culture, and Social Welfare. What is more, the armed forces were busily rearming in the wake of their recent defeat in the Falklands.[29]

The military wanted to slow its retreat from power as much as possible, but political party leaders insisted that the government set a definite timetable for elections. Strikes and demonstrations were almost daily events as, after six years of conformity and fear, Argentine civil society was expressing its pent-up revulsion for the military. The officers were offended. General Nicolaides warned Bignone that resentment was spreading in the barracks, whereupon Bignone squelched the threat by offering to resign. Nicolaides backed off, and Bignone was finally able to announce a definite timetable for turning over power: elections would be held on 30 October, and the new government would take office on 30 January 1984.

The military now sought to protect itself from retribution. On 28 April 1983, the junta published a "Final Document on the War against Subversion and Terrorism," admitting "with the true sorrow of Christians" that "errors" might have been made while "defending the national way of life and the common good." They called for a "national reconciliation."[30] This bit of lugubrious self-justification impressed no one and angered many, especially since it was issued along with an Institutional Act that declared that no one could be punished for acts carried out under military orders during the "war against subversion and terrorism." A few days afterwards, some 30,000 human rights activists marched in protest, while Raúl Alfonsín, the Radicals' presidential candidate, proclaimed his belief that "unlawful acts committed during the repression ought to be judged in the courts, and not just by history."[31]

By now the top officers were truly alarmed. There was grumbling in the junta about how subversives seemed to be infiltrating the protest movements, and rumors about coup plots continued to percolate. It was too late to turn back the transition process, however. Most officers were demoralized and anxious to wash their hands of politics. Instead, the armed forces chiefs went to work on additional legislation designed to protect them from legal reprisals. On 22 September the junta issued Decree Law 22, 924/83, which became known as the Self-Amnesty Law. Article 1 forbid any legal penalties for crimes committed during the "Dirty War," whether by the security forces or by the guerrillas and terrorists. A blanket amnesty was to cover not only those who actually committed the crimes but also those who ordered them, assisted in them, or covered them up. They were to be exempt from both criminal prosecution and civil damages. Article 2, however, held that members of subversive and terrorist organizations who remained outside Argentina were not covered by the law—although if a question arose as to whether an individual was covered, Article 14 gave him the benefit of the doubt. Before the decree was even promulgated, word of it leaked out and, as with the "Final Document," this new attempt to evade responsibility for the "disappearances" of the "Dirty War" was greeted with outrage, culminating in a 24-hour giant March of Resistance around the Plaza de Mayo. Nevertheless, the junta proceeded to issue the decree two days later.[32]

THE ELECTION

The Peronists were confident of returning to power in the upcoming election because they had never lost a general election and they had the working classes' mass voting power. Still, they had never faced an electoral test without Perón behind them. Isabel was still the titular leader, of course, but she now lived in Madrid in semiseclusion and ignored her followers' pleas to speak out in their behalf. Lorenzo Miguel, the old metallurgical union boss, tried to fill the gap but he was no vote getter, only a power broker, and in the end he secured the presidential nomination for Italo Luder, onetime provisional president and leader of the Senate.[33]

The UCR picked Raúl Alfonsín to head its ticket. He was a founding member of the APDH and had been an outspoken critic of the *proceso* at a time when it was dangerous to be so. His principled stands against the military, the AAA, and labor union thuggery made him popular with all those who wanted a clean break with the past. Given Argentina's essentially two-party system, the presidential race would ordinarily have been a simple contest between Italo Luder and Raúl Alfonsín, but there was a third-party challenge as well: Admiral Emilio Massera and his Party for Social Democracy. Unfortunately for Massera, however, his crimes had begun to percolate into the public's attention. He already had been indicted, in August 1982, in the Schoklender murder case, although the judge subsequently left the country after receiving death threats. A month later, former Treasury Secretary Juan Alemann accused Massera, in an interview with *The Buenos Aires Herald*, of ordering the bombing of his home in 1977 to silence his criticism of the junta's extravagant spending on the World Cup playoffs. When Massera responded in a bitter counterattack, Alemann added the charges that Massera was responsible for the murders of Héctor Hidalgo Solá and Elena Holmberg. This time, when Massera tried to counter, Alemann got backing from Gregorio Dupont in another *Herald* interview. Dupont revealed how Holmberg was about to give public evidence of Massera's dealings in Europe with the Montoneros just before she was kidnapped. Furthermore, Dupont went to Elena's brother, Eugenio, with a statement about all that he knew concerning her disappearance, after which the two men had it notarized. Then they went before a judge to lodge a formal accusation against the government. Dupont's brother, Marcelo, disappeared a few days later. His body turned up a week afterwards at a construction site, thrown from the top of a tall building. Although an autopsy showed that Marcelo had been tortured with an electric prod, the investigating judge ruled his death a suicide. (For years afterward, Gregorio Dupont conducted his own investigation of his brother's death, but without success.)[34]

Now, to eliminate Massera from the race, General Cristino Nicolaides found a young federal judge, Oscar Mario Salvi, who was willing to risk his life by prosecuting Massera for the murder of Fernando Branca. Judge Salvi instantly became a public hero by putting Massera under preventative arrest pending a preliminary hearing. Massera complained that all of this was simply a campaign by the Bignone government to eliminate him from the elections, and there were enough people willing to believe this to keep his candidacy viable. Judge Salvi was not to be frightened off the case, however, and to make certain that Massera's candidacy was squelched, he concluded from the hearing that there was enough evidence in the Branca case to hold him for trial. Not until September 1984, a year after the elections, did an appeals courts finally release him.

The presidential campaign was now a two-way contest. Alfonsín attacked the Peronists as men of the past, living off the fading glory of their dead leader.

Luder, a dry, professorial type, came across poorly on television. He seemed colorless and lacking in confidence, in contrast to Alfonsín's robust, likable personality. It also did Luder little good to be seen surrounded by union thugs who called up memories of the AAA. Undecided voters recalled with horror the recent violent past when a Peronist rally set fire to a coffin bearing the inscription "Alfonsín, R.I.P.," and on 30 October 1983 they gave Alfonsín 52 percent of the vote compared to 40 percent for Luder. The Radicals also won a majority of the Chamber of Deputies and six governorships, including Buenos Aires Province. It was not a total debacle for the Peronists, however. They won enough senators to keep the Radicals from claiming a majority of the upper house, and they controlled 12 governorships. The junta dissolved itself on 5 December, putting an end to the *proceso*; on 10 December, General Bignone turned over the presidency to Raúl Alfonsín.[35]

NOTES

1. Gary W. Wynia, *Argentina in the Postwar Era: Politics and Economic Policy-making in a Divided Society* (Albuquerque: University of New Mexico, 1978), 228–30; Troncoso, *El Proceso*, vol. 2, 74, 83–84, 115, 118, 123–24; *Quarterly Economic Report* (January 1981), 3; Túrolo, *De Isabel a Videla*, 99–107, 151–53.

2. Alberto Jordán, *El Proceso, 1976–1983* (Buenos Aires: Emecé Editores, 1993), 231, 265, 271.

3. Túrolo, *De Isabel a Videla*, 269–81; Fontana, "Political Decisionmaking," 122–23; Enrique Baloyra, "Argentina: transición o disolución," in Carlos Huneeus, ed., *Para vivir la democracia* (Santiago de Chile: Academia Humanismo Cristiano, 1987), 111, 117; Uriarte, *Almirante Cero*, 191.

4. *Somos* (5 June 1981), 5–6, 8; (26 June 1981), 51–53; *Review of the River Plate* (10 April 1981), 440, 442, 448; (10 June 1981), 736, 738–39; (30 June 1981), 831–32.

5. Camarasa, et al., *El juicio*, 168–69; Moncalvillo et al., *Juicio*, 114–16; Juvenal, *Buenos muchachos*, 58–62; *Somos* (12 July 1985), 43.

6. Uriarte, *Almirante Cero*, 179–84, 264, 272. The original Schoklender murder investigation concluded with charges being brought against the children, who were accused of wanting the inheritance. The case was reopened in 1982, and this time Massera was accused. However, the judge left the country after receiving a series of death threats. On the evolution of military banditry, see Juvenal, *Buenos muchachos*; Paoletti, *Como los nazis*, 376–77, 391–92; Acuña and Smulovitz, "Militares en la transición argentina," 102, n. 15, 104–5, n. 25 and 29; Graham-Yool, *State of Fear*, 162–63; *Somos* (2 August 1985), 19.

7. Both Bufano and Reisse confessed to carrying out tasks for the Argentine army in Central America, gathering intelligence and laundering money for the Nicaraguan Contras. Martínez also admitted to having participated in three "death flights" over the Río de La Plata, in which the drugged bodies of guerrillas were thrown from the plane. Juvenal, *Buenos muchachos*, 157–58, 161, 164–65, 203–10, 239, 282, 284–86, 289–90; Paoletti, *Como los nazis*, 132–33, n. 4.

8. Gelli himself became an international fugitive until September 1982, when he was arrested in Geneva while trying to draw out some $120 million from a numbered bank

account. Extradited to Italy, he escaped from prison on 9 August 1983, after bribing a guard. Stephen Knight, *The Brotherhood* (New York: Dorset Press, 1986), 272–74; Gerardo Bra, "La 'P-2,' " 8–26; *Somos* (29 May 1981), 18–19; (16 July 1982), 46; (15 October 1982), 6–12; *Latin America* (29 May 1981), 8; (5 June 1981), 2–3.

9. Enrique I. Groisman, *La Corte Suprema de Justicia durante la dictadura (1976–1983)* (Buenos Aires: Centro de Investigaciones Sociales sobre el Estado y la Administración, 1987), 11–12.

10. Graham-Yool, *The Press in Argentina*, 117; Graham-Yool, *State of Fear*, 113–40.

11. Camarasa, et al., *El juicio*, 148–49; *Somos* (7 June 1985), 16; *Review of the River Plate* (10 July 1981), 14–15.

12. *Review of the River Plate* (28 February 1979), 265; (28 December 1979), 1050, 1058–60; (28 March 1980), 432–33; (10 July 1981), 10, 17–19.

13. Emilio Mignone, *Iglesia y dictadura* (Buenos Aires: Ediciones del Pensamiento Nacional, 1986), 50, 59, 62–71, 73.

14. Paoletti, *Como los nazis*, 354–57, 361–62; Mignone, *Iglesia y dictadura*, 80, 245–53; Moncalvillo et al., *Juicio a la impunidad*, 248–49. In 1986 the Angelelli case was reopened and new evidence was presented. On 19 June the examining magistrate affirmed that Angelelli had been murdered, but the perpetrators were unknown.

15. Alison Brysk, *The Politics of Human Rights in Argentina* (Stanford: Stanford University Press, 1994), 46–47, 49–52; Veiga, *Las organizaciones*, 96–97, 102–04, 107, 112, 115–23.

16. Veiga, *Las organizaciones*, 16, 19–20, 24–25, 75–77, 85.

17. Veiga, *Las organizaciones*, 26–54. See also Marysa Navarro, "The Personal Is Political: Las Madres de Plaza de Mayo," in Susan Eckstein, ed., *Latin American Social Movements* (Berkeley: University of California Press, 1989), 249–55.

18. Amnesty International, *Argentina*, 5; Andersen, *Dossier Secreto*, 268–69.

19. Mattini, *Hombres y mujeres*, 485, 501, n. 1.

20. Brysk, *Politics of Human Rights*, 54; Jordán, *El Proceso*, 96, 123–28.

21. "Argentina y la Internacional Socialista: Socialdemocracia versus Montoneros," *Boletín de Notícias* (November 1978), 2. The journal was a Montonero publication.

22. Lars Schoultz, *Human Rights and U.S. Policy Towards Latin America* (Princeton: Princeton University Press, 1981), 75–78; Alison Brysk, "From Above and Below: Social Movements, the International System, and Human Rights in Argentina," *Comparative Political Studies*, vol. 26, no. 3 (October 1993), 267; Pedro A. Sanjuan, "Another American Tragedy—Recent Carter Policies Toward Argentina," in *Argentina—United States Relations and South Atlantic Security* (Washington: American Foreign Policy Institute, 1980), 17–18; Z. Michael Szaz, "United States–Argentine Relations—Alienation or Coming Rapproachment?" in *Argentine—United States Relations*, 28–29.

23. Szaz, "United States–Argentine Relations," 17–19, 30–31, 33–39; Kathryn Sikkink and Lisa L. Martin, "U.S. Policy and Human Rights in Argentina and Guatemala, 1973–1980," in Peter Evans, Harold Jacobson, and Robert D. Putnam, eds., *Double-Edged Diplomacy: International Bargaining and Domestic Politics* (Berkeley: University of California Press, 1993), 330–31, 342–43; Troncoso, *El Proceso*, vol. 2, 7–11, 61–63, 132.

24. On Argentine military participation in Central America, see Juvenal, *Buenos muchachos*, 265–71.

25. Martin Middlebrook, *The Fight for the "Malvinas"* (London: Viking Press, 1989),

1–2, 7–11, 13; Lawrence Freedman and Virginia Gamba-Stonehouse, *Signals of War* (London: Faber and Faber, 1990), 39–83 (especially 41–48), conclude that the Argentine landing party was not entirely innocent in its intentions.

26. Jordán, *El Proceso*, 334–35.

27. Middlebrook, *The Fight*, 47–57.

28. Jordán, *El Proceso*, 361–67; Andrés Fontana, "De la crisis de las Malvinas a la subordinación condicionada: conflictos intramilitares y transición política en Argentina," in Claudio Varas, ed., *La autonomía militar en América Latina* (Caracas: Editorial Nueva Sociedad, 1988), 41–43; *Review of the River Plate* (30 June 1982), 671–72.

29. *Latinamerica Press* (6 October 1983), 7; *Review of the River Plate* (26 February 1982), 202–04; *Somos* (12 February 1982), 4–8.

30. Asociación Americana de Juristas (Rama Argentina), *Argentina, juicio a los militares: documentos secretos, decretoleyes, jurisprudencia* (Buenos Aires: AAJ, 1988), 19.

31. Brysk, *Politics of Human Rights*, 61; García, *La doctrina*, vol. 2. 207; Fontana, "De la crisis," 50–51; Acuña and Smulovitz, "Militares en la transición," 115.

32. Asociación Americana de Juristas, *Argentina*, 22–23; García, *La doctrina*, 211.

33. María Sáenz Quesada, *El camino de la democracía* (Buenos Aires: Tiempo de Ideas, 1993), 189–90; Jordán, *El Proceso*, 399–400, 408–10.

34. Uriarte, *Almirante Cero*, 266–272; Ciancaglini and Granovsky, *Crónicas*, 105–11.

35. Sáenz Quesada, *El Camino*, 206–7; Jordán, *El Proceso*, 410–16; Manuel Mora y Araujo, "La naturaleza de la coalición alfonsinista," *Todo es Historia* (July 1985), 38–45; Ignacio Llorente, "El comportamiento electoral en el Gran Buenos Aires," *Todo es Historia*, 58–67.

Procedures to facilitate prosecution for human rights violations, and revise the penal code to prevent the junta officers from benefiting from its "applicability of the most benign law" provision.[2]

Alfonsín's reform bills finally passed Congress after three weeks of bitter debate. While conservative congressmen argued that the military had done no wrong by crushing the terrorists, the Madres de la Plaza booed and heckled them from the galleries and crowded outside the exits to badger them as they left the floor. Hebe de Bonafini, the Madres' leader, rejected the "two demons" theory because labelling the guerrillas as "demons" played into the military's hands, practically justifying their "Dirty War" tactics. Nevertheless, Congress ratified Decree No. 157, holding the ERP and Montonero leaders criminally responsible for insurrection because they had violated the amnesty of May 1973. Congress also declared that the guerrillas were involved with "foreign interests that selected [Argentina] to apply their forces" with the intent to "obstruct the governance of democratically-elected authorities." Enrique Gorriarán Merlo, Mario Firmenich, Fernando Vaca Narvaja, Rodolfo Galimberti, and Ricardo Obregón Cano were specifically named in the charges.

Decree No. 158 applied to the nine men who had served on the *proceso*'s first three juntas: Lieutenant General Jorge Videla, Lieutenant General Roberto Viola, Lieutenant General Leopoldo Galtieri, Admiral Emilio Massera, Admiral Armando Lambruschini, Admiral Jorge Anaya, Brigadier Orlando Agosti, Brigadier Omar Graffigna, and Brigadier Basilio Lami-Dozo. They were charged with multiple counts of illegal detention, torture, and homicide, and the Supreme Military Council was ordered to bring them to trial. The decree also revised the military code to allow any decision reached by the Supreme Military Council to be appealed to the civilian courts.

Could Congress legally pass such a law and make it retroactive to cover alleged crimes committed in the past? From the very outset, prosecuting the junta leaders got tangled in knotty legal and constitutional questions. For example, although Congress abrogated the Self-Amnesty Law, the Supreme Court previously had recognized the *proceso*'s authority to legislate, including the right to issue binding decrees. Presumably, therefore, the Self-Amnesty Law was constitutional; by abrogating it, Congress was not only overriding the authority of the Supreme Court but opening the way to ex post facto legislation. That, in turn, raised other complicated legal questions. Did all of the legislation decreed by the junta between March 1976 and June 1983 remain null and void, or only selected decrees? Similarly, when Congress revised the military code to allow civilian courts jurisdiction over human rights crimes committed by the armed forces, lawyers for the defense quite properly attacked this too as ex post facto legislation. At the time that the alleged offenses took place, they argued, Article 108 of the Military Code of Justice gave military courts exclusive jurisdiction to try crimes committed by military personnel on military property or when on active duty. There was no right of appeal to civilian courts. Furthermore, they argued, the law was unconstitutional because Article 18 of the Constitution

THIRTEEN

Retribution

During the election campaign, Raúl Alfonsín promised that if he became president he would prosecute all those under the *proceso* who were responsible for human rights violations: both the actual torturers and those who issued the orders. The military's Self-Amnesty Law was "absolutely null." True to his promise, Alfonsín announced on the day before his inauguration that he was preparing two executive decrees for Congress to ratify. One would require the Supreme Military Council to begin criminal proceedings against all those who had participated in the junta from the day of the coup to the appointment of Bignone as provisional president. The second would order the civil courts to begin proceedings against the top leaders of the Montoneros and ERP for crimes committed after 25 May 1973, the date on which Cámpora took office as the constitutionally legitimate president. The country had been flagellated by "two demons," he argued, and both must be exorcised.[1]

Before the decrees could be issued, however, there had to be changes in the laws. First, the military code gave the Supreme Military Council final jurisdiction in criminal matters affecting military personnel. Alfonsín wanted to be able to remove the case to civilian jurisdiction if the Supreme Military Council failed to punish the junta chiefs. Second, Article 2 of the penal code required that accused persons be given the benefit of any doubt and must be charged under whichever law is most favorable to their case. The junta leaders were sure to claim protection under the Self-Amnesty Law. Three days after his inauguration, Alfonsín sent seven bills to Congress that would rescind the Self-Amnesty Law, revise the military code to allow the Supreme Military Council's decisions to be reviewed by the Federal Court of Appeals, revise the Code of Criminal forbids ex post facto laws and requires that the accused be tried by judges "appointed by law prior to the commission of the offense for which he is tried." All in all, the defense lawyers concluded that the entire trial was "political" because it had been initiated by a president whose very attempt to change the law imputed guilt to the defendants.[3]

Nevertheless, the process went forward. On 29 December 1983, Videla, Viola, Lambruschini, and Graffigna were summoned before the Supreme Military Council to hear the formal charges against them. Agosti, Lami-Dozo, Anaya, and Galtieri appeared the following day. Massera, the ninth man, already was in jail, charged with Fernando Branca's murder. The eight retired, formerly high-ranking, officers on the Supreme Military Council had no relish for their task. They had been given six months to deliberate, after which the Federal Court of Appeals could take over the case at any stage of the proceedings "if it notices an unjustifiable delay or lack of progress in the trial." Nor could they agree to General Videla's motion to have the case dismissed. The Supreme Court, "cleansed" and reconstituted with Alfonsín's appointees, already had declared Congress's acts to be constitutional.[4]

In answering the charges before the Supreme Military Council, all the defendants took the position that their actions had been justified by the executive decree issued by Provisional President Italo Luder in October 1975 ordering the military to "annihilate" (*aniquilar*) all guerrilla and terrorist activity throughout Argentina, which is what they had proceeded to do. Because Luder, as provisional president, had the constitutional authority to issue such a decree, the armed forces' officers were acting within the law.

General Videla's testimony before the Supreme Military Council laid down the main arguments for the defense. "I am convinced that I committed no crime in carrying out my duties as commander-in-chief of the army," he told the judges. "I insist on the right to claim that the actions of the government which I headed were political acts; and as such they may be subjects for debate, but not for criminal liability." He reminded the council that terrorists had declared war upon Argentine society and that large segments of that society had applauded the military's acceptance of the challenge. As for any alleged atrocities, or "excesses," committed by the security forces, those were the natural and unavoidable concomitant of war. "Some have called this a 'dirty war,' " Videla said, "but I absolutely refuse to accept that kind of terminology because it seems to imply that there are 'clean wars,' as opposed to 'dirty wars.' But war is war—just that."

He then began describing the mysterious beginnings of the particular war that had taken place in Argentina. When had it started: With the murder of Aramburu? With the *cordobazo*? There were Uturunco guerrillas operating a decade earlier. When did this war end? Indeed, had it ever ended? "I ask myself if, right now, we can say with certainty that, although military operations are suspended, this war has really ended. And I would not dare to offer a definitive answer." Videla also described the war's irregular character. The enemy did not behave like a regular army. It wore no uniforms, flew no flags, operated from no fixed bases, and occupied no definite territory. The Argentine military fought against a hidden foe who blended into the population and struck from ambush without warning. To fight such an enemy, tactics had to be flexible. Orders were issued in very general terms, leaving the commanders in the field free to adjust to any situation. Rather disingenuously, Videla denied any knowledge of "disappearances" or summary executions. The testimony of the other eight defendants followed the same lines. Although it took seven hours in all, the process stretched out to 13 February.[5]

After hearing the defendants, the Supreme Military Council received testimony from people claiming to be victims of the "Dirty War." This procedure dragged on too, through March, April, May, and June. When the allotted six-month period was up, on 28 June, the council asked for more time and was given another thirty days. That was repeated twice more, despite grumblings from the Federal Court of Appeals. Brigadier Luis Fages, the council's spokesman, insisted that the council was not dragging its heels. After all, the junta commanders could not be legitimately sentenced unless the council did a thorough investigation into which, and how many, illicit acts they were responsible for, in order to determine the degree of their culpability. It was clear, however, that the real cause for delay was the council's belief that the defendants were not guilty, as Fages revealed when he added that "the indictments are based on accusations from persons implicated in [subversive] acts, or from their relatives, whose objectivity and credibility are therefore doubtful." He went on to say that certain similarities in the content and style of the accusations had aroused suspicion on the council that there was some sort of collaboration among the accusers, inspired perhaps by interested "third parties."

At the beginning of August the nine defendants were allowed to make their final statements to the council. As before, Videla went first and made the most thorough defense of the junta's actions, although he added nothing new to what already had been said. The next day, 2 August, he was placed under "preventative arrest," to join Massera, Galtieri, Anaya, and Lami-Dozo, the last three having been jailed previously on charges of misconduct over the Falkland Islands War. But if those moves were intended to mollify public opinion's growing impatience with the council, they failed. On 25 September, Alfonsín ordered the Superior Military Council to turn over all its documents in the case to the Federal Court of Appeals. Now the "real trial" would begin.

JUDGES AND PROSECUTORS

On taking office, Alfonsín created a panel consisting of close friends from the UCR to advise him on appointments to the Federal Court of Appeals. The men it recommended were much like themselves: young, "progressive" lawyers in their 30s. Three of them, Jorge Torlasco, Andrés D'Alessio, and Ricardo Gil Lavedra, were UCR activists and already known as "Alfonsín's men," having previously formed part of the Commission of Justice that wrote the revisions to the military code. After making it possible for the Federal Court of Appeals to hear the case, they now would be able to decide its outcome. Jorge Alejandro Valera was Gil Lavedra's colleague at the University of El Salvador Law School. Guillermo Ledesma was a lower court judge and law professor who had been one of the first to attack the military's Self-Amnesty Law as unconstitutional. León Arslanián, the only Peronist in the group, was a personal friend of Jaime Malamud-Goti, who was on the selection panel.[6]

Julio Cesar Strassera would be the chief prosecutor, charged with pinning the blame for the "Dirty War's" atrocities on the junta officers. He rejected their claim that such "errors" happened without their knowledge because of the highly decentralized strategy they used. He was convinced, rightly, that the junta officers knew perfectly well that clandestine torture centers existed and that their current professions of ignorance were lies. Still, he would have to prove that the security forces were acting on orders from above. Because no written orders existed, he would need circumstantial evidence that such orders were given verbally by showing that tactics were similar all over the country and that there was cooperation between the three armed services branches, the National Gendarmerie, and the police. Then he would argue that because the military is a pyramidal organization in which hierarchy, discipline, and obedience are prevailing virtues, the behavior of the lower levels must have conformed to orders from the top.[7]

Strassera had nothing but contempt for Videla's defense that the military was obeying decrees signed by Isabel Perón and Italo Luder. The military could hardly claim to only be following the orders of legitimately constituted authorities when it then forcibly overthrew those same authorities. He also dismissed the military's claim that it was fighting a war. There was never any declaration of war, Strassera countered, and if there was a war then the armed forces had violated the 1949 Geneva Conventions, which protect the rights of civilians and prisoners of war and to which Argentina was a signatory. The military's claim that this was a "new kind of war" requiring "irregular" tactics was no argument either, in his view. Signatories to the Geneva Conventions agreed to avoid "violence to life and person; in particular, murder of all kinds, mutilation, cruel treatment, and torture." Moreover, the *proceso* had also violated the U.N. Universal Declaration of Human Rights, the U.N. Charter affirming faith in "fundamental human rights," and the 1975 U.N. Declaration on the Protection of All Persons from Torture and Other Cruel, Inhuman, or Degrading Treatment or Punishment.[8]

In preparing his case, Strassera had the crucial assistance of CONADEP. Created on 15 December 1983 by Executive Decree No. 187, CONADEP employed more than 120 people who traveled around the country and overseas to interview families and friends of the "disappeared," former prisoners, and human rights activists. They also visited former clandestine detention centers, compiled documents, and prepared the evidence that later would be used by the Ministry of Justice against the military defendants at the Federal Court of Appeals. All of this evidence had to be assembled within 180 days, so CONADEP's employees worked 10-hour days 7 days a week. Even so, the size of the task finally forced Alfonsín to extend its life by another three months. Not until 20 September 1984 did CONADEP's president, Ernesto Sábato, finally present its 50,000-page final report. More than 1,300 military and police officials were targeted for possible indictments, in addition to the junta leaders. For lack of sufficient evidence, the Ministry of Justice narrowed down the actual number of cases to 670.

Like everything else connected with the military trials, CONADEP was a matter of controversy. As a special investigating body, rather than a parliamentary commission, it was said to violate Article 18 of the Constitution, which prohibited the use of special commissions to judge defendants. Nevertheless, Alfonsín had decided that a parliamentary commission would get bogged down in partisan bickering, and he therefore excluded Peronists and conservatives. All of the 13 members of CONADEP's executive committee were radicals and human rights activists. Sábato was a highly regarded novelist—but also, as conservatives pointed out, an outspoken admirer of Ché Guevara and the Cuban Revolution.[9]

Though leaning to the left, CONADEP failed to enlist the support of either Adolfo Pérez Esquivel or the Madres de la Plaza. The Nobel prizewinner refused an invitation to join its executive committee because he suspected Alfonsín of wanting to limit the scope of the trials. The original Executive Decree No. 158 would have allowed a military defendant to plead "due obedience." That would allow lower-level officers who had committed atrocities to escape punishment and limit the trials only to those at the very top of the *proceso*. Congress had eliminated the "due obedience" provision, however, so now Pérez Esquivel and the Madres had more confidence in a congressional investigation than in a commission appointed by the president. The Madres pointed out that CONADEP had no subpoena powers and could not compel testimony; they also recalled that Ernesto Sábato had attended a luncheon hosted by General Videla in 1976 and came away describing him as a cordial and cultivated man. Their real criticism of CONADEP, however, rested on the belief that the entire armed forces, from top to bottom, were guilty of the "Dirty War's" crimes. In their view, those who had remained silent and passive had tacitly acquiesced in the kidnapping, torture, rape, and murder, and so they were as guilty as the actual perpetrators. Thus, they wanted all the officers put on trial.[10]

CONADEP's final report, issued in November, was published immediately by EUDEBA in a five-hundred page edition entitled *Nunca Más* ("Never Again"). It was a thorough description of the kidnappings, torture methods, conditions in the clandestine detention centers, the executions, the robberies and extortions, and the *proceso*'s coordination with other right-wing military regimes in the region. It also included a list of 8,961 persons "known" to have disappeared. In assessing what kind of people those victims were, it rejected the military's claim that the guerrilla organizations had a combined strength of 25,000 activists, of whom 15,000 were fanatical killers. CONADEP pointed out that the military courts condemned only around 350 people of terrorist crimes, and it concluded that the kidnappings and disappearances were "adopted to suppress thousands of opponents, whether they were terrorists or not." In fact, the whole *proceso* was unnecessary, in CONADEP's view. The prologue of *Nunca Más* compared Argentina's experience with terrorism to Italy's and argued that Italy never abandoned the rule of law, despite violence by the Brigada Rossa and various fascist groups, even after the kidnapping and murder of Prime Minister Aldo Moro. Extremists were dealt with through regular law courts, where defendants enjoyed the full guarantees of the law.[11]

Despite its impressive scope and detail, *Nunca Más* came under fire from both Left and Right. The Madres criticized it for not publishing the names of torturers, for not insisting more emphatically that most of the *proceso*'s victims were innocent, for including an introduction that reiterated the "two demons theory," for underestimating the number of "disappeared" (they insisted that the figure was closer to 30,000), and for treating the "disappeared" as dead. On this somewhat curious latter point, the Madres insisted that the "disappeared" should not be considered dead until an accounting was made of the fate of each one. To do otherwise would be to close the book on the "Dirty War," instead of examining the whole social system that produced the *proceso*. To make their point, the Madres continued their weekly marches around the Plaza de Mayo, bearing placards that read "*aparición con vida*" ("produce them alive").[12]

On the Right, a group called the Forum for Studies on the Administration of Justice (FORES) responded in a publication called *Definitivamente . . . Nunca Más*. According to FORES, *Nunca Más* was based on unsubstantiated testimony. CONADEP's investigators never attempted to assess the reliability of their witnesses or their evidence, mainly because they themselves had been, directly or indirectly, victims of repression and therefore were too emotionally involved to be objective. They automatically assumed that the "Dirty War's" victims were almost always innocent, and so their testimony was accepted without question as valid, although such witnesses might have had links to subversive organizations. Horacio Lynch, one of the principal authors of *Definitivamente . . . Nunca Más*, concluded that CONADEP's job should have been carried out by judicial magistrates, who would have deposed the witnesses under oath with potential sanctions for perjury. FORES also considered the comparison of Argentina with Italy to be misleading because Argentina lacked the moral and institutional defenses necessary to fight terrorism under a democracy. In Italy, public opinion supported democratic institutions, which had been in place since 1945, and so the Brigada Rossa was isolated; in Argentina, democracy was weak and the public ambivalent toward it. For decades the rule of law had been violated under both elected and de facto governments when Congress and the courts failed to function as the Constitution indicated. Nor were the terrorists isolated: General Perón originally encouraged them, as did also the Movement of Third World Priests, the Cámpora administration, Congress (with its amnesty), various provincial governments, and a large part of the Argentine intelligentsia. Finally, FORES thought that publishing *Nunca Más* during the trials showed that CONADEP was partisan and trying to ensure a guilty verdict.[13]

THE ARRAIGNMENT

On Thursday, 18 October 1984, Videla and Massera, dressed in civilian clothes, appeared before the Federal Court of Appeals to enter their pleas. Videla refused either to answer the charges or choose a lawyer, making it clear from the outset that he considered the proceedings to be unlawful. The court then appointed a lawyer for him: Carlos Tavares, who entered a plea of not guilty. Massera, by contrast, came with a lawyer, Jaime Prats Cardona, an old-fashioned advocate with flowery speech who also was defending him in the Fernando Branca case. Massera told the court that he was glad to be under the federal judiciary's jurisdiction rather than that of the Supreme Military Council, because he was the target of an army conspiracy to set him up as the villain of the *proceso*. He pleaded not guilty. Questioned by Judge Torlasco, Massera denied that there had been any verbal or written agreements among the armed forces chiefs on common procedures for fighting subversion. He also denied that any human rights violations had occurred under the navy's jurisdiction while he was commander in chief. He had personally inspected all the naval units, and the crimes that were now being alleged could not possibly have taken place. Referring to Massera's testimony before the Supreme Military Council that Argentina had been in a state of war, Torlasco asked him if the armed forces had applied the rules of war to the guerrillas. "Yes, in principle," Massera replied, "but I should point out that there were no existing international conventions with respect to combating terrorism. We applied the Code of Military Justice and the Penal Code. A prisoner was not a prisoner of war; he was an arrested criminal, subject to criminal justice."[14]

Viola appeared the following Monday. His examination lasted an exhausting eight hours. What knowledge did he have about the secret detention centers? Judge Torlasco asked. They were military installations where subversives were kept temporarily, pending a decision on whether to set them free or try them, Viola answered. What about the disappearances? There was no hard evidence that the army was involved, Viola claimed, nor had there been any orders "at the level of commander-in-chief or General Staff Headquarters" to use torture.

On 25 October, after hearing Agosti and Lambruschini, the Court ordered these five defendants to be held for trial. Ironically, they were put in the same prison as Ricardo Obregón Cano, the former governor of Córdoba, who had been arrested in December 1983 for his activities in connection with the Montoneros. Across town, Mario Firmenich was in Villa Devoto prison, having been arrested in Rio de Janeiro on 2 February 1984 and extradited. Meanwhile, the defendants made one last attempt to get the Supreme Court to stop the process on the grounds that Law No. 23,049 violated Article 18 of the Constitution, but they lost their appeal on 27 December, which removed the last obstacle to the trial.

THE TRIAL: OPENING MOVES

There was tight security around the federal courthouse when the trial opened on Monday, 22 April. There were barricades all around the building, and extra police were detailed to keep back the large crowd that had gathered. In the plaza across the way, some two hundred demonstrators were holding a rally, demanding punishment for the junta officers. By afternoon, their numbers would swell to around 50,000. Inside, the courtroom had been refurbished to allow for television coverage. The press boxes were situated against the side walls, while space in the rear was reserved for 75 specially invited guests, many of them leaders of human rights organizations: Hebe de Bonafini, Adolfo Pérez Esquivel, Emilio Mignone, and Augusto Conte. Behind them was a gallery with another one hundred seats for the general public. The judges were on a platform in the middle of the room. To one side were a desk and chairs for the prosecution; opposite was a similar arrangement for the defense. There were two chairs facing the judges, one for the witness and another for a translator, if needed.[15]

Strassera—lean, austere, chain-smoking, with his large moustache and his face lined from the strain of trying to fashion his case from the mounds of evidence—dominated the courtroom with his energy and emotions. Fired by the force of his own convictions, he was more than a match for any one of the defense lawyers, or all of them together. The latter had not bothered to coordinate their defense and had no common strategy. Massera's lawyer, Jaime Prats Cardona, with his pompous, extravagant style, was the epitome of the old-fashioned oligarchy. His literary allusions fell flat, and his attempt to depict his client as an idealist and a stargazer provoked snickers. José María Orgeira, Viola's lawyer, was another Barrio Norte type and was especially inept in his choice of words. When questioning prosecution witnesses, he often referred to each as "the prisoner" (*el detenido*), which only drew attention to the fact that they had been illegally held. He also tried various times to justify torture as a way to get information, referring to it euphemistically as "illegal pressure." That was especially provoking to Strassera, who at one point said that he almost expected Orgeira to tell some witness, "OK, you can take off your hood now." Carlos Tavares, Videla's lawyer, was competent but handicapped by his client's refusal to cooperate. Videla now sat at the defendants' bench, reading a book, usually a catechism, apparently unconcerned about what was happening around him. Massera, on the other hand, was jovial, confident, smiling—exhuberant at being the center of attention. The other defendants watched the proceedings morosely, interchanging nervous looks and whispers.

The first issue to be tackled was the claim that the military had carried out its tactics legally, as authorized by Provisional President Italo Luder's fateful

executive decree of 6 October 1975, which ordered the armed forces to annihilate subversive activity throughout the country. Luder was called to the witness
stand to explain the intent behind the decree. Like the rest of the Peronists,
Luder disapproved of the trial, but on the stand he refused to give the military
the cover that it desired. He denied that the language of his executive order
meant the physical annihilation of the subversives, or that it authorized illegal
methods like kidnapping, torture, or executions. He simply meant, he said, that
the armed forces should render the subversives "incapable of combat" by adding
their strength to that of the provincial police. Even when Prats Cardona asked
Luder whether he had signed the decree because of the "state of war in which
the country was living," the latter fudged his answer: "I don't believe a state of
war existed. There were threats, yes."

The military interpreted *annihilate* differently. Retired Vice Admiral Luis
María Mendía, who had been the navy's chief of operations in 1976, quoted the
Dictionary of the Royal Spanish Academy, which defined the word as meaning
"to destroy, to reduce to nothing." *Annihilation* would indicate the most extreme
type of mission, which is what the armed forces had carried out. "The armed
forces are violent," Mendía insisted. "They don't use half-measures." On cross-
examination, however, Strassera forced the admiral to retreat. Did the order to
"annihilate" authorize torture or the killing of defenseless prisoners? No, Mendía
admitted, not at all.

Nevertheless, the defense made a fairly good showing during the first days
of the trial. General Cristino Nicolaides and Adm. Rubén Oscar Franco stood
their ground on the subject of "excesses." Nicolaides testified that he had punished such acts when they were brought to his attention, but it was always
possible that some wrongs had escaped his notice and gone unpunished. In any
case, such excesses arose through noncompliance with given orders. Both Nicolaides and Franco emphasized the unconventional nature of the war and the
great discretion allowed to the lower-level commanders in the field. Strassera
especially went after Franco to shake his testimony. Would killing an unarmed
prisoner be an act of war? It might occur in the heat of battle, Franco answered.
What about the killing of an unarmed, manacled, and blindfolded prisoner?
Franco claimed to know of no such killings but admitted that such an act would
be brutal. Then Judge Arslanián demanded to know, concretely, whether such
a killing would be considered an act of war. Franco replied that it would not
be an act of war, but it would be an act that could easily occur in a war.

The prosecution made little headway with civilian witnesses, either. Horacio
Domingorena, a UCR politician who currently was president of the state airlines,
recalled a conversation he had with General Viola in which he asked the general
whether he was concerned that arming parapolice and paramilitary groups might
result in their getting out of control. Viola told him that the armed forces were
well aware of the danger. Then he asked about a friend of Viola's, a journalist
named Fernández Pondal, who had disappeared. When Domingorena suggested
that the guerrillas might have kidnapped him, Viola contradicted him: "By no

means! Fernández Pondal was kidnapped by other forces that have nothing to do with the guerrillas. I only hope that someday I'll find out who ordered his kidnapping." Although such evidence hardly presented a favorable picture of the regime, it served to emphasize how little control those at the top had over the machinery of repression. Even more disappointing to Strassera was the testimony of two secretaries of the CGT, Ramón Baldassini and Jorge Triaca. Baldassini, rather than condemning the *proceso*, dwelled on the guerrilla assassinations of Vandor, Alonso, and Rucci. Strassera, surprised and annoyed, wanted to know why he hadn't mentioned Oscar Smith, but he was told by Judge Arslanián to stop leading the witness. Triaca proved even more frustrating. Yes, he was arrested after the coup and held prisoner aboard a naval vessel for almost eight months. "Illegal privation of liberty," Strassera concluded, but then Prats Cardona asked Triaca about the treatment he had received. It was exemplary, Triaca replied. Of course the prisoners' mail was censored and they were not allowed family visits for a couple of months, but as far as personal treatment was concerned, it was cordial and left no feelings of resentment.

There were a few dramatic incidents during the first week. Robert Cox, the former editor in chief of *The Buenos Aires Herald*, flew back from the United States to testify on Wednesday, 24 April, but his nerves were so wrought up that he had to be excused until the following Monday. On Tuesday the 23rd, the prosecution and defense had their first courtroom clash over the appearance of Theodore van Boven, the Dutch former director of the U.N.'s Human Rights Division, who had announced his plans to arrive in Buenos Aires only the previous night, giving the defense no time to prepare. Nevertheless, the judges allowed him to take the stand. Van Boven spoke for four hours; he said that his division had received 3,367 complaints of state violence to which the Argentine government refused to respond. Moreover, the junta had ordered its U.N. ambassador to obstruct any investigations and prevent him from bringing an investigating committee into the country. Defense lawyers countered his testimony by asking if he had tried to verify the reliability of the people making those accusations. U.N. procedural rules did not allow him to expand the scope of his investigations to include the accusers, he replied.

On Thursday afternoon, while Louis Joinnet, a French jurist, was testifying, Augusto Conte entered the courtroom and approached Orgeira, Viola's lawyer, from behind and whispered something in his ear. Suddenly, Tavares, Videla's lawyer, jumped to his feet, almost knocking over his desk. "Señor Presidente!" he told Judge Arslanián, "Deputy Conte has just threatened Doctor Orgeira!" By this time Orgeira was on his feet, too, waving his arms as a loud murmur rose up in the room. Conte, meanwhile, retreated along the aisle and took an empty seat in the fourth row of the guest section, as if nothing had happened. Arslanián ordered Tavares to be seated, while Roberto Calandra, Graffigna's lawyer, restrained Orgeira from stomping down the aisle toward Conte. The latter now arose and denied that he had threatened anyone; he had only reminded Orgeira that Argentina was now a democracy because yesterday Orgeira had asked the police to check the identity of a young, long-haired, bearded man from SERPAJ. Arslanián interrupted to silence him and then shouted down Tavares, who rose again to demand that Conte be removed from the room. At that, Tavares, Orgeira, Calandra, and Andrés Marutián (another of Viola's lawyers) started to walk out in protest. Arslanián ordered the security guards to stop them, which brought thunderous applause from the audience of specially invited guests.

THE TURNING POINT

The first week of the trial had gone better for the defense than might have been expected, but things picked up for the prosecution when the trial resumed on Monday. Cox took the stand and gave vivid details about the life of a journalist under the *proceso*. He had been arrested for publishing information about "disappearances": "They took me in a Ford Falcon. In front was a man with a machine gun. They were talking about the case of a man in whose head they had made a hole, from one side to the other, with a bullet. I figured they were trying to frighten me. They took me to Federal Police headquarters, took away all my clothes, and shut me up in a dark cell. Even so, I was able to make out the words 'national socialism' on the wall, beneath a swastika. That was in June 1977."

Cox also recalled the arrest of Mónica Mignone. "Her parents let her go. They even gave her bus money because they believed their daughter was being taken by members of the Argentine armed forces, in whom they confided, just as I did. She was neither a terrorist nor a leftist." He had spoken on many occasions with General Videla. He was always friendly, and Cox had a high regard for him. Once he had asked Videla for protection for his family because his son, Peter, had been threatened. Videla became nervous and told Cox that those threats were coming from within the military itself. He did not think that anything actually would happen, but he could give Cox no guarantees. That is when Cox decided to get out of Argentina.[16]

As strong as Cox's testimony was, it paled before that of the next witness, Adriana Calvo de Laborde. She had a bachelor's degree in physics and was working as a research assistant at the University of La Plata's Faculty of Exact Sciences when she was arrested on 4 February 1977. A group of armed men broke into her apartment and forced her to go with them to the Investigations Headquarters of the Buenos Aires provincial police. She was more than seven months pregnant, yet they wrapped her head in a sweater, threw her on the floor of the car, and threatened to kill her if she moved. After arriving, she was tortured. During the next several weeks in a cell she was allowed to bathe only once, and many days passed without food. The cell was so crowded with other women that they often slept sitting upright. There were no beds, mattresses, or blankets. Through the walls people could be heard screaming, children crying.

Calvo de Labarde was transferred to another detention center, Pozo de Banfield. During the ride, she gave birth.

I was lying on the floor of the car, my eyes blindfolded. They were insulting me. I told them that my baby was about to come, that I couldn't wait, that they should stop, that it was not my first child and that I knew it was about to come. The driver and his companion laughed. They told me it was all the same to them: they were going to kill me and kill my child too, so what did it matter? Finally, I managed to get my panties off so the baby could emerge—I really don't know how. I screamed. We were going full speed down the road that leads from La Plata to Buenos Aires. The car was going full speed and I screamed to them: "It's born! I can't wait!" And indeed it emerged; my baby was born.

They pulled over on the shoulder of the road. We were exactly in front of the Abbot Laboratories. My baby was born all right. It was very small, but it was hanging by the umbilical cord. It had fallen off the seat onto the floor. I asked them to please let me have it, to let it stay with me. They wouldn't let me near it. They tied up the cord with a dirty rag and we continued down the highway. Three minutes had passed. My baby cried and I continued lying there with my hands tied behind my back and my eyes covered. They wouldn't give it to me, Señor President. That day I swore that if my baby lived and I lived, I would fight the rest of my days to see justice done.

She told her story in a plain, level voice that gave it even more emotional impact. When she was finished, there was no sound in the courtroom. Interviewed at the end of the day, Strassera was very pleased; his witnesses were "devastating," he said. Looking back on the trial later on, he concluded, "I won't claim that I won the case right then and there; but her testimony, coming near the opening of the trial, was a tremendous blow, both for the public and for those who had been defending the Juntas."

Other witnesses who had been kidnapped, tortured, and kept in detention centers followed. One of them, Ana María Saracoche de Gática, had lost a one-year-old child to kidnappers while the child was staying with a neighbor, in March 1977, and the following month she and her newborn baby were seized by soldiers at her apartment. She never saw either of her children again. *Somos* recorded that the testimony of these witnesses caused so much emotion in the courtroom that several members of the audience broke down and wept or were found sobbing on the stairs leading to the outside. The defense lawyers preferred, in most cases, to forgo any questions rather than risk more detailed descriptions. They were limited to complaining that, unlike at a regular trial, the defense had not been presented in advance with a list of witnesses, had not been allowed to depose them, and had not even been given a summary of their accusations against the defendants.[17]

FRUSTRATED DEFENSE

Orgeira accused the judges of being partial to the prosecution by not permitting the defense to ask the witnesses certain questions of fundamental importance. The defense had only one hope of counterattacking witnesses who gave dramatic testimony about torture and abuse in the detention centers: to try to impeach their veracity by linking them to the terrorists. As a rule, however, the court refused to allow the defense lawyers to ask questions that would require a witness to self-incriminate by admitting to subversive activities.[18] For example, Judge Ledesma, presiding on 7 June, intervened to rescue Marta Haydeé García de Candeloro. She had been arrested along with her husband, who subsequently "disappeared." Orgeira was pressing her about her friendships with certain individuals when Ledesma demanded to know where he was leading the witness. Did he have any evidence that the people being named were subversives? Orgeira replied that he was sure they were Marxists. "Marxists?" Ledesma sputtered. "That's not enough, doctor." Nonetheless, Orgeira returned to the attack a few minutes later, demanding to know if it was true that García de Candeloro had been dismissed from the faculty of the University of Mar del Plata in 1975 for her political activities; and hadn't she been a political activist while president of the Provincial Normal School's student center back in 1956? The witness was momentarily stunned. "Where did you get that information?" Strassera then interrupted to demand that Orgeira provide him with this information and its source. Ledesma stepped in, too, and halted the line of questioning.

On another occasion former Lieutenant Ernesto Facundo Urien was on the stand, testifying to the brutal conditions at the La Perla detention center, where he had seen manacled, hooded prisoners. One of Viola's lawyers, Carlos Froment, got Urien to admit that in the early 1970s he had been part of a Peronist military faction led by Lieutenant Julián Licastro, a left-wing officer who eventually was forced out of the army. With a little more prodding Urien admitted that his older brother, Julio César, had been cashiered from the marines in 1972 because of his political activities. Presiding Judge D'Alessio stopped this line of questioning, however, when Froment began asking Urien about his own contacts with the Left, on the grounds that it was just a fishing expedition.

Not only were defense lawyers often frustrated in their attempts to impeach prosecution witnesses, they were also sometimes held up to ridicule. It was easy to stir up laughter at their expense because the audience of invited guests was hostile toward them. Such a situation happened when Orgeira began asking the father of a "disappeared" girl about his daughter's friends. Judge Gil-Lavedra ruled the question out of order, which provoked Orgeira to protest, "The defense has a right to try to determine the character of those who were prisoners." At that point Strassera broke in with a scornful laugh. "Sure, the defense wants to know if they were Montoneros because it's all right to torture Montoneros." Laughter exploded in the courtroom, and afterward there were sarcastic jokes in the corridors that "from now on there are kidnappings that are good and those that are not so good."

Occasionally, though, the defense was able to get a prosecution witness to trip up. Strassera put a former ESMA "slave" of Massera's, Victor Basterra, on the stand. Basterra testified as to how he, a printer by trade, had been put to

work fabricating all kinds of official documents for the criminal types used in
the task forces. In four hours of testimony he described the conditions inside
ESMA, named former comrades who had "disappeared," and related how, starting in 1980, he had been allowed visits to his family once or twice a month.
On those occasions he had smuggled out photographs of officers, prisoners, and
documents, all of which were later turned over to CONADEP. Under cross-
examination Basterra first insisted that he had been arrested simply because he
had participated in a "workers' discussion group," but under the pressure of
questioning by Miguel Angel Buero, Anaya's lawyer, he finally admitted that
he was a member of the left-wing movement called Peronismo de Base. A little
more pressure brought out the confession that Basterra had already known how
to falsify documents before his arrest. Still, he continued to deny that his *compañeros* in the "workers' discussion group" were members of the FAP or that
he had been aware that Peronismo de Base was a Montonero front organization.

Strassera's quickness often enabled him to neutralize a potentially damaging
point. Elena Alfaro, kidnapped in April 1977 and held at both El Vesúbio and
La Tablada, was unfolding a particularly horrible story of being tortured and
raped by her captors. Raping female prisoners was common practice, she explained, even pregnant ones. She herself had been four months pregnant when
captured. Eventually she had her child in prison, and it was baptized on 20
January 1979. Strassera produced the baptismal certificate, which listed Colonel
Franco Luque, whom she identified as one of her rapists as the godfather. Hers
was the sort of emotionally charged testimony that the defense usually preferred
not to cross-examine, but this time Juan Carlos Rosales, one of Galtieri's lawyers, produced a surprise. He had a letter that Alfaro's father had written to
Colonel Luque the year before, a couple of days after she had made some critical
statements to the press about him. "My dear friend," the letter began, "Despite
the passage of time that has elapsed since you returned her to me, alive and
well, I cannot forget all that you did for her, to the point that you were chosen
to be the godfather of her son, Luis Felipe. It is because of all that that I feel
shocked by the statements she made . . . accusing you and Lt. Col. Duran Sáenz
of maltreatment and other atrocities that it were better she had not gone into."

Both Alfaro and Strassera were dumbfounded by the letter, whose existence
they never suspected, but Strassera quickly recovered and pounced on it. "Her
father says, 'You returned her to me alive and well'—what does that mean?
Where did he return her 'alive and well' from? Why the 'return'? Who was
holding her?" "Now I discover the truth," Alfaro added. "My father was my
perfect 'control.' Why, I don't know. I guess he agreed with Luque; that his
ideology is the same as the military's." At that point Rosales mistakenly tried
to push further but only ended up making Alfaro sympathetic once more. Hoping
to smear her as a "loose woman," he returned to the fact that she had been
living with a boyfriend and was four months pregnant when taken into custody.
How free was she with her sexual favors? Had she ever willingly shared them
with Colonel Luque? Presiding Judge Valera Aráoz interrupted to say that the

question was completely improper, but Rosales persisted. Did she ever make love to Lieutenant Colonel . . . ? Visibly angry now, Valera Aráoz ordered Rosales to stop.

BIG NAMES, DRAMATIC MOMENTS

Whatever minor damage the defense may have occasionally made to the prosecution's case, it was buried under a growing pile of evidence about the extent of the *proceso*'s criminal side. The murders of Héctor Hidalgo Solá, Elena Holmberg, and Edgardo Sajón cast a vivid light upon the moral corruption that unchecked power produced, for these were no terrorists or even sympathizers of the guerrilla Left. Indeed, they were part of the "establishment" that originally had welcomed the *proceso*.[19] Carlos Alberto Hours, a former policeman in Buenos Aires Province, admitted to working in a task force led by Col. Ramón Camps. Once you became a member, he claimed, it was almost impossible to get out; men had been killed for trying. In his own case, his sister had narrowly escaped being kidnapped after he had requested reassignment, and he had been warned that she would be "sucked in" if he tried to get out again. So he stayed in, and one of his tasks was to assist in killing Edgardo Sajón, who already had been held at a detention center for 17 months. Sajón was brought to the clubhouse of the Juan Vucetich School for Non-Commissioned Officers, unaware of the fate in store for him. He apparently had been treated fairly well up to then, for he looked healthy and his clothes were better than those of the ordinary prisoner. He and the men detailed to kill him chatted for a while, and then the leader suddenly announced, "I have orders to execute you." Sajón was stripped and stretched across a wet billiard table. One electric cable was attached to his toe and the other inserted in his mouth. Then the current was turned on until he died.

The grim details of the Elena Holmberg murder came out through a parade of witnesses that included Gregorio Dupont, former ambassador Tomás de Anchorena, Silvia Agulla, and General Alejandro Lanusse. Lanusse proved to be a prickly witness. After he was sworn in, Judge Gil-Lavedra asked him if there was anything that would affect his impartiality in giving testimony. "Why do you keep asking me if I'm going to tell the truth?" Lanusse shot back. "I just got finished swearing that I would tell the whole truth, and no one can doubt that I'm going to." He told of going to the cemetery to claim the body of Holmberg and discovering that the badly decomposed corpse was not hers. He added that afterwards he and General Suárez Masón went to the regional police headquarters in Tigre to vent their anger at the chief who made the blunder. "What do you want?" the officer asked Suárez Masón. "You guys have thrown more than eight thousand bodies into that river." That caused a murmuring around the courtroom, but neither Gil-Lavedra nor Strassera followed up this revelation or even asked for the name of the police officer.

Concerning the Edgardo Sajón case, Lanusse described how he went to Videla, Massera, Ibérico Saint-Jean, and Viola to obtain his friend's release. Videla told him that the kidnapping was part of the "left-handed" (*por izquierda*) procedures being adopted by Suárez Masón, Saint-Jean, and Camps to uncover the Graiver millions. Massera told him that Sajón's kidnapping was also connected to the Aluar investigation, because he had been Lanusse's press secretary, and confirmed that Suárez Masón and his friends were to blame. He also informed Lanusse that the "left-handed" procedures taken against the Graiver group were carried out with the authorization of the junta. Judge Gil-Lavedra interrupted to ask if that meant that General Videla was aware of all that was going on. Lanusse exploded again. "Señor, you are talking to a former commander-in-chief and a former president of the Republic! In those positions you can't be unaware of such things." That opened up the possibility of questioning Lanusse about the practice of "disappearances" under his own administration. Strassera began a line of questioning about that, but Lanusse insisted that he had come to testify only about the Elena Holmberg and Edgardo Sajón cases and refused to answer the questions, even when prodded by the judge. On cross-examination, Orgeira asked him specifically whether he knew how subversives were treated when he was head of the army, but the court cut him off.

Other "big names" took the stand. Ragnar Hagelin spoke for two hours about the kidnapping of his daughter Dagmar and his search for her. Jacobo Timerman appeared and provided a little unintentional humor when Judge Ledesma made a slip of the tongue and addressed him as "Señor Graiver." Timerman immediately bristled and demanded to know if the judge was accusing him of something. Hipólito Solari Yrigoyen described his tortures and those of his friend, Mario Abel Amaya. Alfredo Bravo told of his imprisonment at Cotí Martínez and claimed to have recognized General Camps. Patricia Derian flew in from Washington, but when she appeared, all the defense lawyers except for Tavares, who was court appointed, rose and left the room in protest. She told of her three visits to Argentina, during which she spoke with top officials. Massera had put on an act, assuring her that the navy never tortured anyone but that the army and air force did. Grinning, he had made a gesture of washing his hands of them. Videla, by contrast, had spoken to her more seriously. He implicitly admitted the occurrence of human rights violations by reminding her of "the difficulties there are in trying to control lower-level personnel, especially those who had seen their comrades suffer at the hands of terrorists."

The most damaging testimony came from lesser-known people. Pablo Díaz, a La Plata high school student arrested in connection with riots over bus fares, told of his passage through several detention camps, where he was brutally tortured and once made to go through a mock execution. Blindfolded, hands tied behind him, he and some other students were put against a wall. Someone claiming to be a priest asked if they had anything to confess. The girls were crying, and some fainted. One boy shouted, "*Vivan los Montoneros!*" Another said, "*Viva la Patria!*" "I was weeping silently," Díaz said. "They fired; I heard the discharge. I was waiting to feel the blood flow from some part of me. I thought I was dead. . . . It was only a second, but that second was an eternity. . . . I was waiting for the pain; the girls were still crying. After that they took us back to our cells."

Then there was Iris Etelvina Pereyra de Avellaneda, whose testimony lasted only 30 minutes; yet, as *Somos* described it, "on hearing it, a mixture of indignation, impotence, and astonishment was reflected in every face, *without exception*. Some members of the Tribunal pressed their hands to their temples, and everyone listed in absolute silence." On 15 April 1976 five men disguised with wigs and false beards burst into her home, looking for her husband, a Communist Party activist. He had just fled by the rooftops, so they hauled in his wife and 14-year-old son. She was tortured at Campo de Mayo to such an extent," she told Judge Torlasco, "that when I was finally released I couldn't nurse my baby daughter because they had burned out my mammary glands." Like Pablo Díaz, she went through a mock execution. "They said I could ask for three things first. I asked to know about the fate of my son. They told me, 'We've already killed him.' " Eventually she was released and began writing letters to various persons, asking for information about her son. Finally, a friend told her not to ask any more because his body had been found in the Río de la Plata by Uruguayan authorities. His hands and feet were tied, his neck had been broken, and he had been raped.

Pereyra de Avellaneda was followed by Armando Lucchina, a former Federal Police official, who described the procedures at headquarters. "They were not legal interrogations," he told the court, "they were total aberrations. They abused people to the most ignoble extremes. The prisoners were submitted to tortures like 'the submarine,' blows with chairs or wooden clubs, even to the point of violating men. My colleagues felt shocked and disgusted by what went on." He blamed the armed forces. "The robbery of automobiles, the moving of prisoners, the decision to take them up in helicopters to some undisclosed destiny—possibly to throw them in the river—were done so as not to let the police decide. We all knew that it depended on the three armed services." Asked by Tavares why he had not denounced those procedures at the time, Lucchina responded, "To whom? I've been present at a police station when the magistrate called by telephone to ask for 'free zones' for [military] action." A "free zone" was one in which the police stayed out of the way. "To which judge was I to turn?" Lucchina demanded.[20]

The sinister Mansión Seré was the main subject of testimony on 4 June, with various former prisoners and neighbors of the air force's torture center providing details. After the air force razed the house, one neighbor poked through the ruins and found human hair and fingers. A former prisoner testified how he and four other boys escaped on 24 March 1978 while the guards were away celebrating the second anniversary of the coup. They were able to slip out of their handcuffs because their arms had become so thin. In the early morning hours, they managed to loosen the shutters over the window of their second-floor cell and lower themselves to the ground by using bedsheets. Another prisoner testified that, after this escape, the remaining prisoners were transferred to the First Army Regiment in Palermo. Strassera made him emphasize that point, because it indicated that the three services shared a common strategy rather than operating in a completely decentralized fashion. Another ex-prisoner of Mansión Seré, Carmen Graciela Floriani, added details of sexual perversion. She had been violated with a police club on her first day of captivity, she related, and on the day she was finally released she had to engage in oral sex with her captor in exchange for her life. None of the defense lawyers rose to cross-examine her. Orgeira started to but then changed his mind and sat down.[21]

What could they have accomplished, anyway? Repeated attempts to sully the character of witnesses were futile. Even if they had been terrorists, they did not deserve to be victimized in the manner described in that courtroom, and no one doubted the veracity of their testimony. As one of the defense's own witnesses, Máximo Gainza, the publisher of *La Prensa*, summarized it, "In a civilized country people should be judged and, if necessary, shot. But you don't just make people disappear." That fell like an icy shower on the defense, alleviated only slightly by his suggestion that the whole society, including the prosecution and the court, colluded in the *proceso*. "It surprises me," he said, at the end of his testimony, "the number of people nowadays who pretend not to have known what was happening back then. If they didn't know, it's because they didn't want to know." The defense also called Arturo Frondizi as a witness, a fact he considered to be "incomprehensible," because he had lost a brother and three nephews to right-wing violence, and while president he had been challenged by repeated military revolts before being overthrown. Nevertheless, he urged an amnesty for the junta leaders. "Look, Your Honor, I've been through a lot," he told Gil-Lavedra, "but since I'm a man without bitterness or hatred, I've pardoned those who ordered my brother's murder because I believe that if we Argentines allow the rule of revenge to prevail, we are never going to pull this country together." Asked by Buero, Anaya's lawyer, when he thought the war against subversion had ended, Frondizi replied that it never had ended because sooner or later terrorism would return to Argentina.[22]

THE SUMMATIONS AND SENTENCES

At 7:50 P.M. on Wednesday, 14 August, the last witness stepped down from the stand. The testimony had run for 114 days, with 832 witnesses appearing before the court. There would now be a four-week recess while the prosecution and defense prepared their final statements. When the court reconvened on 11 September, Strassera began his argument. He and his principal associate, Luis Moreno Ocampo, would spend five days summarizing their case. The courtroom was packed. Videla, dressed in civilian clothes to show his refusal to recognize the court's right to judge him as an officer, read a book and occasionally glanced up at the chandelier that hung over the room. Galtieri, also in civilian clothes, shifted nervously and glowered at Moreno Ocampo. Viola assiduously took notes. Massera kept glancing around the room, occasionally smiling. A nervous tic made his face twitch, and when Strassera spoke of him, he nodded his head in cadence with the prosecutor's voice. Lami Dozo and Anaya listened intently, poker-faced. Lambruschini kept his attention fixed on petty details—his shoes, his fountain pen, his spotless uniform. Graffigna and Agosti seemed tired and dispirited. The latter leaned forward on his arms and lowered his gaze whenever Strassera referred to him.[23]

After briefly reviewing the main acts of guerrilla violence before the 1976 coup, Strassera described the kidnapping, torturing, and killing that occurred under the *proceso*: the same criminal methods the guerrillas used, but "on an infinitely greater scale." Those were not acts of war. Is it an act of war to torture and kill people who can offer no resistance? he demanded. Or to invade a home and take the relatives of those you are looking for as hostages? Are newborn babies military objectives? Is the robbery of someone's tableware comparable to knocking out the enemy's artillery? In fact, "there was no war; there were no victors, only a gang of bullies that tried to silence anyone who didn't think the way they did." Moreno Ocampo went further, comparing the *proceso* to Nazi Germany and dwelling on the atmosphere of fear that blanketed Argentina.

The prosecution insisted that the junta leaders were responsible for the crimes committed by their subordinates. The Nuremberg war crimes trials and the Adolf Eichmann case established that whoever sets up an organized power apparatus can be considered the author of any criminal acts committed under it, even if he didn't actually commit the crimes himself.[24] Thus, Strassera concluded, either there was no war and the defendants are common criminals, or there was a war and the the defendants are war criminals. Either way, it was necessary to punish them to establish, in the name of the Argentine people, "that sadism is neither a political ideology nor a military strategy, but simply a moral perversion." In the name of 10,000 *desaparecidos*, "Your Honors. *Nunca más!*" With that, the spectators in the gallery, most of the invited guests, and even the reporters in the press box stood and applauded for a full five minutes, ignoring Judge Arslanián's gavel. As they applauded, some began to shout, "Assassins! Assassins!" Videla seemed surprised by the outburst, while Viola stood up to shout back, "Sons of bitches! Sons of bitches!" at the gallery. Order was restored only by the police clearing the courtroom.

The defense summations lasted approximately three weeks, from September 30 to October 21. Just before the defense took the floor, an earthquake hit Mexico City, killing many people. Among the survivors and victims were several Argentines, whose names were published in the press between September 22 and 27. One of Viola's lawyers, Andrés Sergio Marutián, compiled a list of 118 names that were either exactly identical to those on CONADEP's list of the "disappeared" or bore a close similarity. In retaliation, his office was broken into during the night of 4 October, his file cabinets were forced open, and papers were thrown about. Some were missing. The documents were not important, according to Marutián, but because it occurred just as he was preparing his statement, the incident had a psychologically disruptive effect, so the court granted him a week's postponement.[25]

There was little that was new in any of the defense arguments: The trial was illegal and unconstitutional; the events alleged by the prosecution never took place, and there was no evidence to support the charges except that produced by CONADEP; CONADEP's so-called witnesses were either former terrorists or their supporters, knew one another, and had gotten together in CONADEP's offices to concoct and coordinate their stories; there had been a serious terrorist threat, and the armed forces had acted to save the country; there was no centralized, coordinated command at the highest levels and therefore no shared responsibility; there was a war and it was fought in a highly decentralized fashion because it was an unconventional war that could be won only with unconventional methods; innocent people had been hurt and killed along with the guilty, but that happened in all wars; the end result was that Argentina was saved from communism, but now those same subversives were sitting in judgment on those who won the war, and their true aim was to destroy the military so that they could have another try at power.[26]

The most dramatic moment came when Massera rose to speak on his own behalf. Without referring to a single note, he gave an impressive speech that built up tension as it went along, producing even in that hostile courtroom an atmosphere of astonishment and silence. It was not a speech of self-defense, but a flaming accusation:

I didn't come here to defend myself. No one has to defend himself for having won a just war, and the war against terrorism *was* a just war. Nevertheless, I am on trial because we won a just war. If we had lost it none of us—neither you nor we—would be here now. Because long before this the high judges of this Court would have been replaced by turbulent "people's tribunals" and a ferocious, unrecognizable Argentina would have replaced the old fatherland. But, here we are—because we won the war of arms and lost the war of psychology.

The armed forces underestimated the propaganda resources of the enemy, Massera said, so while the war of arms was being won, the enemy's "efficient system of persuasion" transformed the aggressors into victims. The guerrillas, seeing themselves about to lose, switched tactics and began clamoring for "human rights." Those psychological tactics were continuing, helped by the press, which is impossible to counter because there are so few willing to defend the truth against the power of the media. Even the Argentine political class was cowed. "We were convinced that we were defending the nation; and we were convinced and felt that our compatriots not only supported us but, even more, that they encouraged us to victory because it would be a triumph for us all." Now, however, they were all enthusiastic for "human rights." Yet "none of the worthy organizations or the notable persons who lift their voices for human rights—not one of them has ever, *ever* said anything about the victims of terrorism. What is it about the policemen, soldiers, or civilians who were victims, often indiscriminately, of subversive violence? Do they have fewer rights? Are they less human?"

Massera admitted that the armed forces might have committed "excesses," but there was a difference between the legal forces, for whom excesses were exceptional lapses, and subversive terrorism, for whom excesses were the norm. That, he said, was the central point of the trial. Nevertheless, he was resigned to inevitable punishment. "Who would be so naive as to expect a fair trial in the midst of this social pressure? Who would be so naive as to suppose that this is a search for the truth, when my accusers are the very ones we beat in the war of arms?" He ended by expressing his belief that the armed forces would be vindicated by history.[27]

At the end of the defense summaries, the court adjourned for another month to consider its decision. When it reconvened, a few minutes before 6:00 P.M. on 9 December, it began by dismissing the military's argument that the unconventional nature of terrorist subversion created the necessity of using "Dirty War" tactics to suppress it. The Constitution, which provides for state of siege powers; Law No. 14,072, which allows the declaration of a "state of internal war"; and Law No. 16,970, the 1966 National Defense Law, which permits the creation of emergency zones under martial law, all combined to give the Argentine state sufficient legal powers to deal with the threat. Using them, the junta could have issued edicts, detained suspected terrorists without habeas corpus, ordered summary trials, and even applied the death penalty. There was no need to resort to kidnapping, torture, and secret executions. Responding to Massera, the court insisted that "the commanders are on trial, not for winning a victory, but for the means they used in bringing it about." The court also dismissed the defense plea that the military had been carrying out the orders of a constitutional government, especially since the commanders later overthrew that same government. As for the claim that a war existed, if that were so, the junta should have adhered to the principles of the Geneva Conventions, to which Argentina was a signatory.[28]

Then the sentences were read. Videla and Massera were given life imprisonment; Viola got 17 years; Lambruschini, 8; and Agosti, 4. In addition, each of them lost his rights as a citizen to ever vote or hold office, and all were stripped of their military status, meaning their right to wear the uniform or to draw a military pension. The other four defendants—Galtieri, Anaya, Graffigna, and Lami Dozo—were absolved. The verdicts pleased no one. Those who defended the *proceso* could only see someone like Videla as a martyr. It was the Left that expressed the greatest anger, however. There apparently had been some leak about the court's forthcoming decision, because already some two-hundred human rights activists had gathered outside the building to protest the dismissal of the charges against Galtieri, Anaya, Graffigna, and Lami Dozo and also the "light" sentences meted out to Viola, Agosti, and Lambruschini. They passed out leaflets calling on the people to join in a planned protest march. Inside the courtroom, Hebe de Bonafini appeared wearing the white scarf that is the Madres' symbol. Judge Arslanián interrupted his reading of the sentences to demand that she remove it. When she refused, he ordered her out of the room. She left in a loud huff, clearly indicating her contempt for the proceedings.

Strassera, too, expressed his disappointment later in the day that some of the defendants had gotten off and others received too little punishment. That night, Hebe de Bonafini led three thousand demonstrators in a march throughout the center of Buenos Aires, which ended with a sit-in before the Congress. The human rights movement was not finished with the military. For them, the junta commanders' trial was just the beginning.

NOTES

1. Moncalvillo et al., *Juicio a la impunidad*, 28, 39; Camarasa et al., *El juicio*, 24–25, 29.

2. Moncalvillo et al., *Juicio a la impunidad*, 28–30, 36–37, 60; Camarasa et al., *El juicio*, 30–34.

3. Asociación Americana de Juristas, *Argentina*, 25–31; Amnesty International, *Argentina*, 10–11.

4. Amnesty International, *Argentina*, 11–12, 91; Camarasa et al., *El Juicio*, 35, 39; Moncalvillo et al., *Juicio a la impunidad*, 21–24.

5. Jorge Rafael Videla, *Ante los jueces* (Buenos Aires: Asociación Jurídica Argentina, 1984); Camarasa et al., *El juicio*, 47–49, 53–56, 64–66.

6. Camarasa et al., *El juicio*, 25–26, 67–72; Uriarte, *Almirante Cero*, 299–300; Horacio Verbitsky, *Civiles y militares: memoria secreta de la transición* (Buenos Aires: Editorial Contrapunto, 1987), 51.

7. Nestor J. Montenegro, *Será justicia* (Buenos Aires: Editorial Distal, 1986), 19.

8. The United Nations, *The United Nations and Human Rights* (New York: United Nations Department of Public Information, 1995), 144, 153–55; Montenegro, *Será justicia*, 22–23, 26, 29, 31.

9. Camarasa et al., *El juicio*, 28, 56–57, 88; Moncalvillo et al., *Juicio a la impunidad*, 32–33, 45; Brysk, *Politics of Human Rights*, 1994), 69; Carlos Catania, *Genio y figura de Ernesto Sábato* (Buenos Aires: EUDEBA, 1987), especially 110–11, 163.

10. Veiga, *Las organizaciones*, 48; Verbitsky, *Civiles y militares*, 72; Marguerite Bouvard, *Revolutionizing Motherhood: The Mothers of the Plaza de Mayo* (Wilmington: Scholarly Resources Press, 1994), 135; Carlos H. Acuña and Catalina Smulovitz, *¿Ni olvidio ni perdón? Derechos humanos y tensiones cívico-militares en la transición argentina* (Buenos Aires: Centro de Estudios de Estado y Sociedad, 1992), 12–13.

11. CONADEP, *Nunca Más*, 7, 481.

12. Bouvard, *Revolutionizing Motherhood*, 136–37, 147–50; Brysk, *Politics of Human Rights*, 71–72.

13. FORES, *Definitivamente*, 14–15, 18–21, 24, 26–28, 34–37, 40–41, 43–51, 55–56, 109–10, 114–15, 117–18.

14. Camarasa et al., *El juicio*, 73, 75–76; Troncoso, *El Proceso*, vol. 1, 46.

15. For the trial's opening, see Camarasa et al., *El juicio*, 96–100, 107–8, 111, 114–16, 122–25; *Somos* (26 April 1985), 14–15; (3 May 1985), 17; Uriarte, *Almirante Cero*, 297–98, 300–302, 320–21.

16. *Somos* (3 May 1985), 18.

17. Camarasa et al., *El juicio*, 127–28; Moncalvillo et al., *Juicio a la impunidad*, 151–53, 156–57, 162–63; *Somos* (3 May 1985), 16, 18–19.

18. Camarasa et al., *El juicio*, 140–41, 154–55, 160–61, 165–67, 175; Moncalvillo et al., *Juicio a la impunidad*, 160–66, 280–83; *Somos* (17 May 1985), 20; (28 June 1985), 44–48; (26 July 1985), 19; Argentine Republic, *El Libro*, 175–232.

19. For testimony on these murders, see Argentine Republic, *El Libro*, 43; *Somos* (17 May 1985), 19–21; Camarasa et al., *El juicio*, 129, 132–36, 170–71, 173.

20. Moncalvillo et al., *Juicio a la impunidad*, 195–206; *Somos* (24 May 1985), 22; (31 May 1985), 16, 18.

21. Camarasa et al., *El juicio*, 150–52; Moncalvillo et al., *Juicio a la impunidad*, 82–83; *Somos* (7 June 1985), 17.

22. Moncalvillo et al., *Juicio a la impunidad*, 221; *Somos* (24 May 1985), 14–15.

23. For the prosecution's case, see Montenegro, *Será justicia*, 73–74, 82–84; Camarasa et al., *El juicio*, 185–86, 193–98; Moncalvillo et al., *Juicio a la impunidad*, 179–80, 321; *Somos* (20 September 1985), 6.

24. Camarasa et al., *El juicio*, 193–94.

25. *Somos* (9 October 1985), 8; (23 October 1985), 8–10.

26. Ciancaglini and Granovsky, *Crónicas*, 166–67; Camarasa et al., *El juicio*, 199–215; Amnesty International, *Argentina*, 46–49.

27. Uriarte, *Almirante Cero*, 323–26; Camarasa et al., *El juicio*, 203.

28. Amnesty International, *Argentina* 61, 69, 71–72; Camarasa et al., *El juicio*, 11–13.

FOURTEEN

The Endless Denouement

As the Federal Court of Appeals sentenced the junta commanders, it also prepared to try lower-ranking military officers. In its verdict it instructed the Supreme Military Council to apply the same standards of guilt to all those below the junta who had operational responsibilities for any actions. This was a direct challenge to the armed services, for whom hierarchy, discipline, and "due obedience" are essential.

Alfonsín's original draft law protected lower-ranking military personnel by holding that only those who gave orders or exceeded them would be held responsible for human rights violations but Congress inserted the phrase "except where [the accused] committed atrocious or aberrant acts." At the time, that did not seem to be a significant addition, but it would later open the door to a great number of military trials because human rights violations are, by their very nature, perceived to be aberrant and atrocious.[1]

The armed forces were already angry over the trial of the junta commanders and viewed this new move by the courts as an attempt to destroy them. Monseñor José Miguel Medina, the ranking army chaplain, spoke from the pulpit about "subterranean efforts to dismember" the military and police. General Ramón Camps gave press interviews from his cell, calling the Alfonsín government "socialist" and dismissing the trials as a sort of revenge by the Left and its international backers. The military began to close ranks. Much to the indignation of congressmen and human rights leaders, active duty officers showed their solidarity by visiting their jailed comrades. The Supreme Military Council also indicated its unwillingness to participate in the process. When the case of Lieutenant Alfredo Astiz came before it, on 31 May, it deliberated for only one day before setting him free.

The military's anger was stoked by the comparably favorable treatment being accorded to former guerrillas. Many of them had been released under the military's Self-Amnesty Law, but unlike the lower-ranking military officers now being arrested and indicted, they remained free. Notorious examples included 27 former guerrillas arrested in connection with the murder of General Jorge Cáceres Monie and his wife. One of them, María del Rosario Dadano, even got a job in the University of Paraná's Faculty of Education. Oscar Ciarlotti, an *erpista* who had masterminded the kidnapping of Rear Admiral Francisco Alemann, was released from prison on an amnesty obtained by Alfonsín's interior minister, Enrique ("Cotí") Nosiglia, who happened to be the brother of Ciarlotti's mistress. Not only was Ciarlotti set free, he was hired in the Interior Ministry's Social Section on Nosiglia's orders. Nosiglia also arranged the release of Hilda Nava de Cuesta, who participated in kidnapping Admiral Alemann. She was hired by Catalina Nosiglia, Enrique's sister and also a former ERP member, to work in her government-sponsored "literacy program." Yet another member of that same gang, Enrique Ferreira Beltrán, worked in the office of the Presidential Secretariat. His brother, Pablo, was private secretary to Carlos Becerra, the man in charge. Becerra hired many other former *erpistas*. In 1988, while the Alfonsín government refused all appeals to reduce the sentences of the convicted junta officers, Becerra would secure the release of two other terrorists, Francisco Carrizo and Fermín Angel Nuñez, who had been sentenced to life imprisonment for the murder of Major Humberto Viola and his three-year-old daughter, María Cristina.[2]

Anxious to head off a spate of new military trials, Defense Minister Raúl Borrás told the Supreme Military Council's prosecutor that military subordinates should not be tried unless they had exceeded orders from superiors or knowingly committed atrocities. When the Federal Court of Appeals threatened to resign as a body, however, Alfonsín promised Congress that the plea of "due obedience" would not be allowed to protect those who had committed criminal acts. Nevertheless, Alfonsín was able to put a time limit on the process by the passage of the so-called Full-Stop Law (*Punto Final*) in December 1986. No new indictments would be permitted after 60 days from the promulgation of the law. Despite a great outcry from human rights organizations, 23 February 1987 was fixed as the deadline.

Once again, however, the government was confounded as federal courts all across the country waived their customary January holidays in order to receive more than three hundred new indictments. By this time, the military was seething with discontent. In mid-February six naval officers refused summons to appear in court. They were arrested, but the spirit of revolt was in the air. On 13 March, General Juan Sasaín, former commander of the Fourth Airborne Infantry Brigade, refused to enter a plea before federal judges and four days later General Luciano Benjamín Menéndez did the same. General Acdel Vilas, by contrast, defiantly entered a not-guilty plea and launched into a two-week defense of his antiguerrilla campaign in Tucumán. Each of these men, in his own way, touched responsive chords in resentful military hearts.

OPERATION DIGNITY

Open revolt came during Easter Week, on 14 April 1987, when Major Ernesto Barreiro refused to appear in Federal Criminal Court in Córdoba to answer charges that he was guilty of torturing prisoners at the La Perla detention center. When the court ordered his arrest the next day, Barreiro took refuge at the 14th Airborne Infantry Regiment. Despite assurances by the Army General Staff that Barreiro would be arrested, the regiment's commander, Lieutenant Colonel Luis Polo, refused to give him up. Moreover, neither the Air Force General Staff nor the Third Army Corps would force Polo to obey. Meanwhile, Lieutenant Colonel Aldo Rico, a twice-decorated commando of the Falkland Islands War, left his post at the head of an infantry regiment in Misiones and flew to Buenos Aires, where he was met by other rebellious officers and conducted to Campo de Mayo. Once at the base, he took over the infantry school and issued a proclamation demanding an end to all persecution of the military, a change in the army's high command, and amnesty for the rebels. The revolt, known as Operation Dignity, was not against the Alfonsín government or democracy, he said, but was aimed at the army's leaders, who were failing in their duty to protect the institution.[3]

The revolt by the *carapintada* ("painted faces"), as Rico's blackened-faced commandos were called, immediately revealed a vast gap between the soldiers and civilians. The *carapintada* were surprised the next day when more than 300,000 demonstrators from all the main political parties gathered in the Plaza de Mayo to demonstrate their support for the government. On the other hand, Alfonsín discovered that General Héctor Ríos Ereñú, the army chief, was unable to get any military unit to act against the rebels. After a stream of government mediators tried unsuccessfully to reason with Colonel Rico, Alfonsín himself went to Campo de Mayo. Alfonsín later insisted that he made no concessions, but Rico claimed that he laid down his arms only after Alfonsín had agreed to all his demands.

Subsequent behavior by both sides suggests that Rico's version was closer to the truth. In the following week, Alfonsín replaced General Ríos Ereñú with General José Dante Caridi as head of the army. Caridi's appointment did not please many of the rebels, however, and rumblings of discontent suggested another outburst. Rico, who was under arrest at Campo de Mayo, counseled patience. A few weeks later, Alfonsín sent Congress a "due obedience" bill, which exempted lower-level officers from criminal prosecution for human rights violations. It passed by large majorities in both houses and set free some 180 soldiers, policemen, intelligence officials, and other security personnel who were either awaiting trial or had already been condemned to prison. Human rights organizations promptly appealed to the Supreme Court to have the law declared unconstitutional, but they were turned down. They then tried the World Court and the OAS's Interamerican Commission on Human Rights, neither of which was willing to intervene.[4]

Although technically under arrest, Colonel Rico received a stream of visitors and well-wishers every day, including fellow *carapintadas*, journalists, and right-wing politicians. The *carapintada* were still subject to military court-martial, however, and General Caridi was determined to punish them. Little by little, Rico's main supporters were transferred out of their commands, passed over for promotion, scheduled for court-martial, or forcibly retired from active duty. By the end of the year, Rico realized that he was becoming isolated. On 30 December he left the Campo de Mayo after a friendly military judge decided that he could exchange his prison quarters for house arrest. On that same day, however, he was ordered to appear before General Caridi and bring a signed written request for his retirement. Instead of obeying, Rico went to a farm in Buenos Aires Province, accompanied by friends and supporters, including Major Barreiro, who had recently been put on the retirement list. Caridi, furious at Rico's latest act of rebellion, vowed to "put him in a cage." However, the first three military commanders ordered to rearrest Rico refused to move their troops. Eventually, a force of 30 tanks was sent out, but many of them "broke down" on the way, and others stopped for breakfast long enough for Rico to board a small private airplane and head for the Fourth Mechanized Infantry Regiment at Monte Caseros, where the local commander was a *carapintada*.

Once again, the army teetered on the verge of open rebellion. Many units around the country shared Rico's views but there was also an instinctive reluctance to back a junior officer's revolt against the high command. Meanwhile, Caridi, personally directing the operations, encircled the Monte Caseros base with tanks and about two thousand soldiers. He vowed to crush Rico once and for all, but Rico vowed not to surrender. In the end, Rico's friends from the nearby Third Infantry Brigade finally convinced him to avoid needless bloodshed. Rico was sent to Magdalena prison in southern Patagonia, where Videla, Viola, and Massera were detained. Four hundred other supporters were court-martialed, of whom 127 went to prison while the remainder were either discharged or passed over for promotion. Nevertheless, *carapintada* "fever" was still strong throughout the military, and in the meantime Alfonsín's popularity was plunging as inflation, stagnation, and unemployment—rather than human rights or democratic stability—now topped the list of public concerns, making him all the more vulnerable to military pressure.

Phase three of Operation Dignity erupted on 2 December 1988 when Colonel Mohammed Ali Seineldín led 55 commandos from the navy's port police to occupy the infantry school at Campo de Mayo, just as Rico had done. Seineldín's *carapintada* sympathies were well known to the army chiefs, but he had escaped sanctions by being out of the country as a military trainer in Panama. Seineldín was no ordinary military trainer. As a famous commando with service in both antiguerrilla warfare in Tucumán and against the British in the Falklands, he possessed a special mystique. When he trained crack detachments of the marines, the National Gendarmerie, or the Federal Police, he did more than merely impart technique: his men were put through exceptionally rigorous physical training and learned to live under the most demanding conditions, whether in the jungles or in cold windswept mountains. Beyond that, Seineldín insisted on the importance of religion as a source of inspiration and required his men to kneel and pray the rosary with him. Those who survived the course were filled with a fanatical esprit de corps and a sense of belonging to a true elite. Obviously, Seineldín was a man of exceptional energy and leadership ability, and therefore the Argentine Embassy in Panama kept a close watch on him—especially because he received plenty of Argentine visitors, including Major Ernesto Barreiro and various right-wing Peronist politicians and labor leaders.[5]

Seineldín's followers had begun their plans for an uprising even before his return to Argentina and had set up a secret military base in the Paraná delta near the town of Tigre. To avoid the government's informers, he did not fly directly from Panama to Buenos Aires but took a private plane to Montevideo and then proceeded by speedboat to the Buenos Aires harbor, where he was received by the naval police commandos, his former trainees. Two days later, he and his followers left their base in the Paraná delta and took over the infantry school at Campo de Mayo. Proclaiming himself the head of the National Army in Operation, Seineldín called for the release of Colonel Rico and all other jailed *carapintada*, pardons for all those convicted of "Dirty War" crimes, an end to attacks on the military by state-owned television and radio stations, and a complete change in the army's current leadership. In reply, General Caridi ordered the shelling of the infantry school with mortars. Seineldín requested a truce, during which the two officers met in the empty engineering school, next to rebel headquarters. As expected, the two sides publicly disagreed as to what was said, but the upshot was that Caridi agreed to call a cease-fire and allow the *carapintada* to move from Campo de Mayo to the 101st Arsenal Battalion at Villa Martelli, a garrison on the outskirts of Buenos Aires that had declared itself in revolt that morning. As the rebel soldiers moved to their new stronghold, they were joined by a convoy of tanks that had been ordered up from the Magdalena base to crush them.[6]

Villa Martelli was more difficult to attack than the Campo de Mayo because it was situated amidst a sprawling neighborhood of poor homes. Furthermore, Alfonsín and Caridi were discovering that many key units refused to go into action against the *carapintada*. The Fourth Airborne Brigade, which accounted for about 70 percent of the Third Army Corps' firepower, was the first to announce that it would not help to crush the revolt. Then the Campo de Mayo refused to move as did an infantry unit in Mercedes and an artillery unit in Santa Fe. Even those units that obeyed Caridi's orders to surround Villa Martelli refused to fire on the rebels. Meanwhile, dozens of young leftist demonstrators emerged from the surrounding slums to throw rocks and Molotov cocktails against the gates blocking the entrances to the base.

Caridi was forced to turn to General Isidro Cáceres, who was widely respected even by the *carapintada*, as a mediator. At his meeting with Seineldín, Cáceres pointed out the window to the rock throwers, who by now were also taunting the loyalist troops for their inaction, and urged the rebel to consider: if soldiers fought each other, it would be "those people," the remnants of the ERP and Montoneros, who would be the winners. Rather than that, he—Cáceres—would find a solution both sides could accept. After talking with Alfonsín, who had been unable to get any support from the navy or air force, and with Caridi, who informed him that more army units were siding with the *carapintada*, Cáceres returned that afternoon with Caridi to offer the following terms: Caridi would retire by Christmas, no more officers would be tried for "Dirty War" abuses, none of the *carapintada* would be punished, the military would be restored to its former place of honor in society, and there would be a hefty pay raise for the soldiers. Seineldín agreed, but he had some trouble getting his followers to surrender. Many of them recalled how Rico had been double-crossed. Still, they eventually accepted the government's terms, and Seineldín submitted himself to nominal arrest. Before the government troops were withdrawn, however, both they and the rebels suddenly turned on the increasingly aggressive civilian demonstrators and sprayed them with a volley of shots that killed at least 3 and wounded more than 40.[7]

LA TABLADA

The aftermath of Seineldín's revolt left no one satisfied. Alfonsín had to grant a 40 percent increase in military salaries at a time when he was struggling to control inflation, and sacrifice the loyal General Caridi. Beyond those concessions, however, he refused to budge. He would not agree to pardon the junta leaders serving their sentences in Patagonia, nor any of the *carapintada*, although Rico was brought back from Patagonia to Campo de Mayo, where he was much better treated. Alfonsín also passed over Gen. Cáceres, the *carapintadas*'s choice to succeed Caridi, in favor of General Francisco Gassino, the head of Army Intelligence. However, Alfonsín, forbidden by the Constitution to seek immediate reelection, was a "lame duck" president. Moreover, the Radicals' candidate to succeed him, Governor Eduardo Angeloz of Córdoba, was lagging in the polls behind the Justicialist candidate, Governor Carlos Saúl Menem of La Rioja. Anxious to secure support from the nationalist right, Menem sent a stream of emissaries to Seineldín at Campo de Mayo. The fact that both men were Argentines of Arab descent lent credence to rumors that Menem would pardon the *carapintada* and incorporate them into his government if he won.

All of that alarmed the Movimiento Todos por la Patria (MTP), which viewed the three *carapintada* revolts as part of a strategy to get the military back in power. Few people had heard of the MTP before 12 January 1989, but on that day a left-wing daily newspaper called *Página 12* published on its front page a letter from Jorge Baños, one of the MTP's leaders and a human rights lawyer for Emilio Mignone's CELS, in which he accused Seineldín, Menem, and Lorenzo Miguel of plotting a coup to depose Alfonsín. Baños didn't explain why Menem would bother plotting when he was so far ahead in the polls, but the accusation spread quickly by radio, television, and the major newspapers. Menem hotly denied the charge and accused the Alfonsín government of trying to discredit him by spreading false rumors.[8]

Alert readers of *Página 12* might have recalled that the MTP had written to the press once before. On 8 December 1988, the day following Seineldín's surrender at Villa Martelli, both *Clarín* and *Página 12* had published a letter from the MTP accusing Caridi's loyalist troops of collaborating with the *carapintada* to force Alfonsín into issuing a general amnesty for the military. Baños signed the letter, as did Brother Antonio Puigjané, a Liberation Theology monk who worked in the slums; Carlos Alberto Burgos, who edited the MTP's weekly newspaper, *Entre Todos*; Francisco Provenzano and Roberto Felicetti, former *erpistas*; and Enrique Gorriarán Merlo![9]

Gorriarán and his followers had been quietly slipping back into Argentina, working underground through the youth sector of Oscar Alende's Partido Intransigente and infiltrating the MTP. Baños and Felicetti, both of whom were members of the Partido Intransigente, opened the way. By December 1987 the *erpistas* were a majority in the MTP, at which point Gorriarán announced his intention to join. That caused the resignation of several of the original members, who refused to switch from peaceful tactics to guerrilla warfare. Throughout most of 1988, the MTP kept a low political profile, although it was adding activists to its ranks: Luis Segovia, the former metallurgical leader from Villa Constitución; Carlos Samojedny, an ex-*erpista*; Pablo Díaz, formerly of ERP's Juventud Guevarista; and Roberto Sánchez (alias Osvaldo Farfán), a Frenchman who had joined ERP, was jailed by the *proceso* (but released under French pressure), and had followed Gorriarán to Nicaragua.

The first signs that the MTP would turn violent came during Seineldín's revolt, when its youthful demonstrators pitched rocks and Molotov cocktails at the Villa Martelli base and then began pelting the loyalist troops for not attacking the rebels. When both military factions opened fire on them, the MTP had its first martyrs. A few days later there was an attempted bank robbery in Mataderos, an industrial suburb of Buenos Aires, in which one of the bandits, Osvaldo Olmedo, was killed. Olmedo was the brother of Carlos Olmedo, one of the founders of FAR. His death caused a stir on the Left, according to Horacio Verbitsky, *Página 12*'s star reporter, who began interviewing various leftist leaders to discover whether there was any new movement toward armed insurrection. Verbitsky was well connected for the task. A former Montonero himself, and an occasional contributor to *Entre Todos*, his newspaper was owned and managed by ex-*erpistas*. Still, he could discover no violent plans by any of the leftist organizations except for the MTP. One of its militants confessed that, in view of the danger to democracy, it might be necessary to take up arms.[10]

At 6:15 A.M. on 23 January 1989, MTP guerrillas driving a heavy Coca-Cola delivery truck smashed through the gate of the Third Infantry's garrison at La Tablada, on the outskirts of Buenos Aires. The truck was followed by a pickup and five cars: 60 guerrillas in all, wearing army uniforms and blackened faces. Pamphlets spewed from the windows of the pickup and the cars, proclaiming that the attackers belonged to "The New Argentine Army" that supported Rico and Seineldín. After killing the guard, they split into three groups. One headed for the base's headquarters, a second went toward the officers' club, and the third was to take over the enlisted men's club. La Tablada was lightly defended. Many of the soldiers had been given weekend passes, and because of the salary freezes, many officers were moonlighting at second jobs. The 3 officers and 40 men still at the base paid no attention to the first shots because it was common to hear their colleagues at target practice. Repeated shots coming from head-quarters and a grenade shattering one of the barracks windows finally roused them. By that time the headquarters were taken, but only after a fierce fight in which both attackers and defenders were killed. The enlisted men's club also fell to the guerrillas, but the officers' club held out. The guerrillas then set about destroying the tanks located at La Tablada. There was confusion and unorga-nized resistance on the part of the defenders, many of whom were raw recruits. The defenders were also short of ammunition. The guerrillas, on the other hand, were well-armed with Soviet-made rifles, rocket and grenade launchers, and plenty of ammunition. Within an hour the guerrillas were in control. After ra-dioing for help, the defenders abandoned the base, leaving five of their dead behind.[11]

Responding quickly, about a hundred Buenos Aires provincial police soon arrived and took up positions to block the guerrillas' retreat. They were backed by soldiers returning from leave, who, upon hearing the news over radio and television, hurried one by one to the scene with whatever personal weapons they owned. Around 11 A.M. President Alfonsín finally gave General Gassino the go-ahead to bring in army units. A little after midday, the Tenth Infantry Brigade arrived. Now the guerrillas were sealed inside La Tablada, which upset all their plans.

The loyalist forces, now numerically stronger, took the offensive, reinforced by National Gendarmerie units, commandos from Campo de Mayo, helicopters, tanks, and mortars. By midafternoon they had recaptured the guardposts, the infirmary, and the officers' club. The guerrillas still held the enlisted men's club, Company B barracks, and the mess hall. Helicopters flew back and forth over the base, pinning the guerrillas down inside and destroying any vehicles they tried to use. Then tanks and mortars began firing into the base to "soften up" guerrilla positions. The barrage lasted three hours. Finally, at 8 P.M., on a stifling hot summer evening, the commandos went into action, quickly taking the mess hall and Company B barracks. Reporters claimed to have seen, and sometimes actually photographed, commandos shooting wounded or captured guerrillas. Some of those later reported dead or missing were reportedly seen being led away by their captors. In any case, night fell before the commandos could take the enlisted men's club, the guerrillas' last redoubt. Visibility was practically nil, and the attackers had to be extra cautious because the guerrillas were holding 10 hostages: 9 NCOs and an enlisted man. In the morning, the guerrillas agreed to surrender and turn over their hostages, but only in the presence of a doctor and a judge. Both were produced, and moments later the guerrillas surrendered, after almost 30 hours of fighting. The army had lost 8 men and the police 3, whereas 28 guerrillas were found dead and another 11 were missing. Among the dead or missing were Jorge Baños, Luis Segovia, Carlos Samojedny, Pablo Díaz, Carlos Alberto Burgos, Roberto Sánchez, and Francisco Provenzano. Enrique Gorriarán Merlo made another one of his miraculous escapes and disappeared underground.

With the exception of the Madres de la Plaza de Mayo, all the human rights organizations condemned the MTP's attack on La Tablada but they soon took up the cry that the army and police had "overreacted," that they had not allowed the guerrillas an opportunity to surrender, and that some of the guerrillas taken prisoner were later tortured and killed. Brother Puigjané told an investigating magistrate that the MTP had tried three times to surrender, without success, and that when Provenzano and Samojedny surrendered they were summarily executed. Horacio Verbitsky and *Página 12* joined in criticizing the La Tablada attack as "cretinism" but expressed sympathy for the guerrillas, who had acted out of "desperation in the face of the impunity of armed power and their inability to grow under an unjust regime." Emilio Mignone of CELS, Graciela Fernández Meijide of APDH, and Hebe de Bonafini of the Madres also expressed their views in *Página 12*: that the guerrillas' identity was "uncertain," that the military had once again violated humanitarian norms, and that nothing the authorities said was believable. Mignone announced that CELS would monitor the trials of the MTP prisoners to ensure that there was due process, and the communist Argentine League for Human Rights undertook their defense in court.[12]

La Tablada was a severe public relations setback for the Left, since Baños and Puigjané were well-known human rights activists. By contrast, the military's prestige rose, and its violent tactics against guerrillas appeared justified. The Catholic hierarchy also used the occasion to condemn Liberation Theology and Brother Puigjané, although Adolfo Pérez Esquivel insisted that the monk was a "misunderstood and persecuted prophet." Alfonsín had little choice but to distance himself further from his former colleagues in the human rights movement and declare his solidarity with the armed forces. Nevertheless, both Carlos Menem and the *carapintada* suspected that the MTP guerrillas had been encouraged by persons inside the Alfonsín administration—especially Carlos Becerra, given the number of former *erpistas* inside the Presidential Secretariat. In reply, the Radicals accused Menem of conspiring with Seineldín to pardon the jailed junta leaders and *carapintada*.

THE FINAL *CARAPINTADA* REVOLT

On 14 May 1989, Carlos Saúl Menem won the presidency with 47 percent of the popular vote and 310 out of 600 electoral college votes, to Eduardo Angeloz's 32 percent and 211 electors. At the time of his victory, the annualized rate of inflation was 4,924 percent—almost 50 percent in the month of April alone—and the country was on the edge of a total economic collapse. On 28 May, Alfonsín announced a package of emergency measures that included price controls, higher charges for government services, budget cuts, and export taxes—all designed to tackle hyperinflation and balance the budget. It was too late. Many stores already were closed because the merchants were unable to get goods from their suppliers; those that were open were unsure of what prices to charge, so they raised them as high as they dared. The tension that had been building up for months exploded on the day after Alfonsín's decree was issued. Riots broke out in the industrial center of Rosario and in the working class *barrios* of Buenos Aires. Supermarkets and other shops were smashed and looted. Unruly demonstrations broke out in other cities, leading to arson and bloody clashes with the police. Bombs exploded in Buenos Aires's financial district. Alfonsín declared a state of siege, but he obviously was no longer in control. Although Menem's inauguration was not scheduled to take place until 10 December, an exhausted Alfonsín announced on 12 June that he was handing over power early. Menem took office on 8 July.

A few days after taking office, Menem announced that he was considering either a pardon or an amnesty for both the military and the guerrilla leaders. He remained vague for the time being as to exactly what action he would take, preferring to allow public opinion to digest the possibility. Polls showed that 68 percent of the citizenry were opposed to any leniency toward the military, but by the end of July the business community and the Catholic hierarchy were making public statements favoring an amnesty or pardons. General Isidro Cáceres, whom Menem had appointed as army commander in chief to replace Gassino, also urged him to sign an amnesty so as to strengthen his position in relation to the *carapintada*.[13]

Finally, on 8 October 1989, Menem issued a presidential pardon to 277 officers who had been convicted of human rights violations during the "Dirty War," of misconduct during the Falkland Islands War, or of taking part in the three *carapintada* revolts. Among them were Albano Harguindeguy, Luciano Benjamín Menéndez, Reynaldo Bignone, Cristino Nicolaides, Acdel Vilas, Leopoldo Galtieri, Jorge Anaya, Basilio Lami Dozo, Aldo Rico, and Mohammed Ali Seineldín. Sixty-four former Montonero guerrillas also went free or were exempted from prosecution. Excluded from the pardons, however, were Videla, Viola, Massera, Agosti, and Lambruschini, as well as General Camps, General Suárez Masón, and Mario Firmenich.[14]

On Sunday, 9 October, the day following Menem's first pardon, Colonel Seineldín dined at the Presidential Residence in Olivos. He praised Menem for his courage in signing the pardons and talked at length about the internal politics of the army. Menem spoke little, except to ask questions that would draw him out. Seineldín was elated. He and the other *carapintada* were certain that, with Menem in the presidency, their ascendancy in the army was inevitable. After all, Menem had named their choice, General Cáceres, to head the army. Not long thereafter, however, General Cáceres died from a heart attack and his successor, General Félix Martín Bonnet, was heard to express the view that those who disrupt the military chain of command must be punished. The army's Qualifications Board, meeting to consider promotions, assignments, retirements, and disciplinary matters, reviewed 1,600 cases of officers and NCOs involved in the three *carapintada* revolts and resolved to discipline about 125. Most were given 30 days or more of barracks arrest, but 25 officers and 4 NCOs were discharged from the service. Rico was dismissed on 21 October. Seineldín's case came up on 1 November. Bonnet put up a spirited resistance when Menem suggested leniency toward Seineldín: the army couldn't tolerate personalist factions, for there could be no obedience or discipline if barracks were turned into political conventions. If Seineldín stayed in, he would end up as the de facto commander in chief. Because Bonnet was supported by both the defense minister and the interior minister, Menem backed down.[15]

Menem next sounded out Seineldín through emissaries on the possibility of his heading a training school to turn out special units for counterguerrilla warfare and combating drug traffickers. Seineldín was receptive but insisted that the units under him be armed. That ran into General Bonnet's opposition too, for it meant creating a fighting force parallel to the regular army. As Menem wavered, Seineldín and his followers put on more pressure, speaking at various political meetings of nationalists around the country, appearing on radio talk shows and muttering ominous warnings, and holding gymnastic classes in Buenos Aires's Palermo Park. As their gestures became more menacing, Menem turned against them, convinced that there were two Argentine armies, one of them governable and obedient and the other not. To prepare for the inevitable showdown, he announced that there would be a second wave of pardons at the year's end, which most likely would include the junta commanders, and he ordered a salary increase for army officers.

For his part, Seineldín was making a tour of the interior, drawing large crowds wherever he spoke. He had a great deal of ammunition to use against Menem, too, because the president had incorporated a large number of conservative economists and politicians into his administration and was pursuing an orthodox economic strategy that was at complete odds with Peronist tradition and with his own campaign pledges. Menem's popularity in the polls was very low making him more vulnerable to a military coup, and indeed many officers and NCOs were turning out to greet Seineldín on his tour. By the end of November, Seineldín could wait no longer. During the previous few weeks, six active duty colonels had decided to join his revolt, giving him more men actually in command of troops than the *carapintada* had ever had before. The rebels set the date for 3 December, at 2:00 A.M.; Seineldín was not to lead the fighting because he was under barracks arrest for having sent President Menem a letter urging him to change his military policy "before events occur that neither you nor I desire," without first clearing it with General Bonnet and the defense minister. Meanwhile, General Bonnet's loyalist faction was aware that something was about to erupt and began a whispering campaign designed to ensure the loyalty of the bulk of the officer corps. Rumors circulated that a revolt of the sergeants was brewing, and their victory would result not just in the destruction of the military hierarchy but in the "sovietization" of the army.

The last *carapintada* revolt was the bloodiest of all. There had been few casualties previously, and those were usually accidents. This time, with the NCOs providing much of the impetus, the *carapintada* unwisely acted with unaccustomed violence by killing some of the defenders in the installations they took over. They seized the First Infantry ("Patricios") Regiment in Palermo, the First Cavalry Brigade and the Munitions Company at Campo de Mayo, the tank factory attached to the Boulogne Arsenal, and the Army General Staff headquarters, which was housed in the Libertador Building in downtown Buenos Aires. In the latter attack, the NCOs were aided by armed civilians, and in taking over the building they killed two loyalist officers. The news of that swung any wavering officers over to the loyalist side. Meanwhile, a rebel force of 12 tanks and 8 armored personnel carriers, under the command of Major Pedro Mercado, was heading south toward the capital from Entre Ríos Province. Along their route they encountered a broken-down army truck with two loyalist soldiers in it. Both were made to lie down in the road while they were interrogated, and one was shot.[16]

Menem, informed of the revolt while at a party, returned to the Casa Rosada at 4:30 A.M. and called in General Bonnet. "No one is to negotiate with the *carapintada*," he ordered. "This has got to be finished quickly, and no two ways about it." He then declared the entire country to be under a state of siege and gave General Bonnet complete authority to take any measures necessary to crush the revolt. Bonnet's attitude was as hard as Menem's. He told his subordinates that the only terms they could offer the rebels was unconditional surrender. Moreover, "when they surrender, I want them stripped naked and barefoot, and I want them marched in front of the civilians with their hands clasped behind their neck."

While loyalist forces counterattacked, Menem carried on with his normal agenda, receiving the Bulgarian ambassador at the Casa Rosada, even though shots could be heard in the distance. Out at Palermo, the rebel commander was captured and tied to the front of the lead tank as the loyalists moved on the last *carapintada* stronghold there. Heavy fighting at the port finally crushed the marine commandos, the special forces whom Seineldín had trained. By mid-morning the Campo de Mayo and the tank factory were retaken, the Libertador Building was surrounded, and a rebel attempt to free Seineldín from jail was repulsed. The rebel commander at the Fábrica Militar de Tanques (TAMSE) tank factory committed suicide rather than surrender. The tank column from Entre Ríos was slowed by the loyalists blowing up all the bridges leading southward and finally was surrounded. Having heard of the Patricio's Regiment's surrender in Palermo, Major Mercado decided that the revolt had failed and gave up, too. An hour later the *carapintada* holding the Libertador Building surrendered. They were forced to sit in the parking lot while civilians pelted them with stones and garbage.

Shortly after 9:00 P.M., Menem held a press conference to announce the end of the revolt. His speech called for "exemplary punishment" for the rebels. Hauled before the Supreme Military Council on 8 January 1991, the coup leaders, including Seineldín, heard the prosecutor call for the death penalty. Menem himself had said during the revolt that the ringleaders ought to be shot but later he relented. Now he let it be known that he would commute any death sentences. The council therefore sentenced Seineldín and his chief officers to life imprisonment. Other rebels received long sentences, too.

NO RECONCILIATION

After the last *carapintada* revolt, President Menem issued pardons to the remaining junta officers and guerrilla leaders, although they were not actually released from prison until 2 January. The Madres responded with mass demonstrations, and Julio Strassera, now representing Argentina at the United Nations, said he would resign. Former President Alfonsín seized the occasion to castigate Menem, saying that Argentine society didn't need to "reconcile itself with crime" to achieve national unity. Nevertheless, Menem had already weighed the costs and benefits and decided that the pardons would solidify the "professionalists" control of the military.

Most of the released prisoners soon made themselves scarce. Viola took a trip to Rio de Janeiro, as did Firmenich and his family. Massera retired to a country house, where he busied himself cataloguing his extensive library. Interviewed later, he was effusive in his gratitude toward Menem. Only Videla remained defiant. The pardons only lifted the criminal penalties; they did not declare the former junta commanders innocent. On the contrary, they condemned them to a kind of "civic death" in which they could not vote, hold office, sign legal documents, wear their uniforms, or even collect a military pension. Moreover, upon returning to his wife's apartment in Buenos Aires, Videla found a letter from General Bonnet waiting for him, requesting that he not appear at army functions or speak out on military matters. He immediately replied to Bonnet, pointing out that all previous army commanders had demanded the complete revindication of the *proceso*, which had rescued the country from subversion.[17]

Menem was angry upon hearing of Videla's letter. He wanted all of the junta commanders simply to remain out of sight; yet here was Videla writing letters, walking the streets of Buenos Aires, going to Mass, and insisting upon his innocence! Such behavior was bound to provoke the Left. Demonstrations, street marches, and vigils outside the residences of former *proceso* leaders kept the pressure on to repeal the pardons, rescind the Due Obedience and Full-Stop Laws, and reopen the human rights trials.

Such pressure could be resisted in the early 1990s, however, because most of Argentine society was more concerned with the economy than with human rights. Hyperinflation, which had soared under Alfonsín, gradually came under control as Menem imposed a severe austerity program. Government spending was curtailed, state corporations were sold off, tariffs were eliminated, and the peso was linked to the dollar at even par. Dismantling the old populist system was painful, and it especially affected small-business owners, workers, and government employees. It also affected the military, which saw its budgets slashed and its extensive industrial empire sold off. Instead of resisting such efforts violently, as it had done in the past, an exhausted public bowed to the seemingly inevitable but in the struggle of each individual to survive, democratic processes lost much of their former appeal. Rising unemployment and crime rates often made Argentines impatient with gradual solutions. There was more support for policemen who meted out vigilante justice to criminals, and in some provinces, military officers with questionable human rights records found themselves voted into office by people who recalled with nostalgia the *proceso*'s civic action programs and impatience with "red tape." Naval Captain Roberto Ulloa won the governorship of Salta in 1991 and in Chaco Province, Colonel José David Ruíz Palacios was prevented by a technicality from running for governor himself, but his stand-in won. Ruíz Palacios had already been elected mayor of the province's capital. Also in 1991, General Domingo Bussi was barely beaten in his bid for the governorship of Tucumán, only because Menem convinced a popular singer, Ramón ("Palito") Ortega to oppose him. However, in 1995 Ortega was ineligible to succeed himself, and Bussi won easily. In each case, these right-wing military officers won after the financial mismanagement of Peronist and Radical administrations that took over after civilian rule was restored.

By the end of the decade, however, there were some signs that the political pendulum was swinging back to the Left. In 1997 a Spanish judge, Baltasar Garzón, began an investigation into the death and disappearance of some six hundred Spanish citizens living in Argentina during the "Dirty War." In the course of his investigation, he got the cooperation of Swiss authorities, who revealed that several Argentine officers had secret bank accounts where they presumably hid money that they had stolen from the *proceso*'s victims. Garzón then issued subpoenas to around two hundred Argentine officers to come to Spain to give evidence, as well as warrants for the arrest of some of the *proceso*'s leading figures—including Bussi, who was found to have a numbered Swiss bank account.[18]

Those revelations sparked a debate in the Argentine Congress about whether Alfonsín's Full-Stop and Due Obedience Laws ought to be repealed. Menem said at first that he would veto any such attempt, and his Justicialist bloc in

Congress fell in behind him. The opposition was divided. Some radicals who had supported the 1976 coup preferred to avoid the issue, but a coalition of leftist parties called FREPASO (Frente para un País Soldario) demanded repeal. The latter had little hope of success, however, until early in March 1998, when a small-circulation magazine called *Trespuntos* published an interview with the former naval captain Alfredo Astiz in which he not only admitted to certain crimes during the *proceso* but even bragged about them.

Once again, human rights groups rallied as public opinion became outraged at the blatant swaggering of one of the *proceso*'s most notorious figures. Menem, who was weighing his chances for revising the Constitution to permit him to run for a third term, reversed his earlier position and stated publicly that he would not veto a repeal of the Full-Stop and Due Obedience Laws, if Congress insisted. With that, the Justicialist bloc swung around, and the repeal was duly passed. Bussi was ousted as governor of Tucumán two weeks later, on 14 April, as the provincial legislature voted to suspend him from his duties while it looked into his financial affairs. Prosecutors began preparing charges against other officers who previously had been exempt from punishment. Meanwhile, human rights groups claimed to have a list of more than 10,000 names of alleged repressors they wanted brought to trial. They held demonstrations outside the homes of Massera, General Galtieri, and General Harguindeguy, during which the houses were stoned and had graffiti painted on their walls, and they called for Videla's "perpetual imprisonment" as an assassin.

General Videla had been living in obscurity for the past seven years. His name seldom appeared in the newspapers and his life was uneventful, but he was soon to become the center of this new political storm that was brewing. On Tuesday evening, 9 June, the police raided Videla's home in the suburb of Belgrano, searched the premises, and took him to a jail in San Isidro. There he remained overnight, handcuffed, until around 10:00 A.M., when he was taken to be fingerprinted, given a physical examination, and interviewed by a psychologist. By noon his lawyers had arrived, whereupon he was hauled before Federal Judge Roberto Marquevich, who had ordered his arrest. Marquevich charged him, as president of the former military junta, with being the "ideological author" of the army's practice of stealing the children of political prisoners. Videla refused to enter a plea but insisted, through his lawyers, that he should be judged only by the Supreme Military Council. Marquevich ignored this request and ordered Videla to be taken to the main federal courthouse, the Palacio de Tribunales. Handcuffed again, he was led to a waiting police van, but by the time he emerged from the building, a crowd of leftist protesters and human rights demonstrators had gathered. They pelted Videla and his guards with rocks, eggs, and oranges and they did the same to Videla's lawyers. A similar scene awaited Videla and his lawyers when they got to Tribunales: a crowd that had gathered near the entrance threw trash at them and spat on them. From Tribunales, Videla was taken to Caseros prison, where he remained for the next two months, until he was allowed to return home under house arrest. Meanwhile, Marquevich let it be known that he had a long list of other officers whom he intended to arrest, including Admiral Massera and General Suárez Masón.

All of this came as a shock to the armed forces, because many senior active duty officers had once been involved, earlier in their careers, in the "Dirty War." Naturally, it caused great unease among many retired military men. Although General Martín Balza, the army commander, denied that Videla's arrest had any effect on the service, he already had met with defense minister Jorge Domínguez to convey the anger that was growing among his subordinates. Balza's authority was already shaky among his fellow officers because he had publicly apologized for the army's role in the "Dirty War;" now there was muttering in the ranks, including the eight division generals, that unless this new attack on the armed services was halted, they would refuse to turn over any indicted officers or obey any summonses themselves.

President Menem moved quickly to calm the situation. "The specter of hate has reappeared among certain groups that recur to violence as a form of expression," he noted, "but the Government will not permit a return to the past." He blamed the new tensions on the leaders of FREPASO, who only sought to persecute "our suffering men of arms." However, he promised, "we will never cease pursuing the goal of reconciliation." Nevertheless, Argentina was once again divided.

NOTES

1. Acuña and Smulovitz, *¿Ni olvidio ni perdón?*, 12–13, 16; Montenegro, *Será justicia*, 239.

2. Hernández, *La Tablada*, 56–57, 59–60; Horacio Félix Bravo Herrera, *La guerrilla de papel* (Buenos Aires: SIELP, 1992), 68–69; *Somos* (9 June 1985), 28–29; (2 August 1985), 6–11.

3. Hugo Chumbita, *Los carapintada: historia de un malentendido argentino.* (Buenos Aires: Editorial Planeta, 1990), 26–29, 31–32, 38; Héctor Simeoni and Eduardo Allegri, *Linea de fuego* (Buenos Aires: Editorial Sudamericana, 1991), 98–112.

4. Brysk, *Politics of Human Rights*, 83; Simeoni and Allegri, *Linea*, 113–15, 119, 146, 153; Acuña and Smulovitz, *¿Ni olvidio ni perdón?*, 20–21; *Expreso* (26 June 1987), 13–15.

5. Simeoni and Allegri, *Linea*, 190–92; *Somos* (7 December 1988), 4–12, 18–21, 45–51; (14 December 1988), 18–19.

6. Simeoni and Allegri, *Linea*, 194–98, 203–10; Juan Salinas and Julio Villalonga, *Gorriarán, La Tablada, y las "guerras de inteligencia" en América Latina* (Buenos Aires: Editorial Mangin, 1993), 98–99, 101; Chumbita, *Los carapintada*, 113.

7. Simeoni and Allegri, *Linea*, 210–14; Chumbita, *Los carapintada*, 116–17; Acuña and Smulovitz, *¿Ni olvidio ni perdón?*, 27; *Somos* (7 December 1988), 56–57; (14 December 1988), 4–8.

8. Hernández, *La Tablada*, 163.

9. Hernández, *La Tablada*, 76; Bravo Herrera, *La guerrilla*, 40; *Somos* (8 February 1989), 6–7.

10. Salinas and Villalonga, *Gorriarán*, 74–75; *Somos* (21 December 1988), 10–15. *Página 12*'s owner and chief editor, Fernando Rubén Sokolowicz, was an active member in the Jewish Movement for Human Rights, a former activist in PRT-ERP, and once belonged to a youth group linked to FAR. Jorge Ernesto Prim, the newspaper's vice president and general attorney, also belonged to the same FAR youth group and to PRT-ERP. Hugo Ernesto Soriani, the general manager, was an ex-FAR and ex-ERP activist as well. So was Alberto Clodomiro Elizade Leal, one of the comanagers of distribution; the other comanager, Julio Mogordoy, was a former *erpista*. Verbitsky, who used to work with Jacobo Timerman on the editorial staffs of *Primera Plana, Confirmado,* and *La Opinión*, joined the Montoneros and became a collaborator of Rodolfo Walsh on *Noticias*. He broke with the Montoneros in 1977, apparently after providing them with faulty intelligence that led to a failed attempt on President Videla's life, and went into exile for the remainder of the *proceso*. See, Bravo Herrera, *La guerrilla*, 34–36, 48–52.

11. Bravo Herrera, *La guerrilla*, 14–19; Salinas and Villalonga, *Gorriarán*, 66–70, 103–5, 240–43; Hernández, *La Tablada*, 110, 112–15; *Somos* (25 January 1989), 4–13, 15, 46–58; (1 February 1989), 4–14, 18–22.

12. Brysk, *Politics of Human Rights*, 119–20; Hernández, *La Tablada*, 136–37; Bravo Herrera, *La guerrilla*, 106–7; Julio José Viaggio, *La Tablada y el Caso Puigjané* (Buenos Aires: Editorial Cartago, 1990).

13. Acuña and Smulovitz, *¿Ni olvidio ni perdón?*, 32–36; *Somos* (5 July 1989), 8–9; (31 December 1990), 4–6.

14. Chumbita, *Carapintada*, 245–47; *Somos* (26 July 1989), 4–9; (4 October 1989), 4–9.

15. Acuña and Smulovitz, *¿Ni olvidio ni perdón?*, 36–37; Simeoni and Allegri, *Linea*, 244–46; *Somos* (8 November 1989), 16–19.

16. Simeoni and Allegri, *Linea*, 278–334; Hugo Reinaldo Abete, *Por qué rebelde* (Buenos Aires: Librería Huemul, 1997), 129–279; *Somos* (10 December 1990), 4–12; (17 December 1990), 4–8; (31 December 1990), 8–9.

17. *Somos* (17 December 1990), 9; (7 January 1991), 4–9.

18. Latin American Regional Reports, *Southern Cone Report* (3 February 1998), 2–3; (10 March 1998), 2; (21 April 1998), 6.

FIFTEEN

Residues of the "Dirty War"

During a March 1981 visit to Washington, as president of Argentina, General Roberto Viola boiled over at a press conference after a barrage of questions about human rights in his country. "You are suggesting that we investigate our own security forces—absolutely out of the question," he told his listeners. "We fought a war and we were the winners. And you can be quite sure that if the armies of the [Third] Reich had won the last World War the war crimes trials would have been held in Virginia, not Nuremberg."[1] No doubt he was right. Little did he guess, however, that in just a few months the Argentine armed forces would be humiliated in the Falkland Islands and subsequently driven from power, or that in four years he himself would be in the defendant's dock.

The trial of the junta officers settled very little. Furthermore, the *carapintada* revolts that followed it put a stop to the Left's strategy to mortify, if not completely destroy, the armed forces. The country lapsed into a political stalemate in which neither of the "two demons" was exorcised. On every issue connected to the "Dirty War" there were two camps, whose views of the recent past were so divergent as to present two irreconcilable histories.

For example, was there a "Dirty War," and if so, what was it all about? Julio Strassera was quoted after the trial as denying that there ever had been a real war between the guerrillas and the military. "It was simply a rabbit-hunt (*cacería de conejos*)," he asserted, implying that the guerrilla threat had been greatly overblown. Many North American and European writers on the "Dirty War" agree. In his detailed study, *Dossier Secreto*, Martin Edwin Andersen claims that there never was a real war. The armed forces "misrepresented the nature and size of the threat" in order to "bamboozle public opinion both at home and abroad" and thereby justify "their own illegal repression and their seizure of power." The so-called guerrilla threat was never more than "a serious problem of terrorism . . . that could have been handled better, and with a lot less bloodshed, by the police." In fact, by the time the military took power in March 1976, "the military threat from leftist guerrillas had been effectively broken." Moreover, such violence as was attributed to the guerrillas, both before and after the coup, was often really carried out by the military itself or by right-wing death squads and then blamed on the guerrillas. Even when the violent acts could be attributed to the guerrillas, they frequently were encouraged by agents provocateurs who had infiltrated their organizations. The military knew all this before they took power, but they were motivated by a desire for revenge. Beyond that, they were determined to restructure Argentine society, break the power of labor unions, impose a type of unrestrained capitalism, and insert their nation into a global power structure dominated by American capital. In this project they were aided by "an international network of Nazi terrorists" as well as "foreign banks and much of the U.S. foreign policy and security establishment," which was "more preoccupied with profits, order, and internal security than with development and democracy."[2]

Andersen's thesis is generally accepted by the Left, but not by all leftists. Mario Firmenich continues to view the "Dirty War" as simply one phase in a civil war that has been going on between the Oligarchy and the people since the country's independence from Spain.[3] Donald Hodges, in his *Argentina's "Dirty War,"* considers the "Dirty War" to have been a response to the "revolutionary war" that the ERP and the Montoneros—"the two largest, best-organized, and best-financed urban guerrilla formations on record"—already had launched. Moreover, although his sympathies clearly reside with the Left, Hodges is willing to concede that "the Military Process was in fact necessary for victory." Thus, the threat from the guerrillas was not only real, but "not until the end of 1977 did the defeat of the armed resistance [i.e., the guerrillas] appear imminent." Apart from that, Hodges agrees with Andersen that "notwithstanding the military's repeated appeals to Argentina's national being, the ideologies that immediately inspired the "Dirty War" have stamped on them the imprimatur of the Vatican and "made in the U.S.A." The aim was to "annihilate the rear guard of subversion" by purging "the factory floor, universities, political parties, and the rest of Argentine society" of the insidious purveyors of "progressive" ideas, whether trade union organizers, teachers, lawyers, journalists, or psychiatrists.[4]

The Right's viewpoint is perhaps best expressed by General Ramón Genaro Díaz Bessone, who considers the "Dirty War" as part of a worldwide revolutionary war waged by the communists to control the Third World. That revolutionary war had been going on in Argentina since 1956, after the military overthrew the populist government of General Juan Domingo Perón. The communists successfully infiltrated the Peronist underground Resistance, and the guerrilla movements of the 1970s grew out of that. Thus, their appearance can-

not be attributed to the reaction of disillusioned youth to the overthrow of democracy in 1966 by the military because the revolutionary war already was in
progress under the constitutional regime of Arturo Frondizi (1958–62). Neither
the police nor the courts could control it; their efforts to do so were confounded
by politicians who sympathized with the extreme Left. By 1975 the guerrillas
had created "liberated zones," taken over villages, and were launching major
assaults on army bases. In Díaz Bessone's view, the Argentine situation was
more comparable to Cuba or Nicaragua before the communists seized power. If
the army killed innocent people while fighting to keep Argentina from sharing
the fate of those countries, it is of small consequence; innocent people always
die in wars. When faced with aggression, one must either accept that the ends
do indeed justify the means, or else "we'd better prepare to become either saints
or slaves" and "resign ourselves to being eliminated from the category of free
nations on this earth."[5]

That view finds little echo today among academic intellectuals, journalists, or
the cultural elites, either in Argentina or abroad. Indeed, one candidate in the
1999 general elections was dropped from the ticket of a conservative party
because she drew down upon herself an avalanche of media outrage for suggesting that General Videla was a decent man who ought to be left alone by
the courts. That the man who headed that conservative party, Domingo Cavallo,
had himself worked for the *proceso* made no difference. Nor did it make a
difference that, unlike Admiral Massera or General Suárez Masón, Videla never
used his office to enrich himself, or that most of the Radical Party, including
the winning presidential candidate in 1999, Fernando De la Rua, supported Videla's coup in 1976; or that Argentina in the 1990s underwent a free market
capitalist revolution far more extreme than anything that Videla and José Martínez de Hoz ever attempted, and that this revolution has been accepted, however
grudgingly, as unavoidable.

Human rights is the reason that no one can defend General Videla or any of
the *proceso* figures in public—although it is probably true that the junta leaders
were also paying the bill for repeated military interventions since 1930. The
1985 trials revealed a degree of savagery, sadism, and criminality behind the
façade of military professionalism that surely deserved punishment. Videla was
part of that system, and by choosing to stay at the head of the junta he shared
in the guilt, although his resignation would probably have changed nothing
except to bring the hard-liners to power sooner. Thus prosecutors and magistrates continue to indict and jail the *proceso* leaders. At the end of December
2000, General Luciano Benjamín Menéndez was under arrest, as was Admiral
Massera. General Videla was under house arrest. Lower-level task force operatives and torturers like Julio ("El Turco Julián) Simón and Juan Antonio ("Colores") del Cerro were in jail. Meanwhile, foreign courts have joined in the
movement to punish *proceso* officials. Miguel Cavallo, a former naval officer,
was being held in Mexico while an extradition request from Spain was being
debated in court. Another naval officer, Adolfo Scilingo, already resided in a

Spanish jail. Jorge Olivera, a retired army major, was arrested in Italy in August but released a month later on a legal technicality. The Italian press was incensed. However, another Italian court, basing its decision on the testimony of families of the "disappeared," sentenced General Suárez Masón and half a dozen close collaborators to prison in absentia—and promised to hear more cases involving the Argentine military.

No doubt this serves the cause of democracy and human rights by warning would-be military strongmen of the probable consequences of their crimes. However, while academic intellectuals, journalists, and cultural elites quite properly condemn the military for its abuses, there is a contrary tendency for them to explain away, diminish, or excuse the murders, kidnappings, and bombings of ERP and the Montoneros. For them the guerrilla terrorists were either misguided idealists "trying to work towards helping others to live better" (Hebe de Bonafini), or unfortunate "rabbits" whose occasional acts of violence were exaggerated and posed no threat to society (Strassera and Andersen).

The recent campaign in Argentina to free the guerrillas who attacked the La Tablada military base in January 1989 illustrates how selective the Buenos Aires intelligentsia is concerning human rights and how forgiving it is of former terrorists. As a result of the La Tablada attack, 11 guerrillas—including Gorriarán Merlo and his wife, who were captured six years later—were condemned to life imprisonment under a law known as the Defense of Democracy Law. One of the terms of this law, which also had been applied to the *carapintada*, forbade any appeal of the sentences. In 1994, however, a provision was added to the Constitution that guaranteed the right of appeal. The La Tablada prisoners then petitioned for the application of this provision to their case and a pardon. Nothing came of their attempts during Menem's presidency, but in the new administration of President De la Rua there were many sympathizers from the left wing of the Radical Party and from the Radicals' alliance partners, FREPASO. Enrique ("Cotí") Nosiglia was now the Radical Party secretary, while Carlos Becerra became head of SIDE. Both had multiple ties to former *erpistas*.

Interviewed over radio from his jail cell, Colonel Mohammed Ali Seineldín said he was "totally opposed" to any commutation of the La Tablada prisoners' sentences, and he denied that he—who had been condemned under the same law—had ever asked for leniency. The same people who were petitioning to release the ex-*erpistas* were the ones who were behind the January 1989 attack on the La Tablada army base: Nosiglia, who was then minister of interior, and Bercerra, who was Alfonsín's presidential secretary. "The operation was intended to provoke a kind of temporary chaos, with riots, so as to suspend the forthcoming elections until the government had a better chance to win," Seineldín claimed. "It was done with Alfonsín's knowledge, and the operation failed."

Nevertheless, De la Rua urged the courts to grant the La Tablada prisoners a new hearing, with the possibility of reducing their sentences so as to free them in the near future. Meanwhile, Gorriarán and his colleagues began a hunger strike in September to call more attention to their case. Human rights groups swung into action with protest marches and all-night vigils in the Plaza de Mayo, demanding the prisoners' release. Presumably, they were not equally concerned about releasing the jailed *carapintada* chiefs, like Colonel Seineldín, who also were serving life sentences.

Nor were the human rights activists satisfied with peaceful demonstrations. After the courts refused to alter the sentences, President De la Rua asked Congress to legislate on the matter. Congress was soon divided, with the Radicals and FREPASO favoring a law that would free the ex-*erpistas*, and the Peronists opposing it. On 18 October 2000, some 50 activists burst into an evening session of the Senate, waving placards in the galleries and shouting "murderers" and "thieves" at the legislators. There was pandemonium for the next 20 minutes until the building's security guards herded them out of the room. As they left, one demonstrator shouted back at the senators, "My husband is dying!" in reference to the prisoners' hunger strike. In the meantime, the presiding officer called a recess. In the end, the Justicialists blocked any move for revising the prisoners' sentences.

Turned down by both Congress and the Supreme Court, De la Rua finally issued an executive decree at the end of December 2000 that reduced the sentences of 9 of the 11 prisoners. Seven had their sentences reduced to 20 years, making them eligible for release in May 2001. Claudia Acosta's sentence was reduced to 22 years, and Roberto Felicetti's to 25. Gorriarán Merlo and his wife, Ana María Sívori, remained condemned for life. The guerrillas were not satisfied: they wanted their immediate release. Gorriarán Merlo petitioned the OAS Interamerican Commission on Human Rights to rule on the case. Out on the street, most Argentines expressed opposition to De la Rua's decree, according to *La Nación*, retired Lieutenant Colonel Guillermo Nani, who had led the army's forces in retaking the La Tablada base back in January 1989 and had been decorated for it by President Alfonsín, asked for an audience with the president so that he could give back the medal.

BACK TO THE FUTURE

Though Argentine human rights groups advocated clemency for former guerrillas, they insisted on punishing the military. On Tuesday, 6 March 2001, they scored a great success when federal judge Gabriel Cavallo handed down a decision that opened up the possibility of bringing hundreds of officers and their subordinates to trial for "Dirty War" crimes. The case involved a woman whose parents had been kidnapped and "disappeared" in 1978 when she was a small child. Raised by foster parents chosen by the military, she had not discovered the truth about her real parents until a couple of years ago. She then charged two of the interrogators at the "El Olimpio" clandestine detention center with the crime of depriving her of her true identity. Julio Héctor ("El Turco Julián") Simón and Juan Antonio ("Colores") del Cerro, both notorious torturers, appealed to the 1986 "Punto Final" (Statute of Limitations) Law, by which Congress had put a time limit on bringing charges against *proceso* officials. They also cited the 1987 "Due Obedience" Law which exempted lower-level officials from prosecution. Nevertheless, Judge Cavallo declared both laws unconstitutional, on the grounds that Article 29 of the Constitution forbids Congress to pass any law that waives certain inalienable rights. He also pointed to a growing body of international law, to which Argentina was a signatory, that made human rights violations unpardonable.[6]

Naturally, Cavallo's decision was hailed by some people and attacked by others. Horacio Verbitsky, the new head of CELS, which had provided legal counsel for the plaintiff, saw it as a major turning point, for it would allow the 1,180 military men, policemen, and civilian collaborators who had escaped punishment under those two laws to finally be brought to trial. Verbitsky also had in mind some officers who were still on active duty, including the army's commander-in-chief, who recently had been accused of helping to kill seventeen persons during the *proceso*'s intervention of Chaco Province. The Mothers of the Plaza immediately called for the reopening of the case against former naval captain Alfredo Astiz for the kidnapping and murder of two French nuns, Alice Domon and Leonie Duquet. Patricia Walsh, presidential candidate for the United Left in 1999 and daughter of the radical journalist Rodolfo Walsh, said she would soon take former ESMA officials to court to learn where the bodies of her father and other *desaparecidos* were deposited. Praise for Judge Cavallo poured in from the Italian and Spanish press; and former federal judge Jorge Torlasco, who in 1985 had formed part of the tribunal that tried the *proceso*'s top leaders, called Cavallo's 188-page decision "a real legal treatise."[7]

The armed forces were alarmed. General Juan Carlos Mugnolo, chairman of the Joint Chiefs of Staff, complained that, "No country can go on forever blaming itself for its past." Defense minister José Horacio Jaunarena, who also had been Alfonsín's defense minister when the Punto Final and Due Obedience laws were passed, also regretted this digging up of the past. He was certain that laws duly passed by a democratic Congress were constitutional, and he pointed out that the military today was very different in its attitudes than it had been in 1976. *La Nación* thought that Judge Cavallo's decision was a "retrograde step," both "irritating and inopportune." It was also one-sided: after all, the "Dirty War" was started by Leftist terrorists. *The Buenos Aires Herald* called Cavallo's decision "judicial manipulation" and doubted whether it would survive the inevitable appeal to the Supreme Court.[8]

March 24 was the 25th anniversary of the coup that launched the *proceso*: an occasion that was certain to bring out the human rights organizations in full force. The "Day of Memory" was celebrated in all of Argentina's schools and universities with special classes and commemorative acts aimed at teaching students respect for legal authority and hatred of coups. SERPAJ, CELS, APDH, the Families of the Disappeared and Detained for Political Reasons, two factions of the Madres de la Plaza (Linea Fundadora) and the Abuelas de la Plaza held marches and convocations that were attended by political, labor, and artistic figures of the Left. Most of the events were peaceful and solemn, but an afternoon march by the Madres de la Plaza resulted in turmoil when the UCR's youth group, Franja Morada, tried to join. About fifty of the Madres de la Plaza turned on the youths with sticks and knives, presumably because the Franja Morada was linked to the government's party.[9]

Meanwhile, a small counter-demonstration occurred in the Buenos Aires suburb of Belgrano. Led by the actors Elena Cruz and Fernando Siro, about thirty people gathered in front of the apartment house where General Videla lived and sang the national anthem. Videla appeared on the balcony to wave at them, flanked by his wife and son, who is an army officer. The little group cheered and thanked him for saving the nation from communism. The next day, a reporter who saw the event went to the APDH, which in turn filed a petition in court asking that Videla, who was living under house arrest, be returned to jail. APDH also asked the court to ascertain whether Cruz and Siro could be indicted for "advocating criminal behavior."[10]

Thus, the "Dirty War" remains unforgotten and unresolved. None of the principals on either side are repentant; all are certain that the enemy is only biding its time before making a new grab at power. For the Left, human rights is a weapon to wield against the Right to break the political stalemate. As James Neilson, a columnist for *The Buenos Aires Herald* ironically put it: "If a Right-winger tortures a Leftist, that is appalling and anyone who refuses to get angry is a swine who should be dragged before the courts for 'advocating criminal behavior,' but if a Leftwinger does the same to some miserable conservative it probably means that circumstances left him with no other choice." The Right doesn't bother with the language of "human rights"; it prefers the language of right wing populism.

Carlos Ruckauf, formerly Menem's vice-president and now governor of Buenos Aires Province, may be a pariah to the elites, but he is popular in the working class *barrios* (neighborhoods) for his tough stance on crime. During his first year in office, he hired the ex-*carapintada*, Aldo Rico, to be his justice minister; and he hired an ex-cop, Luis Patti, who had been accused of torturing victims, as his special advisor on crime.

Meanwhile, out in Tucumán, where unemployment is high, the electorate continues to vote for General Bussi for various office posts. The elites charge Bussi with being a torturer and murderer, and the Chamber of Deputies refused to let him take his seat after the 1999 elections; but the ordinary citizens of Tucumán seem to mainly remember that during Bussi's eighteen months as the head of the Province he built hospitals, schools, rural clinics, dams, aqueducts, workers' housing, and sports complexes—all by cutting through the usual "red tape." Besides the large number of jobs this created, what captured the local people's attention was how Bussi had forced the wealthiest *tucumaño* families to foot the bill by contributing to a "Patriotic Fund." That some of this apparently found its way into overseas accounts made little difference to Bussi's supporters: corruption has always been endemic in Tucumán, but in Bussi's case the common people got something back for it.[11] Thus, the general is an almost perfect example of the political stalemate. The people continue electing him and the elites keep preventing him from taking office.

However, apart from a few sincere moderates, no one on either side of Argentina's political divide is really interested in human rights as a universal principle. No one is really interested in constitutional procedures, either. The president bribes legislators to pass his bills, or else he ignores them and rules by executive decree. In the meantime, the economy has been wracked by hyperinflation, painful free market adjustments, and most recently by double-digit unemployment that reaches nearly forty percent in some parts of the interior. About half of the Gross Domestic Product goes towards servicing the country's heavy foreign debt. That is a heavy load for a new democracy to carry, and Argentina can be proud of having carried it this far. But unless relief is in sight soon, it is very likely that the solutions offered by Right and Left extremists will become attractive once more—and then the "Dirty War" may be on again.

NOTES

1. Quoted from *La Nación* (19 March 1981), in Veiga, *Las organizaciones*, 97.

2. Andersen, *Dossier Secreto*, 2–3, 12–14, 328, 6; Strassera was quoted in *La Prensa* (14 July 1987), 3, during an interview in Mexico.

3. Donald Hodges, *Argentina's "Dirty War": An Intellectual Biography* (Austin: University of Texas Press, 1991), 288.

4. Hodges, *Argentina's "Dirty War,"* ix–x, 177–78, 205, 282–83.

5. Díaz Bessone, *Guerra revolucionaria*, 9–14, 41.

6. *La Nación Line*—Política: "Procesaron a dos ex represores de El Olimpio," (20 February 2001); "Pidieron la nulidad de las leyes de punto final y obediencia debida," (3 March 2001); "El juez Cavallo anulará dos leyes exculpatorias," (6 March 2001); "Vuelvan a investigar ex represores," (7 March 2001).

7. *La Nación Line*—Política: "El CELS buscará datos sobre el jefe del Ejército," (4 March 2001); "Buscan reabrir otras causas contra militares," (7 March 2001); "En Italia se considera una 'gran noticia,' " (7 March 2001); Garzón pedirá la detención de 48 ex represores argentinos," (7 March 2001); "El juez Cavallo pide que se respete la división de poderes," (8 March 2001); "El fallo del juez Cavallo es un verdadero tratado de derecho," (12 March 2001).

8. *La Nación Line*—Política: "Un fallo que significa un retroceso," (7 March 2001); "Jaunarena afronta su primera prueba," (7 March 2001); "Aumenta la protesta de los militares," (10 March 2001); "Jaunarena dió un contundente respaldo político a los militares," (13 March 2001); "El momento para hablar de golpe," (13 March 2001); *The Buenos Aires Herald online*: "Full Stop for Due Obedience?" (8 March 2001).

9. *La Nación Line*—Política: "Agenda," (24 March 2001); "El recuerdo se instaló en escuelas y universidades," (24 March 2001); "Miles de voces cantaron 'Nunca más,' " (24 March 2001); "Varias generaciones manifestaron que no olvidan ni perdonan," (25 March 2001). The Madres de la Plaza split into two factions in 1988 when some of the members accused Hebe de Bonafini, their leader, of allowing the organization to be

infiltrated by Marxist-Leninists. The Linea Fundadora, led by Nora Cortiñas, claims to be free of communist influence.

10. *La Nación Line*—Política: "Videla salió al balcón a saludar," (25 March 2001); "La APDH solicitó que Videla vuelva a prisión," (28 March 2001); "Citaron a un periodista: El ex dictador Videla podría volver a prisión," (30 March 2001).

11. Echagüe, *El enigma*, 24, 63, 69–70, 78–80, 95–96, 113–14, 118, 124–25, 139–41, 145, 152–54, 198, 201–2, 204–12; Zaremberg and Larrea, "El General ha vuelto," 47–48, 54–58.

Selected Bibliography

Abete, Hugo Reinaldo. *Por qué rebelde*. Buenos Aires: Librería Huemul, 1997.

Acuña, Carlos H., and Catalina Smulovitz. "Militares en la transición argentina: del gobierno a la subordinación constitucional." *Revista Paraguaya de Sociología*, vol. 31 (January–April 1994).

———. *¿Ni olvidio ni perdón? Derechos humanos y tensiones cívico-militares en la transición argentina*. Buenos Aires: Centro de Estudios de Estado y Sociedad, 1992.

Aizcorbe, Roberto. *Argentina, the Peronist Myth: An Essay on the Cultural Decay of Argentina after the Second World War*. Hicksville: Exposition Press, 1975.

Amnesty International. *Argentina: The Military Juntas and Civil Rights*. London: Amnesty International Publications, 1987.

Andersen, Martin Edwin. *Dossier Secreto: Argentina's Desaparecidos and the Myth of the "Dirty War."* Boulder: Westview Press, 1993.

Argentine Republic, Cámara Nacional de Apelaciones en lo Criminal y Correccional de la Capital Federal. *El Libro de El Diario del Juicio*. Buenos Aires: Editorial Perfil, 1985.

Argentine Republic Nacional. *Evolution of Terrorist Delinquency in Argentina*. Buenos Aires: Poder Ejecutivo: 1980.

Asociación Americana de Juristas (Rama Argentina). *Argentina, juicio a los militares: documentos secretos, decretoleyes, jurisprudencia*. Buenos Aires: AAJ, 1988.

Baschetti, Roberto, ed. *Documentos (1970–1973): De la guerrilla peronista al gobierno popular*. Buenos Aires: Editorial de la Campana, 1995.

Beaufre, Andre. *La guerra revolucionaria*. Buenos Aires: Editorial Almena, 1979.

Berger, Martín. *Historia de la lógia masónica P-2*. Buenos Aires: El Cid Editor, 1983.

Bignone, Reynaldo. *El último de facto*. Buenos Aires: Editorial Planeta, 1992.

Blixen, Samuel. *Conversaciones con Gorriarán Merlo: treinta años de lucha popular.* Buenos Aires: Editorial Contrapunto, 1988.

Bouvard, Marguerite. *Revolutionizing Motherhood: The Mothers of the Plaza de Mayo.* Wilmington: Scholarly Resources Press, 1994.

Bra, Gerardo. "La 'P-2' en la Argentina," *Todo es Historia*, no. 214 (February 1985), 8–27.

———. "La noche de los bastones largos: el garrote y la inteligencia," *Todo es Historia*, vol. 18, no. 223 (November 1985), 8–26.

Bravo Herrera, Horacio Félix. *La guerrilla de papel.* Buenos Aires: SIELP, 1992.

Brignone, Carlos S. *Los destructores de la economía.* Buenos Aires: Ediciones Depalma, 1983.

Brysk, Alison. "From Above and Below: Social Movements, the International System, and Human Rights in Argentina." *Comparative Political Studies*, vol. 26, no. 3 (October 1993), 259–85.

———. *The Politics of Human Rights in Argentina.* Stanford: Stanford University Press, 1994.

Buongiorno, Pino. "La internacional del Venerable Licio," *Todo es Historia*, no. 214 (February 1985), 27–37.

Burzaco, Ricardo. *Infierno en el monte tucumaño: Argentina, 1973–1976.* Buenos Aires: R. E. Editores, 1994.

Camarasa, Jorge, Rubén Felice, and Daniel González. *El juicio: proceso al horror.* Buenos Aires: Sudamericana/Planeta Editores, 1985.

Camps, Ramón J. A. *Caso Timerman: punto final.* Buenos Aires: Tribuna Abierta, 1982.

———. *El poder en la sombra: el affaire Graiver.* Buenos Aires: Ro.Ca. Producciones, 1983.

Capdevilla, Irene. *El Caso Graiver, o la historia de los testaferros.* Buenos Aires: Editorial Ágora, 1984.

Castiglione, Marta. *La militarización del Estado en la Argentina (1976–1981).* Buenos Aires: Centro Editor de América Latina, 1992.

Cazes Camarero, Pedro. *El Ché y la generación del 70.* Buenos Aires: Ediciones Dialéctica, 1989.

Chumbita, Hugo. *Los carapintada: historia de un malentendido argentino.* Buenos Aires: Editorial Planeta, 1990.

Ciancaglini, Sergio, and Martín Granovsky. *Crónicas del apocalipsis.* Buenos Aires: Editorial Contrapunto, 1986.

Coggiola, Osvaldo. *El trotskismo en la Argentina (1960–1985).* Vol. 1. Buenos Aires: Centro Editor de América Latina, 1986.

Comisión Nacional sobre la Desaparición de Personas (CONADEP). *Nunca Más: Informe de CONADEP.* Buenos Aires: Editorial Universitaria de Buenos Aires (EUDEBA) 1986.

Crawley, Eduardo. *A House Divided: Argentina, 1880–1980.* London: C. Hurst & Co., 1984.

De Riz, Liliana. *Retorno y derrumbe: el último gobierno peronista.* Mexico City: Folios Ediciones, 1981.

Díaz Bessone, Ramón Genaro. *Guerra revolucionaria en la Argentina.* Buenos Aires: Editorial Fraterna, 1986.

Familiares y Amigos de los Muertos por la Subversión (FAMUS). *Operación Independencia.* Buenos Aires: FAMUS, 1988.

Ferrer, Aldo. "The Argentine Economy, 1976–1979," *Journal of Inter-American Studies and World Affairs*, vol. 22, no. 2 (May 1980), 131–62.

Florit, Carlos A. *Las fuerzas armadas y la guerra psicológica.* Buenos Aires: Editorial Arayú, 1963.

Fontana, Andrés. "De la crisis de la Malvinas a la subordinación condicionada: conflictos intramilitares y transición política en Argentina," in Claudio Varas, ed. *La autonomía militar en América Latina.* Caracas: Editorial Nueva Sociedad, 1988.

———. "Political Decisionmaking by a Military Corporation: Argentina, 1976–1983." Ph.D. dissertation, University of Texas, 1987.

Foro de Estudio sobre la Administración de Justicia (FORES). *Definitivamente Nunca Más (La otra cara del informe de la CONADEP).* Buenos Aires: FORES, 1985.

Fraga, Rosendo. *Ejército: del escarnio al poder (1973–1976).* Buenos Aires: Editorial Planeta, 1988.

Freedman, Lawrence, and Virginia Gamba-Stonehouse. *Signals of War.* London: Faber and Faber, 1990.

Galasso, Norberto. *La izquierda nacional y el FIP.* Buenos Aires: Centro Editor de América Latina, 1983.

García, Alicia S. *La doctrina de la seguridad nacional (1958–1983).* 2 vols. Buenos Aires: Centro Editor de América Latina, 1991.

García, Roberto. *Patria sindical versus patria socialista.* Buenos Aires: Editorial Depalma, 1980.

Gasparini, Juan. *El crimen de Graiver.* Buenos Aires: Grupo Editorial Zeta, 1990.

———. *Montoneros: final de las cuentas.* Buenos Aires: Puntosur Editores, 1988.

Gillespie, Richard. *Soldiers of Perón: Argentina's Montoneros.* Oxford: Clarendon Press, 1982.

Giussani, Pablo. *Montoneros: la soberbia armada*, 8th ed. Buenos Aires: Editorial Sudamericana/Planeta, 1984.

González Jansen, Ignacio. *La Triple-A.* Buenos Aires: Editorial Contrapunto, 1986.

Gorbato, Viviana. *Vandor o Perón.* Buenos Aires: Tiempo de Ideas, 1992.

Goyret, José Teofilo. *Geopolítica y subversión.* Buenos Aires: Ediciones Depalma, 1980.

Graham-Yool, Andrew. *The Press in Argentina, 1973–1978.* London: Writers and Scholars Educational Trust, 1979.

———. *A State of Fear: Memories of Argentina's Nightmare.* New York: Hippocrene Books, 1986.

Groisman, Enrique I. *La Corte Suprema de Justicia durante la dictadura (1976–1983).* Buenos Aires: Centro de Investigaciones Sociales sobre el Estado y la Administración, 1987.

Hagelin, Ragnar. *Mi hija Dagmar.* Buenos Aires: Editorial Sudamericana/Planeta, 1984.

Hernández, Pablo. *La Tablada: el regreso de los que no se fueron.* Buenos Aires: Editorial Fortaleza, 1989.

Hilb, Claudia, and Daniel Lutzky, eds. *La nueva izquierda Argentina: 1960–1980.* Buenos Aires: Centro Editor de América Latina, 1984.

Hodges, Donald C. *Argentina's "Dirty War": An Intellectual Biography.* Austin: University of Texas Press, 1991.

———. *Argentina, 1943–1987: The National Revolution and Resistance.* Albuquerque: University of New Mexico Press, 1988.

Itzcovitz, Victoria. *Estilo de gobierno y crisis política (1973–1976).* Buenos Aires: Centro Editor de América Latina, 1985.

Jackson, Geoffrey. *People's Prison.* London: Faber, 1973.

Jordán, Alberto R. *El Proceso, 1976–1983.* Buenos Aires: Emecé Editores, 1993.

Juvenal, Carlos. *Buenos muchachos: la industria del secuestro en la Argentina.* Buenos Aires: Editorial Planeta, 1994.

Kandel, Pablo, and Mario Monteverde. *Entorno y caída.* Buenos Aires: Editorial Planeta Argentina, 1976.

Kohl, James, and John Litt, eds. *Urban Guerrilla Warfare in Latin America.* Cambridge: MIT Press, 1974.

Landivar, Gustavo. *La universidad de la violencia.* Buenos Aires: Editorial Depalma, 1983.

Lanusse, Alejandro. *Mi testimonio.* Buenos Aires: Lasserre Editores, 1977.

Leuco, Alfred, and José Antonio Díaz. *Los herederos de Alfonsín.* Buenos Aires Editorial Sudamericana/Planeta, 1987.

López, Ernesto. *Seguridad nacional y sedición militar.* Buenos Aires: Editorial Legasa, 1987.

López Echagüe, Hernán. *El enigma del General Bussi.* Buenos Aires: Editorial Sudamericana, 1991.

Martínez de Hoz, José Alfredo. *Bases para una Argentina moderna, 1976–1980.* Buenos Aires: Companía Impresora Argentina, 1981.

Mattini, Luis. *Hombres y mujeres del PRT-ERP.* Buenos Aires: Editorial Contrapunto, 1990.

McSherry, J. Patrice. *Incomplete Transition.* New York: St. Martin's Press, 1997.

Méndez, Eugenio. *Aramburu: el crimen imperfecto.* Buenos Aires: Sudamericana/Planeta Editores, 1987.

———. *Confesiones de un Montonero.* Buenos Aires: Editorial Sudamericana/Planeta, 1985.

Middlebrook, Martin. *The Fight for the "Malvinas."* London: Viking Press, 1989.

Mignone, Emilio. *Iglesia y dictadura.* Buenos Aires: Ediciones del Pensamiento Nacional, 1986.

Moncalvillo, Mona, Alberto A. Fernández, and Manuel Martín. *Juicio a la impunidad.* Buenos Aires: Ediciones Tarso, 1985.

Montenegro, Nestor J. *Será justicia.* Buenos Aires: Editorial Distal, 1986.

Moyano, María José. *Argentina's Lost Patrol: Armed Struggle, 1969–1979.* New Haven: Yale University Press, 1995.

Navarro, Marysa. "The Personal Is Political: Las Madres de la Plaza de Mayo," in Susan Eckstein, ed., *Latin American Social Movements.* Berkeley: University of California Press, 1989.

O'Donnell, Guillermo. *Bureaucratic Authoritarianism: Argentina, 1966–1973, in Comparative Perspective.* Berkeley: University of California Press, 1988.

Ollier, María Matilde. *El fenómeno insurreccional y la cultura política (1969–1973).* Buenos Aires: Centro Editor de América Latina, 1986.

———. *Orden, poder, y violencia (1968–1973).* Buenos Aires: Centro Editor de América Latina, 1989.

Organization of American States, Interamerican Commission on Human Rights. *Report on the Situation of Human Rights in Argentina.* Washington, D.C.: General Secretariat of the OAS, 1980.

Orsolini, Mario Horacio. *La crisis del ejército.* Buenos Aires: Ediciones Arayú, 1964.

Page, Joseph. *Perón: A Biography.* New York: Random House, 1983.

Paoletti, Alipio. *Como los nazis, como en Vietnam*. Buenos Aires: Editorial Contrapunto, 1987.

Pehme, Kalev. *Argentina's Days of Rage: The Genesis of Argentine Terrorism*. New York: Argentine Independent Review, 1980.

Perdía, Roberto Cirilo. *La otra historia: testimonio de un jefe montonero*. Buenos Aires: Grupo Ágora, 1997.

Perón, Juan Domingo. *Perón-Cooke correspondencia*. vols. 1 and 2. Buenos Aires: Gránica Editor, 1972.

Petric, Antonio. *Así sangraba la Argentina: Sallustro, Quijada, Larrabure*. Buenos Aires: Editorial Depalma, 1983.

Pineiro, Armando Alonso. *Crónica de la subversión en la Argentina*. Buenos Aires: Editorial Depalma, 1980.

Pion-Berlin, David, and George A. López. "Of Victims and Executioners: Argentine State Terror, 1975–1979," *International Studies Quarterly*, vol. 35 (1991), 63–86.

Pontoriero, Gustavo. *Sacerdotes para el Tercer Mundo: "El fermento en la masa" (1967–1976)*. Buenos Aires: Centro Editor de América Latina, 1991.

Quinterno, Carlos Alberto. *Militares y populismo: la crisis argentina de 1966 a 1976*. Buenos Aires: Editorial Temas Contemporáneas, n.d.

Revista Somos, *Historia y personajes de una época trágica*. Buenos Aires: Editorial Atlantida, 1977.

Rodríguez Molas, Ricardo. *Historia de la tortura y el orden represivo en la Argentina*. 2 vols. Buenos Aires: Editorial de la Universidad de Buenos Aires (EUDEBA), 1984–85.

Rouquie, Alain. *Poder militar y sociedad política Argentina, 1943–1973*. Vol. 2. Buenos Aires: Editorial Emecé, 1982.

Sáenz Quesada, María. *El camino de la democracía*. Buenos Aires: Tiempo de Ideas, 1993.

Salinas, Juan, and Julio Villalonga. *Gorriarán, La Tablada, y las "guerras de inteligencia" en América Latina*. Buenos Aires: Marngin, 1993.

Santucho, Julio. *Los últimos guevaristas: surgimiento y eclipse del Ejército Revolucionario del Pueblo*. Buenos Aires: Editorial Puntosur, 1988.

Selser, Gregorio. *Perón: el regreso y la muerte*. Montevideo: Biblioteca de Marcha, 1973.

Seoane, María. *Todo o nada*. Buenos Aires: Editorial Planeta, 1991.

Seoane, María, and Héctor Ruiz Nuñez. *La noche de los lápices*. Buenos Aires: Editorial Planeta, 1992.

Sigal, Silvia. *Intelectuales y poder en la década del sesenta*. Buenos Aires: Puntosur Editores, 1991.

Sikkink, Kathryn, and Lisa L. Martin. "U.S. Policy and Human Rights in Argentina and Guatemala, 1973–1980," in Peter Evans, Harold Jacobson, and Robert D. Putnam, eds. *Double-Edged Diplomacy: International Bargaining and Domestic Politics*. Berkeley: University of California Press, 1993, 330–362.

Simeoni, Héctor R. *¡Aniquelen al ERP! La "guerra sucia" en el monte tucumaño*. Buenos Aires: Ediciones Cosmos, 1985.

Simeoni, Héctor R., and Eduardo Allegri. *Linea de fuego*. Buenos Aires: Editorial Sudamericana, 1991.

Timerman, Jacobo. *Prisoner Without a Name, Cell Without a Number*. New York: Vintage Books, 1988.

Trinquier, Roger. *La guerra moderna*. Buenos Aires: Editorial Rioplatense, n.d.

Troncoso, Oscar. *El Proceso de Reorganización Nacional.* 2 vols. Buenos Aires: Centro Editor de América Latina, 1984.

Túrolo, Carlos M. *De Isabel a Videla: los pliegues del poder.* Buenos Aires: Editorial Sudamericana, 1996.

Uriarte, Claudio. *Almirante Cero: biografía no autorizada de Emilio Eduardo Massera.* Buenos Aires: Editorial Planeta, 1991.

Veiga, Raúl. *Las organizaciones de derechos humanos.* Buenos Aires: Centro Editor de América Latina, 1985.

Verbitsky, Horacio. *Civiles y militares: memoria secreta de la transición.* Buenos Aires: Editorial Contrapunto, 1987.

————. *Ezeiza.* Buenos Aires: Editorial Contrapunto, 1986.

————. *The Flight: Confessions of an Argentine Dirty Warrior.* New York: New Press, 1996.

Videla, Jorge Rafael. *Ante los jueces.* Buenos Aires: Asociación Jurídica Argentina, 1984.

Villegas, Osiris. *Tiempo geopolítico argentino.* Buenos Aires: Editorial Pleamar, 1975.

Zaremberg, Gisela, and Pablo Larrea. "El General ha vuelto: un análisis del discurso bussista," in Pablo Lacoste, ed. *Militares y política, 1983–1991.* Buenos Aires: Centro Editor de América Latina, 1993.

Index

About the Author

PAUL H. LEWIS is Professor of Political Science at Tulane University. An authority on Latin American political history, Professor Lewis has published six previous books, including *Paraguay Under Stroessner, The Crisis of Argentine Capitalism,* and *Political Parties and Generations in Paraguay's Liberal Era.*